Ghosts – dead and yet alive, absent and yet present – are able to cross the borders of experience; in literature their evocation has been enduringly important. In *Henry James and the ghostly* T. J. Lustig explores the ghost stories that James produced throughout his career and relates them to the great dynamic forces which may well represent James's most original contribution to literature. The centrepiece of the book is a detailed analysis of James's classic ghost story 'The Turn of the Screw', set in the context of work by earlier Victorian writers, and developments in James's own treatment of the ghostly. Lustig evaluates the ghostly charge attached to the many scenes in James's novels and tales which turn on thresholds, perspectives, windows and doors, and the many moments when James's characters seem almost to encounter the margins of the texts which enclose them.

HENRY JAMES AND THE GHOSTLY

HENRY JAMES
AND THE GHOSTLY

T. J. LUSTIG

Keele University

CAMBRIDGE
UNIVERSITY PRESS

Published by the Press Syndicate of the University of Cambridge
The Pitt Building, Trumpington Street, Cambridge CB2 1RP
40 West 20th Street, New York, NY 10011–4211, USA
10 Stamford Road, Oakleigh, Melbourne 3166, Australia

First published 1994

Printed in Great Britain at the University Press, Cambridge

A catalogue record for this book is available from the British Library

Library of Congress cataloguing in publication data

Lustig, T. J. (Timothy J.)
Henry James and the ghostly / T. J. Lustig
p.   cm.
Includes bibliographical references.
ISBN 0 521 45378 x (hardback)
1. James, Henry, 1843–1916 – Knowledge – Occultism.
2. Ghost stories, American – History and criticism.
3. Occultism in literature.   1. Title.
PS2127.025L87   1994
813'.4 – DC 20   93-38835 CIP

ISBN 0 521 45378 x hardback

CE

For my father and mother

Contents

Acknowledgements

I would not have started work on Henry James without Hermione Lee, who taught a course on James at the University of York, or finished a doctoral dissertation without Tony Tanner, my supervisor at the University of Cambridge. The process of converting a thesis into a book would have been benighted indeed without the advice and suggestions of Ian Bell, of Keele University, and Adrian Poole at the University of Cambridge. I owe a great debt to all of them. I must thank Charles Swann, of Keele University, who read and commented on the Hawthorne portion of my manuscript, and Richard Godden, also of Keele, who drew my attention to Allan Lloyd Smith's work on 'The Turn of the Screw'. I am grateful to Allan Lloyd Smith and S. H. Clark for permission to quote from typescript versions of forthcoming works. I should also like to express my deep gratitude to Michael Black, Alban Harvey, Alan McIntosh, Rod Mengham, Julia Podziewska and Simon Ross, who all, in numerous ways, mitigated the nightmare of writing. Small parts of this book were originally published as the introduction to '*The Turn of the Screw' and Other Stories*, World's Classics (Oxford, 1992).

Abbreviations

CE   *The Centenary Edition of the Works of Nathaniel Hawthorne*, ed. by William Charvat and others, 20 vols. (Columbus, 1962–88)

CT   *The Complete Tales of Henry James*, ed. by Leon Edel, 12 vols. (London, 1962–4)

L   *Henry James: Letters*, ed. by Leon Edel, 4 vols. (vols. I–III, London, 1974–81; vol. IV, Cambridge, Mass., 1984)

LC, I   *Henry James: Literary Criticism; Essays on Literature, American Writers, English Writers*, ed. by Leon Edel and Mark Wilson, Library of America (New York, 1984)

LC, II   *Henry James: Literary Criticism; French Writers, other European Writers, the Prefaces to the New York Edition*, ed. by Leon Edel and Mark Wilson, Library of America (New York, 1984)

N   *The Complete Notebooks of Henry James*, ed. by Leon Edel and Lyall H. Powers (New York, 1987)

NYE   *The Novels and Tales of Henry James*, New York Edition, 26 vols. (vols. I–XXIV, London, 1907–9; vols. XXV–XXVI, London, 1917)

SE   *The Standard Edition of the Complete Psychological Works of Sigmund Freud*, ed. and trans. by James Strachey and others, 24 vols. (London, 1953–74)

Introduction

Ghosts are as old as writing. The shadowy nature of the one – both real and imaginary, literal and figurative, dead and alive, full of meaning but also obscure, out of the past and yet also within the present – is not easily distinguished from the other. In a very general way all writing evokes, revives or resurrects what is not present. In this sense, but also in more specific ones, the history of literature is bound up with the ghostly. When Odysseus voyages to the edges of the world or Ovid's Orpheus descends to Hades, when Beowulf plunges into the pool or Gawain crosses the wild forest, when Piers dreams his dream or Spenser's Guyon steps into the Bower of Bliss, the hero's task, like that of the poet, is to enter the realm of the ghostly, the uncanny or the monstrous. Where philosophy has typically sought to exorcise the irrational and the ghostly, to live in the clear light of truth and reason, poetry and fiction have with an equal consistency been haunted by darkness and the occult.

This book sets out to explore Henry James's ghost stories and to assess the significance of the ghostly for his literary project as a whole. From 'The Romance of Certain Old Clothes' and 'De Grey: A Romance', respectively his eighth and eleventh published tales, to 'The Jolly Corner' and *The Sense of the Past*, the novel he left unfinished at his death, the ghostly in James's fiction is intimately connected to the great dynamic forces which play through his work in its entirety. Indeed, James's thinking about the ghostly played an important role in creating and defining these dynamic forces. 'A good ghost-story', as he wrote in an 1865 review of Mrs Braddon's *Aurora Floyd*, 'must be connected at a hundred points with the common objects of life'.[1] It is a somewhat simplistically phrased argument. But James's early sense of the connection between the supernatural and the natural was still operating in his Preface to volume XVII of *The New York Edition*, in which he recalled how, with

I

'Sir Edmund Orme', he had sought 'the note...of the strange and sinister embroidered on the very type of the normal and easy' (*LC*, II, 1264). The relationships established in the ghost story are no less than a synecdoche of those which obtain in James's fiction as a whole. In a famous passage of his Preface to *The American*, James described those writers of the 'largest responding imagination' who were prepared to commit themselves both to the 'air of romance' and to the 'element of reality' without finally deflecting in either direction (pp. 1061–2). Such writers instead performed a 'revolution', created a 'rich and mixed current' capable of dealing successively with the 'near and familiar' and the 'far and strange' (p. 1062). This vision of a rotary movement which plays from the familiar to the strange and from the unknown to the known, connecting whilst continuing to make distinctions, is vital to James's work and to his ideas about consciousness. For James, consciousness could of course involve experience of the near and familiar. Yet it could also, without the need for literal visits to far, strange lands or the distant past, be a place of wonder, a scene of the fantastic. Indeed, it was only through the medium of a fictional consciousness, within the field of 'second ... exhibition', as James put it in his Preface to volume XVII of the *New York Edition*, that ghosts could be represented effectively (p. 1259).

James believed that the ghostly required subjective mediation to become fictionally effective. Yet this relationship between the supernatural and the psychological could be turned round; Jamesian consciousness could itself be described in ghostly terms. For Sallie Sears at least, 'the human mind is, for James, by definition a haunted mind'.[2] At a very general level a great deal of James's fiction is ghostly in its enigmatic impalpability, its vague precision, its subtle allusiveness, its hovering uncertainty, its fascination with anxiety and awe, wonder and dread. Many of the catalytic moments in James's fiction are profoundly eerie and many of James's characters possess an almost psychic sensitivity to shades: shades of meaning, certainly, but also shades in their sense as ghosts. It is true that neither 'The Romance of Certain Old Clothes', 'De Grey', 'The Last of the Valerii', 'Adina', 'The Ghostly Rental' nor 'The Third Person' were included alongside James's other ghost stories in volumes XII and XVII of the *New York Edition*. Even 'Sir Edmund Orme', as Michael Anesko's tables of the proposed contents of the *New York Edition* show, made a relatively late appearance in this second collection.[3] It is also true that James repeatedly deprecated his ghost stories as pot-boilers. Yet there was meaning and method, as well as a certain amount of disingenuousness, in this modesty. James's ghostly fiction raised distinctly uncomfortable questions about the nature of his literary project, suggested a more one-sided indebtedness to the sensational and to romantic disconnection that he would have liked openly to admit. To disparage it was to cover his tracks and protect the autonomy of his fiction. James defended the idea of imaginative freedom magisterially in a letter to George Bernard Shaw of 20 January 1909, claiming that he had written *The Saloon* (his one-act adaptation of 'Owen Wingrave' for the stage) 'because I happen to be a man of imagination and taste ... and because the imagination ... from the moment direction and motive play upon it from all sides, absolutely enjoys and insists on and incurably leads a life of its own'.[4]

The artist's imagination led a life of its own. Being a writer of the 'largest responding imagination', however, James was also committed to coherence, to establishing limits in the interests of literary form and (paraphrasing the Preface to *Roderick Hudson*) drawing the circle within which relations appeared to stop. The dedication to the centrifugal, to romantic extension and the liberated consciousness, to what the Prefaces called 'the expansive, the explosive principle'; the equal and opposite commitment to the centripetal, to the real, to formal limitation and the exigencies of 'economic mastery': these are the great forces which play through James's work (*LC*, II, 1278). On the one hand, James maintained an intimately collaborative rapport with the fictional centre of consciousness; at the same time, however, there was also a more competitive and even hostile relationship between the writer and the represented subjectivity. It would be all too easy to associate the ghostly in James's work solely with the romantic. In fact, the ghostly defines the changing relationships of his fiction with such comprehensiveness and intensity because it is able to operate during both phases of the Jamesian double dynamic. In 'The Romance of Certain Old Clothes', the ghostly is an explosive force which threatens to break the moulds of James's form. In tales like 'A Passionate Pilgrim' and still more so in 'Sir Edmund Orme', 'The Way it Came',[5] 'The Turn of the Screw' and 'Maud-Evelyn', James countered the explosive threat of the ghostly by containing it within the experience of a particular individual and by an increasing emphasis on formal framing. And yet, in tales such as

'De Grey' and still more emphatically in 'Travelling Companions', the ghostly could also be used as a means to achieve 'economic mastery'. In the latter tale an admonitory ghostly presence seems to patrol the outer edge of the text, confining the protagonist within the circle of the fiction. James's competitive drive to contain and limit the experience of the represented subjectivity was also to take on an uncanny dimension in *The American* and *The Portrait of a Lady*. These two novels stand at the beginning of the least ghostly period in James's career: that between 'The Ghostly Rental' (1876) and 'Sir Edmund Orme' (1891).[6] Nevertheless, ghostly notes continued to sound in *The Bostonians*, *The Princess Casamassima* and *The Tragic Muse*. Even in his most programmatically 'realist' phase, the ghostly was an important figurative resource for James; indeed, one could argue that it became increasingly potent as metaphor rather than literality, as a form of subjectivity rather than an object for subjectivity. Both *What Masie Knew* and 'In the Cage' are concerned throughout with phantasmagoric experiences. Neither *The Sacred Fount*, *The Ambassadors*, *The Wings of the Dove* nor *The Golden Bowl* contain objectified ghosts but the protagonists of each are haunted men and women who frequently themselves become haunting presences. In the meantime, in tales such as 'Sir Edmund Orme', 'Sir Dominick Ferrand', 'Owen Wingrave', 'The Third Person' and to some extent even in 'The Way it Came', the ghostly, far from being a terror, had for James begun to represent the pinnacle of extended, enlarged experience. During the later stages of his career, the ghostly was no longer used exclusively to guarantee the outer edge of his fiction. Instead the ghosts tended to be encountered at its core, where they were closely linked, in 'The Private Life', 'The Real Right Thing' and perhaps in 'The Turn of the Screw', *The Ambassadors* and 'The Jolly Corner', to the figure of the writer. At the same time, through his notebooks, and later in *The American Scene*, his Prefaces and his autobiographical writings, James seems increasingly to be haunting his life and past works, to have become a ghost within his own house of fiction. By enacting his various relationships with his protagonists, James's ghosts always potentially related to, and often directly dramatized, his authorial investment in the work at hand. In what follows, therefore, I will be trying to assess the nature and trace the development of these investments and dynamic relationships.

From what I have already said it will be obvious that I am not interested in isolating the ghostly from James's work as a whole. Although Sidney Lind's unpublished dissertation on James concedes that the ghost stories were more than light-hearted literary exercises, he concludes that they represent 'a special category in the body of his work'.[7] A similar approach is taken by Benjamin Carroll in an earlier and also unpublished dissertation, 'The Supernatural in the Writings of Henry James' and later by Martha Banta in *Henry James and the Occult*. The desire to categorially confine James's ghostly fiction relates to other attempts, which I have also largely eschewed, to define the ghostly in generic terms. It seems to me that the classic debate over 'The Turn of the Screw', besides tending misleadingly to isolate the text as an anomaly in James's fictional output, erred on the side at least of psychological if not literary genre by confining discussion to the question of whether to categorize the narrative as a ghost story or a study in insanity. This is not the place to recapitulate Edmund Wilson's argument that the governess is 'a neurotic case of sex repression' and that Peter Quint and Miss Jessel are 'merely the governess's hallucinations' or to deal in detail with Robert B. Heilman's counter-claim that the ghosts are not hallucinations and that Miles and Flora have indeed been corrupted.[8] For anybody who has had anything to do with 'The Turn of the Screw', even this prefatory hat-tipping to the ever expanding body of critical predecessors has become tediously predictable. Even forty years ago Marius Bewley and others were arguing that questions about the 'reality' of the ghosts or the 'reliability' of the governess were not simply insusceptible of verification but also, given the irreducibly hypothetical nature of literary statements, little better than meaningless. Such critics sought rather to preserve and evaluate than to resolve the tale's ambiguity.[9] The 'erroneous readings' that the debate has generated have also been the subject of critical comment by Christine Brooke-Rose and, more recently still, Paul B. Armstrong takes it as read that the Wilson/Heilman antinomy is now 'incapable of opening new interpretive possibilities'.[10] Armstrong may well be right. What strikes me, however, is the way in which the Wilson/Heilman debate acts out the polarized paradigms of a previous period. The conflicting accounts of the governess in 'The Turn of the Screw' manifest in really rather precise ways an opposition between the madwoman in the attic and the angel in the house: the very terms in which the nineteenth century tended to see women in general and, as I will try to show, governesses in particular. One might add that the classic phase of 'Turn of the Screw' criticism also replicates the ambivalent Victorian response to children: are they pure and innocent (Wilson) or corrupted, guilty, full of impure knowledge (Heilman)? In a literary critical sense, as well, the debate seems to belong to a pre-Jamesian age, confining itself to proposing answers to what Julia Briggs sees as 'the question most basic to the ghost story': '"Was it real or imaginary?"'.[11] In spite of Wilson's 'Freudian' trimmings (and compared to the more recent work of Shoshana Felman they are no more than that) it was hardly a new idea to suggest that ghosts were subjective phenomena. This would have been the view not only of Freud and the psychical researchers but also of Hobbes and Locke. Ghostly or uncanny events had been presented as illusions (albeit with varying degrees of subtlety and usually with less ambiguous conclusions) in the novels of Ann Radcliffe and Walter Scott, as well as in tales such as Hawthorne's 'Young Goodman Brown', George Eliot's 'The Lifted Veil', Guy de Maupassant's 'Le Horla' and Vernon Lee's 'A Wicked Voice'. 'Reality or Delusion?', as the title of one of Mrs Henry Wood's tales succinctly but crudely puts it. In these terms Heilman's hostility to Wilson is somewhat surprising, as is his decision to counter the latter's 'astonishingly *unambiguous* exegesis' with a diametrically opposed one of his own.[12] Yet the misleadingly polarized account of 'The Turn of the Screw' cannot, in my view, be overcome by appealing to the idea of 'ambiguity'. Dorothea Krook's *The Ordeal of Consciousness*, Tzvetan Todorov's *The Fantastic* and Shlomith Rimmon's *The Concept of Ambiguity* all seem to me to employ conceptual models already current in, for example, Scott's essay on Ann Radcliffe: models which do not, I think, help us to achieve an adequate understanding of 'The Turn of the Screw'.

The ghostly is necessarily an insubstantial entity, yet this very openness is of the essence. Attempts to analytically circumscribe the irrational in post-Gothic literature[13] have repeatedly encountered an extraordinary multiplication of themes, and have often virtually resorted to the mere listing of proliferating sources. Even the least ambitious of these studies succeed – often in spite of themselves – in demonstrating the important fact that the irrational is, almost by definition, the illimitable. The ghostly is fundamentally and vitally uncertain and Todorov's argument that this uncertainty is itself a generic hallmark seems to me to categorize the uncategorizable, to classify that which challenges or suspends classification and to ignore the supra-generic features of the ghostly, its ability to slip through conceptual meshes and cross categorial borders. The ghost, the vision, the hallucination, the dream, the fantasy, the metaphor: there is clearly a descending order of what Max Black calls 'ontological commitment' here.[14] Yet the list also provides a continuous sequence of ghostly or ontologically uncertain experience. James, I think, would have appreciated this continuity. Much of his work, as I have already suggested, deals with problematic oppositions and thresholds, and Adrian Poole has argued that James is attracted to the paranormal precisely because it 'raises questions about boundaries'.[15] Indeed, James's interest in the supernatural led Virginia Woolf to say that he had 'only to take the smallest of steps' to find himself 'over the border'.[16]

Boundaries certainly do proliferate in the Jamesian text, and much of my work depends on evaluating the uncanny charge so often attaching to those scenes in James's work which turn on thresholds, perspectives, windows, doors, on those isolated moments of heightened attention which amount, at times, to encounters with the margins of the text. James is undoubtedly raising questions about boundaries. It is in the answers that he provides and, indeed, in the way in which he questions the notion of boundary itself that he makes what I believe are some of his most powerfully unique and original contributions. In order to pave the way for an informed assessment of these contributions and for an evaluation of James's characteristic conceptual manoeuvres I have devoted my first chapter to examining pre-Jamesian handlings of the supernatural. From Plato and Aristotle through Hobbes and Locke to post-Jamesian thinkers like Freud and Girard there is a consistent attempt (which I take to be a procedure typical of philosophy) to distinguish the rational from the irrational, the natural from the supernatural. These oppositions almost always result in the attempted expulsion, subordination or domestication of the second term. Yet ghosts cannot be exorcised without first being raised, and to conjure them up is often to discover that the ghostly and the uncanny are more intimately related to the living, the familiar, than philosophy at least would care to admit. The light of reason requires darkness and obscurity to throw it into relief. I think this was one reason why the ghostly was able to survive the scepticism of thinkers like Hobbes and Locke with undiminished power. Indeed, their troubled awareness that the threshold joins as much as it divides found positive aesthetic valorization in the literature of the sublime, the Gothic and the Romantic, all of which movements typically sought not to impose absolute distinctions but to deal with border-line experiences in mixed literary forms. The culmination of this aesthetics of hybridity is of course to be found in the romance, and one of its most frequently quoted statements appears in 'The Custom-House', Nathaniel Hawthorne's introductory chapter to *The Scarlet Letter*, which speaks of 'a neutral territory, somewhere between the real world and fairy-land, where the Actual and the Imaginary may meet, and each imbue itself with the nature of the other'.[17] In important ways, however, Hawthorne's formulation still belongs to an oppositional understanding of relationships, an under-standing which reaches back at least to Locke. What I want to bring into focus, then, is the contrast between Hawthorne's comparatively static, linear notion of the mid-point and James's own more dynamic and rotary reformulations of the neutral territory, as well as of consciousness, fiction and relationships in general. Yet – and this is particularly true of the ghost stories, from 'The Romance of Certain Old Clothes' and 'The Ghostly Rental' through the tales of the 1890s to 'The Turn of the Screw' if not beyond – James continued to be profoundly influenced by Hawthorne, whose picture of the writer's 'haunted chamber' cast a shadow which stretched from James's account of the 'chamber of consciousness' in 'The Art of Fiction' to his description of the 'house of fiction' in the Preface to *The Portrait of a Lady* (Hawthorne, *CE*, xv, 494; James, *LC*, i, 52; ii, 1075).

I should add a brief note on the texts. Since this is by and large a chronologically arranged study which tries to examine the issues appropriate to each stage of James's career, I have as a rule chosen to cite easily available editions which carry the first book version of the work in question. In the case of the stories (including 'The Turn of the Screw') this means Leon Edel's twelve-volume edition of the *Complete Tales*; in the case of the novels, this means the Library of America series: *Novels 1871–1880* (notably for *The American*), *Novels 1881–1886* (particularly for *The Portrait of a Lady*) and *Novels 1886–1890*, which takes me up to *The Tragic Muse*. For novels written thereafter, I rely where possible on the *New York Edition*. I have used Leon Edel's edition of *The Sacred Fount* (London, 1959). I draw attention to earlier versions of the later *New York* texts when these differ significantly (as they do at one important moment in *The Ambassadors*), as well as to *New York Edition* revisions of earlier texts such as *The American*, *The Portrait of a Lady* and 'The Turn of the Screw'.

CHAPTER I

The threshold

ENLIGHTENMENT AND THE DARKNESS

For John Aubrey, modernity was marked by the disappearance of ghosts. When he was a child, before the Civil War,

> the fashion was for old women and mayds to tell fabulous stories nightimes, of Sprights and walking of Ghosts, &c. This was derived down from mother to daughter ... When the warres came, and with them Liberty of Conscience and Liberty of inquisition, the phantoms vanished. Now children feare no such things, having heard not of them; and are not checked with such feares.[1]

In Aubrey's view it was writing, as well as the war, which had put the ghosts to flight. 'In the old ignorant times, before woomen were Readers, the history was handed down from Mother to daughter', but 'now-a-dayes Bookes are common, and most of the poor people understand letters; and the many good Bookes ... have putt all the old Fables out of doors: and the divine art of Printing and Gunpowder have frighted away Robin-goodfellow and the Fayries' (quoted by Dick, pp. xxix, xxxiii). Acutely aware of the gap between the present and the past, between the printed and the spoken word, modernity and magic, Aubrey sentimentally repudiated the Enlightenment's characteristic expulsion of ghosts and fables. In the *Leviathan* (1651), for instance, Thomas Hobbes had made a sustained attack on miracles and wonders, on 'the demonology of the heathen poets' and 'their fabulous doctrine concerning demons, which are but idols, or phantasms of the brain, without any real nature of their own, distinct from human fancy; such as are dead men's ghosts, and fairies, and other matter of old wives' tales'.[2] Hobbes's assault on the ghosts went hand in hand with his attempt to confine, purge and exorcise language, particularly in its figurative dimension. There was for him a close connection between poetic 'phantasms of the brain' and 'dead men's ghosts', between idols and eidolons. 'Fictitious miracles' and 'histories of apparitions' could be laid at the door of a religion which promoted 'conjuration' (pp. 449, 401–3). Conjuration (as distinct from 'consecration') implied that 'by ... words, the nature or quality of the thing itself, is ... changed', and Hobbes believed that it was an 'abuse' to take such figurative language literally (pp. 401, 402). The transformation effected in the Eucharist, for example, was nothing more than 'an ordinary figure of speech' (p. 402).

But was there such a thing as an 'ordinary' figure of speech, an innocuous rhetoric? Hobbes recognized that one of the functions of language was 'to please and delight ourselves and others, by playing with our words, for pleasure or ornament, innocently' (p. 19). Yet it was difficult to confine this notion of decoration or entertainment. All ideation for Hobbes was fundamentally figurative and language as a whole was a phantasm of the brain, without any real nature of its own. Hobbes described Aristotle's attempt to 'avoid ambiguity and equivocation' by the 'right limiting of ... significations' but criticized the 'doctrine of *separated essences*' because it mapped reality by phantasmatic words and in doing so brought the ghosts to life, 'for it is upon this ground, that when a man is dead and buried, they say his soul ... can walk separated from his body, and is seen by night amongst the graves' (pp. 440, 442). Endeavouring to avoid ambiguity by fixing meaning, Aristotle had played into the spectral hands of language. If the world was treated as a verbal structure then it could be improperly articulated. To believe in dead men's ghosts was to treat the word as flesh, violating the threshold between different realms. Even at the ornamental level Hobbes found such transgressions deeply suspect. His apprehensions were expressed most strongly with regard to what he called the 'compound imagination' (p. 10). This faculty was said to be capable of metamorphosing ordered forms into grotesque figures, enabling a man to 'fancy shapes he never saw; making up a figure out of the parts of divers creatures; as the poets make their centaurs, chimeras, and other monsters never seen' (p. 426). In order to combat the ghostly and the monstrous, the *Leviathan* dispensed with the doctrine of essences and offered in its place a taxonomy of science, the 'knowledge of consequences' (p. 54).

Yet the taxonomic method welcomes parodic extension. Aubrey seems to be behaving reasonably enough when, in the 'Naturall

Historie of Wiltshire', he announces his intention to discuss 'Air, Springs Medicinall, Rivers, Earths, Mineralls, Stones, Plantes, Beastes, Fishes, Birds, Insects and Reptiles, Men and Women' (quoted by Dick, p. xlvi). But in the *Miscellanies* he embarks with extravagant and subversive enthusiasm on a catalogue of 'Omens', 'Dreams', 'Apparitions', 'Voices', 'Knockings', 'Blows Invisible', 'Marvels', 'Magick', 'Visions in a Beril, or Glass' and 'Converse with Angels + Spirits' (quoted by Dick, p. cv). The list rises to 'Extasie' and leaves behind it a strong doubt as to whether the taxonomist's attempt to impose categorial order was motivated exclusively, or even mainly, by rational considerations (p. cv). There were, however, deeper reasons behind the difficulty in fixing the borders on which science relied. Because the light of reason needs to define itself against the ghost-filled dark, there is an important sense in which the categories of philosophy require as their shadowy other the uncanny mixtures and displacements of metaphor and poetry. Order presumes and often evokes a disorder against which it can be defined. As Tony Tanner has written, 'contracts *create* transgressions; the two are inseparable, and the one would have no meaning without the other'.[3] The complicity between order and disorder produced significant tensions in the *Leviathan*. Hobbes argued that language promoted superstitions which challenged 'civil obedience', but also realized that without language there could be 'neither commonwealth, nor society, nor contract, nor peace' (pp. 13, 18). The predicament of the leviathan was an awkward one. In describing the body of the state, Hobbes admitted the rhetoric of monsters. Phantoms and chimeras would have caused fewer problems if there had been an impermeable barrier between order and disorder. Unfortunately for Hobbes, such a threshold was impossible to maintain. The notion of a clear border which might prescribe where the irrational begins and thus protect the rational from infiltration is a deeply problematic and even a paradoxical one. Thresholds only exist within reason; they lie on this side of chaos. Hobbes's admission that it is 'a hard matter ... to distinguish exactly between sense and dreaming' has an exemplary force which extends to all his other distinctions between light and dark, ghosts and men, and at the most general level between poetry's figures and philosophy's forms (p. 11).

In *An Essay Concerning Human Understanding* (1690), John Locke followed up Hobbes's attack on rhetoric and the ghostly. The old wives' tales condemned by Hobbes and mourned by Aubrey duly reappeared in Locke's observation that 'the *Ideas* of *Goblines* and *Sprights* have really no more to do with Darkness than Light: yet let but a foolish Maid inculcate these often on the Mind of a Child, and raise them there together, possibly he shall never be able to separate them again so long as he lives'.[4] Locke stood firmly with his predecessor on the issue of figurative language, permitting it for 'entertainment' or 'pleasure' but arguing that 'if we would speak of Things as they are, we must allow, that all the Art of Rhetorick, besides Order and Clearness, all the artificial and figurative application of Words Eloquence hath invented, are for nothing else but to insinuate wrong *Ideas*, move the Passions, and thereby mislead the Judgment' (III, 10, 34). The problem of the threshold also plays a central role in the *Essay*. Locke calls attention to the difficulty of drawing a line between changelings and human children, rational and irrational souls, on the basis of appearance alone. At what point, he asks, does the 'well-shaped *Changeling*' acquire a sufficient degree of 'the likeness of a Brute' for us to conclude that it is a '*Monster*' with 'no rational Soul' (IV, 4, 16)? Where is the 'just measure' (IV, 4, 16)? Locke saw the need for borders as clearly as Hobbes but he was more anxiously aware than his predecessor of their artificiality and fragility. He believed that the first task of philosophy was 'to take a Survey of our own Understandings' in order to establish 'the Horizon ... which sets the Bounds between the enlightened and dark Parts of Things' (I, 1, 7). All knowledge for Locke was based on the sensations or reflections which together constituted experience, and 'all those sublime Thoughts, which towre above the Clouds, and reach as high as Heaven it self, take their Rise and Footing here' (II, 1, 24). Yet Locke could not limit reflection merely by avoiding 'remote Speculations' (II, 1, 24). His sensations forced him to admit the existence of a 'vast Ocean of *Being*' which stood outside any circle drawn by reason (I, 1, 7). To reflect on this ocean was to become aware that 'what lies within our Ken, is but a small part of the immense Universe' and thus to discover a 'huge Abyss of Ignorance' which existed both inside and outside the self (IV, 3, 24). It was not even certain that knowledge extended to the things that lay to hand. What was the essence of substance? How did matter cohere? In principle 'there must be something to hinder it from scattering asunder' but if the maintenance of cohesion was left to the human understanding there could be nothing but a centrifugal catastrophe (II, 23, 27). Since categories

trictly linguistic entities, an ordered discourse may have no real
hase on the things it attempts to describe. Repeatedly referring
to the difficulty of marking 'the bounds' which limit 'the several
ranks of Beings', Locke is acutely aware of the need to separate the
monstrous figure from the ordered body of philosophical discourse
(IV, 16, 12). He claims that the rational distinctions of philosophy
avoid 'Similitude' and are 'a way of proceeding quite contrary to
Metaphor and Allusion', but he also knows that philosophy cannot
avoid something perilously close to similitude (II, 11, 2). 'Composition' and 'combining several simple *Ideas* into one compound
one', especially in 'mixed modes', are vital operations in a rational
being (II, 11, 6; II, 12, 1; II, 22). Philosophy could not exist without
'comparison' or the perception of '*connexion and agreement*' between
ideas (II, 25, 1; IV, 1, 2). These functions are half of knowledge and
'the end of Language' (II, 22, 5). Yet mixed modes provide a fertile
mould for the growth of rhetorical fungi. Like the chimeras of
Hobbes's compound imagination, examples of mixed modes tend to
become dangerously divorced from sensation and reality. They
name things which have not or could never be seen and therefore
threaten the analogy between understanding and visual perception
which is so important to Locke. Like the changeling who haunts the
Essay, the rhetoric of monsters and the monstrosity of rhetoric refuses
to be detached from human discourse. We repeatedly suppose that
words are '*conformable to some real Existence*' and indulge in '*Fantastical
or Chimerical*' ideas like that of 'a rational Creature, consisting of a
Horse's Head, joined to a body of humane shape' (II, 32, 5; II, 30, 1;
II, 30, 5). There is for Locke, as Paul de Man has shown, something
ineluctably uncanny about the predicative power of mixed modes:
'when one speaks of the legs of the table or the face of the mountain,
catachresis is already turning into prosopopeia, and one begins to
perceive a world of potential ghosts and monsters'.[5] As it had been
for Hobbes, language for Locke is at best a double-edged tool, a
system of tokens in their sense as signs but also of tokens in their sense
as wraiths. Unless rigorous efforts were made to conform ideas to
things then language, 'the great Instrument and common Tye of
Society', would be more like 'that of *Babel*' (III, 1, 1; III, 6, 28). In
many ways, however, reality was already an incomplete, if not a
collapsing tower. In the 'Epistle to the Reader' which introduces the
Essay, Locke describes Newton as one of the 'Master-Builders' in the
'Commonwealth of Learning' but presents himself as 'an Under-

Labourer ... removing some of the Rubbish, that lies in the way to Knowledge' (pp. 9, 10). The broken terrain of philosophical endeavour has begun to resemble a landscape out of Edmund Spenser or Horace Walpole. As forgetfulness eats away at the edges of lucidity and metaphors sprout along the blurred border of reason, our minds for Locke become like 'Tombs ... where though the Brass and Marble remain, yet the Inscriptions are effaced by time, and the Imagery moulders away' (ii, 10, 5). The understanding should have been 'like the Eye' (i, 1, 1). To deploy such a metaphor, however, is to gain insights to make one blink: the eye is a 'curious Organ' which cannot see itself and nourishes an understanding which resembles 'a Closet wholly shut from light' (ii, 7, 4; ii, 11, 17). Ultimately the 'dark side' of ignorance is 'infinitely larger than our Knowledge' and it is 'an hard Matter to say where Sensible and Rational begin, and where Insensible and Irrational end' (iv, 3, 22; iv, 16, 12). The *Essay* had attempted to draw a line between light and darkness and to bound man's nominal essence, reason. But its geometrical longings were thwarted by a predicament which would continue to be explored in the literature of the sublime as well as in Gothic and Romantic writing. The problem was not so much that ghosts, monsters and metaphors were continually invading the circle occupied by man and rational discourse as that, in the absence of any such circle and the uncertainty of any such border, man was not so homely after all: in the chimeras of his language he gazed at an image of himself.

Charles Feidelson has shown that American religious writers of the late seventeenth century were more prepared to grant a limited licence to the figurative. In *Souldiery Spiritualized* (1674), for example, Joshua Moody wrote that 'the Lord is in his word teaching us by such familiar and known *Metaphors* taken from those Callings that we are versed in'.[6] To accord metaphor even this illustrative value would have made Hobbes and Locke, although perhaps not Spenser or Bunyan, distinctly uncomfortable. Although he was somewhat out of sympathy with the English intellectual climate, Aubrey might well have applauded a proposal reported in Cotton Mather's *Magnalia Christi Americana* (1702) to make a systematic catalogue of 'all *unusual accidents* ... all wonderful *deliverances* of the distressed: *mercies* to the godly; *judgments* on the wicked ... with *apparitions, possessions, inchantments,* and all extraordinary things wherein the existence and agency of the *invisible world* is more

sensibly demonstrated' (quoted by Feidelson, p. 81). By the beginning of the eighteenth century, however, attitudes were changing
rapidly. In *A Compleat Body of Divinity* (1726), Samuel Willard was as
sure as Hobbes that 'Rhetorick is but an Ornament of Speech'
(quoted by Feidelson, p. 85).

<h2 style="text-align:center">PHILOSOPHY AND ITS SCAPEGOATS</h2>

Philosophy's suspicion of the ghostly and the figurative is not,
however, by any means a seventeenth- or eighteenth-century development. The subjects of suspicion in the *Leviathan* or *An Essay
concerning Human Understanding* are not unlike those in Plato's *Phaedrus*, where Socrates argues that to rationalize myths by subjecting
them to order and 'the rules of probability' is to run the risk of being
overwhelmed by 'Gorgons and winged steeds ... and numberless
other inconceivable and impossible monstrosities'.[7] Monsters are
seen as the very antithesis of the object of philosophy: knowledge of
one's own nature (see section 229). Their lack of a proper shape and
their grotesqueness is the reverse of philosophical discourse which, as
Socrates argues, ought to have 'its own body and head and feet ... a
middle, beginning, and end' (section 264). Philosophical discourse
operates through order and category, articulating the relations
between genus and species by means of 'regular division' and refusing to mangle the parts of knowledge 'as a bad carver might'
(sections 263, 265). In contrast, the speech of the rhetorician Lysias
possesses a grotesque invertedness which closely allies it with the
unshapeliness of the monstrous (see section 264). Rhetoricians lack
the categorial discipline of philosophers and Socrates comments on
their ability to find 'a likeness of everything to which a likeness can
be found' (section 261). One of the major aims of the *Phaedrus* is to
create an impermeable barrier between philosophical discourse,
conceived of as a 'living creature' (section 264), and arts such as
rhetoric, writing and painting (see section 275). These arts involve
figures or likenesses, and it is significant that there is death in the
etymology of the English word 'like'.[8] Jacques Derrida has argued
that the *Phaedrus* uses the word '*pharmakon*' with reference to various
forms of the figurative, the mimetic and the graphic, which Plato
sees as alien and ghostly.[9] Yet the *pharmakon* does not characterize
what is simply external or dead. The objects of Plato's suspicion
possess a monster's power over the usual articulation of bodies in

space, a ghost's power over time and death, an uncanny ability to cross borders, to infiltrate the living speech of philosophy and contaminate its dream of categorial clarity (see Derrida, *Dissemination*, pp. 110, 143, 152). When Socrates argues that the truths of philosophical discourse are *'graven* in the soul of him who has learned' (*Dialogues*, I, 276; my italics) and that orally communicated teaching is 'the true way of writing' (section 278), Derrida promptly notes that philosophy is being described 'by a "metaphor" borrowed from the order of the very thing that one is trying to exclude' (*Dissemination*, p. 149). For Derrida, Plato's excursions into the figurative, the poetic and the mythical – and in particular the references to the detour through a madness which is for Socrates 'the special gift of heaven' and which leads to philosophical knowledge (*Dialogues*, I, 244) – almost make it possible to speak of 'the "irrationality" of living *logos*' (*Dissemination*, p. 115). Plato's exorcisms involve further forms of occult activity, and Socrates seems to evoke the uncanny figures which ostensibly he wishes to expel.

When Aristotle argues in the *Rhetoric* that good metaphors 'ought to set the scene before our eyes' and 'suggest activity', he seems to be according rhetoric a vitality which Plato wanted to restrict to philosophy.[10] The *Poetics* recognizes the way in which poetic diction 'becomes distinguished and non-prosaic by the use of unfamiliar terms, i.e. strange words, metaphors … everything that deviates from the ordinary modes of speech' (*Works*, XI, 1458. a. 20–5). Aristotle values metaphor but he offers it only a limited licence. For him, 'ordinary modes of speech' necessarily precede deviations. The unfamiliar and the metaphoric are secondary to the familiar and the literal. Metaphors rearrange relationships between genus and species (see 1457. b. 6–9) but, as Paul Ricoeur puts it, they occur for Aristotle within 'an order already constituted in terms of genus and species'.[11] Just as the *Phaedrus* condones writing on condition that the philosopher produces it only 'as the show of a festival' (Plato, *Dialogues*, I, 276), so the *Rhetoric* allows metaphor into ordered discourse only as long as it remains ornamental, the mere 'seasoning of the meat' at a feast (Aristotle, *Works*, XI, 1406. a. 15–20). There is nevertheless a danger that festival will turn into riot and revolt, that figures of resemblance will overthrow systems of distinction. If a discourse were to be taken over by metaphors it would, according to the *Poetics*, become 'a riddle or a barbarism' (*Works*, XI, 1458. a. 25).

The primacy of order and literality is more seriously thrown into doubt when Aristotle admits that metaphor can be used in cases where there is 'no special name', no original and recuperable term from which the metaphoric deviation can begin (1457. b. 25–30). This admission implies that metaphor is not necessarily an ornamental elaboration which temporarily disorders a previous order. I. A. Richards and Max Black were among the first to show that metaphor has a heuristic as well as a decorative dimension.[12] There is nowhere 'outside' metaphor, even in philosophy, and 'order itself', as Ricoeur observes, 'proceeds from the metaphorical constitution of semantic fields, which themselves give rise to genus and species' (*The Rule of Metaphor*, p. 23; see also pp. 197–8). Because it is 'impossible to talk about metaphor non-metaphorically', there is for Ricoeur no controlling inside with relation to which metaphor can be said to be peripheral or external (p. 18). Requiring figures to create its ordered bodies and resemblances as well as differences to found notions of familiarity and literality, philosophy is haunted by what it seeks to exorcise. There is witchcraft in the familiar, something curious or peculiar, perhaps even idiosyncratically idiotic about the notion of property and proper meaning.[13]

The *Poetics* contains a partially concealed analogy between linguistic and literary structure, between the transferences and substitutions amongst genus and species in metaphor and the disruptions and transgressions which power the tragic plot.[14] Aristotle's attempt to limit the deviations necessary to set tragedy in motion anticipates his efforts to prevent discourse from being taken over by metaphor later in the *Poetics*. He argues that tragedy should avoid 'merely monstrous' spectacles and that the 'improbable' should as far as possible be kept 'outside the tragedy' (*Works*, xi, 1453. b. 9; 1454. b. 5–10). Just as Aristotle enlisted metaphor on the side of order by arguing that the unfamiliar term was merely a temporary substitute for an ordinary term, so tragedy is defined as a detour through disorder which leads eventually, by way of catharsis (see 1449. b. 25–30) to the restitution of proper categories. Attempting to capture metaphor for category and to place poetry within boundaries drawn up by philosophy, the *Poetics* subordinates disorder to order in both metaphoric and tragic transgression. When Aristotle writes that 'to be beautiful, a living creature, and every whole made up of parts, must not only present a certain order in its arrangement of parts, but also be of a certain definite magnitude' since 'beauty is a matter of size and order' (1450. b. 34–8), his corporeal analogy subjects the aesthetic to the ordered body first described by Plato in the *Phaedrus* (see p. 16 above).

René Girard would disagree with the connection between metaphor and tragedy outlined above since for him both linguistic and literary practices have their origin in cultural ones: 'modern theory ... speaks of "phantasms" and "poetry" and does not ... realize how real the sacrificial process can be'.[15] In Girard's view, the transgressions of metaphor and tragedy are the by-products or after-effects of violence within culture; linguistic and literary order follows cultural order, whose categories are the products of sacrifice. During the sacrificial process a community unanimously performs an act of violence on a scapegoat from outside the community who replaces a 'surrogate victim' from within (*Violence and the Sacred*, p. 101; see also pp. 79–83). The surrogate victim is himself a token for the community at large. The act of sacrifice represents a culture's ejection of everything which is inimical to its own order; and what threatens order above all, in Girard's analysis, is the mimetic nature of human desire, which leads inevitably to conflict when the desiring subject seeks to appropriate his model's object (see pp. 147–8). The resulting conflict precipitates 'a crisis of distinctions' within the cultural order during which categorial thresholds are overthrown and improper resemblances multiply inexorably, creating 'a formless and grotesque mixture of things that are normally separate' (pp. 49, 160). Girard describes in some detail how the crisis brings with it instances of demonic possession as well as a chaotic influx of twins and doubles, monsters and ghosts (see *Violence and the Sacred*, pp. 57–64, 79, 162–5, 245, 254–6). This list of transgressive and uncanny manifestations seems to owe a great deal to the notion of 'liminality' first outlined by Arnold van Gennep in *The Rites of Passage* and extended more recently in the work of Victor Turner. Van Gennep subdivides rites of passage into 'rites of separation' or 'preliminal rites', 'transition rites' or 'liminal rites' proper, and 'rites of incorporation' or 'postliminal rites'.[16] He argues that rites of betrothal or initiation and even funeral ceremonies are particularly associated with the liminal (see *The Rites of Passage*, pp. 11, 146–7). These rites often incorporate suspensions of the 'usual economic and social ties' such as the sanctioning of theft (p. 114) and also periods of misrule and sexual licence (see pp. 115, 147–8, 170). Turner expands on these ritualized transgressions, associating liminality with the erasure of a wide range of categorial distinctions. During the initiation rites of the Ndembu of Zambia, for example, neophytes are seen as 'neither living nor dead from one aspect, and both living and dead from another'.[17] The same neither/nor/both/and logic applies to distinctions between male and female (see 'Betwixt and Between', p. 98). In other rites the ambiguities and paradoxes of liminality involve the inversion of relations between the sexes, between those of high and low status, between the strong and the weak, and between the young and the old.[18] Liminality is associated with the grotesque and the marvellous,[19] with pollution and anarchy[20] and with the use of 'bizarre and monstrous masks and figures' ('Betwixt and Between', p. 104).[21]

In principle, van Gennep's model of the rites of passage is to be understood as a chronological sequence. The same holds true of the four-stage model proposed by Victor Turner in *Dramas, Fields, and Metaphors* to describe the phases of 'public action' in social 'dramas', which Turner defines as 'units of aharmonic or disharmonic process, arising in conflict situations'.[22] Like van Gennep's preliminal-liminal-postliminal sequence, Turner's four stages – 'breach of regular ... social relations'; 'mounting crisis' with 'liminal characteristics'; a period of 'redressive action' followed finally by the 'reintegration of the disturbed social group' (*Dramas, Fields, and Metaphors*, pp. 38–9, 41) – distinctly resemble Girard's account of the sacrificial trajectory, particularly since, as Turner points out, the fourth stage of reintegration may alternatively involve the 'recognition ... of irreparable schism' (p. 41).[23] The postliminal phase can be one of sacrificial expulsions rather than ritual incorporations and Turner subsequently uses the example of courts martial and excommunication ceremonies to argue that 'ritual degradation occurs as well as elevation' (p. 232). One would not be pushing these ideas much further by suggesting that when the liminal phase is resolved by marriage and/or incorporation it takes a prototypically 'comic' form whilst resolution by death, separation or expulsion would prefigure a 'tragic' path. In a general sense, Turner's work draws attention to the broad relations between ritual and later 'symbolic genres' such as carnival, festival and drama.[24] And of course his use of the concept of social 'drama' is by no means accidental. More specifically, Turner does make cautious analogies between ritual practices and the patterns of comedy and tragedy.[25] I am not qualified to assess the anthropological value of these analogies. I simply want to stress the resemblances between Girard's account of the sacrificial crisis and Turner's descriptions of liminality. In both cases threshold contracts[26] are suspended and categorial distinctions (including even those between the living and the dead) temporarily break down. Yet there is no need to limit the literary analogues of the liminal phase or the sacrificial crisis to tragedy and comedy. The uncanny categorial transgressions I have been describing reappear with some force in Tzvetan Todorov's anatomy of the themes of fantastic literature, amongst which one finds 'the collapse ... of the limit between matter and mind'[27] and of other limits between word and thing, subject and object, real and unreal, literal and figurative (see *The Fantastic*, pp. 112–16, 154, 167). The erasure of these limits produces proliferating examples of violence (see p. 134), madness (see pp. 115, 117), doubles (see pp. 116, 143–4) and transgressive sexual acts (see p. 131).

One could argue that the fantastic is a literary extension of the sacrificial crisis. Alternatively, the sacrificial crisis might itself represent the eruption of the 'literary', with its predicative freedom, its potential for figurative transformation and categorial transgression, within the field of the 'real'. For Todorov, 'rhetorical figures' precede and make possible devils, vampires and other manifestations of the supernatural (p. 82). Girard would strongly object to these notions, since for him even an ancient literary form such as tragedy is positioned some way along a curve of decreasing reality and increasing metaphoricity. The sacrificial crisis evolves from primordial violence through tragedy into mere fantasy (see *Violence and the Sacred*, p. 119). Girard sees the ghosts and monsters as secondary effects, symptoms of cultural repressions, later symbolic or mythological elaborations, metaphors which conceal a 'real' process (p. 297; see also pp. 64–7). It is true that, where Plato opposes the monstrous to the ordered body, myth to philosophy, Girard sees 'the human being who lurks behind the monstrous form' (p. 253). Nevertheless, Girard's analysis of sacrificial expulsion reveals a certain complicity with its subject. Although he knows that cultures are implicated in the monstrous, Girard follows Aristotle in seeing the figurative as a temporary and merely ornamental substitute for the real, the literal, the familiar, the human and the primary. Yet these oppositions and concepts of origin are deeply problematic. Metaphor is not simply 'unreal'; as Ricoeur points out, it combines an 'is' within an 'is not': like a ghost, it straddles being and non-being, inhabits the liminal terrain between polarities (*The Rule of Metaphor*, p. 255). Making his own sacrifices in order to establish an originary reality or literality, Girard refuses to read back from the ghosts and monsters, his scapegoats, to his surrogate victim, the figurative, and then to the body of his own work, whose governing principles – mimetic desire, the erasure of difference during the sacrificial crisis – are vitally figurative. Is the metaphor a projection of the scapegoat or the scapegoat a projection of the metaphor? Do incest, parricide and adultery produce cultural and literary crises or are they not – since Locke uses them as examples of the 'unclean mixtures' found in mixed modes (*Human Understanding*, III, 5, 7) – literalizations or socializations of figurative language and its transgressions?

THE CANNY AND THE UNCANNY

Despite his criticisms of the Freudian model of desire (see *Violence and the Sacred*, pp. 84–8, 190–2), Girard's attitude to poetry and phantasms largely resembles Freud's. Just as Girard wants to discover the 'real origin' of sacrifice (p. 91), so Freud in 'The "Uncanny"' (1919) sets out to find the 'common core' of his subject.[28] Freud defines the uncanny as 'that class of the frightening which leads back to what is known of old and long familiar' (*SE*, XVII, 220). In spite of its shock value, this is a typically philosophical proposition. Freud treats the uncanny very much in the way that Aristotle treated the verbal strangeness of metaphor: as an ornamental detour, a secondary replacement for some more familiar term. He then sets out to translate the strange into the familiar, to read from secondary effects to primary causes, from form to content and from the figurative to the proper. Attempting to reconstruct the 'original arrangement' of the 'elements' in Hoffmann's 'The Sandman', Freud argues that 'the feeling of something uncanny' in the tale is 'directly attached to . . . the idea of being robbed of one's eyes' (pp. 232, 230). Reading the fear of blindness as 'a substitute for the dread of being castrated', Freud believes that he has restored a proper meaning behind the figures of the text (p. 231). He then connects his literary example of the uncanny with common infantile fears and with primitive culture. From here it is only a short step to 'the old, animistic conception of the universe', with its belief in the '"omnipotence of thoughts"' (p. 240). Freud had first mentioned this phrase in 'Notes

Upon a Case of Obsessional Neurosis' (1909) and used it extensively four years later in *Totem and Taboo* (see *SE*, x, 226; xiii, 75–99). In 'The "Uncanny"' the notion at last provides the common core of the uncanny, a single perspective on its manifestations in literature and for children, neurotics and primitives. At last Freud is back on 'familiar ground' (*SE*, xvii, 240).

Freud's announcement of his 'special obtuseness' (p. 220) in relation to uncanny experience links him with Hoffmann's Clara, who reasons that spirits are only 'the phantom of our own selves' whilst anticipating that Nathaniel will accuse her of being 'impervious to any ray of the mysterious'.[29] Freud's attempts to reduce the strange to the familiar also connect him with another figure in 'The Sandman' that he entirely ignores: the professor of poetry and eloquence who, after the destruction of the doll Olympia, asks his audience if they do not 'perceive where the trick lies' ('The Sandman', p. 142). For Freud as much as the professor of rhetoric, the tale is 'all an allegory', a trick to be translated ('The Sandman', p. 142). Hoffmann does not share this attitude to rhetoric, and 'The Sandman' counterpoints the theme of blindness which Freud finds susceptible to allegorical translation with a more glancing treatment of the theme of vision. The narrator of the tale wants to make the reader feel 'as if you had often seen' the objects of his fiction 'with your own corporeal eyes', and Nathaniel tells his friend Lothaire that he wishes he could 'bring the picture plainly and clearly before your eyes' (pp. 124, 110). Neil Hertz is quite right to see 'a grandiose wish for rhetorical power' in these comments.[30] Such desires recall Aristotle's *Rhetoric*, with its description of metaphor's ability to 'set the scene before our eyes' (*Works*, xi, 1410. b. 30–5). Yet Hoffmann, his narrator and Nathaniel want to give Aristotle an extra twist, to produce an imitation which is no mere substitute but which provides a magical illusion of presence and possesses all the affective force of the original. They follow Longinus, who celebrated imagery in which 'you think you see what you describe, and ... place it before the eyes of your hearers'.[31] Freud attempts to explain the multiplication of optical references in 'The Sandman' as instances of the same dread of castration which for him underlies the blindness theme. He points out that dreams are 'fond of representing castration by a doubling or multiplication of a genital symbol' (*SE*, xvii, 235). Doubled or taken away, therefore, eyes are firmly annexed to an interpretation in terms of castration. This is a short-sighted reading, since Hoffmann's tale is equally interested in speculations about literary and visual potency. It is true that Nathaniel eventually becomes the victim of this potency but his death is a response to the sublime and not a product of neurosis. He falls prey not to Coppelius (the 'sandman' who once threatened to steal his eyes) but to Coppola the conjurer, who provides him with a pocket telescope which kindles 'the power of seeing' and brings Olympia's glances to life (Hoffmann, 'The Sandman', p. 132). It is not the threat of physically losing his eyes which drives him to suicide but a sheer excess of vision.

Speaking of 'The "Uncanny"', Derrida has drawn attention to the way in which Freud shares Plato's interest in figures, replicas and ghosts (see *Dissemination*, pp. 219–20, note 32). The refusal of Socrates to accord life to painted representations does partly anticipate Freud's attempt to play down the importance of Olympia. In some ways this is a surprising manoeuvre because Olympia, a living replica, would seem to be the tale's most obvious instance of animism; the 'familiar ground' from which the uncanny is supposed to flower (*SE*, XVII, 240). Freud resists this connection because Olympia does not produce the strong negative responses which should, in his account of the uncanny, be associated with the revival of beliefs which culture has surmounted. The Olympia episode is merely a matter of 'satire' (p. 227). In 'Creative Writers and Day-Dreaming', Freud had written that 'every child at play behaves like a creative writer' (*SE*, IX, 143). Hoffmann presents an example of the creative writer behaving like a child at play; far from resisting animism, he puts something very like it at the top of his aesthetic manifesto. To bring the doll Olympia to life is to behave like the children mentioned in 'The "Uncanny"' who have 'no fear of their dolls coming to life' and 'may even desire it' (*SE*, XVII, 233). This exuberant attitude to fabulation challenges Freud's theory that 'The Sandman' concerns 'the arousing of an early childhood fear' (p. 233). The hinted equation between Nathaniel and Hoffmann which supports this theory (see pp. 232–3, note 1) is an unconvincing one, for there is much of Hoffmann's writerly self in Nathaniel's father and Coppelius, as well as in Spalanzani and Coppola. Freud reads this pair of doubles as two versions of Nathaniel/Hoffmann's ambivalence towards his father (see p. 232). But it is also true that the series father-Coppelius-Spalanzani-Coppola hints at an aesthetic of fragments which blinds as it illuminates, which is both

benign and malevolent, sentimental and sinister, which breathes life
into its figures before mischievously killing them off, which teeters on
the edge of explosion or collapse and works in all cases to forestall
the reductive interpretations offered by professors of rhetoric or
psychoanalysis. Freud complains that the reader of Hoffmann's *The
Devil's Elixirs* is not 'enlightened' by the novel's ending but instead
'falls into a state of complete bewilderment' (p. 234). Yet this is
precisely the point: Hoffmann prevents the return to a familiar
origin and prohibits critical attempts to define his rationale. Calculatedly scattered and indisciplined, his work has no method in its
madness, no reason in its coruscating light.

Freud is fully aware that 'among its different shades of meaning
the word *"heimlich"* exhibits one which is identical with its opposite,
"unheimlich"' (p. 224). He wants to convert this circuitry into a
hierarchy and subordinate the uncanny to the canny, to determine
the *unheimlich* as 'a sub-species of *heimlich*' (p. 226). Sometimes,
however, it is the canny which gets driven underground. Several of
the examples which Freud takes from Sanders's *Wörterbuch der
Deutschen Sprache* use the word *heimlich* in a negative sense: 'she did
not feel too *heimlich* with him' (p. 222). In other citations the canny
occurs *after* something else: 'wild animals ... are trained to be
heimlich' (p. 222). More interestingly still, the canny often seems to
be under threat: 'is it still *heimlich* to you in your country where
strangers are felling your woods?' (p. 222).

Freud claims to have found the 'genetic connection' which leads
from the *unheimlich* to the *heimlich* and from figurative effects back to
literal causes (p. 225). David Carroll, who has analysed Freud's
ideas about origins and his efforts to 'distinguish ... between reality
and fiction', would associate this sort of reading with Freud's earlier
work.[32] In the 'Preliminary Communication' (1893) of *Studies on
Hysteria* (1895) there is no doubt that the trauma at the root of
neurotic symptoms is an 'event' (*SE*, II, 6). By the time of 'From the
History of an Infantile Neurosis' (1918), however, the distinction
between reality and fantasy, and implicitly between the literal and
the figurative, has become less certain. Freud argues that even if the
seduction scene witnessed by the 'Wolf Man' was a fantasy it
nevertheless produced effects 'just as though it had been entirely
real' (*SE*, XVII, 58). Far from being translated into something more
'real', the figures of fantasy may well stand in the place of a literal
source. For Carroll, Freud's inability to reduce the deviations of

fantasy to literal meaning is to be seen as a strength: abandoning his
efforts to achieve absolute interpretative control, Freud discovers
that 'the route taken to the origin is as important as the origin itself'
(Carroll, 'Freud and the Myth of Origin', p. 517). In his *'détour'*
through the Wolf Man's psychical life, Freud reaches the figure and
not the fact (*SE*, xvII, 18). Ultimately, therefore, and in spite of his
continuing attempts to translate the strange into the familiar, literature into psychoanalysis, Freud's version of the analytic path is
different from Plato's detour and Aristotle's notion of metaphoric
deviation. Freud ceases to believe that the royal road which leads
through madness to knowledge, through the symbol to the symbol-
ized and through the figures of the dream to the facts of the
unconscious has any end. He comes to realize that his annexation of
the 'uncanny', which begins typographically as early as the title,
reveals only the strange figurativeness of the inside. The autobiographical anecdote which Freud relates shortly after his discussion of 'The Sandman' represents this new and fruitful hesitancy and
could be seen as a synecdoche of 'The "Uncanny"', since the entire
essay has been for Freud a sort of holiday in a 'rather remote' area, a
'province' of aesthetics (*SE*, xvII, 219).

As I was walking, one hot summer afternoon, through the deserted streets
of a provincial town in Italy which was unknown to me, I found myself in a
quarter of whose character I could not long remain in doubt. Nothing but
painted women were to be seen at the windows of the small houses, and I
hastened to leave the narrow street at the next turning. But after having
wandered about for a time without enquiring my way, I suddenly found
myself back in the same street, where my presence was now beginning to
excite attention. I hurried away once more, only to arrive by another *détour*
at the same place yet a third time. Now, however, a feeling overcame me
which I can only describe as uncanny, and I was glad enough to find myself
back at the piazza I had left a short while before, without any further
voyages of discovery. (p. 237)

Unable to terminate his detour and return to the security of the
familiar, Freud finds himself encountering living symbols of the
figurative, emblems of the kinds of 'subtle invitation to transgression' which, in the view of Hélène Cixous, Freud tries
throughout the essay to resist and which are repeatedly associated
with literature and the uncanny.[33] Meretricious and illicit sup-
plements to licensed desire, the painted women transform sexuality-
as-cause into artifice and effect. They irresistibly recall the figure of
Olympia and the dangerous delights of rhetoric: the speech of Lysias

in the *Phaedrus* which has seduction on false pretences as its *raison d'être*, the '*seducing spirits*' of 'heathen poets' which Hobbes warns against (*Leviathan*, p. 398) and Locke's extended comparison between pleasurable but deceptive eloquence and 'the fair sex' (*Human Understanding*, III, 10, 34). Interrupting the pursuit of truth and knowledge, the painted women gaze out at Freud from their windows and he, more prudently than Nathaniel, attempts to withdraw, to avoid exciting attention by his own excited attention. Yet Freud also subtly accepts transgression. Although he denies himself a literal pleasure in the flesh, his restraint makes possible a subsequent rendezvous in and with fiction, a fascinated circling. His avoidance of literal seduction allows him in a figurative sense to be seduced into telling stories, creating rather than reducing metaphors.

THE SUBLIME

Does philosophy stand alone in trying to exorcise the ghosts and resist being seduced by the figures? It is tempting to argue that poetry seeks to evoke both, and yet, as Derrida argues, the poet may be a 'man of metaphor' who plays with language only 'in order to return to the identity of meaning' (*Margins*, p. 248). Despite Ricoeur's optimism, poetry is not always a domain of figurative freedom in which categorial transgressions abolish old frontiers to create new relations (see *The Rule of Metaphor*, pp. 197, 310–11). A poet like Spenser is preoccupied not by the heuristic force of metaphor but by the ornamental, artificial and ultimately suspect nature of figurative language. The very doubleness of 'Duessa' (deuce – the devil) is a conventional characterization of both evil and rhetoric, and the destruction of the Bower of Bliss in *The Faerie Queene* could be read as an act of self-protective violence, a defence against the seductive phantasms of figurative language. The Bower is a partially avowed emblem of poetry in general, of everything that 'natures worke by art can imitate'.[34] Here as elsewhere, the scapegoat is closely related to the body which expels it. With its ivy of beaten gold, the 'evil' scenery of the Bower is difficult to distinguish from the 'good' landscape of 'Prothalamion', in which the banks of the Thames are 'paynted all with variable flowers' (Spenser, *Works: The Minor Poems*, II, 257, line 13). In spite of a variability which favourably contrasts with the enamelled fixity of the Bower, the link between evil and the artificially imitative unavoidably carries over, so that poetry, insofar as it too produces unreal and painted likenesses, inevitably becomes tainted by rhetoric. Spenser repeatedly falls prey to the guilt of rhetorical flowers, fearing an eloquence which can only be meretricious, an ornamentalism that must be deathly. Signs of his struggle against figurative and ultimately poetic utterance emerge in repeated acts of apparently unconscious self-sabotage so that in 'Epithalamion', for example, the bride's beauty is said to create an astonishment which would affect a spectator in the same way as 'Medusaes mazeful hed' (*Works: The Minor Poems*, II, 249, line 190).

It is perhaps to be expected that monsters tend to lose the subversive impact they may once have had. The centaurs and chimeras mentioned by Hobbes and Locke are the products of such basic categorial permutations that it is somewhat surprising to see them being seriously offered as threats to taxonomic order. Even Aubrey conceded that 'old wives fables are grosse things' (quoted in Dick's introduction to *Brief Lives*, p. lxv). In a *Spectator* essay of 14 March 1711, Joseph Addison followed Hobbes and Locke more willingly than Aubrey when he wrote that 'Stories of Spirits and Apparitions' were merely 'old Womens Fables'.[35] Ghosts were clearly a threatened species; nevertheless, the ghostly had not entirely disappeared. In the *Spectator* (6 July 1711), Addison described how he had wandered at dusk through the estate of Sir Roger de Coverley. He wrote with distinct relish that the grounds of the abbey were 'one of the most proper Scenes in the World for a Ghost to appear in' (*The Spectator*, I, 453). Ruins were 'scattered up and down on every Side, and half covered with Ivy and Eldar-Bushes, the Harbours of several solitary Birds which seldom make their Appearance till the Dusk of the Evening' (p. 453). In the churchyard there were 'Graves and Burying-Places', and there was 'an Eccho among the old Ruins and Vaults' (p. 453). Committed equally to delineating the literal features of an external scene and expressing a mood, an interior landscape, this passage dwells on the blurred border between day and night, nature and culture, silence and sound, the archaic and the modern. No ghosts appear but there is an overwhelming sense of the still reverberating presence of the past. Addison's echo reminds one of the 'eccho' in the 'Epithalamion', but the later writer shows little of Spenser's drive to fracture the Orphic voice, the self-present song, to enforce the visions of catastrophe and collapse which haunt the 'Two Cantos of Mutabilitie' and 'The Ruines of Time'. Spenser's echo is a necessary failure or pious renunciation whereas Addison's is a triumph of the stimulated sensibility. The ivy in the Bower of Bliss sacrilegiously mimics nature but Addison's ivy returns the cultural to nature in a partial effacement of boundaries which makes for aesthetic pleasure rather than theological horror.

Locke had casually compared the mind to a tomb (see p. 15 above) but for Addison literal tombs and ruins prompted less rigorously rational speculations concerning the nature of imaginative experience. Aubrey had already discussed the gratification which could be derived from a combination of 'stately Ruines' and 'Prospects' where the eye had 'roome to guesse' and this pictorial interest in scenes which combine a natural panorama with foregrounded cultural details returns in still more intermingled ways in Addison's explorations of the sublime (quoted in Dick's introduction to *Brief Lives*, p. 1). From Sir Roger de Coverley's abbey to the ruined structures of Gothic fiction and Romantic poetry, the literature of the sublime showed a continuing fascination with conceptual and geographical spectra, with uncertain borders and with the interplay between thought and things. Sublime experience resembled reading in that it often involved the reception and resurrection of partially decayed but still potent signs. It emerged from feelings of what Harold Bloom would call 'belatedness'[36] and often aimed at creating a sense of hauntedness. Just as Addison listened for echoes of the archaic, so Thomas Gray attempted to disinter 'the voice of Nature' in 'Elegy written in a Country Churchyard' whilst Oliver Goldsmith searched for a 'voice prevailing over time' in 'The Deserted Village'.[37] Both these poems endeavour to stage transactions across the threshold between the present and the past and in this they prefigure what Geoffrey Hartman calls the 'antiphonal style' of Wordsworth's poetry.[38] Wordsworth's notion of poetry as a passage of meaning manifests itself in dramatized encounters between the teller of a tale and a listener ('The Female Vagrant', 'Hart-leap Well'), in the uncanny encounters of 'Lines composed a few miles above Tintern Abbey' and 'Resolution and Independence', and in the belated quest for an experience of 'The ghostly language of the ancient earth' in *The Prelude*.[39]

The *Poetics* had argued that beauty cannot exist either in 'a very minute creature' or 'in a creature of vast size' (Aristotle, *Works*, xi,

1450.b.35–9). Edmund Burke's conception of the sublime coincided precisely with what Aristotle expelled from the realm of the beautiful: 'as the great extreme of dimension is sublime, so the last extreme of littleness is in some measure sublime likewise'.[40] Writing in the *Spectator* some forty-five years before the publication of *A Philosophical Enquiry*, Addison had already argued that one of the pleasures of the imagination lay in its attempt 'to graspe at any thing that is too big for its Capacity' and also to 'discover in the smallest Particle of this little World, a new inexhausted Fund of Matter' (*The Spectator*, III, 540, 576). In defiance of Locke's injunction to keep thought within the bounds of reason, Addison believed that sublime experience enabled the soul to become 'delightfully lost and bewildered in a pleasant Delusion' (p. 546). Hobbes had argued that the ravages of compound imagination particularly afflicted those who were 'much taken with reading of romances' (*Leviathan*, p. 10). But Addison positively wanted to 'walk about like the Enchanted Hero of a Romance' (*The Spectator*, III, 546). Nevertheless, the pleasures of the imagination were not entirely unmixed. The sublime fused pleasure and pain in ways which would have interested the author of 'The "Uncanny"' and 'Beyond the Pleasure Principle'. This fusion was related to the old aesthetic problem of how, in the words of the *Poetics*, 'we delight to view the most realistic representations' of objects which may in themselves 'be painful to see ... the forms for example of the lowest animals and of dead bodies' (Aristotle, *Works*, XI, 1448. b. 10–15). For Addison the 'Mixture of Delight in ... Disgust' was made possible by the spectator's safety (*The Spectator*, III, 540). Burke agreed that the representation of pain could be a source of delight but argued that the spectator's safety was a necessary but not sufficient condition for pleasure. Sublime terror created 'an unnatural tension and certain violent emotions of the nerves' (*A Philosophical Enquiry*, p. 134). Provided it was not excessive, nervous tension provided beneficial exercise for 'the finer organs' (p. 136). To emphasize the salubrity of sublime experience was, however, to ignore more important aspects of Aristotle's point about the delight in represented pain. In a sense this delight was the purest of aesthetic moments since it set the world of representations free from the world of objects and released mimetic pleasure, the ability to 'delight in works of imitation', in possibly its most intense form (Aristotle, *Works*, XI, 1448. b. 5–10). To enjoy seeing likenesses was to enjoy seeing phantasms, to recognize, as Addison put it in the *Spectator*

(1 July 1712), that imaginative pleasure occurred when 'we do not care for seeing through the falsehood, and willingly give ourselves up to so agreeable an imposture' (*Works*, III, 423). Addison's argument was eventually to culminate in Coleridge's comments in the *Biographia Literaria* (1817) on the 'willing suspension of disbelief' with regard to poetry in general and the supernatural in particular.[41]

Sublime experience released what Burke described as 'a richness and profusion of images, in which the mind is so dazzled as to make it impossible to attend to that exact coherence and agreement of the allusions' (*A Philosophical Enquiry*, p. 78). Burke's phrasing owes a great deal to Longinus's advice that metaphors should be used when 'the passions roll like a torrent and sweep a multitude of them down their resistless flood' (*On the Sublime*, p. 121). At its deepest level the explosion of the figurative in sublime experience was for Burke a matter of epistemological vertigo rather than psychological callisthenics. Ravished by aesthetic experience, the spectator's mind was 'so entirely filled with its object, that it cannot entertain any other' (*A Philosophical Enquiry*, p. 57). It encountered an 'irresistible force' which swept away its capacity to reason and to limit itself to particulars (p. 57). Because the sublime transported experience beyond the boundary of reason it was closely connected with 'obscurity', with 'uncertain, confused' descriptions and with 'apparent disorder' (pp. 58, 59, 78).

Although Burke and Addison knew that the sublime was often a pleasurable element of experience, they feared the implications of categorial crisis as much as they were fascinated by them. One could derive imaginative pleasure from represented pain, but the pleasure itself was mixed with pain. The sublime did not involve a naive delight in sheer anarchy and in many ways it was quite close to Locke's uneasy contemplation of the shadows. One could even argue that sublime aesthetic theory was the ambitious child of Lockeian rationalism, that it haunted the darkness which Locke had not been able to subject to light and pondered the consequences of his failure to fix the 'just measure'. Although Addison and Burke investigated the areas of experience left unexplained or defined as inexplicable by Hobbes and Locke, they too were committed to drawing their own boundaries. Although the genre sublime was in principle the genre which exceeded genre, the category in which the categories collapsed, the analysis which addressed the unanalysable, its signs and tokens were fated to settle into patterns. The objects of the sublime became (in, for instance, the novels of Ann Radcliffe) conventional pictorial archetypes, orthodox and familiar rhetorical strategies. The literature of the sublime seemed merely to have extended the realm of the sayable and left its real object out of reach beyond the threshold.

THE NOVEL AND THE ROMANCE

At the same time as the romances condemned in the *Leviathan* and modestly celebrated in Aubrey were being transformed into Addison's ghostly scene and Burke's sublime, a further metamorphosis was under way in the Aristotelian conception of the pleasure in 'realistic representations' of things that 'may be painful to see' (Aristotle, *Works*, xi, 1448. b. 10–15). Daniel Defoe's 'A True Relation of the Apparition of one Mrs Veal' (1706) preceded the publication of *Moll Flanders* (1722) and *Roxana* (1724) and could be seen as the forerunner of the novelistic realism often said to begin with the later texts. Sir Walter Scott was later to compare the writing of Defoe to Flemish paintings, 'where, though the subjects drawn are mean and disagreeable, and such as in nature we would not wish to study or look close upon, yet the skill with which they are represented by the painter gives an interest to the imitation upon canvass which the original entirely wants'.[42] Scott devoted more attention to 'Mrs Veal' than to any other of Defoe's works because it best exemplified his 'plausibility', his 'matter-of-fact, businesslike style' and his 'art of recommending the most improbable narrative, by his specious and serious mode of telling it' (Scott, *Novelists and Fiction*, pp. 179, 176, 175).

James Sutherland has argued that Scott's view of Defoe is misleading and that 'Mrs Veal' is 'factually true in almost every detail'.[43] Such a view does not, however, refute the idea that the 'truth' of Defoe's relation needs to be fabricated in the right way. Defoe showed neither Locke's disapproval nor Addison's delight in the imposture which lurked behind the mimetic relation. His account made no overt attempt to reach beyond the borders of understanding, to entertain what Locke had called 'those sublime Thoughts, which towre above the Clouds' (*Human Understanding*, ii, 1, 24). The ghost of Mrs Veal did not belong to a shadowy beyond or to a nostalgic sense of the past. She was simply imported into the heart of what purported to be commonplace reality. History became a *trompe l'oeil* illusion, although it was only later, with *Moll Flanders*, that fiction began to pose as history. Because the appearance of Mrs Veal's ghost leads one to accept the fact that Mrs Bargrave, the ghost seer, is barred from the grave and therefore not herself a phantasm, one could argue that the ghostly actually strengthens the verisimilitude of the narrative. I agree with Todorov when he argues that, 'far from being a praise of the imaginary', fantastic literature 'posits the majority of a text as belonging to reality' (*The Fantastic*, p. 168). But one could also argue in somewhat different terms that literal instances of the supernatural deflect attention from the more significant if less specific ghostliness of other fictional presences. What is the difference between Mrs Veal, the postulated apparition, and Mrs Bargrave, herself a phantom raised by the text? What, after all, is a 'true relation'? In *Gulliver's Travels* (1726), the Governor of Glubbdubdrib tells Gulliver that the ghosts will certainly tell him the truth, 'for Lying was a Talent of no use in the lower World'.[44] Cassirer has shown how the Sanskrit word for 'lie' (*druh*) develops into the German *Traum* and 'recurs also in the Germanic designations for demons and ghosts (Old Norse, *draugr* – ghost, OHG *troc*, *gitroc*, etc.)' (*Mythical Thought*, p. 245, note 10). Ghosts may be born out of what the religious consciousness wants to dismiss as lies (a 'fetch' is a ghost but also a trick) but although they are equivocal or illusory in sensory terms they are rarely deceitful in terms of meaning. In *Macbeth* and *Hamlet*, in Schiller's *The Ghost-Seer* and Byron's 'Oscar of Alva', to name but a few, ghosts return to point out their own murderers, to reveal the truth. In Aubrey's tale of Francis Fry (see *Brief Lives*, p. 109) and in Oldbuck's tale of Rab Tull in Chapter 9 of Scott's *The Antiquary*, ghosts appear in order to indicate the whereabouts of a missing will or to enforce its terms.[45] Ghosts may of course riddle truth, and Swift's narrative wittily places the truth of the ghosts within a hoax document, raising possibly deeper questions than Defoe. Mrs Veal's pious posthumous recommendation of Drelincourt seems, at least in part, to have been merely an ingenious marketing strategy even though, as Manuel Schonhorn has shown, it was factually if inconsistently supported by other sources.[46] 'Mrs Veal' uses ghostly truth as a vehicle for moral instruction, and it seems that Addison was defining society's use of the ghostly as accurately as Hobbes when he remarked in the *Spectator* (6 July 1711) that tales of the afterlife promoted 'the study of virtue' in those credulous enough to accept them (Addison, *Works*, II, 443).

Like the ghost of Hamlet's father, the ghost of Mrs Veal has become a touchstone and a test case in discussions of the nature and function of fiction. For Freud, Frye, Ricoeur and Frank Kermode, the spectre exemplifies in various ways the predicative power of fiction, the hypothetical nature of literary statements and the ability of writing to manipulate and stimulate the reader.[47] A discussion along these lines had already begun in Fielding's *Tom Jones* (1749). When Partridge attends a performance of *Hamlet*, he is at first unruffled by the appearance of the ghost, who for him is merely a man in 'strange Dress'.[48] Yet the naturalism of Garrick's acting soon infects him with Hamlet's fear in the face of his father's ghost. Unable to conceive of mimesis in terms of a correspondence which allows represented pain to become the source of pleasure, Partridge jumps from total disbelief to its opposite. Having been unwittingly seduced into judging art like life, his sleep is destroyed for weeks. For W. K. Wimsatt and Monroe C. Beardsley, the fear of fictional ghosts would be conclusive evidence of aesthetic primitivism, of an adherence to what they somewhat dismissively term the 'affective fallacy'.[49] It is certainly true that the physiological account of the aesthetic moment in Longinus, Burke and Hoffmann is also frequently found in descriptions of ghostly experience. In both cases there is an attempt to describe the effect of the disembodied in terms of automatic physical responses on the part of the spectator. There is a common emphasis on the feeling of having 'really seen' something, together with a standard set of references to creeping or prickling flesh, tingling spines, sensations in the pits of stomachs and hearts in mouths.

Burke had not yet completed his essay on the sublime when the novelistic readjustment to theories of the representation of the commonplace began to harden into a manifesto. Early in 1741 Samuel Richardson wrote to Aaron Hill about his attempts to 'introduce a new species of writing' in *Pamela*, the first two volumes of which had been published in the previous year.[50] He had excluded 'the improbable and marvellous' in his attempt to get away from 'the pomp and parade of romance-writing' (Richardson, *Selected Letters*, p. 41). In his Preface to the two-volume sequel to *Pamela* (1741), Richardson again pointed out his adherence to 'NATURE' and his avoidance of 'romantic flights, improbable surprises, and irrational machinery'.[51] Richardson's conception of fiction might almost have satisfied Hobbes. Remarkably, however, Horace Walpole (whose literary aims were so different to those of Richardson) initially appears happy to accept his predecessor's terms with only minor terminological adjustments. In the Preface to the second edition of *The Castle of Otranto* (1765), he distinguished between the ancient romance, in which 'all was imagination and improbability', and the modern romance, in which 'nature is always intended to be ... copied' and which attempted to maintain 'a strict adherence to common life'.[52] By the time of Scott, the familiar opposition of 'romance' and 'novel' has at last been adopted, although the definitions are largely the same as those of Walpole or Richardson. Romance dealt with 'marvellous and uncommon incidents', whereas the events of a novel were 'accommodated to the ordinary train of human events, and the modern state of society'.[53]

It is not my intention to criticize these generic definitions. To formulate the essential nature of a genre in a phrase is inevitably to construct a simplistic, non-specific model, and yet, as Adena Rosmarin has argued, the schematic nature of generic definitions is precisely what gives them their 'explanatory power'.[54] The important point is that Richardson, Walpole and Scott are invoking a number of the borderlines which I have attempted to explore in this chapter, in particular those between the real and the unreal, the literal and the figurative, and between commonplace, contemporary actuality and the ghostly realm of the past. Yet there is no neat opposition between Richardson and Walpole. This is not simply because the probable, the natural and the contemporary are relative concepts and that from Scott's point of view Richardson's novels were 'but a step from the old romance' and still dealt in 'improbable incidents' (*Novelists and Fiction*, p. 52).[55] What separates a writer like Walpole from one like Richardson is not the way in which they define the romance and the novel or the way in which their work may or may not obey the definition but their conception of their own position within the romance/novel spectrum. Having bisected the fictional landscape, Richardson claimed that his own work fell exclusively within the territory of the novel. But Walpole did not adopt an opposite position by devoting himself to pure irrationality and improbability. Instead he described his literary project in the Preface to the first edition of *Otranto* (1764) as an attempt to *combine* the 'preternatural events' of ancient romance with a naturalism which ensured that his characters 'comport themselves as persons would do in their situation' (*Otranto*, p. 4).[56]

Combining, mingling, counterbalancing: these were to become the most characteristic manoeuvres of the romancer, and they could of course be seen as somewhat faint-hearted compromises. Clara Reeve dutifully sought to hold the potential extravagances of romance in check by her fidelity to 'the manners of real life' and her determination to keep within the '*verge* of probability'.[57] Dorothy Scarborough's description of the Gothic novel as 'a protest against the excess of rationalism and realism in the early eighteenth century' does little to explain the genre's deep need for law.[58] There are few if any Gothic novels in which the descent into disorder is not ultimately recuperated, in however artificial or revealingly unsatisfactory a manner, and Walpole is far more apologetic about his improbabilities than Defoe. Horace had distinguished between poetic licence and the irresponsible multiplication of centaurs and mermaids in poetic ideas which, 'like a sick man's dreams, are all vain and fictitious: so that neither head nor foot can correspond to any one form'.[59] But in his epigraph to the second edition of *Otranto*, Walpole did not evince the fierce perversity required to claim these sick dreams and shapeless fancies as his own. Instead, as W. S. Lewis has pointed out, Walpole's epigraph 'reverses Horace's meaning' to suggest that the idle fancies are ' "assigned to a single shape" '.[60] Walpole recoups fancy's monstrous permutations for the unified body of order. In a curious sense, therefore, Defoe's stylistic realism is more radically 'romantic' in its unapologetic use of the supernatural within a contemporary setting than Walpole's displacement of the ghosts into the remote period before protestantism dispelled 'the empire of superstition' (*Otranto*, p. 3).

Richardson would have argued that the novelist could afford to ignore romance. The romancer, on the other hand, wanted to negotiate a space between divergent tendencies and actively sought out the interstices between the past and the present, the natural and the preternatural. This desire was formulated once again in the opening chapter of Scott's *Waverley*, which claimed that the work was 'neither a romance of chivalry, nor a tale of modern manners'.[61] Neither, nor, but something of both: a hybrid form in which the claims of reality and the imagination, of chivalric conventions and those of the contemporary novel of manners could be productively played off against each other. What Scott and other romancers were promoting was a literary form in which, as George Dekker puts it, 'cross-cultural alliances' and 'relationships ... across party lines' could be constructed for the purposes of irony, ambivalence or mediation.[62] Yet the longing for a mid-point involved problems and dangers as well as compromises and resolutions. In its fictional revival of the marvellous and through its transformation of what David B. Morris sees as the 'figurative elements of the sublime style into principles of narrative structure', Gothic literature, in spite of its commitment to order, inaugurates a crisis in which 'words and images grow radically unstable' and 'meaning is continually in question'.[63]

HAWTHORNE

Charles Feidelson has argued that Jonathan Edwardes stands at the beginning of a tradition in American literature which endorses symbolic meaning and breaks decisively with the antipathy towards rhetoric shown by many American writers of the eighteenth century (see *Symbolism and American Literature*, pp. 98–101). Emerson is the culmination of the new tradition and his 'sweeping sense of poetic fusion' and tolerance of paradox transcend the polarities and fixed categories aimed at in Lockeian thought (p. 120). Yet the belief of the New England liberals that 'mutually exclusive ideas may be equally true' was, as Feidelson demonstrates, only a short step from the fear that such ideas were equally untrue (p. 98), that acts of synthesis presumed the existence of antitheses (see pp. 50, 126, 135–7) or that symbolic unity led to formlessness and a 'proliferation of metaphor' (p. 148). In these circumstances, as Tony Tanner points out, the attitude of innocent wonder often found in American writing can give way to a reign of terror, 'a shockingly abrupt disillusion, a very sudden sense of blighting deprivation, an impotent gloom'.[64] A strong sense of post-Romantic pessimism appears in *Moby-Dick* (1851) and the chapter entitled 'The Whiteness of the Whale' even seems to project the doubts of Hobbes and Locke concerning rhetorical artifice onto the world at large. 'Nature', writes Melville, 'absolutely paints like the harlot, whose allurements cover nothing but the charnel-house within'.[65] Poe's awareness that 'the boundaries which divide Life from Death are at best shadowy and vague' combines fascination with an anxiety about categorial instability that is typical of the English Enlightenment.[66]

For Michael Davitt Bell the philosophical presuppositions of American romance are directly descended from the intellectual tradition which runs from Locke to Hartley. Haunted by this tradition and its deep-rooted suspicion of rhetoric and the imagination, writers such as Brown, Irving and Hawthorne 'often painfully denigrated not only the order of imaginative experience but their own status as writers of fiction'.[67] Bell argues that the attitude of the romancers towards their own literary activity was too ambivalent for them to adopt anything but an at best defensive posture in response to attacks on fiction such as that of Thomas Jefferson, who in 1818 wrote to Nathaniel Burwell about the 'inordinate passion prevalent for novels' (quoted by Bell, p. 11). For Jefferson this passion was a 'poison' which led the mind to reject 'reason and fact, plain and unadorned', creating a 'bloated imagination' and a disgust for 'the real business of life' (quoted by Bell, p. 11). The generation of Jefferson was, as Leslie Fiedler puts its, 'pledged to be done with ghosts and shadows'.[68] Once again, however, exorcism involves raising spectres: a bloated imagination has poisoned the lives of numerous American heroes and heroines from Charles Brockden Brown's *Wieland* (1798) and Washington Irving's 'The Adventures of the German Student' (1824) onwards.

When Nathaniel Hawthorne formulated the distinction between the romance and the novel in his Preface to *The House of the Seven Gables* (1851) he echoed the terms of Walpole, and for that matter of Reeve, Shelley and Scott, with an almost weary exactitude. The novel was 'presumed to aim at a very minute fidelity, not merely to the possible, but to the probable and ordinary course of man's experience', whereas the romance claimed 'a certain latitude' in form and subject (*CE*, II, 1). Like his predecessors, Hawthorne then argued that although the romance departed from a minute fidelity it 'sins unpardonably, so far as it may swerve aside from the truth of the human heart' (*CE*, II, 1). It was in 'The Custom-House' that Hawthorne made his most explicit bid for the threshold or mid-point of romance, envisaging his study as 'a neutral territory, somewhere between the real world and fairy-land, where the Actual and the Imaginary may meet, and each imbue itself with the nature of the other' (*CE*, I, 36). Formally, thematically and epistemologically, though perhaps not geographically, these comments amply justify Richard Chase's description of the romance in America as 'a kind of "border" fiction'.[69] But far from being a safe haven, a place of fusion in which hostilities were suspended and oppositions became reconciled within literary form, Hawthorne's neutral territory was potentially a place of disturbing confusions and compounded tensions. In 'The Custom-House', Hawthorne argued that his 'wiser effort would have been to diffuse thought and imagination through the opaque substance of to-day' (*CE*, I, 37). In practice, however, he found himself committing the 'folly' of creating 'the semblance of a world out of airy matter' (p. 37). Even in his letter to Longfellow of 4 June 1837, Hawthorne had felt that his attempt to give 'a lifelike semblance' to his 'shadowy stuff' was 'not easy' (*CE*, xv, 252). These reservations about the project of romance set Hawthorne at a considerable distance from the *Biographia Literaria*, in which Coleridge describes his attempts to foster 'poetic faith' (*Collected Works*, VII, 2, p. 6). Coleridge had endeavoured to give his 'supernatural' or 'romantic' characters 'a semblance of truth' and to suspend disbelief in his 'shadows of imagination' (p. 6). He had not for a moment fallen prey to fears that the plan adopted in the *Lyrical Ballads* was foolish.

For Hawthorne the conjuring of semblances was not only difficult or absurd: it was also frequently sinister, virtually criminal. In 'The Devil in Manuscript', the author Oberon develops 'a horror of what was created in my own brain' and shudders at 'the manuscripts in which I gave that dark idea a sort of material existence' (*CE*, xi, 172). Michael Anesko argues persuasively that when, in a letter of April 1860 to James T. Fields, Hawthorne talks of the 'Devil' in his 'inkstand', he is referring simply to his failure in writing genial and commercially successful books (*Friction with the Market*, p. 69). The devil here would not represent the evil of writing but the evil of not being able to make a living by it. One could of course extend this argument back to Oberon, seeing the 'devil' of the title in relation to unpublishable manuscripts rather than dark ideas. I would agree with Michael J. Colacurcio that the 'Oberon' pieces are 'thoroughly ironic' and that 'The Devil in Manuscript' 'reads off best as comedy'.[70] Oberon's comments on writing are indeed exaggerated almost to the point of absurdity. Yet surely the irony behind Hawthorne's comedy is that the manuscripts actually do have a dangerously inflammatory effect – although not in the ways that Oberon might have thought. An ironic recognition of the power of fantasy does not entirely erase that power, and there was, I think, for Hawthorne, an unnervingly fine line between the romancer's fidelity to 'the truth of the human heart' and the plotting Chillingworth's cold-blooded violation of 'the sanctity of a human heart' in *The Scarlet Letter* (*CE*, II, 1; I, 195). In his paintings, John Winslow of 'The Prophetic Pictures' is able to conjure 'phantoms at will, and keep the form of the dead among the living' (*CE*, IX, 169). His mimetic ability sponsors a blasphemous pride and a manipulative egotism; he becomes 'a magician, controlling the phantoms which he had evoked' (p. 182). The artist's power to create replicas and 'striking counterfeits' enables him to exercise a malign influence over the lives of his originals (p. 169).

Representation has its risks, but observation brings analogous dangers and temptations. 'A cold observer' like Ethan Brand experiments on the living, converting them into his puppets (*CE*, XI, 99). 'The Unpardonable Sin', as Hawthorne wrote in a notebook entry of 27 July 1844 which paved the way for 'Ethan Brand', 'might consist in a want of love and reverence for the Human Soul; in consequence of which, the investigator pried into its dark depths, not with a hope or purpose of making it better, but from a cold philosophical curiosity ... only desiring to study it out' (*CE*, VIII, 251). The dangers of representation and observation here give way to those of interpretation. Hawthorne's description of the unpardonable sin contains a double bind, for it is made possible by the coolly investigative stance which it condemns. To diagnose the unpardonable sin or to represent it in fiction is to inspect the dark inspecting depths of other souls and to run the risk of committing a second such sin. This insight is given extended treatment in *The Blithedale Romance*, in which Hollingsworth accuses Fourier of having committed 'the Unpardonable Sin' and is then himself convicted by Coverdale of a 'terrible egotism' and of believing in a 'cold, spectral monster' of a theory (*CE*, III, 55). Coverdale subsequently finds himself in turn being accused by Zenobia of 'a cold-blooded criticism ... a monstrous scepticism' and of 'groping for human emotion in the dark corners of the heart' (pp. 170, 214). Coldly ignoring emotions or coldly seeking them out, the characters of *The Blithedale Romance* seem doomed to commit either the sins of partisanship or those of scepticism. For Hawthorne, the predicament of the artist was much the same. If analysing the unpardonable sins of others meant implicating oneself in such sins, if pointing to monsters was well on the way to being one, then the writer of *The Blithedale Romance* was only the outermost circle in a spreading series of concentric crimes. Hawthorne showed little faith in the efficacy of catharsis. Instead of isolating, fixing and removing evil, the scapegoat transformed its persecutors into images of itself.

Hawthorne's suspicions of observation and analysis, creation and control, magic and magicians, are focussed with great clarity in 'Rappaccini's Daughter', a tale which is haunted by an almost Spenserian guilt about semblances and artifices. A latterday Bower of Bliss, Rappaccini's garden and its flowers stands at one level for literature and its tropes. Rappaccini is specifically compared to an artist (see *CE*, x, 126) and the plants in his garden seem to Giovanni to be 'no longer of God's making, but the monstrous offspring of man's depraved fancy' (p. 110). Rappaccini's art does not license a marriage between the actual and the imaginary but instead creates a licentious confounding, an orgiastic proliferation of monstrous hybrids produced by 'adultery of... vegetable species' (p. 110). The dream of a neutral territory turns into a nightmare of uncanny figurative fusion, a 'lurid intermixture' of light and dark (p. 105). The tale presents something very like the sacrificial crisis: 'not a synthesis of elements', as Girard puts it, 'but a formless and grotesque mixture of things that are normally separate' (*Violence and the Sacred*, p. 160).

Like the aristocratic wraith in Irving's 'The Adventures of the German Student', Beatrice Rappaccini is cousin to Hoffmann's Olympia. One of the differences between the German writer and his American followers is, to use the terms of 'The "Uncanny"', that between the infant's desire to bring dolls to life and the adult's fear of fictional animism. Hawthorne shares the anxieties of Hobbes and Locke concerning the seductive power of rhetorical flowers and those of Freud regarding painted women. He seems more capable than Irving of entertaining and exploring his ambivalent attitude towards fantasy within fantasy but he has little of the mad confidence with which Hoffmann promoted a modern version of the sacrificial crisis as a programme for literature. Like Giovanni, he was at one level searching for stable categories, attempting to bring the literary, as Giovanni wants to bring Beatrice, 'rigidly and systematically within the limits of ordinary experience' (*CE*, x, 105). Unlike Giovanni, however, Hawthorne knew that the imposition of the fixed limits of the actual was as fatal an affair as the adulterations of the imaginary. Poisons could cure in the person of Chillingworth, who is in spite of himself, as Fiedler points out, responsible for driving Dimmesdale 'toward confession and penance' (*Love and Death*, p. 236). But cures could also poison: Baglioni's antidote causes the death of Beatrice. Even when they pry into other souls with the hope of making things better, those who administer the cures which convert evil into good themselves become poisonous. Beatrice's evil 'will pass away like a dream' but Giovanni must live with the fearful meaning of her final question: 'was there not, from the first, more poison in thy nature than in mine?' (*CE*, x, 127).

One could argue that Hawthorne feared the monstrous more than he feared the ghostly. The orderly procession of spectres in 'Howe's Masquerade' is quite unlike the grotesque mobs featured in 'My Kinsman, Major Molineux' or 'Lady Eleanore's Mantle'. Bell argues that the two latter tales concern Hawthorne's perception of 'the essential connection between the unleashing of fantasy and the unleashing of revolutionary violence' (*The Development of American Romance*, p. 171). The ghosts of 'Howe's Masquerade', on the other hand, stand for sequence and control, enabling Hawthorne to represent the past as an unfolding tableau, a line of meaning. At one point or another almost all of Hawthorne's characters and a good many rooms, fireplaces and pictures are described in ghostly terms. In some ways this stylistic tic displaces the anxieties associated with monstrosity and anarchy. In *The Scarlet Letter* and *The House of the Seven Gables* Hawthorne repeatedly suggests that American life attenuates the European stock. The living become ghostly reductions of their ancestors, losing the fatal sexual potency embodied in a European like Beatrice Rappaccini. Zenobia is the Beatrice Rappaccini of *The Blithedale Romance* but even as she makes her first appearance Coverdale is claiming that 'I can now summon her up like a ghost, a little wanner than the life' (*CE*, III, 15). Whereas Rappaccini's art monstrously confounded the actual and the imaginary, the neutral territory described in 'The Custom-House' was designed to create ghostly but regulated transactions between the two, spiritualizing the actual by rendering it translucent and mysterious whilst actualizing the imaginary by giving it a certain dimensionality and opacity. When Hawthorne's 'familiar room' was 'spiritualized' by cool moonlight he was able to feel that 'ghosts might enter here without affrighting us' (*CE*, I, 35, 36). In practice, however, things did not always work out so happily. Actuality might become entirely spiritualized; reduced to its vanishing point, the real world became a dream. Correspondingly, the imaginary might become the only actuality, shadow the only substance. One can see neutral relationships beginning to turn into interchangeable ones in Hawthorne's letter of 4 October 1840 to his fiance Sophia Peabody. In his old study in Salem, the imaginary had taken on actuality as Hawthorne's 'visions' became 'visible to the world' (*CE*, xv, 494). Yet far from achieving the romancer's 'latitude', Hawthorne had found himself in a 'lonely chamber' equipped with 'viewless bolts and bars' (*CE*, II, 1; xv, 495). His room had become a more disturbingly ghostly place, a 'haunted chamber' in which he had felt as if he were 'already in the grave' (*CE*, xv, 494). Those who accuse others of being monsters are themselves monstrous, but it seems that those who conjure ghosts themselves become ghostly, personally suffering the interstitial existence which they had hoped to establish in their work. The problem of the neutral territory is still more explicitly described in 'The Haunted Mind', in which the writer's heart becomes 'a tomb and a dungeon' (*CE*, IX, 306). An anxious reverie set in the 'intermediate space' between the past and the future, the tale presents a 'disconnected' series of imaginative phantasms which cannot be governed by the 'power of selecting or controlling' ideas (pp. 305, 308, 306). In contrast to the regulated column of apparitions in 'Howe's Masquerade', ghostliness in 'The Haunted Mind' is more uncontrollable, threatening and pervasive.

The neutral territory was more of a problem than a solution, more a conceived need than an achieved form, and often as much a fear as a desire. Hawthorne remained true to his uncertainties and 'apparently opposite peculiarities' (Preface to *Twice-Told Tales*, in *CE*, IX, 6). Time and again, however, this meant losing himself between the available oppositions or representing the failure of attempts to open out a creative space. Everything gave way to his haunted and haunting perception of a universal ghostliness, and the writer – to adapt a motif which haunts later works such as 'The Ancestral Footstep', 'Grimshawe', 'Septimius Felton' and 'The Dolliver Romance' – was condemned to leave a bloody footprint on every threshold.

I recognize that this brief account of Hawthorne is not likely to endear me to sympathetic readers of Michael J. Colacurcio's *The*

Province of Piety. My reservations about Colacurcio's reading of
Hawthorne relate, not to what he puts in, but to the way in which he
justifies what he wants to leave out. The account of Hawthorne's
knowledgeable and profoundly ironic engagement with American
history is completely convincing. The demonstration of the way in
which Hawthorne sets about deconstructing provincial mythologies
and typologies is revelatory. What disturbs me is that Colacurcio's
emphasis on the importance of an American theological legacy is
often made at the expense of a European and specifically British
aesthetic and philosophical legacy. The former has a historical value
which seems not to be accorded to the latter. There is of course a
case for righting the balance, since the philosophical inheritance has
been one of the mainstays of Hawthorne criticism, most recently in
books such as Michael Davitt Bell's *The Development of American
Romance* and George Dekker's *The American Historical Romance*. I
suspect that Colacurcio refuses to deal seriously with Hawthorne's
problematic relation to and filtration of Enlightenment and Romantic thought because he believes that this aspect of the influence
(through the aesthetics of sensation, the sublime and the romance)
leads eventually to, or has at least been appropriated by, a psychological or psychoanalytical interpretation of Hawthorne which promotes what Colacurcio dismissively calls the 'dismal chamber' or
'haunted chamber' view of Hawthorne (see *The Province of Piety*, pp.
29, 52, 501, 549 note 74). I accept that Colacurcio's reconstruction
of the 'Story Teller' series intriguingly suggests the possibility that
Hawthorne had been creating narrators and narratives which exist
outside the chamber of literary solipsism, mobile, in the world and
untroubled by the 'Sin of Art' (p. 501). Colacurcio's rectification
complicates one's picture of Hawthorne but does not necessarily
justify abandoning critical interest in the haunted chamber, for this
would merely be to opt for a new simplicity. The force of *The Province
of Piety* often seems to depend on opposing supposed psychological
shadow to historical substance, purportedly ungrounded theorizing
to solid empiricism, the general to the specific and similarity to
difference. These strategies support the inclusion of American theology and the exclusion of European philosophy. Colacurcio reports
the critical arguments which discuss Hawthorne's 'failure' to be a
good Romantic and specifically a good Coleridgean but, rather than
dissenting from them, seems rather to dismiss them as comparatively
unimportant (see pp. 9, 487–8). What he wants to emphasize is that

Hawthorne's dealings with Puritan history should not be seen in terms of failure and a retreat into the past (see pp. 9, 156). But if this is true of Hawthorne's theology – and I think it is – the same may well go for Hawthorne's philosophy. The reservations about Coleridge might be seen, not in terms of failure and a retreat from the 'imagination' to 'fancy' but rather as a productive engagement. 'Fancy' would relate to an encounter with association, memory and history rather than to a Romantic flight into atemporal imaginative originality. Colacurcio takes Hawthorne's language of fancy relatively lightly. For him it suggests 'that . . . curious and shaky world of pre-Coleridgean mistrust of the *absolutely* truthful power of the imagination alone' (p. 55). For me this mistrust is one of the great strengths of Hawthorne's writing. Colacurcio claims that we will 'think better of Hawthorne's intelligence' if we accept the pervasiveness of his irony with regard to Puritanism (p. 209). But surely we can only think less of Hawthorne's intelligence by denying it an ironic or at least critical perspective on the Lockean tradition. Towards the end of *The Province of Piety*, Colacurcio argues that the 'parodic' intentions of 'The Haunted Mind' do in fact point to the existence of revisionary impulses with regard to 'the embattled Scottish model of association' (p. 488). Such an understanding would, as he points out, place Hawthorne's sketch 'a good deal closer to something we might call "history"' (p. 488). By depicting the disappearance of the subject and exposing the emptiness of their own terms, 'Wakefield' and the other 'haunted' sketches begin to specify psychological generality and 'throw us back on "the historical" as the only suitable model of mental completion' (p. 492). Perhaps so; this would at least represent the point of departure for any historicization of Hawthorne's relation to philosophy. But it is, on Colacurcio's part, a belated and somewhat perfunctory recognition.

One could argue, perhaps unfairly, that Colacurcio's attack on metaphor, imagery, dream, myth, spectrality, ambivalence, perhaps even romance, and on philosophical or psychological readings demonstrates precisely the Oedipal dynamic (*vis-à-vis* Crews in particular: the sins of the fathers become a particularly potent critical anxiety of influence) whose explanatory power with regard to Hawthorne he spends so much time qualifying. I suspect that on occasion Colacurcio is himself ironically rehearsing the old Puritan problem of finding what one had wanted to exclude within what one d defined as the uncorrupted centre. He certainly relishes tactically describing Puritanism in terms of paranoia (see pp. 214, 439), *idées fixes* (see p. 345), hysteria (see p. 440) and psychosis (see p. 441). He claims that 'the perception that the Puritan world "in declension" was bound to be fraught with Oedipal anxiety belongs to the order of history as surely as to the order of psychoanalysis' (pp. 291–2). This would be incontrovertible were it not for the implication that history and psychoanalysis are mutually exclusive categories. Colacurcio appears to believe that the material world exists in time in a way that the mind does not. In order to define his own position with oppositional clarity, Colacurcio accepts psychoanalytic criticism's dubious evaluation of itself as fundamentally and essentially trans-historical. Addressing 'The Minister's Black Veil', he makes the strictly temporary admission that 'even the historical critic seems constrained to admit that Hooper's Puritan problem of Sin everywhere threatens to lapse into a more general problem of Self' (p. 351). He then moves on to a persuasive, historically specific account of the problem of self in the tale, but in doing so decisively disproves the idea that there is anything fundamentally, essentially or necessarily general and ahistorical in the concept of self. It would be unwise to deny that the 'powerfully general formulae' of self, subjectivity, anxiety, and all the other 'post-Freudian categories' are underlain or overwritten by other categories, contrary as well as complementary specificities (p. 371). Few would quarrel with the idea that the self is not a 'fundamental "reality"' (p. 371). Yet what Colacurcio almost seems to be doing is to be making out a case for Hawthorne's prescient historicist critique of Freudianism and of the Oedipal nature of American psychopolitics (see pp. 4, 150–2) without accepting the inevitable assumption of Hawthorne's prescient debt to Freudianism, a debt which compels one to conclude that for Hawthorne the historical and the psychological are always vitally and significantly related. Colacurcio's argument is that the psychoanalytical notion of the self as fundamental category is itself indebted to Puritan hermeneutics (see p. 372). On this controversial but intriguing reading, the psychological subject is part of the problem which Hawthorne recognizes, ironizes and deconstructs in order to reveal that there is only the most scattered and attenuated self outside historical circumstance. For Colacurcio, Hawthorne breaks decisively with the epistemology of Puritanism. His ironies register distance, detachment and difference rather than shades of implication and interrelation.[71] Yet not only does Hawthorne's critique of Puritanism, psychologism and proto-Freudianism in favour of a richer, more adequate historicism presume a debate which the oppositional tenor of Colacurcio's entire argument works to deny, it also, curiously enough, suggests that Freudian terminology is in fact adequate to describe the Puritan mind, since it is in some sense a product of it.

The Province of Piety shows with compelling detail the way in which Hawthorne is not simply perpetuating a 'national legend' or helping to create a 'national mythology' (p. 41). Yet in some ways, whilst embedding the language of psychoanalysis still deeper in Puritan history, Colacurcio works to remove Hawthorne from history. It is as if Hawthorne's originality as a moral historian enables him to transcend his status as a subject of history, to stand outside traditions and conventions which, for Colacurcio at least, seem entirely to lack internal differences. By arguing for Hawthorne's imaginative originality as a moral historian, Colacurcio subtly underplays Hawthorne's engagement with the philosophy and psychology of associationism and reinforces the misleading idea that what Hawthorne departs from is a tradition which lacks internal difference. I cannot see that in principle it is any better for Colacurcio to resist a philosophical or psychological reading of Hawthorne in order to promote his status as historian than it is for the critics he opposes to resist historical readings in the attempt to preserve Hawthorne's status as a literary artist. The problem in both cases is that difference is the product of polemics: the arguments of the other side are expelled rather than engaged. The relentless assertion that discussion of Hawthorne must deal either with theology or European philosophy finally reminds one of what Colacurcio calls 'the fatal either/or of Puritan logic' (p. 197). It is an either/or that seems ultimately to work against history, since with his emphasis on the tight specificities of the 'province' of piety as opposed to the loose generalities of psychology, Colacurcio effectively redefines historicism as localism. It is also an either/or which works against exceptions and differences within the body of Hawthorne's work. A particularly disturbing feature of *The Province of Piety* is Colacurcio's willingness to write off those tales which are 'merely' conventional and cannot 'be made to yield a sense of deepening historicity': a list that includes *Fanshawe*, 'Sights from a Steeple' and to some extent 'The Hollow of the Three Hills', 'The Wives of the Dead' and 'An

Old Woman's Tale' (p. 46). A perturbing distinction between
originality and conventionality (with the latter naturally subord-
inated) seems to haunt _The Province of Piety_ and I at least begin to feel
that Colacurcio does to Hawthorne's aesthetics precisely what he
criticizes James for doing to Hawthorne's theology: arguing that it is
inherited thoughtlessly, automatically and as a cultural given
(compare pp. 6 and 52; see also p. 169). _The Province of Piety_ subjects
the 'Gothic' to exactly the reduction that Colacurcio accuses James
of doing to 'Puritanism'. For Colacurcio, Gothic fiction as the mode
of excess and 'extreme literary stimuli' is essentially a matter of
surface, machinery and literary convention (p. 45; see also pp. 15,
42, 46, 95–6). Yet why is it that what is conventional in literary
terms (assuming for a moment that Colacurcio's definition is
correct) has no historical status? Surely convention implies chron-
ology and thus the possibility of historicization. Does it really matter
that the Gothic tradition 'almost never' values 'real time-and-place
settings' (p. 50)? For Colacurcio this means that Gothic fiction has
no authentic purchase on historical reality. He accordingly underplays Hawthorne's investment in the Gothic and, once again, frees
the moral historian from history by putting the stress on Hawthorne's differences from the conventional, on his imaginative
originality. It is this imaginative quality that surely ought to remove
Hawthorne from Colacurcio's province. The faculty of imagination
is virtually denied any historical status in _The Province of Piety_, since
Colacurcio associates it exclusively with the timeless universalisms of
philosophy and psychology.

In spite of his commitment to the range of Hawthorne's American
influences, Colacurcio does in fact make persuasive use of Hawthorne's by no means slavish debts to Spenser (see pp. 90, 97, 295,
305), Bunyan (see pp. 97, 305), Milton (see pp. 280–1, 305) and
Lamb (see pp. 651–2, note 20). There is, as one might expect, 'a
specific American context' for this (p. 306). But I fail to see how one
can fully historicize Hawthorne without also at some stage evaluating a general and potentially non-American context. Colacurcio
wants to show that Hawthorne's sense of history is a sense of
something 'more than convention or costume' (p. 41). To argue that
the conventional is somehow beneath the dignity of a fully-fledged
historicism is, however, a dangerous manoeuvre. Discussing 'An Old
Woman's Tale', Colacurcio speculates that the eponymous narrator
may well have been intended to serve as framing device 'for the

"Seven Tales" project itself' (p. 47). Despite her potential structural importance, however, Colacurcio writes the figure of the old woman off as 'a frank literary convention' who 'calls our attention ... to the timelessness of imagination as such' (p. 47). I cannot agree with this proposition. Far from calling our attention to the timelessness of imagination, the figure of the elderly female narrator comments on, belongs to and possibly dissents from a convention which relates, in very specific literary historical ways, to the attack on fancy, the uncanny and the ghostly mounted by writers like Hobbes and Locke. Colacurcio inveighs against the 'timeless "haunting"' view of Hawthorne but this is largely because he does not want to analyse the way in which the idea of the ghostly, like the concept of imagination, enter into time, into a broad but complex history (p. 486). Towards the end of *The Province of Piety*, Colacurcio says that 'we begin to realize' the way in which history and the Gothic 'were never truly opposing categories' for Hawthorne (p. 485). Finally, it would seem, one still has to think through the problematic relationships encountered by Hawthorne the historical romancer: a figure who is not entirely subsumed by Colacurcio's description of Hawthorne the moral historian.

CHAPTER 2

The chamber of consciousness

'THE ROMANCE OF CERTAIN OLD CLOTHES'

On the day of Hawthorne's death in the summer of 1864, Henry James (as he was later to recall in *Notes of a Son and Brother*) sat down on a 'belated bed' within his own 'cherished chamber of application' and 'positively and loyally' cried.[1] To a large extent the fate of the haunted chamber and of the ghostly figures which crossed its threshold or lurked within now lay in the hands of a twenty-one-year-old who had as yet published only a single story, 'A Tragedy of Error'. James's first comments on the ghost story came a year after Hawthorne's death, in an 1865 review of Mrs Braddon's *Aurora Floyd*. Declaring that 'the supernatural ... requires a powerful imagination in order to be as exciting as the natural', he argued that 'a good ghost-story ... must be connected at a hundred points with the common objects of life' and would derive half its force from its 'prosaic, commonplace, daylight accessories' (*LC*, 1, 742). James displayed only a limited degree of appreciation for the 'romances pure and simple' of Mrs Radcliffe (p. 742). Yet the commonplace on its own was almost equally unattractive. It was only by making connections between the ghostly and the prosaic that significant force could be generated. In this early review James was already beginning to explore the legacy of the neutral territory and to formulate the balances, borderlands and relationships to which he would repeatedly return throughout his career.

Invoking Harold Bloom's notion of literary influence and the poetics of anxiety ('the process of misprision by which any latecomer ... attempts to clear an imaginative space for himself'), John Carlos Rowe has argued persuasively that the beginnings of James's literary project are to be found in his resistance both to the influence of American romance, particularly to Hawthorne, and to mid-

Victorian realism, as exemplified by Trollope.[2] One could of course question Rowe's somewhat idiosyncratic invocation of Trollope as James's main Victorian predecessor. Clearly James owes a great deal to George Eliot in a novel like *The Portrait of a Lady* and it is especially significant that this debt concerns the representation of uncanny or ghostly experience. The recurrent anxieties and terrors felt by the archer Gwendolen Harleth in *Daniel Deronda* anticipate those of Isabel Archer. Sir Hugo Mallinger's reference to the 'ghosts of the old monks' haunting the abbey on his estate and Deronda's later comments on suffering made in his stepfather's picture-gallery are later coupled by James in chapter 5 of *The Portrait of a Lady* when, in the gallery at Gardencourt, Isabel asks whether the house has a ghost and Ralph replies that one must have suffered to see it.[3] James more or less explicitly acknowledges the connection between the two novels by quoting (inaccurately) from *Daniel Deronda* in the Preface to *The Portrait of a Lady*. Yet it seems to me that the Eliot influence, or at least the influence of *Daniel Deronda* (1876), was exerted a little later in James's career. More importantly, James's relation to Eliot is a matter of an influence largely accepted. I can see little significant misprision in the fact that James renders Eliot's 'delicate vessels' as 'frail vessels' (*Daniel Deronda*, p. 160; *LC*, II, 1077). In the case of Hawthorne and Trollope, by contrast, James is more fundamentally questioning and challenging the work of his predecessors.

In an 1872 review of Hawthorne's posthumously published *French and Italian Note-Books*, James described his predecessor as 'a man of fancy' (*LC*, I, 310). He was to repeat this phrase, though surrounding it with some qualifications, seven years later in *Hawthorne* (see *LC*, I, 365), the critical biography in which he quoted Hawthorne's 'haunted chamber' letter appreciatively (see p. 358) before going on to argue rather more acerbically that the narrator of many of Hawthorne's tales had been 'a disembodied spirit, imprisoned in the haunted chamber of his own contemplations' (p. 419). Yet if Hawthorne's work tended to be over-fanciful, that of Trollope, according to an 1865 review of *Miss Mackenzie*, 'could not possibly' have been written by 'a man of imagination' (*LC*, I, 1315). One of the tasks for the 'man of imagination' – a figure that James made all his own in later life[4] – was to address subjectivity without losing touch with actuality, as Hawthorne repeatedly feared he had done, and to represent reality without restricting himself to the merely mundane, like Trollope. For the young James, the tales of Mérimée, which he described in an 1865 review of Harriet Spofford's *Azarian* as 'eminently real' and the work of Balzac ('literally real') appeared to offer a way of avoiding these twin dangers (*LC*, I, 607, 608). In 'Honoré de Balzac' (1875), James was to dismiss Balzac's 'lively interest in the supernatural' (*The Wild Ass's Skin*, 'Louis Lambert' and 'Seraphita') as a product of his 'adventurous fancy' but Mérimée's 'The Venus of Ille' may well have suggested the notion that there was no necessary incompatibility between what might be called imaginative realism and the ghost story (*LC*, II, 48).[5] For the 1865 reviewer of *Aurora Floyd*, at least, ghost stories required realistic treatment in order to become effective.

'The Romance of Certain Old Clothes' (1868), James's first ghostly tale, could be read as an attempt to counter Trollope by evoking ghosts in the midst of the mundane and simultaneously to overcome Hawthorne by rewriting the colonial history of Massachusetts with Mérimée's detached worldliness and rhetorical restraint. In mixing his masters, however, James overlooked the methods by which Hawthorne and Mérimée had succeeded in distancing and mediating the supernatural. A story like 'Young Goodman Brown' refracts supposedly supernatural events by suggesting that their nature and meaning are subject to various interpretations. In 'The Venus of Ille', Mérimée had formally mediated the supernatural by his use of a dramatized first-person narrator to relate the series of events which culminate in Alphonse de Peyrehorade's death on his wedding night.

Yet 'The Romance of Certain Old Clothes' did attempt to connect the ghostly with the 'common objects of life' in the manner recommended in the review of *Aurora Floyd* (*LC*, I, 742). The 'ribbons and top-knots and furbelows' deployed by Viola and Perdita Willoughby in their struggle to attract Arthur Lloyd establish the prevalent tone of domesticity.[6] The piece of lace given to Perdita by Viola after the former reveals her engagement bears the burden of representing quintessentially 'prosaic, commonplace, daylight accessories' (*LC*, I, 742). The 'romance' of the old clothes begins only when the newly-married Perdita discovers that Viola has dressed herself in the wedding veil and wreath, 'a hideous image of their old rivalry come to life again' (*CT*, I, 308). At this point, however, it begins to seem that, rather than counterbalancing the ghostly, commonplace fabrics are suddenly being transformed into supernatural agents. The clothing in Perdita's chest refuses to belong to the mundane world and instead becomes the means to punish Viola's 'insatiable love of millinery' (p. 307). In the final lines of the story, Lloyd, who has married Viola after the death of Perdita, discovers his second wife in front of the opened clothes chest, her face disfigured by terror and 'the marks of ten hideous wounds from two vengeful ghostly hands' (p. 319).

One could argue, with some justification, that 'The Romance of Certain Old Clothes' reads like a lurid foreshadowing of 'The Way it Came' and *The Wings of the Dove*. Rather more specifically, Leon Edel has seen the tale as a study of the rivalry between James and his elder brother William, an instance of the 'recurring theme of reversal of role and usurpation' in James's early work.[7] In these terms the tale symbolically suggests that James achieves his victories through some form of posthumous existence.[8] Allying himself with Perdita, James becomes a ghost who inscribes, who wounds, who retreats to a haunted chamber within the heart of the house of fiction.[9] Nevertheless, the fantasized fulfilment of James's wish for a virtually spectral power seriously damages the connections which, according to the *Aurora Floyd* review, he was trying to establish. As he crosses the threshold in the final scene of the tale, Lloyd comes upon an explosion of absolute alterity. Ejected almost bodily from the text, the disfigured Viola is the victim of a shift from the prosaic textiles of a rather crudely-conceived realism to the ghostly fabrics of a garish romance. James seems to have done both more and less than was required by his theory of the ghost story, and if he is at some level the ghost at the heart of his fiction, he is also, like Lloyd or Viola, an observing presence at its edge. Opening the Pandora's box of romance, James discovers that in practice there is a contradiction, or at least an incompatibility, between realism and the ghost story. In *The Scarlet Letter*, the stigma on Dimmesdale's breast nudged the limit of the romancer's latitude and was only just contained by Hawthorne's use of allegory and indeterminacy. The ghost-inflicted wounds of 'The Romance of Certain Old Clothes', on the other hand, rupture the fabric of the text. James shrinks from overt allegory but if anything Viola's wounds inadvertently symbolize the injury to his literary project. They create too definite a signature, leave too overt a trace of the writer's uncontainable presence.

THE EXPLOSIVE PRINCIPLE AND ECONOMIC MASTERY

James's ghost stories were his furthest ventures into the romance and towards Hawthorne's 'fairy-land' (*CE*, I, 36). In the Preface to volume XII of the *New York Edition* James described 'The Turn of the Screw' as a 'sinister romance', a 'fairy-tale pure and simple' (*LC*, II, 1183). The Preface to volume XVII added that 'the "ghost-story" ... has ever been for me the most possible form of the fairy-tale' (p. 1257). Although the ghost story was a possible form, it posed different and arguably greater risks in James's fiction that it did in Hawthorne's. Reviewing Julian Hawthorne's *Idolatry: A Romance* in 1874, James deplored 'the exaggerated modern fashion of romancing', wondering whether it was 'running away with the human mind, and operating as a kind of leakage in the evolution of thought' (*LC*, I, 298). The final scene of 'The Romance of Certain Old Clothes' had certainly produced leakage of a sort. James's first ghost did not emerge from the relatively ordered transactions between the actual and the imaginary which ideally took place in Hawthorne's neutral territory. It represented crisis and chaos, ruptured any smooth relationship between the natural and the supernatural, tipped the text into sensational death and grotesque injury. Far from providing a processional unfolding of historical meanings, the ghost burst into the present with more power than significance, more violence than sense. Rather than standing for a convenient sexual etiolation, a spiritualization of the flesh, the ghost perpetuated sexual struggle beyond the grave and was closely connected with transgressive or uncontainable desires.

The importance which James attached to establishing a relationship between the ghostly and the human was again revealed in an 1874 review of *Dernières Nouvelles*, which argued that some of Mérimée's best tales were 'those in which a fantastic or supernatural element is thrown into startling relief against a background of hard, smooth realism' (*LC*, II, 564). More than thirty years later James had dropped this naive and doctrinaire approach to realism but was still examining balances (not to mention textile metaphors of the text) in his Prefaces. The note that he had sought in 'Sir Edmund Orme' was 'that of the strange and sinister embroidered on the very type of the normal and easy' (*LC*, II, 1264). To present the supernatural directly and objectively was to imperil its effect, which was preserved only when prodigies loomed through 'the indispensable history of somebody's *normal* relation to something' (p. 1259). To have the supernatural 'straight', as in Poe's *Narrative of Arthur Gordon Pym*, was to reveal a quite literal tendency towards the south pole of romance which abolished all latitude and tropic charge (p. 1259). The climax of *Pym* failed 'for want of connexions', and these connections could only be preserved by representing the supernatural through the 'human consciousness' (p. 1259).

The Prefaces emphasized that the ghost story should be 'neat' and possess 'the compactness of anecdote' (pp. 1257, 1183). Such tales had at all costs to avoid any tendency towards 'the long and loose', towards the overflowing, improvisatory nature of the *Arabian Nights* tales (p. 1183).

Nothing is so easy as improvisation, the running on and on of invention; it is sadly compromised, however, from the moment its stream breaks bounds and gets into flood. Then the waters may spread indeed, gathering houses and herds and crops and cities into their arms and wrenching off . . . the whole face of the land – only violating by the same stroke our sense of the course and the channel, which is our sense of the uses of a stream and the virtue of a story. (p. 1184)

Flooding; breaking bounds; violating; wrenching off the face: these expressions remind one of the dangers which James had failed to circumvent in 'The Romance of Certain Old Clothes' and of the leakage which he had warned against in his review of Julian Hawthorne. In 'The Turn of the Screw', by contrast, he set himself the task of improvising 'with extreme freedom and yet at the same time without the possibility of ravage, without the hint of a flood' (p. 1184).

Orderly channels and chaotic floods; looseness and cathected compactness; the articulation of a charged fulcrum involving the strange and the familiar: the question of the ghostly focussed the dynamic relationships of Jamesian fiction in general. One of the most revealing and concise expressions of these relationships is to be found in the Preface to volume XVIII of the *New York Edition*:

The simplest truth about a human entity, a situation, a relation, an aspect of life . . . strains ever . . . toward the uttermost end or aim of one's meaning . . . struggles at each step, and in defiance of one's raised admonitory finger, fully and completely to express itself. Any real art of representation is, I make out, a controlled and guarded acceptance, in fact a perfect economic mastery, of that conflict: the general sense of the expansive, the explosive principle in one's material thoroughly noted, adroitly allowed to flush and colour and animate .. but with its other appetites and treacheries, its characteristic space-hunger and space-cunning, kept down. (*LC*, II, 1278) In its most basic form the explosive principle related merely to the matter of length, to practical questions of magazine serialization and to the 'developmental' tendencies of certain subjects (*LC*, II, 1239). Yet it was also closely linked to the centrifugal nature of what the Preface to *The American* called the 'air of romance' (*LC*, II, 1061). Fiction which committed itself to the romantic depicted 'experience liberated ... disengaged, disembroiled, disencumbered' (p. 1064), represented 'disconnected and uncontrolled' forms of subjectivity (pp. 1064–5).

For each of these different but closely connected principles there was an equal and opposite force. For the explosive principle there was economic mastery. For the 'developmental' there was the 'anecdotic' (p. 1239). For the air of romance there was the 'element of reality' (p. 1061). The first of these great pairings to emerge – and arguably the seed of all the relations which followed – was the balance struck in the ghost story between the strange and the familiar, the abnormal and the commonplace, the supernatural and the human consciousness. The ghost story involved chaotic and explosive forces, yet to counteract and channel romantic strangeness through brevity, the point of view and the use of commonplace, prosaic accessories was to practise a form of 'economy' and thereby to achieve an effective dynamic balance (Preface to volume XVII of the *New York Edition*, in *LC*, II, 1260).

The description and evaluation of the forces outlined above has been one of the major tasks of Jamesian criticism. For some critics James's central subject is freedom and liberated experience;[10] others see only his 'despotic and dictatorial' tendencies.[11] Some writers emphasize James's commitment to control, containment, compression, compactness, form, unity and closure.[12] For others his works are open, plural and polysemic, full of an endless unfolding of meaning.[13] For some critics the Prefaces reveal a James whose knowledge of the purpose and character of his work is 'calm, full, and ordered'.[14] For others the Prefaces are dominated by 'the tenor of crisis',[15] riddled with 'blind spots', displacements, failures of mastery and of memory.[16] Partial in themselves, these approaches to James – one responding to economic mastery and the other to the explosive principle – should be taken together or at least, since they are by no means incompatible, be successively pursued. To take freedom as one's subject is necessarily to investigate what threatens freedom; to be committed to control is inevitably to ponder the forces which struggle against control. Stuart P. Sherman was quite right to see James's work as 'an escape from the undesigned into the designed, from chaos into order' and to draw attention to the other side of the coin, the 'illimitable effluence and indefinable *aura* of things' in James's fiction.[17] In the Prefaces, James can represent himself as a Newtonian 'master-builder' (*LC*, II, 1141; see p. 14 above). Yet he can also be a more anxious Lockeian under-labourer who 'builds all vainly in the air' (p. 1051). 'By a geometry of his own' he can draw the circle limiting the endless expansion of relations but he can also recognize that the novel becomes 'more true to its character in proportion as it strains, or tends to burst, with a latent extravagance, its mould' (pp. 1041, 1075).

Numerous attempts have been made to describe the relation between James the romancer and James the realist. It is of course perfectly accurate and appropriate to draw attention to the fairy-tale motifs in James's work,[18] his use of the melodramatic, sensational and grotesque,[19] his indebtedness to Gothic literature,[20] to the romance[21] and to Hawthorne.[22] Yet the criticism which argues that James opts for some static point between realism and romance or a resolved mixture of the two genres[23] seems as unsatisfactory as the criticism which sees his work exclusively in terms either of economic mastery or the explosive principle. Charles Feidelson's analysis of the 'problematic interplay' between James's 'Romantic premises' and his premises as 'a "realistic" social novelist' is perhaps the most suggestive of all these accounts in its conclusion that James's 'roundabout realism ... is almost indistinguishable from a roundabout romanticism'.[24] Feidelson's conception of Jamesian interplay and rotation certainly shares much with the Preface to *The American*, in which, with lucid and resolute ambiguity, James argues neither for romance nor reality but (citing Scott, Balzac and Zola) for the writer's commitment 'in both directions ... by some need of performing his whole possible revolution' (*LC*, II, 1062).

Although Hawthorne is conspicuous by his absence in the Prefaces, one could argue that James's promotion of the writer's commitment in both directions is in part descended from the descriptions of romance put forward by writers like Walpole and Hawthorne (see pp. 35–6, 38–9 above). Hawthorne's efforts to place himself in a neutral territory where the oppositions between the actual and the imaginary could give way to a meeting and partial mingling anticipate James's attempts to span polarity, to make use of current and counter-current, 'the warm wave of the near and familiar and the tonic shock ... of the far and strange' (*LC*, II, 1062). Yet resemblance does not preclude difference, and the governing relationships of James's fiction do not finally place him alongside Hawthorne. James's version of the neutral territory of romance turned out to be neither neutral, nor a territory, nor a romance. It gave rise to charged interminglings, had no fixed borders and initiated a 'revolution' which connected the real and the romantic in a circuit of meaning (p. 1062). Whereas Hawthorne's Preface to *The House of the Seven Gables* somewhat reluctantly recapitulated a comparatively rigid and linear distinction between romance and the novel, James argued that it was 'as difficult ... to trace the dividing-line between the real and the romantic as to plant a milestone between north and south' (*LC*, II, 1067).[25] Whereas Hawthorne had seen the 'latitude' of the romancer shrink to the compass of a dungeon, James found all the latitude in the world between north and south. Being forces and not points, principles not genres, there was no single, absolute or final dividing-line between the real and the romantic. Indeed, since there are as many milestones as one likes between north and south, James was able to make the seemingly paradoxical claim in *Hawthorne* that his predecessor testified to 'the sentiments of the society in which he flourished almost as pertinently ... as Balzac and ... MM. Flaubert and Zola ... testify to the manners and morals of the French people' (*LC*, I, 321). And if romancers could be presented alongside the realists, then the realists showed a corresponding tendency to romance: in an 1888 essay on Stevenson, James declared that Zola's literary doctrine became fruitful only insofar 'as in practice he romantically departs from it' (*LC*, I, 1248).

Michael Davitt Bell has argued that James transcended the 'fundamentally dualistic' outlook of American romance and inherited a characteristically Romantic valuation of the imagination as 'a major foundation of ... truth' (*The Development of American Romance*, pp. 31, 91). James's thinking was 'truly unitary' because there was for him 'no dissociation of form from life, of imagination from "reality"' (p. 154). Bell is quite right to point out that the Preface to *The American* recommends that the romance should not 'flagrantly betray' its 'sacrifice of community' because James is intent on sustaining the fictional illusion and not because he wants, like Hawthorne, to conceal a subversive departure from reality into the imaginary (*LC*, II, 1064; see *The Development of American Romance*, pp. 7–8). Bell's idea that James's valorization of the imagination represents a typically Romantic strand in his thought seems quite plausible,[26] and a number of critics have described James as a unitary thinker[27] or suggested that either his practice as a writer or his conception of the imagination owes much to Coleridge's.[28] Although the word 'fancy' possessed an inferior sense to the word 'imagination' long before Coleridge,[29] the difference between Hawthorne the man of fancy and James the man of imagination (see p. 51 above) implicitly makes use of the distinction between imagination and fancy put forward by Coleridge in the *Biographia Literaria* (see *Collected Works*, VII, 1, pp. 293, 304–5). When James connects the fanciful element in Hawthorne to his predecessor's taste for 'conceits and analogies', for 'allegory' ('quite one of the lighter exercises of the imagination') and for 'symbols and correspondences' which do not seem 'spontaneous' and are later said to be 'mechanical' (*LC*, I, 365–6, 407), he is more plainly, although still rather loosely, indebted to the related distinction between allegory and symbolism made by Coleridge in 'The Statesman's Manual' (see *Collected Works*, VI, 28–30).

Was the Jamesian man of imagination a committed Coleridgean? In the *Biographia Literaria*, Coleridge had described the poet who in '*ideal* perfection' was able to balance or reconcile 'opposite or discordant qualities', who 'diffuses a tone, and spirit of unity, that blends, and ... *fuses*, each into each, by that synthetic and magical power, to which we have exclusively appropriated the name of imagination' (*Collected Works*, VII, 2, pp. 15–16). When, in the Prefaces, James describes the writer as a 'modern alchemist' in whom 'the old dream of the secret of life' was renewed, he shares Coleridge's perception of the imagination as a magically transforming power (*LC*, II, 1141). The Prefaces repeatedly return to the importance of fusion, synthesis and the abolition of artificial oppositions (see, for example, pp. 1091, 1107, 1110, 1135, 1195, 1236). It is only by fusion that James achieves the 'sublime economy of art' and only by economy that he finds intensity (p. 1139; see also pp. 1048, 1084, 1090, 1110, 1162, 1237, 1297, 1313). Establishing a centre or 'point of command' (p. 1050; see also pp. 1068, 1112, 1153, 1297, 1313), he selects (see pp. 1041, 1138), compresses (see pp. 1048, 1116, 1137, 1177, 1238) and foreshortens (see pp. 1048, 1110, 1155) in order to arrive at a 'science of control' (p. 1237; see also p. 1137).

The path from fusion to a science of control would be a surprising one from Coleridge's point of view, and J. A. Ward has analysed the surprising manner in which James employs scientific and mechanistic terms alongside Romantic and organic ones.[30] Yet one could go further: Jamesian fusion initially seems to echo Coleridgean fusion but soon begins to act in an exactly opposite direction. Whereas Coleridge speaks of a synthesis which centrifugally *diffuses* unity, James's fusions act inwards in the interests of economic mastery, providing the centripetal force of infusion and reduction to counter an 'expansion' which the Prefaces equated with the 'inorganic and thin' (p. 1155). Inorganic expansion? Coleridge had spoken of the innate 'organic form' in Shakespeare, which 'shapes as it developes itself from within' (*Collected Works*, v, 1, p. 495). In the Preface to *The Tragic Muse*, James similarly proclaimed his appreciation of 'organic form', yet he also possessed a counterbalancing delight in a 'deep-breathing economy' (*LC*, II, 1108; see also pp. 1127, 1171, 1302). James's centripetal drive to compress and control distinguishes him from Hawthorne, who in 'Rappaccini's Daughter' had expressed fears that the act of confounding and compounding gave rise to monstrous and adulterous hybrids, the products of a 'depraved fancy' (*CE*, x, 110). Yet it differentiates him quite as much from Coleridge, whose version of unitary thought was for James a matter of expansion without counterbalancing compression, fusion without corresponding tension. James repeatedly spoke of the major figures of Romanticism in terms of formlessness and the centrifugal.[31] In an 1875 review of Stopford Brooke's *Theology in the English Poets*, he described Coleridge as 'loosely reflective' (*LC*, I, 772). Frank Saltram of 'The Coxon Fund', who in the Prefaces is defined as a member of 'the S. T. Coleridge *type*', is said in the story itself to resemble 'a jelly without a mould' (*LC*, II, 1236; *CT*, IX, 170). By contrast, one of James's most rapidly expanding and potentially extended consciousnesses – Lambert Strether of *The Ambassadors* – is profoundly aware of the inevitability of limits and the necessity of moulds (see pp. 194–5 below).

When, in 'The Art of Fiction' (1884), James described the novel as 'a living thing, all one and continuous, like any other organism', he was not exclusively emphasizing the centrifugal and the developmental: living bodies grew, but they also had form (*LC*, i, 54). If the forces of expansion were allowed to hold sway, as in Thackeray, Dumas or Tolstoy, then the novelist created what the Prefaces called 'large loose baggy monsters' (*LC*, ii, 1107). In contrast to Hawthorne, it is unrestricted expansion which leads to the monstrous in James, the 'rank vegetation' of power in the romance which sounds the note of 'Rappaccini's Daughter' (Preface to *The American*, in *LC*, ii, 1067). When James argues that the failure to maintain an 'organic centre' condemns the novel to 'the disgrace of legs too short ... for its body' (p. 1108), his recognition of the importance of articulation and structure looks back less to Coleridge than to Plato's *Phaedrus*, in which discourse was compared to 'a living creature, having its own body and head and feet' (*Dialogues*, i, 264; see p. 16 above; see also pp. 18–19 and 36 above for the analogies between literary form and the human body put forward by Aristotle and Horace).

The great principles of James's fiction – the strange and the familiar, the romantic and the real, the explosive principle and economic mastery – cannot, therefore, finally be understood either in terms of Hawthorne or of Coleridge, either through the dualistic or the unitary. Avoiding absolutes of difference or identity, James's thinking is relational or proportional. It seeks neither to fix nor to cancel nor to transcend static oppositions but, as several critics have recently shown, to articulate relationships in terms of connections and distinctions, contrasts and comparisons. Having analysed the tensions in James's work, Carren Kaston speaks of fusion rather than dualism in relation to *The Golden Bowl*.[32] Examining James's by no means merely naive or hostile sense of the literary market-place, Michael Anesko argues that James's fiction was informed by 'a state of charged suspension' in which James negotiated the claims of self and society, freedom and fixity, in far from oppositional or simply melodramatic terms.[33] Relating desire to the explosive principle and love to economic mastery, David McWhirter argues that 'the clash between these two forces usually results in a dynamic alternation of impulses rather than in any consistent or peaceful compromise'.[34] Sharon Cameron demonstrates the way in which James's novels question conventional distinctions between mind and matter, internal and external, subjective and objective, putting in their place an 'interactive' and 'interpenetrated' sense of relationships.[35] Ian Bell rightly argues that James 'refuses the comfort of taking sides'.[36] For

Adrian Poole, James's imagination is in 'perpetual motion' between 'multitude and unity . . . anarchy and autocracy' (*Henry James*, p. 9).

It was precisely the lack of opportunity for creating a play of fusions and tensions which led to James's disillusionment regarding the fictional possibilities of the 'international' relation between Europe and America. The Prefaces speak of the 'scant results' achieved by confronting positives with negatives, 'the fruits of a constituted order with the fruits of no order at all' (*LC*, II, 1149). Only if order was opposed to order could James focus 'the correspondences and equivalents that make differences mean something' (p. 1149). The 'interest and the tension of disparity' could only exist 'where a certain parity may have been in question' (pp. 1149–50). Such parities and disparities were, however, markedly present in the notion of the '*visitable* past' which James set out in the Preface to volume XII of the *New York Edition* (*LC*, II, 1177). Indeed, the idea of the visitable past raises the question of the relation between the strange and the familiar that plays so important a part in James's comments on 'Sir Edmund Orme' and in his consideration of the real and the romantic in the Preface to *The American* (see p. 2 above). 'We are divided', he writes, 'between liking to feel the past strange and liking to feel it familiar' (*LC*, II, 1178). His difficulty in 'The Aspern Papers' had been to catch this relation 'at the moment when the scales of the balance hang with the right evenness' (p. 1178).

The relation between the Old World and the New; the strangeness and familiarity of the visitable past; the revolution between the real and the romantic; the play of centrifugal and centripetal force: in no aspect of his fiction was James seeking to establish fixed and absolute borders. The thresholds which did exist were the effects of intersecting fields of energy; they did not make meaning possible: they *were* meaning. It is, I believe, this awareness of the movable, permeable and charged nature of thresholds which distinguishes James from the writers examined in the previous chapter. James did not attempt to draw a single line between the light and the dark, like Hobbes and Locke.[37] Nor did he expel the ghostly and the figurative in the interests of order, like Plato and Aristotle. Although he was as fascinated by the relation between the strange and the familiar as Freud in 'The "Uncanny"', he did not subordinate the former to the latter in the interests of proper hierarchies and one-way translations. James knew that the explosive principle did not make sense without economic mastery and that economic mastery was nothing without the explosive principle: both forces reciprocally required and intensified each other.

There is, however, a further and vitally important double dynamic which plays through James's work and which directly returns us to the question of the ghostly. This is the variously collaborative and competitive relation which James establishes between himself and the centre of consciousness. These engagements and disengagements could be seen as a function of James's efforts to weigh the claims of involvement and detachment: the 'two instincts' which Tony Tanner describes as being 'endlessly at work' in James's fiction and his representation of character.[38] On the one hand, James and his protagonists are intimately involved with each other. Isabel Archer's 'mild adventure' (*LC*, II, 1083) is closely connected to the 'adventure' experienced by James in writing 'The Art of Fiction' (*LC*, I, 61) and to the metaphors of romance and adventure used with reference to writing throughout the Prefaces (see, for example, *LC*, II, 1040, 1060, 1232, 1286). In the collaborative phase of his engagement with the protagonist, James extends his own adventures of consciousness to the fictional subjectivity, sponsoring imaginative extension and underwriting a romantic liberation of experience. All James's centres of consciousness seek in some sense, to adopt the expression used by Ralph Touchett in *The Portrait of a Lady*, to 'gratify their imagination'.[39] To be able to do this is, according to Ralph, to be made 'free' (p. 379). In its quest for subjective freedom, the Jamesian centre of consciousness is at some level aspiring to the position occupied by James the writer, yearning for the 'boundless freedom' of artistic consciousness (Preface to *The Portrait of a Lady*, in *LC*, II, 1075). It was in 'The Art of Fiction' that James first spoke of the 'revelation' of freedom reserved for the artist (*LC*, I, 59). From this essay onward, he was to find it increasingly difficult and, by the time of 'Is There a Life After Death?', finally impossible to conceive of consciousness except as a faculty that aimed towards the greatest possible extension; that aimed towards artistic, or in other words Jamesian consciousness. Whilst Sartreian man wants to be God, James's men and women want to be James. The ghostly encounter represents a particularly intense adventure of consciousness, an access of liberated and disencumbered experience, and one could argue that it brings the ghost-seer extremely close to James himself. When the narrator of 'The Way it Came' talks of ghostly experience as 'a rare extension of being' (*CT*, IX, 400), she anticipates James's description of the artist's 'great extension' in the Preface to *The American* (*LC*, II, 1061) and his reference in 'Is There a Life After Death?' to the 'great extension' offered by the possibility of a posthumous existence.[40]

There is, however, a second and counterbalancing phase in the relation between James and the fictional subjectivity. A unilateral commitment to collaboration and intimacy would have provided comparisons between James and the centre of consciousness but no corresponding contrasts, likenesses without differences. James often expressed reservations about autobiography and the autobiographical form in fiction.[41] These reservations are closely connected to the question of the romantic and William Goetz has cogently argued that for James both the first-person form and the romance lack 'the intersubjective relations that alone can impose a check or a control on the individual experience'.[42] As I have tried to show, controls and checks are as necessary for James as liberations and extensions. The other phase of his relation to the centre of consciousness therefore involves detaching himself from the fictional subjectivity, containing or restricting rather than entertaining imaginative aspiration, emphasizing the real and not the romantic, economic mastery and not the explosive principle. Hyacinth Robinson of *The Princess Casamassima* cannot be allowed to feel and know too much for verisimilitude and his 'proper fusion with the fable' (*LC*, II, 1095). If he was not bewildered he would have partaken of 'the superior nature of the all-knowing immortals' (p. 1090). Maisie's 'small expanding consciousness' must also be a 'limited consciousness' (*LC*, II, 1157, 1159). Likewise the Preface to *The Tragic Muse* finds James recalling his need to invoke dramatic 'protection' against the 'usurping consciousness' (*LC*, II, 1112).

One could argue, to return for a moment to the terms of René Girard, that James is an 'involuntary tyrant' (*Violence and the Sacred*, p. 147). Positing himself as the model for the centre of consciousness, he issues an invitation to 'Imitate me!' and a contradictory injunction: 'Don't imitate me!' (p. 147).[43] The centre of consciousness is, as the Preface to *The Golden Bowl* points out, 'the impersonal author's concrete deputy or delegate, a convenient substitute or apologist for the creative power otherwise so veiled and disembodied' (*LC*, II, 1322). This sounds like a generously empowering 'Imitate me!'. Yet James's notion of delegation often extends to sacrificial substitution.

Discussing James's view of the centre of consciousness in terms of Girard's theory of desire, William Goetz argues that the Jamesian subject yearns for the veiled and disembodied creative power, tending to attribute a 'godlike plenitude' to others, and in particular to literary master-figures (*Henry James and the Darkest Abyss*, p. 161).[44] The paradox of the ghostly in James's work is that it would both promote and prohibit imitation, realize and defeat desire. Articulating the double dynamics of his fiction with the greatest intensity, ghosts in James would represent the explosive principle but they would also stand for economic mastery. On the one hand, the ghostly would erase the distance between James and the fictional protagonist, authorize subjective privilege and romantic extension, call up the formless energies and mould-breaking tendencies which are so vital in James. Yet ghosts would also – and this is a further instance of their ability to cross borders – create a gap between James and the protagonist and assist in the centripetal phase of the subjective adventure, during which wonder gives way to bewilderment and dread, liberation to limitation. To paraphrase the subtitle of Tony Tanner's *Adultery in the Novel*, the ghosts would be associated both with expansive transgressions and with the contractions implied in the notion of contract. In James's future work, ghosts would offer the prospect of collaboration but they would also appear in the interests of competition and in order to prevent the centre of consciousness from attaining or usurping the position occupied by the artist. Foreclosing on the spreading subjectivity, those authoritative and even authorial ghosts would raise the 'admonitory finger' on behalf of James (*LC*, ii, 1278). Rather than bursting outwards from within they would guard the outer edge of the text, maintaining forms, structures and patterns, exerting pressure inwards to ensure the character's 'proper fusion with the fable'.

It would be misleading to argue that ghosts in James always represent *either* the explosive principle *or* economic mastery. The final scene of 'The Romance of Certain Old Clothes' is the most intensely centrifugal ghostly encounter in James, yet the ghost also intervenes authoritatively in order to defeat Viola's desires, prosecuting the competitive principle from beyond the grave and bringing the tale to a bewildering and dreadful close. From text to text, then, James strikes subtly different balances. It is these texts which must now be examined in detail.

EARLY GHOSTS: FROM 'DE GREY' TO 'THE GHOSTLY RENTAL'

James addressed the supernatural for a second time in 'De Grey: A Romance' (1868). When Margaret Aldis discovers that her fiancé's family carry an inherited curse which has resulted, generation after generation, in the death of a de Grey's first love, she curses the curse in 'a prodigious act of volition' (*CT*, 1, 416). Losing her 'appealing weakness', Margaret becomes a powerful figure, 'intoxicated, electrified, by the unbroken vigilance and tension of her will' (pp. 418, 421). Perversely, however, the curse can be 'shifted, but not eluded' (p. 425). Margaret's very resistance becomes fatal to Paul. 'She ... drained the life from his being. As she bloomed and prospered, he drooped and languished. While she was living for him, he was dying for her' (p. 425).

Blooming and drooping; prospering and languishing; living and dying: 'De Grey' is an early study of the countervailing dynamics that play through James's fiction. When Paul asks to hear of Margaret's adventures she replies that she has never had any. 'That in itself is an adventure', returns Paul, antedating by many years the more famous formulations of 'The Art of Fiction' and the Preface to *The Portrait of a Lady* (*CT*, 1, 408). It is perfectly appropriate that Paul's comment has James's signature written all over it, since even in this early story Margaret's adventure has its centrifugal and centripetal aspect. The collaborative phase of James's engagement involves representing her desire to cut loose from the past and triumph over the uncanny curse. Yet the tale moves on to a second stage during which Margaret realizes that she is doomed to smother and drain Paul, to perpetuate restrictive patterns even as she inverts them.

'De Grey' is still 'A Romance' but it avoids the awkward shift from the natural to the supernatural which had marred 'The Romance of Certain Old Clothes'. Paul de Grey is not merely the victim of a malign supernatural agency and is 'dying' for Margaret in more ways than one (p. 425). Previously the curse meant the death of the desired object; Margaret turns its operation and kills the desiring subject. In registering this revolution the tale moves gradually towards a linguistic crisis in which difference collapses and opposites come to resemble each other. Love becomes 'a damning passion' and Margaret develops a 'feverish gayety', a 'potency of loveliness' which fills Paul with 'dreadful delight' (pp. 413, 417, 418). Margaret undergoes 'feverish transitions from hope to fear, from exaltation to despair' and compares her wedding dress to a shroud, causing Father Herbert to feel 'mingled tenderness and horror' (p. 420). The marriage and the funeral become equivalent; love and death are paradoxically joined; the erotic and the mortuary seem to belong to the same dynamic.

In such tales as 'The Wedding Knell' and 'Dr Heidegger's Experiment', Hawthorne examines similar pairings. Offering alternatively natural and supernatural explanations for the events depicted, these tales move towards climactic final scenes in which the oppositions confront each other in ironic and grotesque tableaux. In 'De Grey', on the other hand, James conceives of the relation between the natural and the supernatural, as well as between love and death, in terms of a seamless interpenetration. Linking the commonplace and the ghostly in a perverse and ambiguous dance of resemblance, he has begun to transform the legacy of the neutral territory and to convert Hawthorne's pendulum into a revolution, a charged circuit of significance.

'Paris ... haunts my imagination': so wrote James to Thomas Sergeant Perry on 27 March 1868, a year before leaving America on his first adult trip to Europe (*L*, 1, 82). Even in his first two stories of the supernatural James had needed European support. 'The Romance of Certain Old Clothes' gave the Willoughbys an English origin, brought Arthur Lloyd out from England and depicted an America still under colonial rule. In 'De Grey', a curse which originated in the Europe of the Crusades provided the motor force of the tale. Life in America, on the other hand, had been summed up in the calculatedly prosaic image of Mrs De Grey knitting 'undergarments for the orthodox needy' and carrying on a 'dull life' which James had suggested was 'no life at all' (*CT*, 1, 390). Morally speaking, Paul's mother has 'no history' (p. 389). In many ways America was simply a land of the dead. But Europe was alive with history, full of ghostly echoes of the past. James arrived at Liverpool on 27 February 1869. By the end of March he had surveyed 'the haunts of departed and mortalized royalty' at Hampton Court and found Bushey Park to be a 'spectral and delightful prospect' (*L*, 1, 104). In Europe it seemed to James that 'the aesthetic presence of the past' was perpetually conjured up or could repeatedly be invoked (*L*, 1, 143). Frequently using the vocabulary of the ghostly to convey his sense of the past and its presence, James wrote to his

father on 19 March 1870 that he wanted to 'exorcise this Italian
ghost that haunts me', adding that if he were physically fit he would
'never rest from scribbling until I had written the life out of him'
(*L*, I, 214).

James returned to the family home in Quincy Street on 10 May
1870 and began his exorcism with 'Travelling Companions' (1870).
In the opening scene, Brooke, the tale's narrator and protagonist,
invokes the 'restless ghost' of Leonardo's 'Last Supper' in Milan
(*CT*, II, 172). He imagines that 'out of the depths of their grim
dismemberment', the figures within the painting 'trembled into
meaning and life' (p. 172). Brooke is a romantic, but a somewhat
crude and complacent one. Towards the end of the tale, however, in
one of the seminal ghostly moments in early James, Brooke takes a
ride on the Campagna and encounters something that affects him
more deeply than the fanciful aesthetic ghosts he had conjured up in
Milan:

> The aspect of all this sunny solitude and haunted vacancy used to fill me
> with a mingled sense of exaltation and dread. There were moments when
> my fancy swept that vast funereal desert with passionate curiosity and
> desire, moments when it felt only its potent sweetness and its high historic
> charm. But there were other times when the air seemed so heavy with the
> exhalation of unburied death, so bright with sheeted ghosts, that I turned
> short about and galloped back to the city. (p. 221)

Passing beyond the feckless amusements of the tourist, Brooke
realizes that Europe is not so much a museum in which to acquire
however finely felt a knowledge of the history of art but a place in
which there are no easy frontiers between art and life, or indeed
between both of these things and the deathly. Leaving the merely
picturesque behind him, he encounters the dissolving borders and
mixed feelings which are so characteristic of sublime experience.
The 'sheeted ghosts' recall Horatio's reference to the 'sheeted
dead'[45] but signal the onset of an individual rather than a social
crisis. Inside and outside, desire and death, enter a circuit of impacted ambivalence, and Brooke's 'mingled sense of exaltation and
dread' is strongly reminiscent of Margaret Aldis's 'feverish transitions ... from exaltation to despair' in 'De Grey' (*CT*, I, 420). But
Brooke's crisis is an achievement for James, who has suddenly begun
to use the ghostly in the interests of economic mastery rather than
the explosive principle. The ghost in 'The Romance of Certain Old
Clothes' burst outwards from within. In 'Travelling Companions',

by contrast, the ghosts wait for Brooke at the outer edge of the text's geography, forcing him to return to the city and settle for the 'stern prose' of marriage to Charlotte Evans (*CT*, II, 218). Brooke's retreat is not an absolute failure: by turning back he avoids the facial disfigurement suffered by Viola. Nevertheless, the encounter with the sheeted dead completes Brooke's adventure, brings him to the edge of a circle which represents a limit imposed on his desire for liberated experience. He cannot satisfy his imaginative requirements. Turning short about, he does not, to put it perhaps too bluntly, go over to the ghosts and become a writer.

In 'Travelling Companions' it was Europe and not America which offered, in Addison's words, 'one of the most proper Scenes in the World for a Ghost to appear in' (*The Spectator*, I, 453; see p. 28 above). It was here, in such tales as 'The Last of the Valerii' (1874) and 'Adina' (1874), that James was able to examine the relation between the past and the present, to posit the past as a threatening presence and to represent his characters in the act of exorcising their Italian ghosts. For his own part, James seems to have been engaged in bringing the ghosts to life rather than laying them to rest: *Transatlantic Sketches* (1875) is a series of impassioned invocations and evocations of the past's 'ghostly presence'.[46] The Europe of *Transatlantic Sketches* is a landscape of wonder which offers subtly shifting exchanges between culture and nature, the actual and the imaginary, involved and detached experience. In Rome, James finds himself leading a 'double life' (*Transatlantic Sketches*, p. 138). This is a significant phrase, for it was at this period that James began to explore in more detail the temperamental dualities which he had already addressed in 'Poor Richard' and 'A Light Man'. Tales such as 'Madame de Mauves' (1874) and 'Benvolio' (1875) were structured around scenes of choice and the theme of alternatives.[47] At the same time, James's critical writing was developing an increasingly dynamic sense of balances and relationships.[48]

Dualities, possibilities, partial selves and split selves: in *Roderick Hudson*, *The American* and even in *The Portrait of a Lady* these themes were opened up by the encounter between America and Europe. 'A Passionate Pilgrim' (1871) was one of the first of these transatlantic studies of duality. At the beginning of the tale Clement Searle comes across a tramp at Hampton Court and feels that he has seen his *doppelgänger* (see *CT*, II, 243). For Searle, Europe is the field in which to track his other self, to assess his ancestry and to interrogate his kinship with the past. For the narrator of the tale and for James himself the European locale also offers opportunities to travel across a strangely familiar (and therefore potentially uncanny) landscape which is unknown and yet has already been seen 'in books, in visions, in dreams' (p. 227). 'A Passionate Pilgrim' also involves new relationships between the explosive and economic. At one level the tale stages a qualified return to the sort of ghostly encounter which took place in the final scene of 'The Romance of Certain Old Clothes'. Searle has returned with the narrator to an inn near Lockley Park, the home of his English ancestors. Flinging open the door of communication to the narrator's room and standing on the threshold, Searle claims to have seen the ghost of a woman, a curate's daughter once seduced and abandoned by his ancestor and namesake (see p. 287). Rather than being turned back at the outer edge of the text, like Brooke in 'Travelling Companions', Searle is centrifugally driven outwards from a central chamber. On this occasion, however, in contrast to 'The Romance of Certain Old Clothes', James succeeds in counterbalancing the explosive principle and in containing romantic leakage. Although Searle's sudden access to an unbearably intense subjective privilege ruptures his sanity, he is not the victim of literal injury. Although Searle feels that he is trembling away into 'waves – waves – waves', his flood of experience does not break the banks of the text (p. 287). To a greater extent than was true with Lloyd in 'The Romance of Certain Old Clothes', the narrator of 'A Passionate Pilgrim' filters the immediacy of Searle's experience through the medium of his own consciousness. Maintaining a connection between the familiar and the strange, the narrator reflects that whilst Searle has seen 'but the transient, irresponsible spectre', he has himself witnessed 'the human subject, hot from the spectral presence' and that his own vision has been 'the more interesting of the two' (p. 288). By representing both the ghost and the ghost-seer through the medium of the narrator's consciousness, James more than obeys the principle later outlined in the Preface to volume XVII of the *New York Edition* (see pp. 2, 54–5 above).

Written shortly after James took up permanent residence in Europe, 'The Ghostly Rental' (1876) looks back on the period of his apprenticeship, on the balances he had already set, the ghosts he had raised. Whilst out walking at the beginning of the tale, James's narrator comes upon a 'blank, bare and vacant' New England house with a 'blighted and exhausted aspect' (*CT*, IV, 52). He fancifully endows the house with a ghostly 'eloquence' (p. 52) that distinguishes it from another house nearby which has 'no sinister secrets, and knows nothing but blooming prosperity' (p. 53). At some level the second, materially prosperous house acts as an emblem of America, echoing the Preface to *The Marble Faun*, in which Hawthorne spoke of 'the difficulty of writing a Romance' about his native land, with its openness, its daylight and its 'common-place prosperity' (*CE*, IV, 3). For James, it was not so much that writing romance in America was difficult; indeed, in one sense it was virtually impossible to write anything else. 'De Grey' and 'The Romance of Certain Old Clothes' could only represent America by romancing it. In 'The Ghostly Rental', the story cannot cohere round the house without sinister secrets. The narrator is inexorably drawn towards the other house, which stands not simply for America, as Peter Buitenhuis has argued,[49] but for the need to conjure eloquence out of blankness, to transform bareness and vacancy into a 'little adventure' (*CT*, IV, 54). The haunted house, accordingly, represents something like the American house of fiction, the house of romance, the house of James's early literary career. It is owned by Captain Diamond, who is said to resemble 'a figure out of one of Hoffmann's tales' and whose troubles have 'detached him from the world' (pp. 56, 60). Diamond has apparently been driven from his home by the ghost of his daughter, from whom he collects a quarterly rental. It would be restrictive to allegorize the tale too relentlessly, but it is only a short step – phonetically and generically – from Hoffmann to Hawthorne and there is an important sense in which 'The Ghostly Rental' sets out to assess the nature of Hawthorne's captaincy, his ownership of the house of romance, the status of his ghosts and the validity of his fears.

The narrator of 'The Ghostly Rental' is a student, an aspirant, an applicant. Approaching the haunted house, he takes 'a puerile satisfaction in laying my hand on the door-knob and gently turning it' (pp. 52–3). At first the door remains closed against his 'impertinent fumblings with the latch' (p. 54). Later, however, at Diamond's invitation, he enters the house and perceives 'a thing of thick shadows' (p. 75). 'I had got what I wanted', he reflects: 'I was seeing the ghost' (p. 75). Yet the narrator's encounter is an unsatisfactory one. In retreating from the house he shows none of Searle's ecstasy. The apparition produces 'vulgar' fear and not poetic

'Dread, with a capital letter' (p. 75). There is something 'trivial' and 'familiar' about the apparition (p. 76). Some months later, the narrator agrees to enter the house for a second time on behalf of Captain Diamond. On this occasion he exposes the ghost as Diamond's still-living daughter:

What I saw before me was not a disembodied spirit, but a beautiful woman, an audacious actress. Instinctively, irresistibly, by the force of reaction against my credulity, I stretched out my hand and seized the long veil that muffled her head. I gave it a violent jerk, dragged it nearly off, and stood staring at a large fair person, of about five-and-thirty. (p. 83)

Following Cornelia Pulsifer Kelley, who detects traces of Poe's 'The Fall of the House of Usher' in 'The Ghostly Rental', both Sidney Lind and Howard Kerr have argued that James's tale sets forth his differences with American romance.[50] That tradition is indeed being demystified here, and the narrator's reaction against his credulity suggests something of James's disillusionment regarding the possibilities of the romance tradition, its sacrifice of relations and connections, the disappointment produced by presenting the supernatural without mediation. In a revised version of the final scene in 'The Romance of Certain Old Clothes', the narrator of 'The Ghostly Rental' exposes and violently masters the fake apparition, ruptures the veils, contests and defeats the supernatural force which had previously been invested in old clothes. Yet the references here are not primarily to Poe and not only to James's earlier work. The narrator's unveiling of the false ghost distinctly recalls Zenobia's tale of 'The Silvery Veil' in *The Blithedale Romance*. In Zenobia's story, Theodore faces the same double bind as the characters in Hawthorne's novel: either he can kiss the Veiled Lady without looking on her face, an act which will prove his 'faith' and his 'pure and generous purpose' but may also demonstrate his uncritical partisanship, his unthinking tendency to take things at face value and to be seduced by surface (*CE*, III, 113). Or he can lift the veil to look behind the outer envelope of things, an act which commits him to the spectator's crime of 'scornful scepticism and idle curiosity' (p. 113).[51] Knowledge before faith or faith before knowledge? Theodore must make his choice: 'grasping at the veil, he flung it upward, and caught a glimpse of a pale, lovely face, beneath; just one momentary glimpse; and then the apparition vanished, and the silvery veil fluttered slowly down, and lay upon the floor' (p. 114).

'The Ghostly Rental' rewrites Zenobia's legend: when James's narrator drags away the veil which covers the face of Diamond's daughter, he does not encounter the ethereal, ephemeral presence of a disembodied spirit but something far more fleshly and mundane: 'a large fair person, of about five-and-thirty' (*CT*, IV, 83). Unveiling an unveiling, James appears to be suggesting that both Diamond and Hawthorne have been the victims of a delusion, a confidence trick; that behind the fluttering rhetorical tissue of romance and superstitious faith there is, or should be, something real and palpable, something solidly if somewhat anticlimactically substantial.

Yet 'The Ghostly Rental' can by no means be read simply as an emblematic account of how James aggressively sides with a sceptical spectatorship in pursuit of his vocation as a 'realist'. In the very act of demystifying romance, James's narrator and James himself become implicated in the moral of Zenobia's tale. Having lifted the veil, Theodore is punished for his lack of faith: the vanishing apparition becomes his 'evil fate' and, haunted by what he has tried to exorcise, he is destined 'to pine, forever and ever, for another sight of that dim, mournful face' (*CE*, III, 113, 114). Far from rewriting this moral, 'The Ghostly Rental' inscribes it even more forcefully. When Captain Diamond's daughter claims to have encountered the ghost of her father at the foot of the stairs, it seems that James's narrator has exorcised one apparition only to raise another, which he sees as 'the punishment of my indiscretion – of my violence' (*CT*, IV, 84). Following the example of 'The Passionate Pilgrim', James mediates this second ghost and its seer through the consciousness of the narrator. Yet although Diamond's ghost materializes in an unseen space beyond a threshold, and in spite of the fact that the living Diamond has been deluded by his own child, the violence of James's narrator puts Diamond into undisputed possession of the haunted house. It is as if, at another level, James's attack on Hawthorne's captaincy has guaranteed his predecessor a place in the house of fiction, made him, in the words of Diamond's housekeeper, 'as big a ghost as any of them' (p. 86). The unveiling depicted in 'The Ghostly Rental' is, therefore, no naively Oedipal assault on Hawthorne. James is seeking to clear imaginative ground for himself, to exorcise the ghosts of his predecessors, but his tale has a properly problematized awareness of the implications of such acts. By revising Hawthorne, James finds himself repeating him and indeed even becoming a sort of Theodore, a character in the text set forth by Hawthorne. Like Margaret Aldis, James discovers that in breaking with the past he has implicated himself in that past and its patterns; in laying ghosts he has become haunted. The revisitation which 'The Ghostly Rental' anticipated was to be acted out in James's future career. If the tale looked back on his early work, it also provided a myth for the middle years. James wrote no further ghost stories until 'Sir Edmund Orme' (1891). Nevertheless, from *The American* to *The Princess Casamassima*, James continued to rely on the ghostly as a root metaphor whether he was extending or restricting the experience of his protagonists, collaborating with or competing against them. If literal ghosts vanished, they almost immediately began to reappear as figures of speech, states and stages of subjective experience. By the time of *The Tragic Muse*, the stage had been set for a revisitation which was to affect the remainder of James's literary career.

THE MIDDLE YEARS: FROM *THE AMERICAN* TO *THE TRAGIC MUSE*

I have examined the explosive force of the ghostly in 'The Romance of Certain Old Clothes' and its tendency to promote centrifugal forms of subjectivity in 'A Passionate Pilgrim'. In a tale such as 'Travelling Companions', on the other hand, James was, as we have seen, also capable of using the ghostly in the interests of economic mastery and in order to preserve limits. The governing principles of James's work are, as I have tried to show, not always superimposable. Although the supernatural is closely connected to the romantic it may counteract the centrifugal force generated by that principle, contributing to the text's dynamic balance by limiting subjective extension. Conversely, a tale such as 'The Ghostly Rental' uses the supernatural to counter the narrator's centripetally directed efforts to unveil and master the mystery of the haunted house.

The American also shows allied principles working in different directions. Anticipating the link between romance and the wish-fulfilment dream made by Northrop Frye,[52] the Preface to the novel speculates that an infallible sign of the romantic may be the 'rank vegetation of the "power" of bad people that good get into, or *vice versa*' (*LC*, II, 1067). Romantic power involves the ability to make the world tractable to one's desires and, for good or ill, to satisfy the requirements of one's imagination. Curiously enough, however, James argues that if *The American* had stuck to the real it would have been a romance: Christopher Newman's wishes would have been fulfilled since the Bellegardes would 'positively have jumped' at his wealth (p. 1066). By representing the failure of Newman's desires (and following the lost illusion trajectory often associated with realism) James paradoxically deviates into romance and affronts 'verisimilitude' (p. 1067). In the act of countering Newman's power, the economic master finds himself cutting the cable and, in spite of himself, invoking the 'bold bad treacheries' which he describes as 'the stalest stuff of romance' (p. 1056). For its author at least, the text ends up as a leaking vessel, a ship with 'a hole in its side' (pp. 1053–4).

Throughout much of *The American*, James allows Newman to penetrate the 'fantastic privacy' of the Hôtel de Bellegarde and enables him to feel that he has 'pulled away the curtain'.[53] In the final chapter of the novel, however, collaboration turns to competition. James literalizes the border which separates himself, the man of imagination, from Newman, whom William Stowe has called a 'Man of Little Imagination'.[54] As in 'The Ghostly Rental', unveiling is followed by a retributive reimposition of thresholds. Entering 'a region of convents and prisons', Newman passes through 'streets bordered by long dead walls' and is finally confronted by the 'high-shouldered blank wall' of the Carmelite convent in the Rue d'Enfer: the place where Claire de Cintré has quite literally chosen to take the veil (*Novels 1871–1880*, p. 867).[55] Reaching 'the goal of his journey' (p. 867), he finds 'release from ineffectual longing' (p. 868). His longing is for Claire de Cintré but also for a world which conforms to his desire. Since the object of this desire is unattainable, Newman turns away, performing the renunciation which is one of the most characteristic gestures of the Jamesian protagonist.

In a letter of 30 March 1877 to William Dean Howells, James argued that the final scene of the novel merely erected the 'tall stone walls' which exist in reality and 'fatally divide us' (*L*, II, 105). Yet James's later Preface makes it clear that this somewhat doctrinaire realism over-simplifies matters: in fulfilling his own wishes as realist and economic master, James replicates the patterns of romance on another level. Indeed, Newman's earlier vigil at the Carmelite chapel in the Avenue de Messine owes much to Ann Radcliffe's *The Italian*, in which Vivaldi hears Ellena di Rosalba singing in the Carmelite convent at San Stefano.[56] Like Vivaldi, Newman imagines that he can hear his imprisoned lover. It is true that James immediately adds that Newman is mistaken, since Claire is not yet a member of the sisterhood. Nevertheless, the somewhat heavy-handed authorial intrusion reveals James's unease concerning his debt to generic romance, his repetition of its stock motifs.

Although the return of romance is one of the revisitations predicted by 'The Ghostly Rental', there is another and more significant surfacing of the uncanny in the novel's final chapter. There are no obvious ghosts in this passage, and indeed Newman specifically returns to Paris in order to lay the 'stubborn ghost' of his yearning (*Novels 1871–1880*, p. 865). Yet we can by now justifiably anticipate that such an exorcism will provoke the usual effect: a ghostly manifestation. Accordingly the scene does seem to introduce the shadow of an apparition, a faint but distinct sense of presence. The last chapter of *The American* shows James adopting the ghostliness he obliquely imputed to Hawthorne in 'The Ghostly Rental', representing his own authorial presence in spectral terms. The walls which separate Newman from Claire are dead and blank but they are also 'high-shouldered' – partially humanized (p. 867). If Newman turns back, one could argue that James, indirectly and symbolically, is blankly turning his back on the protagonist he had previously backed. Of course, many people turn their backs on James and for many different reasons.[57] Yet the act is above all associated with artists, with ghosts and with figures who are both artists and ghosts. In the final chapter of *The American*, James is an absent presence rather than a full-fledged apparition, a present absence. Nevertheless, the artist who turns his back or conceals himself behind walls and closed doors was to take on a more distinctly apparitional form in such works as 'The Real Right Thing', *The Ambassadors* and 'The Jolly Corner'. The narrator of 'The Private Life' opens a door and, 'checking myself on the threshold' with 'a feeling of bewilderment', finds himself in the presence of Clare Vawdrey's literary *alter ego*: 'his back was half turned to me, and he bent over the table in the attitude of writing' (*CT*, VIII, 205). According to the Preface to *The Tragic Muse*, this attitude is that of the artist '*in triumph*': all one sees of him is 'the back he turns to us as he bends over his work' (*LC*, II, 1118).

The final chapter of *The American* looks forward to these later artist-ghosts, and in this it represents an intermediate point between Hawthorne's description of the writer's 'haunted chamber' and James's account of the 'chamber of consciousness' in 'The Art of

Fiction' (Hawthorne, *CE*, xv, 494; James, *LC*, I, 52; see p. 43 above). Hawthorne had felt entombed in his study, but within the chamber of consciousness James enjoys limitless experience, an almost post-humous extension of being, finding through his work 'an immense increase – a kind of revelation – of freedom' (*LC*, I, 59). It seems odd to use the figure of a chamber to convey the idea of freedom and limitlessness, to erect walls in order to experience the centrifugal romance of artistic consciousness, but the last chapter of *The American* effectively turns the interior of the Carmelite convent into an exterior, an inaccessible place beyond the margins of the text. Like Brooke in 'Travelling Companions', Newman comes up against the edge of the fiction, the limit of its circle of relations. Whereas Brooke retreats from the outer margin of the text, Newman turns away on reaching the inner margin. Yet in spite of the contrast between the fearfully open horizon of the Campagna and the nar-rowing perspectives of Paris, both Brooke and Newman fall victim to the economic master, who wishes to place his protagonists within the latitude provided by the text and ensure their 'proper fusion with the fable' (*LC*, II, 1095).

By countering Newman's romance and authoritatively limiting the rank vegetation of his power, James inevitably perpetuates the play of power and commits himself to romance. His freedom under-cuts Newman's; his own reservoir of privileged privacy is the obverse of Newman's privation; his withdrawn fullness leaves Newman with an uncanny sense of emptiness and exposure. Newman wants to be where James is, but the high-shouldered walls block the path of mimetic desire, terminating his career as an aspiring consciousness. Because Newman voluntarily turns away, he avoids a face-to-face encounter with the hostile and violent force which exerts its power in the final scene of 'The Romance of Certain Old Clothes'. Unlike Viola, Newman remains on his side of the threshold and does not force his way into the inner chamber. In his tactful renunciation Newman anticipates Spencer Brydon of 'The Jolly Corner', who pauses before the closed door which separates him from his *alter ego*, realizes 'the value of Discretion' and turns away to make an orderly escape (*CT*, XII, 218). The revised version of *The American*, produced in 1906 at about the time James wrote 'The Jolly Corner', draws out the connections between the two texts, emphasizing still further the uncanny quality of Newman's experience in the final chapter. The 1877 version of the novel has Newman 'strolling soberly' away from

Notre Dame 'like a good-natured man who is still a little ashamed' (*Novels 1871–1880*, p. 869). In the revised text Newman becomes much more like Brydon as he leaves the cathedral 'to the quiet measure of a discreet escape, of a retreat with appearances preserved'.[58]

In both 'The Ghostly Rental' and *The American*, an initial unveiling gives way to an uncanny reimposition of thresholds. James finds himself invoking the ghosts which at some level he had wanted to exorcise and even imbuing himself with ghostliness. In some ways, however, James was still acting out rather than acting on the insights of 'The Ghostly Rental'. He distinctly resembles the narrator of that tale in his continuing efforts to convert blankness and bareness into eloquence. Just as the narrator of 'The Ghostly Rental' sees himself as a character in the *Arabian Nights* (see *CT*, IV, 78), so Felix Young of *The Europeans* fancifully compares Boston to Cairo and is later likened to Prince Caramalzaman (see *Novels 1871–1880*, pp. 884, 894). James uses these picturesque figurative importations and exotic transfusions with wit and irony, but this seems only to emphasize his uneasy awareness of their artificiality. Like the narrator of 'The Ghostly Rental' James is reacting against earlier credulities. Yet the larger problem at issue here, I think, lies not in James's uneasiness about converting blankness into eloquence *per se* but in his awareness of the radical disjunctions between 'real' and 'romantic', 'imaginary' and 'actual' which seem to obtain in America as set against the richer and less polarized interpenetrations of Europe. To be a romancer as Hawthorne had been was, for James at least, to invite disconnection, to move away or even be excluded from the house of blooming prosperity, to become the victim of an oppositional schematism rather than the proponent of relational circuitries. In *Hawthorne* (1879), James conceded that one was 'beguiled into believing' the author of 'Howe's Masquerade' when he drafted in the ghosts of the ancient governors of Massachusetts (*LC*, I, 369). By the time of *Washington Square*, however, the Hawthornean 'infusion of colour' (*LC*, I, 369) has receded to a small area in New York which for James is touched with 'the tenderness of early associations' (*Novels 1881–1886*, p. 15). In subsequent tales, James was again to perform the aggressive unveilings of 'The Ghostly Rental', to depict the material bareness and blankness which so radically counterposed the eloquence of American romance, to offer American cityscapes which were unhomely but

also unhaunted. In 'The Point of View' (1882), Louis Leveret
describes Boston as 'crude', 'peeled', 'raw' and 'hard', whilst in 'A
New England Winter' (1884), Florimond Daintry finds the same
city 'denuded', 'solid', 'frozen' and 'stiff' (*CT*, IV, 500; VI, 128). This
adjectival assault culminates in *The Bostonians*, which all but drops
the point of view to present Boston as 'desolate', 'bald', 'vacant' and
'bare' (*Novels 1881–1886*, p. 963). It is almost as if James is ignoring,
defying or perhaps even at some level inviting the revisitations
predicted in 'The Ghostly Rental' and the legend of the Veiled
Lady. True to these prophetic parables, the revisitations were
indeed to persist, particularly in the European context. To demonstrate the disconnection between the familiar and the strange in
America was increasingly to find, in the European scene, the strange
within the familiar and the familiar within the strange. Already in
'Daisy Miller' (1878), the 'adventure' at the Château de Chillon
stirs distinctly 'romantic' undercurrents for 'a man of imagination'
like Winterbourne (*CT*, IV, 167). It is true that Daisy herself cares
little for 'feudal antiquities' or 'dusky traditions' (p. 168). But when
Château gives way to Colosseum, one might well argue with Leslie
Fiedler that James's Europe reinvents the haunted castle of Gothic
literature (see *Love and Death*, p. 131). As in *The American*, these
Gothic touches do not themselves introduce the explosive forces
which James often associates with the romance. Instead, they act in
the interests of economic mastery, providing images of enclosure,
containment and circumscription.

The echoes of generic romance in 'Daisy Miller' are largely
transformed into images and metaphors, but they are no less powerful for that and are certainly not used with the calculated incon-
gruity of the *Arabian Nights* references in *The Europeans*.[59] *The Portrait
of a Lady* follows 'Daisy Miller' in its use of a figurative and psychological Gothicism. Initially, however, and in contrast to 'Daisy
Miller', James does seem to be invoking the Gothic for ironic
purposes and in order to reveal Isabel Archer's naivety. When
Ralph Touchett points out Lord Warburton in chapter 2 of *The
Portrait of a Lady*, Isabel exclaims that 'it's just like a novel!' (*Novels
1881–1886*, p. 205). This is the sort of response one would expect from
the heroine of Jane Austen's *Northanger Abbey*, and Isabel reminds
one of Catherine Morland even more forcibly when she informs
Ralph that Gardencourt ought to have a ghost because it is a
'romantic old house' or when she tells Henrietta Stackpole that her

'idea of happiness' can be summed up in the image of 'a swift carriage, of a dark night, rattling with four horses over roads that one can't see' (pp. 237, 361). Elsa Nettels draws attention to the parallels between Isabel and Catherine Morland but goes on to argue that, by refusing to marry Lord Warburton, Isabel shows a growing ability to reject stereotypical romance conventions.[60] In many ways, however, Isabel's problem is not that she has read too many romances as that she has not read them well enough. Unlike Catherine Morland or Emily St Aubert in Ann Radcliffe's *The Mysteries of Udolpho* (and for that matter unlike Newman, at least until the closing chapters of *The American*), Isabel has in spite of her love of knowledge, 'a natural shrinking from raising curtains and looking into unlighted corners' (*Novels 1881–1886*, p. 395). As a child, she never opens the bolted street door in the house at Albany, 'for this would have interfered with her theory that there was a strange, unseen place on the other side – a place which became, to the child's imagination . . . a region of delight or of terror' (p. 214).[61] The desire to remain on the nearer side of the threshold is the condition of imaginative experience for Isabel, yet it also belongs to a dangerous propensity to lump delight and terror together indiscriminately. In marrying Osmond, one could argue that she mistakes terror for delight. It is not until she finds herself returning in a swift carriage to Gardencourt at the end of the novel that she sees what lies behind her earlier idea of happiness, apprehends and is assailed by 'the truth of things, their mutual relations, their meaning, and for the most part their horror' (p. 768). This horror is by no means fanciful or delusory: Isabel's experience actually does have a Gothic quality, and far from being a misleading guide to reality, a de-literalized Gothicism ultimately provides an accurate and appropriate description of her situation.

One of the finer ironies of *The Portrait of a Lady* is that, having seen her idea of happiness turn to horror, and therefore having come to a more 'realistic' assessment of her predicament, Isabel finally encounters the ghost of Gardencourt, and thus becomes the subject of a 'romantic' experience that she had once anticipated with naive pleasure.[62] In the last chapter of the novel, Ralph appears to her in 'the cold, faint dawn', a 'dim, hovering figure in the dimness of the room' (p. 787). Although this vision depends on suffering, on having a past to be haunted by, it seems that Gardencourt does become, in a new and more sombre sense, a 'romantic old house'. The apparition provides no grounds for a return to Isabel's youthful romanticism, and she shows none of Clement Searle's ecstasy. But this is not to say that Ralph's ghost is a hostile, competitive figure like the apparitions encountered in 'The Romance of Certain Old Clothes' or 'Travelling Companions'. Indeed, Ralph is the very embodiment within the novel of the collaborative James.[63] He acts as the mediator in the 'Imitate me!' phase of the relation between the model and the desiring subject described by Girard (see p. 64 above). Giving Isabel the chance to fulfil the requirements of her imagination by investing her with sufficient wealth to set her free from circumstantial limitations, Ralph represents the James who is committed to extending Isabel's experience. He passionately wants her to spread her wings and rise above the earth (see p. 419). His 'boundless liberty of appreciation' (p. 228) looks forward to the freedom described in 'The Art of Fiction' (see p. 77 above) and to the novel's Preface, which speaks of the artist's 'boundless freedom' (*LC*, II, 1075).

In spite of her ambivalence towards the world on the other side of the bolted street door, liberty is the goal which Isabel is programmed to pursue. She has 'a fixed determination to regard the world as a place of... free expansion' (*Novels 1881–1886*, p. 241). Yet a 'fixed' view of free expansion (as opposed to a 'boundless liberty') presumes the limits it wants to surpass, invokes the immobility it wants to leave behind. Madame Merle is a creature of forms, but she knows that the self 'overflows into everything that belongs to us – and then ... flows back again' (p. 397). In contrast, Isabel's set vision of freedom only sharpens her awareness of thresholds, making her aware that her belongings are 'a limit, a barrier' (p. 398). Limits and barriers rather than boundless freedom: there is, as one might expect, a second dynamic in the play of mimetic desire, a contrary movement which is expressed in the injunction 'Don't imitate me!'. In the vigil scene, 'haunted with terrors', Isabel finds herself trapped in a 'labyrinth' (p. 628). Her project of expansion and ascension collapses, and she is barred from the path which leads to 'the high places of happiness' (p. 629). Cut off from what Ludwig Binswanger would call the 'ethereal world' – always the imagined destination of the extravagant self – Isabel enters a 'grave world'.[64] Rather than rising above the ground, she descends below the earth. She feels that she is following a 'dark, narrow alley' which leads 'downward and earthward, into realms of restriction and depression' and which comes to an end in a 'dead wall' (*Novels 1881–1886*, p. 629). Trapped

within her marriage and the world of conventional forms, Isabel
seems (like Newman before her) to have reached the edge of the text,
the limit of her possibility. It is at this point that one catches a
glimpse of another, near-ghostly but now more explicitly hostile
presence on the further side of the threshold: Osmond's 'beautiful
mind' seems to Isabel to 'peep down from a small high window and
mock at her' (p. 633). If Ralph acted as James's proxy by sponsoring
extension, then Osmond could be seen as the presiding spirit of the
phase of contraction.[65] Collaborative and fraternally touching,
Ralph's 'pleasant perpetual smile' stands in marked contrast to
Osmond's malicious and competitive mockery (p. 539).[66] James
allies himself with Ralph, but there is also an analogy (albeit a
partial and a problematic one) between a man of forms like
Osmond, and James, a man of imagination who maintains literary
form by restraining the centrifugal force which works towards the
gratification of imagination and desire. James instigates explosive
forces, but he also sustains his economic mastery by turning his back,
and it is perhaps significant that the letters in Osmond's name can
be rearranged to spell *mon dos*. Just as Osmond looks down on Isabel
from a small high window, so the writer in the Preface to *The Portrait
of a Lady* is a 'watcher' who looks out through windows in the house
of fiction, 'mere holes in a dead wall, disconnected, perched aloft'
(*LC*, II, 1075). Osmond frames Isabel, and he uses deception in order
to do so; but James also frames his protagonist, albeit in aesthetic
and formal ways.[67] Osmond and James are by no means identical
and in many ways the former merely blocks Isabel's attempts to
reach the position occupied by the latter, prevents access to that high
place of happiness from which, Isabel feels, 'one could look down
with a sense of exaltation and advantage, and judge and choose and
pity' (*Novels 1881–1886*, p. 629). It is too simplistic to say that
Osmond stands for economic mastery and Ralph for the explosive
principle, that James collaborates with Isabel in the first half of the
novel and then sets out to pull the rug from under her feet in the
second half. As always, James is involved with conditional relationships rather than absolute polarities. Unlike Osmond, he views
Isabel with 'pity' and to this extent there is still a degree of involvement in his detached judgements and discriminations. Similarly, the
revised version of the novel creates an element of detachment in
Ralph's involvement (see note 66 to this chapter). One would
perhaps like to be reassured that James regards Isabel less with
Osmond's desire to appropriate than with Ralph's impulse to invest,

less with Osmond's mockery than with Ralph's pleasant smile. But the novel refuses such easy comforts. James must represent himself through Osmond as well as a Ralph. He is quite prepared to implicate himself in the unpardonable sin, and creates in Osmond a latterday Rappaccini who already owns a flower in Pansy but wants to advance his horticultural experiments by turning Isabel into 'a small garden-plot' annexed to his own intellectual park (p. 636). Even Osmond's mockery is not entirely foreign to James, who is perfectly capable of defining the artist's stance in terms of derision. In his 1874 review of *Ein König Lear des Dorfes*, James had described Turgenev – a writer who significantly resurfaces in the Preface to *The Portrait of a Lady* (see *LC*, II, 1072–73) – as 'the author in the background' who emits a 'chuckle' as he winds up his 'dismal demonstration' of 'disappointment, despair ... and blighted hopes' (*LC*, II, 993). This is the laughter of the detached writer, and it is to return in 'The Figure in the Carpet'. The narrator of that tale imagines that Corvick is playing chess against the 'ghostlier form' of the writer Vereker. 'Wearily secure' in his position, Vereker the master leans back with 'a smile on his fine clear face' (*CT*, IX, 292). The literary disciple is unable to achieve the position of the mocking god, that liberated spectre, incapable of unlocking his secret.[68] James's depiction of such masterful characters was not without its tensions. In an 1865 review of Louisa M. Alcott's *Moods*, one finds him attacking the character of Adam Warwick as a hackneyed unreality. Warwick is the 'cynical bachelor or widower' with the 'quiet smile', and James finds him a 'monstrous' figure (*LC*, I, 90). Osmond is precisely such a monster, but he cannot for this reason be disconnected from James. Alfred Habegger argues that Osmond represents James's partial investment in and capitulation to the 'dark side' of his father's ideas about women and marriage.[69] The writer who began *The Portrait of a Lady* as a 'bid for freedom' finally 'turns against freedom', transforms himself into 'the manipulative middle-aged guardian-lover he detested' (*Henry James and the 'Woman Business'*, pp. 140, 143, 181). There are, however, quite different artistic stances. In an 1883 essay, James speaks of Daudet's 'expressive and sympathetic smile' (*LC*, II, 237).[70] This collaborative humour resembles that of Ralph Touchett rather than that of Osmond. Yet James makes it clear that half his affection for Daudet's benevolence, expressiveness and lack of reserve 'comes from the fact that he writes in a way in which I would not write even if I could' (p. 233).

Is James associating himself with Turgenev's detached derision, perhaps even with Osmond's? If James is chuckling in the background of *The Portrait of a Lady*, his amusement cannot finally be identified with Osmond's mockery since it does not represent an unequivocal commitment to a one-sided formalism. James's strategies of mastery exist by virtue of an underlying recognition of dynamism and life, and one could even argue that they do much to create such vitalities. The Osmond in James kills off the Ralph but cannot prevent the latter's ghostly return. Unless contained and put under pressure by James's attempts to achieve economic mastery, centrifugal forces would merely dissipate and diffuse. Isabel's desire for freedom makes limits appear, but it seems that these limits are themselves the condition of a certain sort of freedom. Like 'Daisy Miller', the vigil scene is rich in images of enclosure and fixity. Yet it also represents the novel's most concentrated rendering of Isabel's adventure. As the Preface points out, her apprehension of her situation is 'as "interesting" as the surprise of a caravan or the identification of a pirate' (*LC*, II, 1084). The scene focusses the point at which James's centrifugal and centripetal dynamics intersect; according to the Preface, it possesses 'all the vivacity of incident and all the economy of picture' (p. 1084). Isabel's literal motionlessness and figurative entrapment provide the grounds for a subjective extension which calls up the imagery of romance. In one sense the vigil is the triumph of Isabel's consciousness, the point at which her experience is finally liberated and her imagination pierces the veil of delusion. It is precisely through being trapped that she acquires what Tony Tanner calls an 'internal' freedom.[71] Yet this is a freedom within form, a liberation which involves the recognition of failure. Like Newman, Isabel is released, but only from a yearning whose ineffectiveness the novel demonstrates. She does not fulfil the requirements of her imagination so much as acquire a more accurate and relatively capacious imagination. If Isabel had achieved supreme imaginative control by reaching the high place of happiness she would simply have disappeared, become as unrepresentable as the artist in triumph, an observing presence rather than an observed figure. In order to give her the 'impress that constitutes an identity', James had, in the words of his Preface, to ensure that she was 'confined by ... conditions' and 'engaged in the tangle' (p. 1076).

James's next three major novels – *The Bostonians*, *The Princess Casamassima* and *The Tragic Muse* – were worldly and public in scope and theme, ironic in tone. Nevertheless, their analysis of experience was not complete without the ghostly and the uncanny. In *The Bostonians*, which Alfred Habegger has described as 'James's ultimate ghost story', James poured scorn on the grotesque figure of Selah Tarrant, the mesmeric healer whose wife fakes his special effects whilst consoling herself with the thought that she 'ministered to a belief in immortality' (*Henry James and the 'Woman Business'*, p. 209; James, *Novels 1881–1886*, p. 867). But he was also capable of suggesting rather more seriously (and Habegger sees this as an instance of James being haunted by the ghost of his father) that Basil Ransom is 'inhabited by some transmitted spirit of a robust but narrow ancestor, some broad-faced wig-wearer or sword-bearer' (James, *Novels 1881–1886*, p. 975; see Habegger, *Henry James and the 'Woman Business'*, pp. 204–8). Although he mocked the trance-lecturer Mrs Ada T. P. Foat, said to have discoursed on a 'Summerland' to which she has since apparently departed (p. 866), James could also give Olive Chancellor a 'spectral face' (p. 823).

Amongst the political and social themes of *The Princess Casamassima*, the ghostly resurfaces with increased force. Indeed, Adrian Poole describes the book as James's 'most spectral novel' (*Henry James*, p. 58). In a somewhat incongruous generic aside, Medley acquires a 'haunted chamber ... where a dreadful individual at certain times made his appearance – a dwarfish ghost, with an enormous head, a dispossessed brother, of long ago' (*Novels 1886–1890*, pp. 265–6).[72] It seems that Captain Sholto was gathering 'horrible ghost-stories' for the Princess long before he began to collect revolutionaries on her behalf (p. 306). When Hyacinth visits Paris after Miss Pynsent's death, a perception of the uncanny moves to centre stage. Hyacinth is haunted by a 'constant companion': the spirit of his grandfather who gazes at him 'with eyes of deep, kind, glowing comprehension' (p. 338).

Beneath the interrogation of art and politics in *The Tragic Muse*, uncanny paternal visitations erupt once more. After being elected Member of Parliament for Harsh, Nick Dormer senses 'the revived spirit of his father' (*Novels 1886–1890*, p. 874). At Beauclere he becomes aware of the ghostly hand of the past (see p. 902). But it is not until near the end of the novel that James brings his middle period to an end in what is probably the single most significant revisitation of his entire career. In order to prove to himself that he has not fabricated the figure of Gabriel Nash, Nick wants to make a sketch of his Mephistophelian mentor, 'a photograph of the ghost'

(p. 1233). Nash is plainly uneasy about being the subject of pictorial representation and shortly afterwards disappears. It is then that Nick imagines that his picture too is beginning to fade, that 'the hand of time was rubbing it away little by little (for all the world as in some delicate Hawthorne tale), making the surface indistinct and bare – bare of all resemblance to the model' (p. 1236). 'The moral of the Hawthorne tale', as James adds in the final lines of the chapter, would be that Nash 'would come back on the day when the last adumbration should have vanished' (p. 1236). Nash never does return, and Nick eventually puts the portrait back in a corner 'with its face against the wall' (p. 1243). But James was to enact the moral of the Hawthorne tale in his fiction of the 1890s.

REVISITATIONS: FROM 'SIR EDMUND ORME' TO
'THE WAY IT CAME'

'The supernatural story', wrote James to Vernon Lee on 27 April 1890, 'is not the *class* of fiction I myself most cherish' (*L*, III, 277). He added that he favoured instead 'a close connotation, or close obser-vation, of the real – or whatever one may call it – the familiar, the inevitable' (p. 277). These comments were written before *The Tragic Muse* had completed its run in the *Atlantic Monthly*. A decade later, James had written 'Sir Edmund Orme', 'Nona Vincent', 'The Private Life', 'Sir Dominick Ferrand', 'Owen Wingrave', 'The Way it Came', 'The Turn of the Screw', 'The Real Right Thing', 'Maud-Evelyn', 'The Third Person' and the opening sections of *The Sense of the Past*. James's letter to Lee apparently lacks prescience, yet perhaps the most surprising thing about it is not that he fails to foretell his return to the supernatural story in the 1890s but that (unlike his 1865 review of *Aurora Floyd* or his later Preface to volume XVII of the *New York Edition*) he seems to maintain a clear-cut distinction between the 'supernatural' and the 'real', the 'familiar'. In the next decade, such distinctions were to be questioned, placed in new dynamic relationships, and even overthrown.

I will shortly be examining the way in which the ghost stories of the 1890s relate to James's literary project as a whole. Yet there is also, of course, a more general cultural and social background to his renewed interest in the ghostly at this time. Since the mid-century and well into the early decades of the twentieth century, periodicals like *Blackwoods*, the *Cornhill*, *Household Words*, *All the Year Round*,

Temple Bar and the *Strand* had assiduously cultivated and supplied the demand for ghostly fiction.[73] To this list we should add, in James's case, *Black and White* ('Sir Edmund Orme'), the *English Illustrated Magazine* ('Nona Vincent'), the *Atlantic Monthly* ('The Private Life', 'Maud-Evelyn'), the *Cosmopolitan Magazine* ('Jersey Villas', later republished as 'Sir Dominick Ferrand'), the *Graphic* ('Owen Wingrave'), the *Chap Book* and *Chapman's Magazine of Fiction* ('The Way it Came') and *Collier's Weekly* ('The Turn of the Screw' and 'The Real Right Thing'). It would, I think, be only a slight exaggeration to assert that hardly a major writer between, say, 1850 and 1930, did *not* at some stage experiment with the ghost story. James's letter to Vernon Lee was written after receiving *Hauntings*, her own collection of such tales. From *Dr Jekyll and Mr Hyde* (1886) through *The Picture of Dorian Gray* (1890) to *Dracula* (1897) and beyond, the last years of the nineteenth century saw an extraordinary explosion of fiction dealing with the supernatural and the paranormal. One can relate this fascination, as Alan Gauld has done, to the religious uncertainty which followed Darwin's discoveries and the attacks on the authenticity of the Bible made by nineteenth-century scholars.[74] One can find in the literature of the fantastic, as Todorov does, 'nothing but the bad conscience of this positivist era' (*The Fantastic*, p. 168). One can see in the theme of the *doppelgänger*, of the hidden, bestial self, the crumbling edges of the Victorian edifice, the selves which lie behind its assumptions of integrity, the violence and discontent which both created and terrified its civilization.[75] Mesmerism, animal magnetism, reincarnation, hypnotism, clairvoyance, telepathy, possession, trance, hallucination, the divided self, the split consciousness, amnesia, hysteria: these were the limit phenomena and borderline states which fascinated writers, scientists, researchers and charlatans in the age before (and after) Freud. In *The Bostonians*, James had of course already explored the extraordinary nexus of spiritualism, feminism and political radicalism described in Howard Kerr's *Mediums, and Spirit-Rappers, and Roaring Radicals*. Indeed, he had been ironically interested in spiritualism since before 'Professor Fargo' (1874).[76]

In his Preface to volume XII of the *New York Edition*, James was to claim that he had made no attempt to keep the ghosts in 'The Turn of the Screw' 'on terms with the to-day so copious psychical record of cases of apparitions' (*LC*, II, 1186). A number of critics have shown, rightly I think, that this claim is somewhat misleading;

James may have followed Andrew Lang in regretting the fact that the ghosts reported by the psychical researchers were, from the writer's point of view, singularly undramatic, but he had in fact more than a layman's knowledge of the Society for Psychical Research.[77] He knew F. W. H. Myers, Edmund Gurney and Henry Sidgwick (all founder members of the SPR). On 23 December 1886 he told his brother William and sister-in-law Alice that he had bought a copy of Gurney, Myers and Podmore's *Phantasms of the Living* although he had not yet 'read a word of them' (*L*, III, 152). William James had been a member of the American branch of the SPR since 1884 and was to be its President from 1894 until 1896. James certainly had personal familiarity with the 'learned meetings' of psychical researchers alluded to by the narrator of 'The Way it Came' (*CT*, IX, 396), having delivered his brother's paper on the medium Mrs Piper to a meeting of the SPR on 31 October 1890.[78]

James's return to the ghostly, therefore, was not staged in literary or cultural isolation. James possessed personal knowledge of various aspects of the diffuse but profound contemporary interest in the paranormal. There was a market for ghostly fiction and, probably, on his own part, a desire to keep up with the Vernon Lees, the Stevensons, the Wildes and the Kiplings of the contemporary fictional scene. There were also, of course, the personal reasons. Despite the assurance of his letter to Lee, James had entered a period of crisis. The deaths of friends and relatives, his troubled theatrical ventures (culminating in the *Guy Domville* fiasco on 5 January 1895 – a week before James made his notebook entry on 'The Turn of the Screw') and his disenchantment with a culture which seemed to him increasingly brazen and distorted were to prompt a growing sense of otherness, of extinction and of the general uncanniness of life. 'I see ghosts everywhere', he wrote to Francis Boott on 11 October 1895 (*L*, IV, 24).[79] As always, though, James's anxieties and fascinations were primarily literary ones. The ghost stories of the 1890s cannot be seen merely as a rearguard action against what a notebook entry of 4 March 1895 called 'the great modern collapse of all the forms and "superstitions"'.[80] They were, rather, a positive investigation of the haunted house of late-Victorian culture. The exploration of the ghostly which James conducted between 'Sir Edmund Orme' and 'The Way it Came' laid much of the groundwork for his representation of the haunted, phantasmagoric consciousnesses which inhabit the vast and shadowy spaces of his later novels.

Nevertheless, the James of 1890 was facing, if not a collapse, then at least an exhaustion of forms. In *The Portrait of a Lady*, the international theme held centre stage as James's great narrative, the governing myth of his fiction. By the time of 'Lady Barberina' (1884) and *The Reverberator* (1888), however, the international theme was deemed suitable for treatment only on the scale of the *nouvelle*; after that, in 'The Solution' (1889–90), it became confined to the short story. On 29 October 1888 James wrote to his brother that he was 'deadly weary of the whole "international" state of mind' (*L*, III, 244). The fallacies and imperfections of the theme form one of the recurrent subjects in the Prefaces (see *LC*, II, 1149–50, 1197–98, 1212–13).

There were also problems in other areas of James's work. When the serialization of *The Tragic Muse* was completed, he felt, as he later recalled in the novel's Preface – probably his most perturbed – that he had 'launched it in a great grey void from which no echo or message whatever would come back' (*LC*, II, 1104). Yet it was not just a matter of public indifference. Once again, as in the case of the international theme, there were difficulties in the dynamic equations of James's fiction. *The Bostonians*, *The Princess Casamassima* and *The Tragic Muse* were James's great realist novels, but their devotion to the close observation of the familiar and the inevitable did not entirely satisfy the exigencies of economic mastery. In the matter of length, and more importantly in that of structure, the novels are, at least for many of their critics, centrifugal, loose, uncontrolled and unbalanced.[81] These somewhat surprising manifestations of the explosive principle help to explain James's decision to devote himself to shorter fiction after *The Tragic Muse*. The intention 'to do nothing but short lengths' was announced in a letter to Robert Louis Stevenson of 31 July 1888 and James's notebooks for the next few years were filled with exhortations to produce compressed and foreshortened works, reminders of his renewed devotion to 'economic necessity' (*L*, III, 240; *N*, p. 144 (21 December 1895); see also *N*, pp. 54–5, 57, 65, 77–8).

The new emphasis on compactness and brevity did not of course preclude those 'developments' which, as James wrote in his notebook on 8 September 1895, were his 'temptation and ... joy' (*N*, p. 130). In one sense, centripetal pressure only intensified the explosive principle. On 11 March 1898 James wrote to A.C. Benson, admitting that his 'unbridled imagination' had caused him to 'see the inevitable development of the subject' in 'The Turn of the Screw'.[82] A letter to William Dean Howells of 11 December 1902 placed *The Spoils of Poynton* and *What Maisie Knew* alongside 'The Turn of the Screw'. All of these works resembled *The Sacred Fount*, which had grown by 'a rank force of its own' (*L*, IV, 251). But the move to shorter fiction did correspond to an increasingly dramatic concentration on point of view, and this had major thematic consequences for James. In such tales as 'The Author of "Beltraffio"', 'The Aspern Papers' and 'The Liar', he had already returned to the realms of private psychopathology, to the themes of possession and vampirism which had marked early stories such as 'The Romance of Certain Old Clothes' and 'De Grey'. In this sense, 'Sir Edmund Orme', James's first ghost story since 'The Ghostly Rental', does not represent a decisive break in his work. I have already argued that the middle years were marked by a series of ghostly revisitations, and it is certainly true that James's interest in this aspect of his work was developing throughout the 1880s. He may, like William Dean Howells, have been working after the manner of the naturalists; yet he too, as he put it in a letter to Howells of 21 February 1884, was 'haunted with romantic phantoms' (*L*, III, 28). Indeed, if anything, the hauntedness applied more to James than to Howells, who was (at least in James's view) more exclusively the Trollopeian actualist, being animated, as James wrote in an 1886 essay on his friend, 'by a love of the common, the immediate, the familiar and vulgar elements of life' (*LC*, I, 502). Howells looked askance at 'exceptions and perversities', but James argued that life 'by no means eschews the strange' (p. 503). James's 1888 essay on Robert Louis Stevenson drew attention to the 'astounding combinations' to be found in everyday marriages and divorces, to the 'strange accidents', 'odd specimens and tangled situations' which were part of the most ordinary families, and to the value for the novelist of the 'uncommon', the 'wonderful', the 'improbable' and the 'extraordinary', insofar as they were represented through consciousness (*LC*, I, 1249). Indeed, 'the novelist who leaves the extraordinary out of his account' was, for James, 'liable to awkward confrontations' (p. 1249).

One can therefore see on James's part a gradual return to the ghostly. The crucial moment in this transitional period occurs in the passage from *The Tragic Muse* that I have already referred to (see pp. 85–6 above). At some level James appears to be reminding himself of the prophetic insight achieved in 'The Ghostly Rental'.

The 'delicate Hawthorne tale' invented by James towards the end of the novel represents the revisitation of a predicted revisitation (*Novels 1886–1890*, p. 1236). It suggests that the moment at which James supersedes or effaces his predecessor in terms of literary form, succeeds in making his surface 'bare of all resemblance to the model' and innocent even of the slightest adumbration, is precisely the moment when Hawthorne returns as a vital force (p. 1236). When James wrote 'Sir Edmund Orme', he took his idea from a sketch recorded in his notebooks on 22 January 1879 (see *N*, p. 10). Although he claimed in his Preface to remember 'absolutely nothing' of the tale's origin, Sidney Lind has shown that the entry was almost certainly inspired by James's research for *Hawthorne* (*LC*, II, 1263; see Lind, 'The Supernatural Tales of Henry James', pp. 114–16). In the *American Notebooks* (7 September 1835), Hawthorne recorded an idea for a story in which a heartless young man wins the love of a girl only to find that he has 'conjured up a spirit of mischief' (*CE*, VIII, 13). In itself, this is a rather unpersuasive source for 'Sir Edmund Orme'. But James's note is preceded by another, derived more directly from a second entry under the same date in Hawthorne's notebook. 'In an old house', Hawthorne had specu-lated, 'a mysterious knocking might be heard on the wall, where had formerly been a doorway, now bricked up' (p. 13). 'Imagine a door', writes James in his own notebook more than forty years later, 'either walled-up, or that has been long locked – at which there is an occasional knocking' (*N*, p. 10). Hawthorne's tale of visitation becomes James's revisitation, and the actual, external origin of his projected story becomes its internal theme as the entry continues. After having 'ceased to heed' the noises, the occupant of the house undergoes 'some great and constant trouble' and the knocking increases (p. 10). Eventually the door is broken open 'and the trouble ceases – as if the spirit had desired to be admitted, that it might interpose, redeem and protect' (p. 10). Three years after 'The Ghostly Rental' it is almost as if James is symbolically mapping out the later stages of his career, creating a projective, mythic history of what will happen after he has built his own chamber in the house of fiction. After the break with Hawthorne, after the long and only partially successful suppression, during which slight ghostly erupt-ions and Hawthornean knockings disturbingly persisted, the revisi-tation and readmission of the interposing spirit is actually invited or solicited during a period of crisis.

The story of the knock at the door was never written, although it returns in a notebook entry made by James on 16 May 1899 (see *N*, p. 183). In a sense, however, all James's ghost stories of this period acted out the unwritten tale's theme: the invocation or admission of the past and of Hawthorne. On 22 August 1837 Hawthorne noted down an idea for a story in which a man and a girl meet. Each is 'in search of a person to be known by some particular sign' (*CE*, VIII, 153). They watch and wait together until 'at last some casual circumstance discloses that each is the one that the other is waiting for' (p. 153). Decades later and in the hands of James, this germ develops into 'The Way it Came' and 'The Beast in the Jungle'. Yet James was not simply raiding the notebooks of his predecessor for subjects to use in a difficult, uncertain period; nor was he merely repeating Hawthorne. Although his reinvestigation of the house of romance was mounted without the aggression manifested in 'The Ghostly Rental', James continued to scrutinize and transform Hawthorne's germs. As Sidney Lind points out, the sketch for 'Sir Edmund Orme' and the tale itself reverse Hawthorne's arrangement of characters, making the woman, Mrs Marden, the one who conjures the persecuting spirit (see 'The Supernatural Tales of Henry James', p. 116). This is a relatively unimportant adjustment, but 'Owen Wingrave' (1892) stages a more challenging revision of Hawthorne, and in particular of *The House of the Seven Gables*. Owen's observation that the portrait of Colonel Wingrave 'fairly stirs on the canvas' reminds one of the scene in *The House of the Seven Gables* when the image of Colonel Pyncheon seems 'on the point of descending bodily from its frame' (James, *CT*, IX, 34; Hawthorne, *CE*, II, 198). Colonel Wingrave's death recalls that of Colonel Pyncheon, and Sir Philip, whose status as a 'relic' contrasts with the 'vigorous' portrait of his ancestor, echoes Judge Pyncheon, who is likewise a reduced version of Colonel Pyncheon (James, *CT*, IX, 20, 38).[83] Both *The House of the Seven Gables* and 'Owen Wingrave' examine the nature of the past and its influence on the present and Wingrave resembles Hawthorne's Holgrave in more than name. Both characters give voice to a desire to escape from the past, from restrictive traditions and oppressive family ghosts. Holgrave eventually accepts that he will build a house for his family and 'conform myself to laws' (*CE*, II, 307). Optimistically fantasizing a resolution to the tainted conflicts of the past, Hawthorne seems to end the novel by forgetting the failed flight of Clifford and Hepzibah Pyncheon and the insights this scene offers into the impossibility of escaping from the house of the past. In contrast, 'Owen Wingrave' engages the problems which Hawthorne's novel resolved so unsatisfactorily. Owen triumphs not by exorcising the ghosts but by invoking them. He frees himself from the past not by moving somewhere else but by entering the haunted chamber. Whilst Phoebe Pyncheon brings liberating light to the house of the Pyncheons, Kate Julian literally locks Owen into the shadowy chamber of the past. 'Owen Wingrave' endorses 'The Ghostly Rental' and the notion that one becomes implicated in the past in the very act of breaking with it. By fighting the traditions of his family, Owen inevitably perpetuates their martial history: displaying 'a military steadiness under fire', he becomes in death 'a young soldier on a battle-field' (*CT*, ix, 34, 51). Maule's curse acted on the Pyncheon family from without, and was finally lifted by marriage. The curse on the Wingraves is entirely internal and can be resolved only by loss of life. Since Owen is the last of his line, his death offers no hope for a new generation. Indeed, the ghost that Owen lays *is* the family. At another level, however, James is repeating Hawthorne in the act of revising him: the name 'Owen Wingrave' recalls Owen Warland in Hawthorne's 'The Artist of the Beautiful'. Like his near-namesake, James's character achieves a symbolic triumph through sacrifice and converts defeat into a sort of victory (see Lind, 'The Supernatural Tales of Henry James', p. 208). It is also significant that Wingrave, the focus of these revisions, revisitations and repetitions, acquires his name through the resurrection of a revision: in the version of 'The Romance of Certain Old Clothes' included by James in volume III of *Stories Revived* (1885), the name of the family was altered from Willoughby to Wingrave.

When Isabel sees the ghostly figure of Ralph Touchett in the final chapter of *The Portrait of a Lady*, the scene is an emblem of experience undergone. To see the ghost is a sign that through suffering Isabel has acquired a knowledge she lacked at the beginning of the novel. In 'Sir Edmund Orme', by contrast, the ghostly is no longer a rite of passage: it is the passage itself. To see ghosts in 'Sir Edmund Orme' is, at least for the narrator if not for Mrs Marden or her daughter, to have a 'distinction' conferred upon one, to be privileged with a 'mystic enlargement of vision' (*CT*, viii, 137). Far from seeing the ghost as a restrictive figure, the ironic token of a certain imaginative failure, the narrator of the tale exults in the word *haunted* 'as if it represented the fulfilment of my dearest dream' (p. 135). It is an astonishing fact that, except perhaps for the final chapter in *The Portrait of a Lady*, Orme is James's first fully visualized and dramatized apparition. Furthermore, for the first time in James's fiction, except perhaps in 'A Passionate Pilgrim', the ghostly encounter is presented as the quintessence of experience.

Subjective privilege; the enlargement of vision; the fulfilment of wishes: the ghostly in 'Sir Edmund Orme' manifests various aspects of the explosive principle. It is true that Orme is experienced through the medium of a human consciousness, but unlike 'A Passionate Pilgrim' or 'The Ghostly Rental', the ghost-seer and the 'I' narrator in 'Sir Edmund Orme' have merged into one. These centrifugal forces seem to have demanded additional forms of mediation. 'Sir Edmund Orme' is the third of some thirteen tales and the first of five with ghostly or uncanny themes to be equipped with a 'frame', a passage supposedly written by another narrator (or the same narrator in later life) and placed before the main first-person narrative.[84] In one sense, of course, all James's fiction was framed. In the Preface to *Roderick Hudson* he spoke of the artist whose 'exquisite problem' was, 'by a geometry of his own', to draw the circle within which relations appeared to stop (*LC*, II, 1041). In the Preface to *The Awkward Age* he spoke of isolating these relations, of attempting 'to surround with the sharp black line, to frame in the square, the circle, the charming oval' in order to make his 'arrangement of objects' become a 'picture' (p. 1123). In the rather more specific and technical sense in which I am using the word, however, the device of the frame, which may well be a vestige of the ghostly sub-plots in Gothic novels, has often been employed in tales of the supernatural.[85] The frame takes various forms and in some writers, though never in James, either the frame itself or the core narrative which it encloses may be told in the third-person form. Generally and most obviously speaking, the introductory frame ambiguates the main narrative by drawing attention to its unverifiability. The central narrative is often although not always presented as a piece of writing, a document and not an immediate reality. Its narrator is often but not always dead, and therefore unavailable for questioning. Although frame narrators often testify to the authenticity of the main narrative and give it an air of circumstantiality, they usually implicitly raise the issue of what constitutes a 'true relation'. Although ghosts, in the tradition of Defoe, may have the effect of guaranteeing and delimiting the real by, as Todorov puts it, positing 'the majority of a text as belonging to reality', they had themselves to be controlled and delimited (*The Fantastic*, p. 168; see p. 33 above). For James, the frame was in addition, as I have already suggested, an important economic device; in terms of form it contained the explosive force of the inner romance, displacing the core narrative into the past and promoting compressed, foreshortened effects.[86] Ghosts enabled him to explore the effects of the past on the present without needing to represent intervening periods of time.[87]

There is, however, a further and more significant economic dimension to James's deployment of the frame. In such tales as 'Master Eustace', 'The Sweetheart of M. Briseux', 'The Path of Duty', 'The Visits', 'The Way it Came', 'The Turn of the Screw' and 'Maud-Evelyn', James appears to be using the device partly in order to avoid identifying himself with the first-person female narrators of the main narrative. To an extent, no doubt, this is simply a matter of creating an effective distance between James's own position as author and that of his possibly dubious or manipulative female narrators. Yet the formal, masculine framing of the female voice provides insights into James's attempts to restrict the explosive force of the ghostly. What he is seeking to economically master in both cases is not only liberated romantic experience, the desire for extension, but desire itself, often specifically female desire, and in particular transgressive, 'abnormal' or violent forms of that desire. Almost all the frame stories and the ghost stories feature women who are not confined within the structures of marriage or the family, women who attempt to escape from traditional forms or are expelled by the representatives of those forms, who place themselves or are placed beyond the pale, who use or are used by 'normal' society. 'A Landscape-Painter' deals with the machinations of a female fortune-hunter. 'Gabrielle de Bergerac' is the narrative of an illicit affair. In 'The Romance of Certain Old Clothes', Viola becomes the wife of Perdita's husband and the victim of her sister's posthumous revenge. In 'De Grey', Margaret Aldis is an orphan who tries to break with the past of the family she is marrying into; Paul droops and languishes in the face of her thriving sexual power. The ghost in 'A Passionate Pilgrim' is that of a woman seduced by Clement Searle's ancestor and cast out by his family. The frame stories and the ghost stories are awash with widows and unmarried women, with coquettes and manipulators, with sexual shames and disgraces, seductions, illegitimate children, elopements and ruptured engagements. It is of course true that James wrote numerous works containing female victims or violators which were neither ghost stories nor frame stories. Nevertheless, the centrifugal tendencies of the ghost story, its tendency to break its bounds and get into flood (see p. 55 above), are closely allied with one of James's most famous, though perhaps not most original, descriptions of the upsurge of female desire.[88] In the final chapter of *The Portrait of a Lady* (a novel whose title, as I have already pointed out, suggests that a kind of framing is again at work), Isabel is terrified by the 'rushing torrent' of her own released desires (*Novels 1881–1886*, p. 798). Just as James channels the ghostly and preserves 'the virtue of a story' (*LC*, II, 1184), so Isabel flees from this fearful flood and dedicates herself to the 'straight path' (*Novels 1881–1886*, p. 799).

Allon White has argued that James's ghosts are one of a number of 'displaced forms of representation' which obscure an original scene of sexual intimacy or, in James's terms, vulgarity.[89] This argument could be extended to the frame stories as a whole, which screen or filter ghosts, women, transgressive desires, and also scenes of violence. It is notable how often, from 'The Romance of Certain Old Clothes' to 'Owen Wingrave', 'The Way it Came', 'The Third Person' and 'The Jolly Corner', James's ghost stories feature wounds. In this context it is significant that the beginning of James's literary career is closely linked to the 'obscure hurt' recalled in *Notes of a Son and Brother*, an injury sustained by James whilst fighting a fire in Newport on the night of 28 October 1861 (*Autobiography*, p. 415).[90] Frames and ghosts do not only obscure the violent or sexual nature of origins; they also represent James's uneasy but by no means merely prudish response to the hackneyed nature of sexual transgression, the unoriginal nature of originating plots. Leslie Fiedler has called the ghost story a 'rather vulgar' form, and James himself is often dismissive of his work in this genre (*Love and Death*, p. 303). Yet it is not only a matter of aesthetic vulgarity, since other forms of obscurity or obscenity are frequently at issue in the ghost stories. To call 'The Turn of the Screw' a 'shameless pot-boiler', as James did in a letter to F. W. H. Myers of 19 December 1898, or to refer to 'Owen Wingrave' as 'an obscure pot-boiler', as he did in a letter to George Bernard Shaw of 20 January 1909, is subtly to raise the issue of sexual as well as literary vulgarity (*L*, IV, 88, 512). The ghost seen by Searle in 'A Passionate Pilgrim' is that of a curate's daughter who, 'turned ... forth ... into the storm', dies with her illegitimate baby 'in the deep snow' (*CT*, II, 272). This incident is sheer melodramatic cliché, a scene of aesthetic and sexual 'vulgarity' which James then obscures by using the ghost, Searle, the narrator and the frame as interposing and mediating layers. The false ghost encountered by the narrator of 'The Ghostly Rental' also follows in the wake of a hackneyed sexual catastrophe: cast out by her father, Diamond's daughter has supposedly been murdered by her lover, 'a young man with whiskers from Boston' (*CT*, IV, 66). It is, as the daughter herself later puts it, 'an old story', and James's uneasiness with such stories extends to his narrator, who experiences 'vulgar' fear when he encounters the mock ghost (pp. 85, 75). White's concept of displacement is clearly valuable, and Alfred Habegger has written interestingly on the 'blank wall' in James's fiction which often conceals some form of sexual secret, something which can seem 'formulaic and subliterary, the stock-in-trade of cheap romance, melodrama, or detective fiction'.[91] Taken too far, however, such readings can become violent ones if they claim to restore proper, familiar or original meanings behind merely secondary, figurative or ghostly manifestations. According to Ned Lukacher, the Jamesian frame focusses 'the question of the origin', but it also simultaneously puts 'the nonoriginary in the place of the origin'.[92] Frames and ghosts do indeed often displace or obscure 'vulgarity', but they also defend against readings which reduce the text to sexual and aesthetic clichés. The economic master mediates or blocks such clichés, but in doing so he acts on behalf of productive secrecies rather than reductive translations or explanations. Ghosts obscure the origin, but they also transform the unrepresentable and the literal into the literary. The frame controls explosive forces, but it also acts as a reverberating membrane which remembers and re-presents. Like scar tissue, ghosts and frames provide new skin for old wounds, covering but also advertising some previous injury, obscuring but also repeating.

Repetition is certainly and markedly present in 'Sir Edmund Orme', perhaps most noticeably in terms of gesture. Characters in the tale are repeatedly described as looking away and looking back or looking down and looking up (see *CT*, VIII, 129, 131, 134, 139). They are continually getting up and sitting down (see pp. 122, 128, 138–40), described as being pallid or rosy in complexion, said to blush or to go pale (see pp. 121–5, 128, 134, 135). Similar stage directions are used to punctuate dialogue throughout James's work. Yet they are particularly significant in terms of the framed ghost story, since they dramatically establish a play of declaration and retraction, veiling and revealing, hinting at 'terminations' and 'embarrassments', to use the terms of two of James's short story collections during these years. These repetitions function as revisitations, allowing the return of the deathly and also of the sexual. 'I've seen him again – I've seen him again!', the narrator imagines himself telling Mrs Marden after an encounter with Orme (p. 141). 'He's here – he's here', she responds (p. 141). 'What on earth *is* the matter with you?', the narrator imagines Charlotte asking her mother (p. 124). Later in the tale Charlotte actually does ask the narrator and her mother 'what on earth is the matter with you?', adding that it is as if they had seen a ghost (p. 134). 'Don't say that – don't say that!', murmurs Mrs Marden when the narrator suggests that her daughter is a coquette (p. 122). This is a particularly interesting and almost self-contradictory repetition, for what it reiterates is a command to be silent and what Mrs Marden desires is an end to repetition. Charlotte already has 'looks and movements and tones' which act as 'a reflection, a recall' of Mrs Marden, who spends her life hoping that her daughter will not 'reproduce her mother in character as vividly as she did in face' (pp. 121, 146). The possibility that her daughter is a coquette must therefore be emphatically blanked out, and this repeated injunction to be silent also applies to the ghostly. 'Hush!', commands Mrs Marden in the church at Tranton after the narrator's first view of Orme (p. 129). 'Hush', she says later as Orme and her daughter approach (p. 132). Shortly afterwards, Mrs Marden describes Orme as 'a perfect presence' (p. 135). She apparently refuses to use the word 'ghost', which she describes as one of 'twenty vulgar names' (p. 135). Perfection therefore stands in for vulgarity just as the presence stands in for an absence. Yet the silence surrounding Orme, the fact that he is an 'unmentionable presence', continues to point towards some other form of unmentionability, some vulgarity concealed behind Mrs Marden's 'scrupulous blandness' (pp. 145, 141). What haunts Mrs Marden's marred and repetitive speeches is the intimate and dishonourable secret of her past coquetry. What she repeatedly blanks out is a scene of sexual coercion which led to a ruptured engagement and Orme's suicide, leaving her haunted by repeated revisitations, unutterable ghostly reminders of an unmentionable sexual guilt. Yet this original situation and indeed Orme's origin as a ghost seem distinctly un-original. Just as the originating elements of 'The Ghostly Rental' are 'an old story', a sexual and aesthetic cliché, so, for the narrator of 'Sir Edmund Orme', the ghost points to and springs from 'an old story, of love and pain' (*CT*, IV, 85; VIII, 145).

'An old story, of love and pain *and death*', added James in the revised version of the tale (*NYE*, XVII, 401; my italics). James's revision is a precise and appropriate one, for what the tale sets in motion is a series of category-confusions which threaten the distinction between the erotic and the mortuary. This erasure of difference recalls 'De Grey', and Mrs Marden's 'strange mixture of dismay and relief' certainly reminds one of Margaret Aldis's 'feverish transitions from hope to fear, from exaltation to despair', not to mention Brooke's 'mingled sense of exaltation and dread' in 'Travelling Companions' (*CT*, VIII, 131; I, 420; II, 221). The oxymoronic mingling and mixing in 'Sir Edmund Orme' suggests that the tale's repeated gestural oppositions (looking away and looking back, looking down and looking up, getting up and sitting down, blushing and going pale) come to much the same thing. Charlotte's 'rosy blankness' simultaneously obscures and reveals, superimposes the absence and presence of signs, indicates that ghostly anxiety and unmentionability is not easily distinguishable from signs of health, embarrassment or desire (*CT*, VIII, 121).

The characters in 'Sir Edmund Orme' repeatedly clutch, seize and embrace each other (see pp. 120, 133, 135, 147–9). The hands employed in these transactions may be possessive ones, as when the narrator sees the 'interlocked hands' of Charlotte and her mother and guesses that 'the grasp of the elder one was violent' (p. 123). They may also be imploring or appealing, as when the narrator feels Mrs Marden's hand 'pressing my arm in a way that might have been an involuntary betrayal of distress' (p. 123). One might expect these two sorts of grasp to be even more emphatically opposed in the final scene of the tale. Charlotte gives the narrator her hand and then, as Orme appears for the last time, throws herself into the narrator's arms. He finds himself 'bending over her' whilst Orme 'leaned over Mrs Marden' (p. 150). But are these two embraces really to be understood in terms of an opposition between the giving of hands in marriage and the dead hand of the past? The two embraces also suggest a parallelism between the narrator and Orme. Shortly before she holds out her hand, Charlotte seems to have 'recognised

something ... felt a coercion' (p. 150). Is this an anticipation of
Orme's materialization or an effect of the narrator's presence? The
tale implies that the latter possibility is at least as likely as the
former. Discussing 'Sir Edmund Orme' in his Preface, James argued
that he had set out to embroider 'the strange and sinister' on 'the
normal and easy' (*LC*, ii, 1264). Yet by superimposing the strange
and the normal James discovered possibly unforeseen relations and
rotations. Ostensibly the normal element in the tale, the narrator
gradually begins to seem distinctly sinister. His gallantry only partially conceals predatory, manipulative tendencies and it is he at
least as much as Orme who subjects Charlotte to 'a compulsion that
was slightly painful' (*CT*, viii, 139). Supposedly the sinister element
in the tale, Orme takes on an increasing degree of normality. No
monstrous alien, he is actually a figure of 'perfect propriety' (p.
145). It is true that his presence records and recalls imperfection and
impropriety, but this 'old story' is itself a very familiar, an archetypically Victorian tale.

Old stories of love and pain and death are again at work in 'Owen
Wingrave', although they seem to be focussed on heads rather than
hands. Owen's father died when an Afghan sabre came 'crashing
across his skull' and Colonel Wingrave killed his son with 'a blow on
the head' (*CT*, ix, 20, 37). In these circumstances it seems ominous
that the hopes of the Wingraves are 'collected on the second boy's
head' (*CT*, ix, 19). When Owen disappoints these hopes by raising
objections to a career in the army, he transforms family relationships
into military ones. 'Tactics' are adopted to make him conform,
'supplies' are cut off, and Owen goes to see his aunt Jane Wingrave
as if 'marching up to the battery' (pp. 22, 31, 25). Whether on the
battlefield or in the house, the Wingrave traditions are made up of
repeated acts of violence. These recurrent head wounds are accompanied by a rather different form of fatality. Colonel Wingrave's
dead body is found to be 'without a wound, without a mark' and
Owen himself dies without apparent physical injury (p. 37). Nevertheless, unruptured corpses belong equally to the traditions of the
Wingraves: overt violence runs alongside blankness and silence.
Confined to an asylum, Owen's brother has become 'a little hushed
lugubrious legend' (p. 19). Colonel Wingrave's attack on his son is
'hushed up' (p. 37). When he visits the Wingrave family home for
the first time, Coyle has the sense of 'names never mentioned'
(p. 21). The unmentioned names suggest a respect for the fallen,

but they also point to the vulgarity and unmentionability of military, not to mention erotic, violence. Sir Philip's 'scrupulous forms' only make him 'more terrible'; his 'studied courtesy' makes it 'impossible not to feel that beneath the surface he was a merciless old warrior' (p. 20). 'A passage of some delicacy' once took place between Jane Wingrave and Captain Hume-Walker, after which she 'had broken with him and sent him off to his fate', apparently a 'horrible' one (p. 21). It is supposed by Jane Wingrave that a marriage between Owen and Kate Julian, Captain Hume-Walker's niece, would heal this 'tragic breach' (p. 36). In fact, however, the relation between Owen and Kate merely leads to a further 'violent passage' (p. 43).

So eager are the Wingraves to spill the blood of the family in order to preserve their traditions that they are scarcely capable of perpetuating it or them. Of all the parent-child relationships mentioned in the tale, only that between Mrs Julian and her daughter consists of two living members, and even in this case the mother is a widow. Scrupulous courtesy and merciless violence; erotic and military injury; broken heads and broken engagements; hushed stories of death and madness: the Wingrave traditions are built on paradoxical equations and a comprehensive indifference to difference. These self-consuming and self-perpetuating practices find expression in the name of their house. 'Paramore' implies something both consistent with and contrary to 'mores', hinting at customs established both in spite and because of discontinuities. 'Paramore' also suggests both 'with' and 'against' love, an erotic ambivalence present in Jane Wingrave's feelings for the army, 'the passion of her life', which mingle love and pain, desire and suffering, aggression and remorse (p. 22). Owen's aunt appears to associate 'Paramore' with her family's 'paramount valour', but the word also contains an extra-familial glimpse of 'paramour', and in this context it is perhaps appropriate that in rejecting the army it is as if Owen has 'fallen in love with a low girl' (p. 23). So compendious are the paradoxes of the Wingraves that such hinted improprieties, as well as the coolness between Owen and Kate, are not the result of Owen's assertion of his independence but, rather, a symptomatic involvement with the broken engagements and violent passages of the Wingrave mythology.

Both 'Sir Edmund Orme' and 'Owen Wingrave' show the patterns of the past being simultaneously repeated and transformed in paradoxical equations of violence and desire. 'The Way it Came' (1896) develops similar themes, and the narrator of the tale is finally to equate being 'abjectly in love' with being 'sick almost to death' (*CT*, IX, 400). The 'tiny vertical scar' near the left eye of the narrator's female friend is said to be 'the mark of a caress from her husband' (p. 392). Like 'Sir Edmund Orme' and 'Owen Wingrave', 'The Way it Came' concerns family stories which are also ghost stories: both the narrator's friends have seen ghosts – one of her father and the other of his mother. Yet the tale does not so much concern old stories of love and pain and death as the evaluation of such stories. James's subject shifts from the field of history to that of hermeneutics, from the patterns imposed by tradition to those imposed by interpretation. His narrator is a geometer of relationships who analyses life in terms of oppositions and repetitions. In 'Sir Edmund Orme', Charlotte Marden resembles her mother, and in 'Owen Wingrave' the relation between Owen and his grandfather is analogous to that between Colonel Wingrave and his son. In 'The Way it Came', by contrast, the perception of resemblance forms the starting-point for a more elaborate theoretical enterprise. The narrator draws attention to the similarities between her two friends. Both have seen ghosts and are in numerous ways 'awfully alike' (p. 377). Yet the fact that her male friend has seen the ghost of his mother and her female friend has seen that of her father suggests an opposition as well as a parallelism. By some 'strange law' her friends are 'alternate and incompatible': like mirror images they can approach but never meet (p. 377). The narrator's efforts to bring her two friends together succeed only in keeping them apart. Her manipulation of these patterns gradually becomes as life-threatening as the family traditions in 'Owen Wingrave', as coercive as the narrator's behaviour in 'Sir Edmund Orme'. It is no accident that a death almost immediately follows her arrangement and her postponement of a meeting between her two friends. The tale contains slight but unmistakable indications of the narrator's unreliability. She tells her fiancé that her friend looked at his photograph during their final meeting whereas in fact this incident occurred during a previous visit (see pp. 384, 379). She claims she had said to herself that there was a 'relation' between her two friends whereas it was her female friend who spoke of the 'relation' (pp. 388, 383). These minor manipulations run alongside the narrator's larger attempts to control events. But her efforts to construct a satisfactory predictive geometry are doomed to failure. 'Laying the ghost' by sabotaging a projected meeting between her two friends she lends the patterns a vitality which escapes her (p. 381). Shortly after the sudden death of her female friend the law of incompatibility which the narrator at first resisted and then tried to enforce is threatened when her fiancé claims to have seen the woman on the night of her death. Determined that this meeting did not occur 'in the body', the narrator asserts that her fiancé has seen a ghost (p. 390). This further attempt to impose a certain reading of events produces another perverse twist: by forcing her theories on her fiancé the narrator raises a ghost between them. Endeavouring to separate her two friends, she succeeds in uniting them after death, becoming a medium rather than a barrier. In the final paragraph, after yet another ruptured engagement, the narrator greets the news of her ex-fiancé's demise as 'a direct contribution to my theory': he was indeed sick to death with love (p. 401). One might conclude that the tone of theoretical triumph struck in this closing comment verges on inhumanity if not insanity. To read the narrator's reading in such a way, however, is inevitably to risk repeating her own dubious attempts to fix meaning.

From 'De Grey' to *The Sacred Fount* and beyond, James's fiction repeatedly involves perverse laws of repetition and inversion. His characters attempt to forecast the operation of these principles but discover that the law is an evasive thing, that it always holds a final and unexpected twist in reserve. The tales which feature these elusive dynamics are not always ghost stories but, from 'The Diary of a Man of Fifty' and 'The Wheel of Time' to 'The Altar of the Dead' and 'The Beast in the Jungle', they are powerfully uncanny ones. The ghost stories of the 1890s are deeply and centrally concerned with uncanny patterns: to the 'strange law' of 'The Way it Came' one could add the 'insidious logic' acted out in 'Sir Edmund Orme' and the paradoxical rotary movement of 'Owen Wingrave', in which to avoid military service is to become a soldier (*CT*, IX, 377; VIII, 146). 'The Turn of the Screw' (1898), a tale whose very title evokes a possibly perverse rotation, treats this theme with unparalleled sophistication, and it is here that many of the other themes studied in this chapter achieve their fullest flowering. James's most elaborate frame story is also his most rhetorically complex in its use of repetition and inversion. Paradoxically full of absences, of charged silences, obscured and displaced forms of violence and transgression, the tale takes the erasure of difference so typical of James's ghostly fiction to new lengths. It is here that James radically problematizes set ideas of oppositions and thresholds, here that the double dynamic of the explosive principle and economic mastery enters into a relationship involving new tensions and fusions, here too that James renews and re-evaluates his authorial investment in the ghostly. 'The Turn of the Screw' is above all a story about reading. At one level the text explores and dramatizes the interpretative problem already outlined in 'The Way it Came': namely, that the reader of the text tends to condone the aggressive reading strategies of the tale's narrator in the very act of rejecting them. But the tale does not simply set in motion a hermeneutic vortex. 'The Turn of the Screw' reverberates with echoes of other texts and, whilst the governess tries to revise Bly in the light of these revisitations, she is herself repositioned by old stories, which seem to resist her reading and to counteract her efforts to fix meaning by their own dynamic movement.

CHAPTER 3

'The Turn of the Screw'

HADDON HALL, NEWMARCH, BLY

One evening in the June of 1872, James found himself walking along the bank of the Wye towards Haddon Hall in Derbyshire:

> The twilight deepened, the ragged battlements and the low, broad oriels glanced duskily from the foliage, the rooks wheeled and clamored in the glowing sky; and if there had been a ghost on the premises, I certainly ought to have seen it. In fact, I did see it, as we see ghosts nowadays. I felt the incommunicable spirit of the scene with almost painful intensity. The old life, the old manners, the old figures seemed present again. (*Transatlantic Sketches*, p. 26)

Joseph Addison would have had no difficulty in placing this landscape alongside his own account of the abbey on Sir Roger de Coverley's estate as 'one of the most proper Scenes in the World for a Ghost to appear in' (*The Spectator*, I, 453, see p. 28 above). I am not suggesting that Addison is in any sense the 'source' for the Haddon Hall passage.[1] Nevertheless, James and Addison do possess a similar fascination with the uncertain border between day and night. Both seem to have wandered onto some stage set erected in the midst of life. The attention of both writers plays between the tokens of nature and those of culture, between ancient buildings and shadowy vegetation, whilst intermittent and distant sounds reinforce the growing sense that the border between the present and the past has been partially effaced. James succeeds in bringing out the mingling of pleasure and pain which is so characteristic of sublime experience. His evocation results in a simultaneous sense of detached observation and involved participation in a moment of emergent meaning. For a few instants James's consciousness is entirely adequate to and absorbed in the objects of its awareness. He is haunting a landscape which is itself glimmering into ghostly life. Poised on a penumbra between the light and the dark, his thought meets no resistance from things and even begins to create the world it inspects: 'ought to have seen' gives way to 'did see'.

A similar moment occurs in *The Sacred Fount* (1901). At the mid-point of the novel, the narrator takes a walk at dusk through the grounds of Newmarch. His eye travels from tree-tops to pinnacles, from the crests of the 'motionless wood' to those of the 'chimnied roof'.[2] He listens to 'the last calls of birds' and begins to feel that he is roaming round 'some castle of enchantment' (p. 97). He is reminded of 'the days of fairy-tales', of the way in which, for the 'childish imagination', the strange '"came true"' (p. 97). Apart from the somewhat sinister note of the bird-song, which is compared to the splashes made by 'divers not expecting to rise again', virtually nothing seems to limit the gratification of the narrator's imaginative needs or to impede the omnipotence of his thoughts (p. 97).[3] He feels that some 'wheel' has 'revolved', enabling him by a 'romantic stroke' to conjure or create the real (p. 97). The climactic moment of his adventure occurs when he succeeds in summoning up Mrs Server, the 'haunting principle' of his thought (p. 97).

The narrator's evocation of Mrs Server's almost ghostly figure is far closer to James's rendering of the moment at Haddon Hall than it is to the first ghostly encounter of the governess in 'The Turn of the Screw', yet the basic elements of this third scene – a summer's twilit walk in the grounds of a large house – are very similar to the other two.[4] During her first days at Bly the governess likes the hour of dusk better than any other. She appreciates the fading light, the lingering day and 'the last calls of the last birds', enjoys 'the beauty and dignity of the place' almost with 'a sense of property' (*CT*, x, 35). She too begins to feel that she has entered 'a charming story', that she is about to meet the master, who will 'stand before me and smile and approve', show a 'kind light' in his 'handsome face' (p. 35). At this point, however, 'The Turn of the Screw' begins to deviate from *The Sacred Fount* and the Haddon Hall passage. Although the governess has compared Bly to 'a castle of romance' she is not, like the narrator of *The Sacred Fount*, to realize her fairy-tale (p. 27). Whilst the narrator of *The Sacred Fount* meets the very person he has been looking for, the governess has an unexpected encounter with somebody quite different. Unlike the narrator of *The Sacred Fount*, who triumphs imaginatively at the moment when May Server shows herself at the end of a vista, the governess becomes the subject of another's gaze. She receives a 'shock' which makes her gasp, has 'a violent perception' (p. 36) of her mistake in supposing that 'my imagination had ... turned real' and that the fantasy of the master's appearance has come true (p. 35). The governess's sense of imaginative control is 'arrested' and shown to be mistaken; mellow appreciation gives way to a 'bewilderment of vision' (pp. 35, 36). In the ample consciousness represented in *The Sacred Fount* there is a play of tensions and fusions, an oscillation between detachment and involvement, pleasure and pain. In the case of the governess, consciousness tips towards the singleness of dread, isolation and emptiness. Wonder becomes bewilderment, a generalized sense of interfusion gives way to violently contradictory emotions. For the governess, the whole scene seems 'stricken with death' (p. 36). This encounter with the deathly strongly reminds one of the experience of Brooke in 'Travelling Companions' or Newman in *The American*. I have tried to suggest that these earlier uncanny incidents in James could be read as encounters with the admonitory presence of the writer as economic master (see pp. 68–9, 75–8 above). Standing at the prescribed edge of the plot, the ghostly representative of this figure prevents the protagonists from gaining complete imaginative control over their lives. Both Shoshana Felman and William Goetz have associated James with the figure of the uncle in 'The Turn of the Screw'.[5] In the governess's fantasy the master is a kindly, approving presence. He therefore appears to represent the collaborative James in rather a similar way to Ralph Touchett in *The Portrait of a Lady*. Yet the links between James and the master do not preclude the possibility of further links between James and Quint, between the master and the master's servant or delegate. Quint appears instead of the uncle and his elevated observational stance seems to connect him to the competitive phase of James's engagement with the centre of consciousness and to echo the vigil scene in *The Portrait of a Lady*, in which Isabel imagines that she is being watched from above by the hostile figure of Gilbert Osmond. Unlike that semi-ghostly presence, Quint displays no derision: after watching the governess for some time he simply turns away. Nevertheless, this turn distantly but distinctly relates him to James's description of the triumphant artist and 'the back he turns to us as he bends over his work' (*LC*, II, 1118). A further connection between Quint and the authorial presence can perhaps be detected in the circumstance that James wryly casts himself in the role of 'an adventurer' as he approaches Haddon Hall on his 'sly pilgrimage' (*Transatlantic Sketches*, pp. 26, 25). One of the governess's first explanations of Quint's presence is that he is an 'unscrupulous traveller, curious in old houses' who has quietly made his way into Bly in order – it is a distinctly Jamesian pleasure – to enjoy the prospect from 'the best point of view' (*CT*, x, 39). The analogy between Quint and James is by no means complete; nor is it exclusively a matter of economic mastery (see pp. 181–4 below). If Quint is 'the hideous author of our woe' this may leave the master or James himself as the author of her weal (p. 137). Furthermore, one cannot forget that the governess is herself an observer and an author. Quint may enjoy the best point of view, even to some extent the artist's point of view, but it is the governess who suffers the actual point of view; she who claims to see Quint 'as I see the letters I form on this page' (p. 37). To see Quint is to write him and to write him is to see him. Yet in the act of representing herself and of being represented as a writer, the governess loses the capacity to disappear like a ghost or a triumphant artist. To see Quint is also to read him as writing, as the trace left by another author.

Of course, James himself can also be a reader and his experience at Haddon Hall is closely related to that of the governess at Bly. Both wander the grounds of a large house whilst entertaining speculations about the life that has been lived within. James remembers that Dorothy Vernon had eloped from Haddon Hall with Lord John Manners and feels that this old story contributes to 'the romance of the spot' (*Transatlantic Sketches*, p. 26). It is significant that these reflections on past transgressions are accompanied by none of the horror and sense of lingering corruption which preoccupy the governess in her meditations. By comparing text with text and vision with vision it is difficult to avoid the suspicion that the governess's response to the improprieties of the past is a somewhat limited one. Miss Jessel is merely 'infamous' (*CT*, x, 59). In *A Small Boy and Others*, on the other hand, the fact that James's French governess had been exposed as an '"adventuress"' only increased his interest and pleasure: Augustine Danse had brought the figure of Becky Sharp in Thackeray's *Vanity Fair* to life (James, *Autobiography*, p. 174; see also pp. 185–6).

In a notebook entry of 16 March 1892, James recorded an idea for a tale about a servant who is thought to do 'base' things such as the 'reading of letters, diaries, peeping, spying, etc.' (*N*, p. 65). The tale was never written but fragments of it seem to return in 'The Turn of the Screw': Mrs Grose asks whether Quint 'only peeps' and Miles opens the governess's letter to the master (*CT*, x, 46; see pp. 133–4). The influence of the notebook entry on 'The Turn of the Screw' would be hardly worth mentioning were it not for the fact that the twist in James's sketch involved the servant being *wrongly* suspected of sinister activities and 'turning out utterly innocent' (*N*, p. 65).

'THE TURN OF THE SCREW' AND 'GABRIELLE DE BERGERAC'

Is the governess right to jump to the conclusion that Quint is a corrupt and malevolent figure?[6] Since the question is not susceptible of absolute proof it may be a meaningless one, but the possibility gains added plausibility in the light of one of James's earliest tales. In 'Gabrielle de Bergerac' (1869), M. de Bergerac recalls how, as a nine-year-old child, he witnessed the developing relationship between his twenty-two-year-old sister Gabrielle and Pierre Coquelin, who has been employed by his father the Baron as a tutor. Marked with 'the genuine plebeian stamp', Coquelin possesses 'a certain masculine freshness and elasticity' (*CT*, II, 114, 115). He is a disciple of Rousseau's ideas on education and takes his charge on long walks, during which, 'without perverting my signorial morals or instilling any notions that were treason to my rank and position, he kindled in my childish breast a little democratic flame' (p. 130). Part way through the tale, the young M. de Bergerac is taken on a visit to a castle by Gabrielle and Coquelin. The castle has 'two great towers', and the boy watches his tutor climb one of them and stand 'on the summit of the edifice, waving his hat' (pp. 142, 148). When Coquelin and Gabrielle eventually confess their feelings for each other the latter recognizes the 'criminality' of her love and has 'no desire to realize her passion' (pp. 157, 156). Feeling that he could only remain 'on the footing of a thief and impostor', Coquelin decides to leave his employer's family (p. 156). Shortly afterwards the Baron forces his son to reveal the truth about the relations between Gabrielle and Coquelin (p. 159). Gabrielle finds herself rejected by her family and is accused of having tried to 'pollute' her younger brother (p. 166). She marries Coquelin, moves to Paris, and is executed alongside her husband during the Reign of Terror.

A young boy; a transgressive relationship between a woman and a socially inferior man; a castle with two towers: a number of elements in 'Gabrielle de Bergerac' anticipate 'The Turn of the Screw'. The resonances between the two tales (both frame stories) are at their most intense in the resemblances between Pierre Coquelin and Peter Quint. One is a tutor; the other, according to Mrs Grose, used to behave as if he were a tutor (see *CT*, x, 64). One accuses himself of being a virtual thief; the other, again according to Mrs Grose, may well have been an actual thief (see p. 47). The governess remarks that Quint looks 'like an actor' (p. 47). The name 'Coquelin' itself belonged to an actor that James had known as a boy.[7] Both Quint and Coquelin are seen on the tops of towers and there is a suggestive echo which plays between French 'Pierre' and English 'Peter', between 'Coquelin' and 'Quint'. M. de Bergerac tells Coquelin that he is 'not a gentleman' (*CT*, II, 103) and when Mrs Grose asks the governess whether Quint 'was ... a gentleman?', she replies in the negative (*CT*, II, 103; x, 45).

Imagine that at the end of 'Gabrielle de Bergerac' the scene shifts to England. M. de Bergerac, now ten years of age, acquires a younger sister. The Baron dies and his brother, who lives in Harley Street, engages a governess to bring up his potentially polluted wards. Extended in this admittedly fanciful way, 'Gabrielle de Bergerac' begins to look like an account of what happened at Bly before the arrival of the governess. Read through 'Gabrielle de Bergerac', Miss Jessel's departure from Bly, like Coquelin's initial decision to rectify his false position by leaving the de Bergeracs, could be read as an attempt to avoid the criminality of a continued liaison. Far from being 'infamous', Miss Jessel would become a sad victim of class barriers (*CT*, x, 59). Read through 'Gabrielle de Bergerac', Quint might be a type of 'masculine freshness and elasticity' and not a 'horror' (*CT*, II, 115; x, 45). The relationship between Quint and Jessel would become an example not of corruption and depravity but of what Coquelin calls the 'tragedies, sorrows, and cruelties' which constitute 'the ghost of the past' (*CT*, II, 144). The time that Miles has spent with a social inferior like Quint would not in the least have perverted his 'signorial morals' but might instead have kindled a 'democratic flame' (*CT*, II, 130).[8] If the governess can be seen as a reader of 'Gabrielle de Bergerac' then she is an extremely unsympathetic one. Unlike Coquelin she is no devotee of Rousseau and describes the fact that Miles has lied and been impudent as an outbreak of 'the little natural man' (*CT*, x, 66).[9] Coquelin's democratic beliefs would not have been attractive

to the governess, who finds the very idea of freedom deeply suspicious. Quint's hatlessness is a 'strange freedom' (p. 37). His presence on the tower suggests that he has taken 'a liberty rather gross'
(p.39). When Mrs Grose tells her that Quint was 'much too free', the
governess experiences 'a sudden sickness of disgust' (p. 50). On this
basis, Miles's attempt to gain 'more freedom' will later confirm her
worst fears (p. 95). Read through 'Gabrielle de Bergerac', the
governess's attitude to past events at Bly as well as her attempts to
extract a confession from Miles begin to resemble the actions of the
inflexible Baron and the self-interested Gaston de Treuil who, by
forcibly drawing a confession from the young M. de Bergerac and
then attacking a perceived source of pollution in Gabrielle and
Coquelin, effectively force the young lovers together, making
inevitable the transgression they had sought to avert.

To read a later work in terms of an earlier one is, of course, almost
always to simplify both and often to use the original text as an
improvised key to pick the lock of the later.[10] 'The Turn of the
Screw' is by no means a straightforward extension of 'Gabrielle de
Bergerac', and naturally there are numerous differences, deviations
and mismatchings between one tale and the other. Neither the
reader nor the governess can ever say with certainty that things at
Bly did or did not happen in the way they happen in 'Gabrielle de
Bergerac'. What is significant is that the governess's awareness is
only of corruption and her response only one of horror. The
governess is unique amongst James's ghost-seers in viewing the
apparitional as a manifestation of unmitigated evil.[11] The uncanny
and semi-ghostly encounters of 'Travelling Companions' or *The
Portrait of a Lady* inspire in Brooke and Isabel a fear not so much of
evil but of limitation, an awareness not so much of corruption but of
the failure of imagination and desire. 'Sir Edmund Orme' and
'Owen Wingrave' go much further, presenting the ghostly encounter as a potential privilege. Even the narrator of 'The Way it Came',
who closely resembles the governess in her determination to enforce
a univocal reading of events, accepts that ghostly experience is 'a
rare extension of being' (*CT*, IX, 396, 400).

THE GOVERNESS AND HER CRITICS

'The Turn of the Screw' raises far more disturbing questions about
the consequences of constructing and enforcing rigid interpretations

than the 'The Way it Came', and these questions extend beyond the governess to her critics. Many of the conceptual strategies adopted in analyses of 'The Turn of the Screw' seem already to have been problematized within the text. For the governess and the critics it seems that 'The Turn of the Screw' is an epistemological whirlpool where escape can only be achieved through interpretative violence: an aggressive single-mindedness, a hostility to uncertainty and a willingness to impose rigid and polarized schemata. For Paul B. Armstrong, the debate over 'The Turn of the Screw' demonstrates the way in which criticism shapes texts in accordance with its own beliefs, revealing the metaphysical conflicts which underlie and undermine attempts to constitute and validate meaning. This is quite correct; but if the critics fit 'The Turn of the Screw' to their own needs, it is also true that the text manipulates its critics. The earlier criticism of 'The Turn of the Screw' might, following Shoshana Felman, be seen less as a catalogue of errors than as an example of the way in which the narrative of the governess produces a spreading ripple of interpretative problems and temptations, a widening ring of analogous analytical strategies.

   In the introductory chapter of 'The Turn of the Screw', Douglas tells his listeners that 'the story *won't* tell . . . not in any literal, vulgar way' (*CT*, x, 18). His comment deflects suggestions that the governess was motivated either by fear or desire, and seems by extension gently to discourage interpretations which seek to explain the text either on the basis of apparitions or of hallucinations. Yet for the earlier critics of 'The Turn of the Screw', Douglas's reservation seems to act as a challenge. Positing a univocal solution to the mysteries of the text in order to make it literally tell, such critics almost inevitably define the evil which James merely adumbrates. Ceasing to read out of the text, they proceed, as James wrote in his Preface, to read into it 'more or less fantastic figures' (*LC*, ii, 1188). Both Edmund Wilson and Robert B. Heilman assume that to read 'The Turn of the Screw' is to establish *the* reading and if necessary to defeat other readings. This assumption is shared by the governess, and Felman has drawn attention to the way in which the critics of 'The Turn of the Screw' so often repeat the conceptual ploys of the governess and the 'lexical motifs' of the text.[12] Even as he rejects the governess's interpretation, a critic like Wilson adopts a similarly single-minded defence of the coherence of his own position, demonizing the governess with something of the vehemence with which she herself demonizes Peter Quint and Miss Jessel. To doubt the governess is to share her techniques of suspicion if not her interpretations. Not to suspect the governess (like Heilman) is to share her meanings if not necessarily to share her methods. The play between Wilson, Heilman and the text becomes even more noteworthy when Heilman, who attacks psychopathological readings, himself accuses Wilson of 'hysterical blindness', seeming to play Wilson to Wilson's governess ('The Freudian Reading', p. 434; see also Felman, 'Turning the Screw of Interpretation', p. 100). And when Heilman claims that 'The Turn of the Screw' is 'worth saving', the debate has taken on the salvational undertones of the novel itself ('The Freudian Reading', p. 443). Heilman now seems to be playing the governess to Wilson's Quint, and one pictures the former desperately clutching the text in his arms and forcing it to confess to its ghosts whilst the latter looms into view to deny that they exist.

The governess's attitude to the sublime minglings of Bly at twilight is considerably more negative than the reactions to similar scenes in *Transatlantic Sketches* or *The Sacred Fount*. This objection to the effacement of clear borders partially re-emerges in Wilson's essay, which challenges Jamesian ambiguity on the grounds that it is 'confusing', 'unpleasant and irritating' ('The Ambiguity of Henry James', pp. 397, 403). A similar hostility to uncertainty is found in several other critics of 'The Turn of the Screw'.[13] It is tempting to see such attitudes as defensive responses to the readerly anxiety that a text like 'The Turn of the Screw' creates. Such hostility is by no means universal. Dorothea Krook appreciates Jamesian ambiguity as an expression of 'the unavoidable, unalterable mixed motive of all human action' and describes how James arranges the elements of 'The Turn of the Screw' so that 'they could with perfect self-consistency yield two distinct and ... contradictory meanings, one confirming the validity of the interpreter's point of view, the other putting it in doubt'.[14] Shlomith Rimmon does not share Krook's ethical concerns and believes that James's ambiguity should be seen as 'a self-reflexive meditation on the medium of art'.[15] Rimmon does, however, argue along similar lines to Krook that the ambiguous text organizes its data into 'two opposed systems which leave little or no room for further "play"' (*The Concept of Ambiguity*, p. 13).[16] Both Krook and Rimmon analyse the operation of ambiguity in 'The Turn of the Screw' without moving towards a univocal resolution. Nevertheless, their use of static and mutually exclusive binary relationships recalls the style not of James but rather of the governess, who, as several critics have pointed out, tends to deal in artificially absolute polarities and is apparently unable or unwilling to recognize the existence of a middle ground (see pp. 128–36, 169–77 below).[17]

Tzvetan Todorov's positioning of 'The Turn of the Screw' as an example of the 'fantastic' would seem to represent a significant advance on the approaches outlined above, for Todorov believes that the fantastic text occupies 'a frontier between two adjacent realms': the 'marvellous' and the 'uncanny' (*The Fantastic*, p. 44; see also p. 105). In the genre of the uncanny, apparently supernatural events are ultimately explained in terms of natural laws. In the marvellous, on the other hand, the events can only be explained as supernatural. Only in the fantastic is a hesitation or uncertainty concerning the nature of the depicted events sustained throughout the text (see *The Fantastic*, p. 41). Christine Brooke-Rose and Tobin Siebers have raised serious and valid questions about Todorov's notion of genre but these do not directly concern me here.[18] The most arresting aspect of Todorov's conception of the fantastic midpoint in this context is that it strongly reminds one of descriptions of the romance from Walpole to Hawthorne (see pp. 35–6 and 38–9 above). Todorov seems to be applying the criteria of the romance by placing the fantastic text in a neutral territory between an actual world based on known laws and an imaginary world in which unknown laws apply.[19] Although Walter Scott's essay on Ann Radcliffe initially argues that for a writer not to give 'a defined or absolute opinion' as to whether exhibited phantoms are real or imaginary is merely 'an evasion of the difficulty', Scott finally concludes that leaving such matters 'in shade' may well be 'the most artful mode of terminating . . . a tale of wonder' (*Novelists and Fiction*, p. 116). I would wholly concur with George Dekker in seeing Scott's artful shading as a clear anticipation of Todorov's notion of hesitation.[20] Todorov does not force a univocal interpretation of 'The Turn of the Screw' and shows no overt hostility to uncertainty. Yet even though he sees the fantastic in more complex terms than those of static opposition, his conceptual schema belongs to pre-Jamesian strategies of representing the supernatural and therefore seems less well suited to explore the work of a writer like James, who conceives of the relation between the real and the romantic or the familiar and the strange in terms of charged circuitries, double dynamics, tensions and fusions. One could even argue that the applicability of

Todorov's linear and static generic model is contested by the rotary movement evoked in the very title 'The Turn of the Screw' (see pp. 177–84 and 204 below for further discussion of the title).

I am not trying to argue that 'The Turn of the Screw' only produces critical failure. There is in fact a sense in which, rather than simply replicating the questionable interpretative strategies of the governess, criticism does indeed (often in spite of itself) express the Jamesian circuit, the turn of his tropes. The ontological choice between an explanation on the basis of hallucinations and one on the basis of apparitions does not necessarily correspond to the moral choice between theories which conclude that the governess is good and those which conclude that she is bad. Neither of these choices can be equated with psychological attempts to decide whether the governess is mad or sane or legalistic efforts to assess whether she is a reliable or an unreliable witness. It is a violent argument which says that the governess is hallucinating and is therefore mad, bad, and, as it were, dangerous to know. And if one begins to speculate that the ghosts may not be evil, then all these ambiguities and the potential play of their inter-relationships double up all over again. Even as such interpretations multiply they do not necessarily move away from polarized responses towards any close appreciation of James's conceptual subtlety, the line-by-line accumulation of proliferating uncertainties.[21] Collectively, however, the criticism of 'The Turn of the Screw' does begin to register minute shifts and intermediate positions, inadvertently expressing what Felman describes as the tale's 'incessant *sliding* of signification' ('Turning the Screw of Interpretation', p. 172). Heilman believed that the governess was a tragically flawed saviour. But to reject the hallucination theory is not necessarily to share his estimation either of the tragedy or the flaw. N. Bryllion Fagin describes the governess as a 'Guardian Angel', Joseph J. Firebaugh as an 'inadequate priestess', and John Lydenberg as a 'false saviour'.[22] Nor are critics devoted to the hallucination theory united in their opinion of the governess: Oscar Cargill can point to her 'befuddled heroism' whilst John Silver paints a picture of a calculating liar.[23]

BLANKS

If 'The Turn of the Screw' is concerned with slippages and turns of meaning, it is also deeply preoccupied with gaps and voids: James wrote in his Preface that the 'values' of the story were 'positively all blanks' (*LC*, II, 1188). Shlomith Rimmon has argued that 'The Turn of the Screw' constructs its ambiguity around 'a central informational gap' (*The Concept of Ambiguity*, p.51).[24] But this notion of an absent core, a single and central enigma, seems to secure its lucidity by avoiding any explication of the teeming voids which haunt 'The Turn of the Screw'. Few fictions deploy such extensive and disparate lacunae, and 'The Turn of the Screw' uses its blanks to undermine all attempts to establish relations and to join references into a coherent pattern. One could even argue that the tale blanks its overt blanks. 'Blankley' is the name of a country house in 'The Wheel of Time'. In 'The Turn of the Screw', by contrast, the revealing blank is elided and contracted into 'Bl...y', a placename as suggestive as 'Paramore', though a more reticently monosyllabic one.[25]

'The Turn of the Screw' is repeatedly concerned with the act of telling. More often than not, however, its predicament is that of not being able to tell. Fragmented and vestigial, the existing text looks like the ruined remains of a fuller story. The introductory chapter of 'The Turn of the Screw' begins just after a story has been told and ends just before a story is about to begin. It occupies a space between two acts of telling, framing and mediating a narrative which, as Douglas points out, takes up the tale 'at a point after it had, in a manner, begun', and which ends in the air, with a death whose consequences are not registered in the narrative of the governess, except in the sense that her narrative is the effect of that death (*CT*, x, 19). The formal beginning and ending of the introductory chapter and of the main narrative do not conclude with actual, absolute, chronological beginnings and endings: they are, as Christine Brooke-Rose puts it, 'truncated, at both ends' (*A Rhetoric of the Unreal*, p. 184; see also note 34 to this chapter).

The frame chapter serves to mediate a further mediation, since it seems that the events at Bly do not constitute a complete and discrete story so much as a border between a past defined in terms of social relations and a future made up of literary or textual relations. Miles and Flora are passed from their dead parents to their disappearing uncle and on to Quint and Jessel, who die to make way for an evanescent nursemaid, a temporary school, Mrs Grose and the governess herself.[26] Some time after the events of the main narrative the governess tells her story directly to Douglas. The story is subsequently written down by the governess and sent to Douglas before her death. Douglas reads the governess's narrative to the circle gathered in the old house and in turn transmits it, before his own death, to the narrator of the introductory chapter, who finally makes an 'exact transcript' of the manuscript (*CT*, x, 19). The events at Bly thus form the mid-point in a sequence of transmissions, each of which begins and ends in death or absence, all of which lead away from genetic sources and reproductive pairs to single parental substitutes and from primary spoken narratives to written, read and copied ones.[27]

The spaces which intervene between the separate events of this skeletal history are complete blanks – mere spaces of time – but the events themselves are almost equally shadowy, permeated and punctured by the voids which they supposedly separate. At first sight the attempt to date the sequence of events following those at Bly seems to meet with some success, although Douglas simply informs his listeners that the governess was ten years older than him, that she has been dead for twenty years (see p. 17) and that she answered the uncle's advertisement 'at the age of twenty' (p. 19). Only by relying on Griffin's assertion that it is forty years since the governess told Douglas her story (see p. 18) and assuming that Douglas, at Trinity, was about twenty 'on ... coming down the second summer' can one relate the succession of events to an independent chronological scale (p. 17). The governess, it appears, told Douglas her story at the age of about thirty, approximately ten years after the events at Bly and twenty years before her death at the age of fifty. The events occurred about half a century before the Christmas house party, at which Douglas is approximately sixty years old. Importantly, however, no information is provided as to how much time elapses between the reading and the narrator's reception of the manuscript shortly before Douglas's death, or between these events and the production of the transcript 'much later' (p. 19). Positioned at the end of the sequence of events, the frame narrator's silence produces a retroactive ripple of uncertainty which, as Edwin Fussell points out, prohibits all attempts to tie the beginning of the narrative to a fixed date.[28]

A similar reticence affects the frame narrator's account of the series of events in the old house. Only three evenings are dramatized in the introductory chapter and with reference to the first of these (Christmas Eve) the narrator initially states that Douglas's reading occurred 'two nights later', that is to say on 26 December (p. 15). Speaking of events on the second day (25 December), however, the narrator now affirms that Douglas received the manuscript 'on the third of these days' and began to read it 'on the night of the fourth' (p. 19). This implies that the reading took place on 27 December, or even (if the narrator is counting from the second day, of which he is speaking at the time) on 28 December.[29] Such a discrepancy is particularly odd because the narrator subsequently repeats his first assertion that Douglas's reading occurred 'the next night' after the second dramatized evening (p. 22). If the reading did in fact take place on 26 December, then one is left with an apparently super-fluous reference to a gap which does not exist. If the reading took place on 27 or 28 December, however, the gap now consists of a mysteriously undramatized period. No hypothesis which adheres to one date for the reading can close these mutually exclusive refer-ences, and yet these contradictions are not directly related to the field occupied by 'ambiguity' in 'The Turn of the Screw', at least as it is usually formulated.

Naturally no fiction is required to take out a stop-watch and calendar to account for its chronological lapses and transitions. Nor is a novel bound to represent time as a smooth linear succession of events: in *The Ambassadors*, as both Ian Watt and Charles Thomas Samuels have shown, James repeatedly employs proleptic and ana-leptic shifts.[30] One would be tempted to dismiss the temporal dis-crepancies in the frame chapter as oversights on James's part were it not for the fact that he rarely made such errors and for the far more important fact that the frame chapter seems to act as a small-scale model of the temporal uncertainties of the governess's own narra-tive, which contains, or rather skirts, a chronological haemorrhage consisting not of days but weeks. The governess arrives at Bly in June and the final scene of the tale occurs in November (see pp. 23, 129). All the dramatized scenes in the main narrative (which thus covers a minimum four-month period) occur on one of a mere thirteen days.[31] The first six dramatized days must all take place in June since on the day of Quint's second appearance the governess tells Mrs Grose that she saw Quint for the first time 'about the middle of the month' and she has already made it clear that this first apparition was encountered 'at the end of a long June day' (pp. 46, 35). The last six dramatized days take up a longer period – one of some seven weeks – but are as unequivocally accounted for as the first six days. The governess's discovery of Miles on the lawn at night (Day 9) takes place on the 'eleventh night' following Quint's third appearance on Day 8 (p. 74). Days 9 and 10 succeed each other, 'a month' separates Days 10 and 11, and the last three days are also successive (p. 84). The first six and the last six dramatized days therefore occupy some eight weeks of at least sixteen spent by the governess at Bly. On either side of the seventh dramatized day (that of Miss Jessel's first appearance), therefore, and lying at the dead centre of the sequence of represented days if not of the chapter plan, two transitional passages (one between Days 6 and 7, the other between Days 7 and 8) must bear the burden of accounting for a blank period of at least two months which lasts throughout July and August and occupies up to a half of the narrative's predicated timespan.

Mrs Grose's tears on the evening of the sixth dramatized day are followed by frequent conversations with the governess 'for a week' and the imposition of a 'rigid control' (p. 52). Since this period of 'disguised excitement' lasts only until it is 'superseded by horrible proofs', one might plausibly conclude that only a week separates Day 6 from Miss Jessel's first appearance on Day 7 and that seven of the missing eight weeks remain to be accounted for (p. 53). But the transitional passage between Days 7 and 8 sheds little light on this blind spot. The last word of the governess on the seventh dramatized day and at the end of chapter 8 is that she 'must just wait' (p. 66). chapter 9 almost immediately begins with the news that 'a very few' days in the company of Miles and Flora were sufficient temporarily to allay the governess's anxieties (p. 66). Because the governess continues to describe the effects of the children's companionship, it seems that her allusions to 'this period' and 'these days' relate to the same few days (pp. 67, 68). If this is true then it would appear that the remaining seven weeks flash past with a reference to a further 'lull' separating Days 7 and 8 (p. 69).

The governess seems to compensate for the hole at the heart of the time-scheme by multiplying her references to specific periods of time. These references either have an ungrounded precision or refer simply to intervals between events, to gaps in which nothing happens. The governess tells Mrs Grose that Miss Jessel appeared 'two hours ago, in the garden', but there is a strange disparity between this scrupulous chronological precision and her admission that she 'can give no intelligible account' of how she has 'fought out the interval' (p. 56). Occasionally the governess's temporal references are simply inaccurate: on the twelfth dramatized day she refers to Miss Jessel's first appearance on Day 7 as 'the other day', although by her own account this event occurred at least six and possibly up to thirteen weeks previously (p. 110).

I have tried to show that the history of the children before Bly, like the history of the governess's narrative after Bly, is a telescoped series of circles within circles. Given the chronological lacunae in 'The Turn of the Screw', this concentric patterning might provide a succession of reassuring enclosures. Examined more closely, however, the line of circles begins to seem more like a run of blanks within blanks. There is a social 'circle' at Bly and Douglas's audience make up a 'hushed little circle' (pp. 89, 19). Unnervingly, however, it is impossible to determine the contents of these circles. Besides the narrator, Douglas and the Griffins, the frame section introduces an unspecified number of 'ladies whose departure had been fixed' (p. 18). On the first evening in the old house they voice their intention to stay on for Douglas's reading. Referring a little later to the events of the second day, the narrator mentions the fact that the ladies departed before the reading 'in a rage of curiosity' produced by the 'touches' with which Douglas had 'already worked us up' (p. 19). Almost immediately, however, and apparently referring exclusively to the second evening, the narrator goes on to relate 'the first of these touches' (p. 19). Evidently the 'departing ladies' are still present and leave at some point before the night of the reading (p. 19). One might assume that it is one of these departing ladies who remains (after her own disappearance has been narrated) to issue the two remarks attributed to 'one of the ladies' on this second evening (p. 22). This cannot be the case, however, because 'the same lady' puts a further question to Douglas on the very night of the reading (p. 22). To acquire even the shadowy identity of the departing ladies is nevertheless something of an achievement in the old house. Six remarks are made by voices identified simply as 'somebody' (pp. 15 (twice), 17, 18) or 'someone' (pp. 15, 21). It is not possible to establish whether these speeches belong to guests already mentioned, to six separate voices or to a single otherwise unidentified speaker.

Does this vagueness matter? Narratives indicate but do not have to catalogue their worlds. Yet the fact that a similar tenuity affects the edges of the circle at Bly reinforces one's sense of a strategy in the blanks. According to Douglas, the master informs the governess that, besides the housekeeper Mrs Grose, Bly is staffed by a cook, a housemaid, a dairywoman, a pony, a groom and a gardener (see p. 21). Aproned and with a room which smells of lately-baked bread (see pp. 33, 98), Mrs Grose seems to take over the role of the cook, who does not appear in the narrative of the governess, although presumably somebody must have provided the roast mutton consumed by Miles and the governess after the housekeeper's departure in chapter 21 (see p. 127). The solitary housemaid mentioned by the master is almost immediately replaced by a 'pair of maids' in the governess's narrative and a reference is subsequently made to 'a couple of the maids' as if there are even more than two (pp. 22, 126). The governess does mention a pony (see p. 86) but it belongs to the Hampshire vicarage where she was brought up and not to Bly. The dairywoman, groom and gardener do not appear in the main narrative. Instead one encounters a bailiff (see p. 100) who may or may not be 'Luke' (p. 109) and a nursemaid who temporarily replaced Miss Jessel but seems no longer to be present (see p. 32).

These are not the only disparities and blanks amongst the peripheral members of the cast in 'The Turn of the Screw'. The governess makes two allusions to her brothers (see pp. 69, 85) although according to the frame narrator, Douglas speaks of her only as 'the youngest of several daughters' (p. 19). Both Douglas and the governess mention the latter's father (see pp. 19, 85) but neither speak of her mother. The uncle mentions his mother (see p. 20) but not (at least in *The Two Magics* text of 1898, which is used in Edel's edition of James's *Complete Tales*)[32] his father, and refers to the children's father (see p. 20) without mentioning their mother. 'Mrs' Grose has no conspicuous husband. The relationships between the frame narrative and the main narrative, therefore, and the relationships which each of these narratives in turn postulate give rise to a perturbing, subliminal sense of mutual discontinuity if not of open conflict.

Considered in its entirety, 'The Turn of the Screw' systematically blanks out beginnings and endings. This overall strategy is replicated on a reduced scale in many of its parts. Hardly a chapter of the tale possesses a beginning or ending which coincides with the initiation or completion of a distinct structural unit, whether this is a time, a place, a scene, an action or a dialogue. The interstices which separate the chapters are an active part of the text and occasionally its most charged moments. Like the final chapter, chapters 3, 6 and 10 break off suddenly at points of crisis. Events following these crises, like the narrative as a whole, are reported subsequently and indirectly. This sometimes creates the curious impression that the governess is not simply recalling the events at Bly but remembering *remembering* those events. In contrast to the chapters which lack endings, chapters 5, 10, 15, 19, 20, 23 and 24 seem, rather like the first chapter of the governess's narrative, to take up the tale after it has already begun. The formal breaks which separate these chapters from their immediate predecessors occur within a single piece of consecutive action.

Whenever texts and writings crop us as objects within the narrative, they too are almost always characterized by emptiness and incompletion.[33] Letters in 'The Turn of the Screw' tend not to be written or, when written, not to be sent or, when sent, to be unmentioned or unmentionable. 'Not a word. I'm off!' writes the master to the governess, dropping her a line only to sever their correspondence and speaking only to preserve and enforce silence (p. 28). His note encloses a letter from Miles's headmaster which apparently makes no charges to back up the boy's dismissal from school and of which the governess decides to say 'nothing' – 'nothing' to the uncle and 'nothing' to Miles himself (p. 33). The governess receives 'disturbing letters from home' but goes into no details about their contents (p. 41). She allows the children to write to their uncle but keeps their letters. When she does eventually write to the master she simply describes herself as sitting before 'a blank sheet of paper' and later claims that her letter contained only 'the bare demand for an interview' (pp. 101, 124). Miles confirms the bareness and blankness of this letter when he admits that he has found 'nothing' in it (p. 134):

'Nothing, nothing!' I almost shouted in my joy.
'Nothing, nothing,' he sadly repeated. (p. 135)

There are so many 'nothings' in 'The Turn of the Screw' that the negative begins to define the positive rather than vice versa. The governess's story can only be spoken of in terms of its blanks. It has 'not been out for years'; 'nobody' but Douglas has ever heard of it and 'nothing' that he knows touches it (p. 16). But it is not even that nothing touches it for 'sheer terror': it is 'not so simple as that' and Douglas seems 'at a loss how to qualify it' (p. 16). The experience is not his own and nor is the record of it, since he took down 'nothing but the impression' (p. 16). The governess did not tell Douglas that she had 'never told anyone' her story (p. 17). 'Neither' he nor the governess mentioned the reasons for her silence and nor does the manuscript, which, as Douglas points out, '*won't* tell' (pp. 17, 18).

Whatever it was that Miles said at school, the negative manner in which he alludes to it resembles nothing so much as Douglas's way of speaking about the governess's manuscript. Miles admits that he 'said things' but cannot remember to whom he said them (p. 135). It was not to everyone, nor to many, but he cannot recall their names. He 'didn't know' that they would tell and the governess confirms that his masters at least 'never told' (p. 137). When the governess comes upon Quint, she can only define him in the same negative way that Douglas defines her manuscript and Miles speaks of what he said at school.³⁴ The figure on the tower is 'not the person I had precipitately supposed' and the governess has 'not seen it anywhere' (p. 36). She can arrive at 'no living view' of the bewilderment produced by the apparition, at 'no account whatever' of it (pp. 36, 39). She does not mention the incident to Mrs Grose and cannot explain her reasons for this reticence (see p. 39). The figure is nobody from Bly and nobody from the village: 'nobody – nobody' (p. 45). Indeed, Quint looks 'like nobody' (p. 46). He has 'no hat', wears clothes that are 'not his own' and is connected with 'missed' waistcoats (pp. 46–7). He is 'never – no, never! – a gentleman' and resembles an actor, although the governess has 'never seen one' (p. 47).

For a narrative which is so concerned with remembering (the verb is used in the first lines of the frame chapter and the first words of the governess are 'I remember'), 'The Turn of the Screw' records a great deal of forgetting (p. 23). The governess is 'unable ... to remember' what plans she made for the resumption of Miles's studies (p. 34). She forgets what 'remarkable person' she was playing in Flora's Sea of Azof game (p. 54). She has 'no subsequent memory' of 'what first happened' after Miss Jessel's final appearance (p. 117). The governess repeatedly draws attention to the difficulty of narrating her experiences, resorting to certain phrases because she 'can express no otherwise' what she means, 'can call them nothing else', 'can use no other phrase', 'can describe only as' (pp. 40, 88, 117, 133). She asks herself with perplexity how she can 'express' and 'describe' events (p. 40). She wonders how to 'retrace' her experiences (p. 87). She searches for 'terms' which will adequately convey the action but feels that her language 'represents but grossly' what actually occurs (pp. 88, 133). She becomes aware that she can 'scarce articulate' and later finds 'no sound on my lips' (pp. 56, 80). She is faced with the 'unspeakable' (p. 86), the 'unutterable' (p. 56) and the 'indescribable' (pp. 58, 75), with things that 'no words can translate' (p. 106). At various points she is unable to 'name' (p. 137), 'say' (pp. 37, 38, 70, 102), phrase (see p. 39), 'speak' (p. 43), 'tell' (p. 65), 'express' (pp. 67, 71, 131), explain (see p. 68), present (see p. 81), represent (see p. 78) and 'convey' (p. 79).

Blanks occur even at the phonemic level of 'The Turn of the Screw'. On the first night in the old house Douglas exclaims that the garden in which he had once heard the governess's story 'wasn't a scene for a shudder; but oh – !' (p. 17). This 'oh' syllables the inexpressible, offers a vestigial emblem of the absent. On the second evening in the Griffins' house another 'oh' is said to be 'the only other word of importance contributed to the subject' until, on a subsequent night, Douglas opens the governess's album and admits that he has no title for the narrative (p. 22). 'Oh, *I* have!' exclaims the narrator in the final utterance of the introductory chapter (p. 22). The narrator's 'oh', echoing back through the other oh's, returns in a full circle to the first utterance of the frame chapter. 'If the child gives the effect another turn of the screw', Douglas then asked, 'what do you say to *two* children – ?' (p. 15). The narrator's final 'oh' therefore seems to act as a suspended reference to the title of the text and by implication to the narrative itself – one long 'oh' of hung meaning.

The play of circles within circles and of blanks within blanks does not, however, end with the 'oh'. Flora's first lesson from her new governess consists in being given 'a sheet of white paper, a pencil and a copy of nice "round O's"' (p. 29). This first act of writing in the main narrative acts as a token of the blankness and circularity which affects the other writings recorded by the text, repeats a bordered void in the same way as the frame narrator's copy of the governess's manuscript. Simultaneously present and absent, Flora's O's are, however, by no means the final stage in the run of lacunae. Below even the letter as message and the letter as character or cipher stands the typographic mark ' – '.[35] One could say that the long dash bears a metonymic relation to the text as a whole; it certainly operates as an effective index of the extent to which the narrative becomes pitted and vesicular at times of crisis. The ghostly in particular tends to be accompanied by an almost telegraphic scattering of dashes, and it is especially appropriate that Quint first emerges from between the lines by means of the dash. 'I mean that's *his* way – the master's', says Mrs Grose, leaving the governess with the 'impression of her having accidentally said more than she meant' (p. 31). In a sense, Quint is a ghost created by the predicative power of language, which, as Darrel Mansell points out, 'can never quite get rid of the thing it says does not exist'.[36] Yet it is not only the language but the silence or pause implied by the typography ('*his* way – the master's') which directs attention to a space occupied by a 'he' other than the master.

There are some sixty uses of the word 'oh' in 'The Turn of the Screw', but there are over 600 long dashes. The average of twenty-five dashes per chapter is considerably exceeded in chapter 21 (forty-five) and the frame chapter (forty-three). But it is particularly apt that the void in the time-scheme, located either before or after Miss Jessel's first appearance, is associated with the highest density of dashes in chapter 6 (fifty-four) and chapter 7 (fifty). Passages of dialogue account for approximately 280 dashes but the average of eleven per chapter is significantly exceeded in chapters 7 and 21, with forty dashes apiece. Douglas's reference to the 'turn of the screw' occurs in the first of seventy-five speeches in the text which peter out in the long dash, emphasizing the ' – ' as well as the 'oh' connotation of the phrase (p. 15). The remaining 360 or so dashes occur in passages of narrative, the average of approximately fourteen per chapter being notably exceeded in chapter 6 (forty-one), chapter 3, that of Quint's first appearance (thirty-four) and in chapter 4, that of his second appearance (twenty-seven).

MULTIPLICATIONS

Many of the blanks described above may seem incidental, peripheral, even unimportant. It is unlikely that clearing up the vagueness about the staffing arrangements at Bly would resolve some central enigma in 'The Turn of the Screw', and Miles makes an astute point when he remarks that the other members of the community at Bly 'don't much count' (p. 129). If the governess does wait ten years after the events at Bly to tell Douglas her story and another twenty years before writing it down, if Douglas indeed keeps her manuscript under lock and key for a further two decades, it is only to present a sequence of absences which invite, without rewarding, speculation. To map the uncertain edges of these blank areas is simply to secure the border of nothing – of a mere interval, a lapse. The blanks do not offer significance so much as pierce it; to the extent that they signify at all, they are signs only of the disappearance of forthright meanings. Yet the blanks do not only shatter, riddle or impair the narrative. They also permit an extraordinary multiplication of references to the impossibility of reference. Faced with the unrepresentable, the governess does not simply stop: she begins to elaborate, to find terms which describe the state of being unable to describe. Although the blanks in her narrative blot sense they also reiterate its absence, and one's impression is not of emptiness and silence but rather of a voluble swarm of surrogates and replacements. One of the most notable absences in the narrative of the governess is that of the word 'ghost'. The only use of the word in the text occurs when Douglas speaks cautiously, and with reference only to Griffin's story, of a 'ghost, or whatever it was' (p. 15). Instead of 'ghosts', the governess offers a host of variously suggestive or euphemistic terms: apparitions (see pp. 55, 71, 75, 88), demons (see pp. 82, 114, 133), fiends (see p. 84), figures (see pp. 55, 57, 71, 76, 116), horrors (see pp. 45, 138), others (see pp. 82, 88), outsiders (see p. 88), presences (see pp. 71, 74, 86, 115, 133, 138), spectres (see p. 96), visitants (see pp. 62, 137) and visitors (see pp. 55, 72, 87).

'The Turn of the Screw' is a matter of circles as well as blanks. Whereas the word 'ghost' is virtually excluded from the text, the word 'turn' is repeatedly and markedly present. 'Ghost' gives way to a play of alternative words; 'turn', on the other hand, remains verbally intact but instead seems to open a proliferation of alternative senses. Characters are said simply to turn (see pp. 71, 78, 83) but they also turn their backs (see pp. 32, 55, 95, 105), turn away (see pp. 46, 76, 136), turn round (see pp. 46, 59, 125, 128, 130), turn off (see p. 104), turn in (see p. 41), turn into (see p. 23) and turn out of (see p. 85). They turn faces on each other (see p. 137) and expressions at each other (see p. 114). They turn pale (see pp. 43, 58), turn things over in their minds (see pp. 38, 39, 83, 92, 104, 124, 137), take 'noiseless turns' (p. 74), have 'quick turns' (p. 29) and 'dreadful' turns (p. 115). They are turned out, both in the sense of being clothed (see p. 90) and of being expelled (see p. 136). Staircases have turns (see p. 70) and paths also have turns which one might approach whilst taking 'a turn into the grounds' (p. 35). 'Matters' are liable to turn (see p. 86) and events to occur 'in turn'

(p. 113). Corners and pages are turned (see pp. 42, 70), summers turn (see p. 86) and Peter Quint dies on a 'turn mistaken at night' (p. 52).[37]

'Turn' is only one member of a slippery lexicon of repeated terms in 'The Turn of the Screw'. Verbs such as 'to return' and 'to repeat' continually return and are repeated in the narrative. If one includes derived forms, 'return' and 'repeat' turn up on twenty-five and twenty-one occasions respectively. Naturally, re-prefixed words like 'remember', 'recall' and 'recollect' will frequently be on the lips of any retrospective narrator. Yet the narrative of the governess also reveals a significant recurrence of re-prefixed verbs and derivatives such as 'to recognize' (eighteen usages), 'to refer' (eight usages) and 'to reflect' (fifteen usages).[38]

Covertly and obliquely, the frame chapter establishes a pattern not only of blanks and limitless multiplications but also of more restricted pairings and doublings. Two ghost stories are told before Douglas mentions his own, which is the second example of a ghost appearing to a child. Douglas's tale contains two children, and if one child gives the effect a single 'turn of the screw' (the first of two uses of this expression in the text), then two children will apparently produce 'two turns' (p. 15). Douglas originally heard the governess's story during his second long vacation from university and expects to receive the manuscript by the second post (see p. 17). He tells his audience that the governess took 'a couple of days' to decide whether to accept the job at Bly but that on a 'second interview' she committed herself (p. 21).

Events in the main narrative show a similar tendency to double up. The governess produces not one but 'two distinct gasps of emotion' in the first of two incidents in which characters look up at the older of the two towers at Bly (p. 36; see also p. 76). Quint appears outside the same window in two scenes (see pp. 42, 133). Two conversations with Mrs Grose follow Quint's second appearance (see pp. 43, 49). A pair of conversations also follows Miss Jessel's first appearance (see pp. 56, 63). Miss Jessel appears twice at the lake (see pp. 54, 113). Two apparitions occur on the stairs (see pp. 70, 74). Flora gets up at night in two scenes (see pp. 72, 75). The governess twice waits outside Miles's door (see pp. 75, 101). She also has two conversations with the boy in his room (see pp. 73, 101).

The governess shows a pronounced tendency to use several negative terms (usually pairs) within a single speech. There are examples of the emphatic repetition of words like 'no' (see pp. 45, 57, 111), 'nobody' (see p. 45), 'never' (see p. 47) and 'nothing' (see pp. 33, 134–35). But she is just as likely to use pairs of positive terms or affirmations such as 'yes' (see p. 29), 'I know' (see p. 49), 'they know' (see p. 56), 'I see' (see pp. 80, 93, 119), 'you see' (see p. 73), 'I will' (see p. 99) and the exclamatory 'there!' (see pp. 114, 138). On occasions the narrative tautologically turns in upon itself. The ghosts are said to come 'from where they come from' and the governess reaches the conclusion that when Quint 'had gone, he had gone' (pp. 57, 72). Miles tells her that 'when I'm bad I *am* bad' (p. 80).

Generally speaking, however, neat pairings are not the final destination of the narrative. Although at points of crisis the dialogue does seem to relapse into pure repetition its echoes are in fact almost always marked by slight shifts and turns. What is spoken again is not exactly what was said before:

> 'Take me away, take me away – oh, take me away from *her*!'
> 'From *me*?' I panted.
> 'From you – from you!' she cried. (p. 116)

Panted repetition brings difference with it and the returns of the phrase are accompanied by shifts in punctuation, case and sense. 'Away,' becomes 'away – ' and then 'away from'. 'From' then sets up a further sequence in which '*her*!' gives way to '*me*?', 'you – ' and finally 'you!'. Similar variations occur when events in the narrative are repeated. Miss Jessel's second appearance by the lake reverses the spatial relationship between her and the governess which obtained during the first appearance. The first of the two apparitions seen on the staircase is that of Quint, who stands facing the governess near the top of the stairs. The second is that of Miss Jessel, who sits at the foot of the stairs with her back turned to the governess.

OPPOSITIONS

Christine Brooke-Rose has observed that 'The Turn of the Screw' makes extensive use of oppositions between, for example, far and near, up and down, out and in (see *A Rhetoric of the Unreal*, p. 165). The governess begins her narrative by remembering the 'succession of flights and drops' with which she first approached Bly (*CT*, x, 23).

This oscillation between up and down is to continue: the governess repeatedly draws herself up in order to act and then collapses or sinks down. In chapter 10 alone she records how she 'dropped', 'sprang again to my feet' and 'lay myself down' only to 'sit straight up' (pp. 72–4). Stable oppositions are replaced by alternations, and alternation seems in turn to give way to a situation in which movement upwards appears to cause movement downwards and vice versa. 'Up' and 'down' in 'The Turn of the Screw' are not merely stage directions of a purely spatial value but also concepts which possess considerable connotative density for the governess. When she speaks of her succession of flights and drops, she appears to be opposing the confident certainties of her flights to the bewilderment and nervousness of her drops, her exaltation and excitement to her depression and her doubt. Shortly afterwards, however, her 'little see-saw of the right throbs and the wrong' suggest moral rather than emotional associations, and these are to intensify throughout the narrative as up and down come increasingly to include salvation and damnation within their connotative field (p. 23). The vertical axis is also a chord which vibrates with social significances. Quint is 'dreadfully below', a 'base menial' (pp. 59, 64). Miss Jessel, on the other hand, is a lady who appears to have fallen victim to some 'abasement' (p. 59). What happened at Bly, in the governess's reconstruction of past events, was that the gap between social superiors and inferiors vanished: Quint's appearance on top of the tower is in itself sufficient to indicate the disordering of such hierarchies. Yet it seems that by promoting oppositions based on the vertical axis, the governess is able to measure only the disappearance or transgression of distinct and stable oppositions. 'Up', in the discourse of the governess, ought to connote 'right' and likewise 'down' should suggest 'wrong'. But the text repeatedly disorders such neat pairings, and the succession of flights and drops might just as well be a succession of drops and flights. In a world of reiteration and spreading association, the governess begins to discover that up and down might simultaneously characterize a single position. She herself reaches the edge of the semantically orthodox by seeing the children's 'advantage' peep up from the 'depths' of their tenderness and sociability (p. 87). She subsequently becomes aware that one can 'plunge into the hideous obscure' as well as 'float ... into a darker obscure' (pp. 127, 136). At this point movement in either direction on the vertical axis seems to lead to much the same thing. Meanwhile, a single 'up' might characterize two ostensibly opposed states. The governess is 'lifted aloft on a great wave of infatuation and pity' but such an ascent bears an unnerving resemblance to the 'strange, dizzy lift or swim' felt during moments when she believes the children to be exposed to the corrupting ghosts (pp. 33, 88). The climax of alternation and conflation in relations defined by the vertical axis occurs during the final scene. At first the governess is figuratively above Miles, who is 'standing at the bottom of the sea and raising his eyes to some faint green twilight' (p. 135). Within a few pages this relation is reversed: Miles utters 'the cry of a creature hurled over an abyss' and the governess, now metaphorically beneath Miles, feels herself 'catching' the boy 'in his fall' (p. 138).

Besides attempting to enforce hierarchical distinctions, the governess spends much of the narrative attempting to create stable and impermeable boundaries between the inside and the outside. Initially, at least, and in spite of sounds heard 'not without, but within', Bly is 'a castle of romance', a 'great drifting ship' (pp. 25, 27). The children must be 'enclosed and protected', offered a fancied future in 'a romantic, a really royal extension of the garden and the park' (p. 34). The governess then describes how Quint 'suddenly broke into' these imagined enclosures, shattering her secure possession of the interior (p. 34). Quint's 'intrusion' is followed by a second appearance 'on the other side of the window and looking straight in' (pp. 39, 42). In order to prevent such incursions and to maintain a distinction between the inside and the outside, the governess believes that she must herself act as a threshold: 'I was a screen – I was to stand before them. The more I saw, the less they would' (p. 53). To become a screen is, for the governess, 'a magnificent chance' – a chance to gain the master's approval but also a chance to enforce or stabilize distinctions and to create a satisfactory moral, epistemological and atmospheric chiaroscuro (p. 53). Almost immediately, however, the protected enclosure of Bly is violated by the appearance of another 'alien object' (p. 55). The apparition of Miss Jessel leads the governess to conclude that she does not in the least 'save or shield' the children (p. 60). 'The others, the outsiders' continue to 'shorten the distance and overcome the obstacle' and the governess even comes to feel that 'it was I who was the intruder' (pp. 88, 83, 97). The governess's day-dreams of distinct interiors turn into increasingly dangerous enclosures. At various points Bly becomes a gaol (see pp. 90, 133), a children's hospital (see p. 102), a nearly wrecked ship (see p. 125) and an arena (see p. 132).

If one cannot keep the out outside then one can only enforce thresholds by keeping the in inside. Yet the governess's attempt to 'fence about' the children often becomes a struggle to contain herself (p. 50). She tells Mrs Grose that 'there are directions in which I must not for the present let myself go' (p. 65). She has to 'shut myself up to think' (p. 39), finds herself and the housekeeper 'shutting ourselves up ... to have everything out' (p. 48) and shuts herself up in her room to fling herself about (see p. 88). Far from being a place of 'rigid control' (p. 52), Bly is repeatedly subject to outbreaks or breakdowns (see pp. 60, 61, 67, 84, 88, 122), to snaps and bursts (see p. 90), collapses (see pp. 94, 117), metaphorically overflowing cups and smashed panes of glass (see p. 113). People burst into tears (see pp. 52, 60). Things break into (see pp. 34, 69, 97, 104, 115, 122), break out (see pp. 69, 73, 86, 127) and are brought out (see pp. 30, 46, 59, 82, 105, 113). At one point the governess reminds herself of the 'art' required to make things 'distinct' (p. 33). Yet it seems that enforcing a border between the inside and the outside is either to legislate transgression into existence or to become aware of the border only by its crossing. Attempts to control the frontier between the inside and the outside produce effects opposite to those intended. The governess prefers 'the fulness' of her own 'exposure' to the ghosts and shortly ceases so to be exposed (p. 87). She finds Miles in 'a sharp trap' but then discovers that 'it was I who fell into the trap!' (pp. 79, 80). To 'provide against some danger of rebellion' is immediately and 'unmistakeably' to be faced with 'revolution' (pp. 90, 91). By trying to bring Miles 'much nearer', the governess produces a perverse effect of 'added separation' (p. 136). To predicate an 'in' seems to provide grounds for an immediate movement to an 'out', and vice versa. The governess tells Mrs Grose that she 'came' to Bly 'to be carried away' (p. 26). Playing at charades, Miles and Flora are described as 'going out ... in order to "come in"' (p. 69). When Miles negatively affirms his love for Flora he repeats himself – and here the governess seems to adopt the French idiom 'reculer pour mieux sauter' – 'as if retreating for a jump' (p. 93). Such see-saw statements skirt flat contradiction to suggest once again the instability and fusibility of absolute oppositions.

To be a screen seems to involve flattening one's identity to a mirroring thinness. Although the governess perhaps seems only fretful when she talks of steadying (see pp. 55, 129), assuring (see pp. 55, 70) or stiffening herself (see p. 71), the self-reflexive form becomes charged with deeper ontological anxieties when she speaks of finding (see pp. 23, 25, 26, 29, 38, 54, 67, 70 (twice), 71, 72, 125, 128) or hearing herself (see pp. 56, 97, 113, 131, 137).[39] In her own eyes the governess develops the opacity of another being, speculating that she 'seemed to see' something, that she 'seemed literally to be running a race' (pp. 91, 93; see also pp. 60, 116, 132). Towards the end of her narrative she writes that 'I seemed to myself ... to have mastered it, to see it all' (p. 124). One wonders how she can believe in a mastery founded on such seemings. Treating her intellectual and emotional states as external presences, the governess notes that her fortitude 'mounted afresh' (p. 23). On other occasions she is 'possessed' by 'a portentous clearness' (p. 49), 'held' by a 'thought' (p. 75) and 'harassed' by her 'inductions' (p. 88). These would normally be sufficiently ordinary expressions but in 'The Turn of the Screw', the 'dead' figures of speech seem everywhere to be coming to life.

The governess frequently weaves textile metaphors into her narrative. She follows threads in her 'pensive embroidery' and offers Mrs Grose 'a view of the back of the tapestry' (pp. 68, 78). In fabricating these veils, the governess appears to achieve a degree of figurative control over the situation at Bly. Having detected the existence of 'a small shifty spot on the wrong side of it all', she is (unlike Isabel Archer) aware of 'the importance of giving the last jerk to the curtain' (p. 63). When the textile metaphor is turned on herself, however, it becomes considerably more problematic. The idea of being a 'screen' between the children and the ghosts is for the governess 'an image richly material' (p. 53). Yet one feels that the material possibilities of this image tend less towards the distinct and the concrete than towards the tenuously interstitial, the elusively occluded or occluding. It is almost as though the governess's image prompts only ghostly materializations. Certainly her literal acts of sewing and knitting are always closely connected to the appearance of ghosts (see pp. 41, 54, 129, 132). To be a screen is to separate the children and the ghosts, but to see ghosts is also to become a screen, if only a blank and not a richly material one: after the governess sees Quint for the second time she is, according to Mrs Grose, 'as white as a sheet' (p. 44).

The governess is nevertheless quite right to see external screens and borders as the site of significant tensions at Bly.[40] The house abounds in registered surfaces, and there are numerous references to curtains, draperies, counterpanes, sheets and window-blinds (see, for example, pp. 23–34, 72). So multiplied are these surfaces that one's sense of specific locations – the space created by the surfaces – begins to dissolve. It is impossible to discover where the schoolroom is in relation to the governess's room or the housekeeper's room in relation to the dining-room. Space at Bly is disarticulated by those borders which usually divide it into distinct parts. One has little sense of geographical relationships but it is hard to ignore the corridors and passageways which wind through the governess's narrative, the doors which open and close between one space and another, the thresholds on which characters repeatedly pause before entering or leaving (see, for example, pp. 23, 29, 32, 51, 66, 109, 118, 124). Doors at Bly are variously watched (pp. 70, 75), listened at (pp. 25, 75, 101), metaphorically closed to avoid the question of the return of the dead (p. 85) and literally opened to encounter ghosts (pp. 42, 96). This multiplication of opaque borders is accompanied by a proliferation of references to windows open and closed, covered and uncovered, looked in through and looked out of (see, for example, pp. 24, 31, 59, 73, 75, 76, 121). Quint's second and fourth appearances turn on a play of glances through 'the haunted pane' of the dining-room window, whilst his third appearance is staged near 'the tall window that presided over the great turn of the staircase' (pp. 130, 70). The apparition of Miss Jessel is also connected with surfaces and borders, although these are horizontal rather than vertical, liquid rather than vitreous: on two occasions she materializes near the 'blank, haunted edge' of the lake (p. 117). The haunted pane of glass and the haunted edge of the lake: these are two spatialized manifestations of the 'O' which dramatize the blanks and turns of the text and re-enact the framing of the narrative at large. Expanses of glass and stretches of water resemble pieces of paper in that they occur in the form of sheets, making letters and ghosts possible, creating junctures and disjunctions between the present and the absent, the liquid and the solid, inside and outside, author and reader.

'The Turn of the Screw' focusses with such intensity on the way in which thresholds simultaneously divide and connect that borders seem to occupy the whole field, to prevent simple oppositions between the outer and the inner rather than making them possible.[41] The narrative tends to make any sort of surface into a spreading web, a network of associations and transitions. Certainly the associations of the in and the out tend to multiply, turn and slip in unnerving ways. I have already described the way in which the governess sees the external, the unenclosed and the free as deeply suspicious (see p. 111 above). After Quint's first appearance she increasingly sees herself as the defender of an interior space. Whatever is outside – the outsiders in particular – must necessarily be sinister. Yet if enclosure is such a good thing, one wonders why the governess compares Quint to 'a sentinel before a prison' in the final scene, suggesting that the internal is criminal (p. 133). And if freedom is so bad, then why (albeit with an enclosing embrace) does the governess feel impelled to convert Miles's dismay into 'the very proof of his liberation' (p. 137)? If the governess wants to distinguish between inside and outside, then one might suppose that her use of the word 'between' would reveal some investment in underlying notions of division and separation. In fact the opposite is the case. On one page alone things are 'agreed', 'passed' and (in James's revised text) 'conveyed' between the characters (*CT*, x, 25; *NYE*, xii, 161). The governess discovers that there was 'something between' Peter Quint and Miss Jessel but when Mrs Grose informs her that there was 'everything' between them in spite of their difference of rank, the 'between' suggests improper liaisons and not socially or sexually impeding borders (*CT*, x, 59). 'Between' does not separate but provides a fertile field for transgressions and transformations, fusions and connections; 'between' unites.

A similar dynamic affects the interface between day and night in 'The Turn of the Screw'. The narrative runs approximately from the spring to the autumnal equinox, and many of its scenes take place at dawn or dusk. The governess often seems quite literally to inhabit a borderland between the light and the dark. This equinoctial predicament recalls that of Locke, and the governess certainly faces similar difficulties in marking and justifying borders. Quint is first encountered at twilight, on a cusp or penumbra which the governess speaks of as 'afternoon', 'dusk' and 'evening' (pp. 35–6). The governess notes both the 'fading light' (p. 37) and the 'clear twilight' (p. 36), asserts both that 'light faded' and that 'day lingered' (p. 35). The problematic border between day and night becomes even more uncertain when the governess refers to the *evening* of Quint's first appearance as her '*dawn* of alarm' (p. 38; my italics). If dusk can be dawn, then dawn can also be dusk: on her first night at Bly the governess refers to the early morning light as 'fading dusk' (p. 24; the unusual if not incorrect usage is repeated on p. 70). Because the symbolism of light and dark is rather more obvious than that of up and down or in and out, the fusion or inversion of the values attached to day and night seems even more telling. Remembering the night of her arrival, the governess looks forward to later apparitions: 'the light, or the gloom, I should rather say, of other and subsequent matters' (p. 25). She describes Quint's second appearance as a 'flash of something it would scarce have done to call light' (p. 127). Yet to resist describing the ghosts in terms of inappropriate figures of light is not to secure occupancy of the connotative field which the governess apparently wishes to inhabit. Rather than working on the side of light she attempts to keep the children 'in the dark' (p. 67). She struggles against her 'new lights', yearns for the 'comparative dusk' of her pew in church, develops 'the will to shut my eyes as tight as possible to the truth that what I had to deal with was ... against nature' and, in a penultimate transformation of the syllable 'bly' (the final one occurs in the Preface, where James describes the ghosts as 'blighted presences'), becomes 'blind with victory' (*CT*, x, 67, 93, 127; *LC*, II, 1186; *CT*, x, 136).

Ghostly experience radically problematizes perceptual categories and sensory distinctions. The governess *hears* an 'intense hush' (p. 36), *sees* Quint 'disappear' into 'the silence itself' (p. 71) and even, in her most complex synaesthetic formulation, becomes aware of 'palpable hushes' through 'quickened recitation', a 'stillness' through a 'louder strum' (p. 88). Her narrative is a gradually mounting crisis of distinctions in which the oppositions typical of ambiguous structures give way to paradoxical conflations. It seems significant, for example, that the governess is able to see 'little difference' between the 'new' and the 'old' towers at Bly, despite the fact that they flank 'opposite ends of the house' (p. 36). This collapse of abstract oppositions is accompanied by an increasing interfusion of distinct and almost contradictory emotional states. The governess finds her 'curiosity' deepen 'almost to pain' (p. 29). A little later, pained curiosity becomes 'a confusion of curiosity and dread' (p. 38). The governess notices that Flora can, 'in the oddest way', be 'brave' about her 'timidity' (p. 25). Soon the governess herself is 'boldly' to say that she is 'afraid' of Quint (p. 45). Some chapters later she will speak of her 'dreadful boldness of mind' (p. 65). As the crisis intensifies, 'relief' and 'despair' are superimposed (p. 88); 'jubilation' and 'terror' become indistinguishable (p. 105) and the governess is able simultaneously to attack and renounce the enigmas before her (see p. 106). The effacement of categorial and hierarchical distinctions in 'The Turn of the Screw', as well as the doublings and multiplications which I examined earlier, seem to recall (or rather anticipate) Todorov's work on the themes of fantastic literature and the descriptions of ritual put forward by Arnold van Gennep, René Girard and Victor Turner. Indeed, Turner's work on the inversion of youth/age and strong/weak relationships during the liminal phase (see p. 20 above) closely resembles Donal O'Gorman's account of the imagery of misrule in 'The Turn of the Screw', which draws attention to the reversal of relations between children and adults and servants and masters at Bly.[42]

Yet one could argue that the crisis at Bly does not result simply in reversal. Shortly before Miss Jessel's final appearance, the governess's logic becomes one of pure oxymoron:[43]

'He found the most divine little way to keep me quiet while she went off.'
'"Divine"?' Mrs Grose bewilderedly echoed.
'Infernal, then!' I almost cheerfully rejoined. (p. 108)

DEVIATIONS

Possessing an almost infinitely suggestive porousness, 'The Turn of the Screw' is rich in fractured seams of reference to many other texts besides 'Gabrielle de Bergerac'. E. A. Sheppard may well be right to raise and accept 'the possibility of reference beyond reference' in 'The Turn of the Screw', although the tale's references are couched as implicit hints, covert glimpses, distant echoes which participate in the blanks and turns of the text.[44] The governess is not allusive in the cultured, sophisticated manner of the narrator in 'The Aspern Papers'. Indeed, in terms of evident quotations, 'The Turn of the Screw' is rather austere. In spite of this, criticism has succeeded in bringing numerous literary sources to the light.[45] These sources have usually been identified in order to fill in the blanks of the tale or to provide grounds for a univocal interpretation. Little attention has been given to the way in which 'The Turn of the Screw' transforms its literary inheritance or to the shifts and turns which lie buried in its quiet quotations.

Harold C. Goddard once argued that the governess is bent on staging her own 'heroic drama' at Bly.[46] The governess does seem to look on her surroundings as a reservoir of archetypal possibilities. She believes that her situation demands an 'extraordinary flight of heroism' (*CT*, x, 53). What sort of heroine does she want to be? In his Preface, James compared 'The Turn of the Screw' to fairy-tales like 'Bluebeard' and 'Cinderella' (see *LC*, II, 1183–84). The narrative of the governess likewise makes a number of generalized references to fairy-tales and legends (see *CT*, x, 27, 34, 35, 40, 54, 68, 78, 80, 81, 107). It also contains a rather subtle allusion to one of the motifs found in both 'Bluebeard' and 'Cinderella'. In her room at Bly the governess finds a set of 'long glasses in which, for the first time, I could see myself from head to foot' (p. 24). This is a suggestive if not a portentous image, since one of the best rooms in Bluebeard's castle contains 'Looking-Glasses, in which you might see yourself from Head to Foot' and Cinderella's stepsisters have 'looking-glasses so large, that they might see themselves ... from head to foot'.[47] To sound the note of 'Bluebeard' and 'Cinderella' both in the text and in the Preface is to suggest two roles for the governess: either, to put it schematically, she can kill a threatening male figure as in 'Bluebeard' or, as in 'Cinderella', marry an attractive one. But 'The Turn of the Screw' opens these archetypal possibilities only to deviate from both of them. As the youngest of several daughters who has never seen a full-length mirror, the governess might put in a good claim for the part of Cinderella. Unfortunately, however, there are to be no glass slippers and no marriageable, no zealously searching princes in 'The Turn of the Screw'. Nor are there any married monsters as in 'Bluebeard'. There is at least, in Miles, a 'little fairy prince' (*CT*, x, 80). Yet ultimately, in a perverse collision of 'Bluebeard' and 'Cinderella', it is the fairy prince who dies, who is treated like a monster. The looking-glass in the governess's room links the governess as much to Cinderella's stepsisters as to Cinderella herself. 'A vulgarly pert little girl in the street' who rolls away from Bly in a coach with her down-to-earth fairy godmother, it is Flora who begins to look like Cinderella, a fairy-tale princess seen through notably unsympathetic eyes (p. 116).

When the governess refers to the 'gingerbread antiquity' of the towers at Bly, one catches a brief glimpse of 'Hansel and Gretel' (p. 36). Yet the governess seems unable to control the archetypes which she invokes. 'Hansel and Gretel' provides no role for the governess except that of the cruel stepmother who sends the children into the forest or the wicked witch who imprisons them. When the governess raises the ghosts of other stories, these seem indirectly to impugn her interpretations. In her view the situation at Bly is quite unlike that in 'Hansel and Gretel' and the children are only pretending to be 'lost in their fairy-tale' (p. 81). But the faint echoes between the two texts also suggest a repetition of the similar, and one wonders whether the children are not actually abandoned in a fairy-tale within which the governess has taken on a distinctly unheroic role: only a few pages earlier she has imagined herself proposing 'to mix a witch's broth' (p. 78).

Shortly after the governess sees Quint for the first time she wonders whether there is 'a "secret" at Bly – a mystery of Udolpho or an insane, an unmentionable relative kept in unsuspected confinement' (p. 38). Oscar Cargill has argued that this passage, with its reference to *The Mysteries of Udolpho* and its distinct allusion to *Jane Eyre*, clearly focusses the ambiguity of 'The Turn of the Screw', the choice between 'a supernatural explanation, such as confronts the reader of *The Mysteries of Udolpho* or a natural one such as is given him in *Jane Eyre*'.[48] One could of course object that precisely the reverse is the case, since Mrs Radcliffe's mysteries are always eventually explained in rational terms, whilst the cry from Rochester which reaches Jane at Marsh End is not subjected to such an explanation, although it is 'the work of nature' rather than of 'superstition'.[49] The essential point, however, is that the allusions to *Udolpho* and *Jane Eyre* are not templates to map what the narrative is but quicksilver glints of what it fails to be. 'The Turn of the Screw' does, of course, repeat a number of recognizably 'Gothic' motifs. When the governess's candle goes out during her third encounter with Quint (see *CT*, x, 70), one meets a relatively conventional and typically Gothic suspense device used, for example, by Clara Reeve in *The Old English Baron* and already the subject of parody in Jane Austen's *Northanger Abbey*.[50] The scene in which the governess wakes to find her candle extinguished (see *CT*, x, 75) is prefigured in Sheridan Le Fanu's *Uncle Silas*.[51] Further examples could be multiplied but they would not explain how the repetition of the Gothic in 'The Turn of the Screw' is so often accompanied by a deviation from Gothic patterns, from what Bruce Robbins calls the 'romance script' of the governess.[52] 'The Turn of the Screw' creates, but does not give up, its secrets. It depicts a socially alienated protagonist but refuses to promote her to wealth and status through the discovery of lost relatives or missing wills. To read 'The Turn of the Screw' through *Udolpho* is to suspect that, despite a shrewdness and occasional cynicism of which Emily St Aubert is incapable, the governess loses that balance of sensibility and sense which in Emily is threatened but ultimately preserved. In *Udolpho* it is the servants who recount ghostly legends to their mistresses. Although sensitive to 'ideal terrors', Emily warns her maid Annette that an undue interest in ghosts leads to 'the misery of superstition', remaining silent about her own uncanny experiences in order to avoid seeming as credulous as a servant.[53] 'The Turn of the Screw' turns these relatively stable post-Enlightenment relations upside-down, for here the governess temporarily remains silent in order to make sure that she is not being 'practised upon by the servants' before exposing the housekeeper to her own terrors (*CT*, x, 39). Whether real or imaginary, whether related to the governess or the ghosts, the irrational in 'The Turn of the Screw' is not working from the bottom up but from the top down.

It would be easy to see the allusion to the insane, unmentionable relative of *Jane Eyre* as a mere flourish in 'The Turn of the Screw', an incidental enrichment of the *mise en scène*, a polite gesture of broad indebtedness to a generic precursor. Examined more closely, however, the relationship between the two texts becomes an intricate play of likenesses and differences. 'The Turn of the Screw' is haunted by *Jane Eyre* and Charlotte Brontë's novel both orders and disorders the narrative of James's governess. One tends to feel that *Jane Eyre* belonged to the unanalysed and possibly forgotten taproots of James's imaginative inheritance, that Charlotte Brontë's treasure, like that of Dickens, had been 'hoarded in the dusty chamber of youth', as James put it in *A Small Boy and Others* (*Autobiography*, p. 68). Yet James had already employed surprisingly specific elements derived from *Jane Eyre* in *The Spoils of Poynton* (1896). As E. A. Sheppard has shown, the fire in the final chapter of *Poynton* distinctly recalls Jane's return to the charred ruins of Thornfield in Charlotte Bronte's novel (see *Henry James and 'The Turn of the Screw'*, p. 46). Sheppard has also pointed out that James would have been reminded of *Jane Eyre* when he discussed Clement Shorter's *Charlotte Brontë and her Circle* (1896) in one of his 'London Notes' (dated 15 January 1897) for *Harper's Weekly* (see *Henry James and*

'*The Turn of the Screw*', pp. 47–9; James, *LC*, 1, 1391–2). Bly indubitably recalls Thornfield and James's portrait of the governess is, as Sheppard and a number of other critics have pointed out, certainly informed by Jane.[54] Jane's arrival at Thornfield (the introduction to the housekeeper Mrs Fairfax, the first night and first day, the early lessons with Adèle, the tour of the house and the visit to the leads) strongly anticipates the opening chapters of 'The Turn of the Screw'. Almost immediately, however, slight slippages and mismatchings between the two texts and the two governesses begin to emerge. Although she is later to reverse her opinion, the governess initially sees Miles as an 'angel' (*CT*, x, 41). Jane Eyre, in contrast, is not subject to such radical shifts of position because she has never held with 'solemn doctrines about the angelic nature of children' (*Jane Eyre*, p. 131). On her first night at Thornfield, Jane sleeps 'soon and soundly' (p. 118). The next day, surrounded by 'no circumstance of ghostliness', she first hears Bertha Mason's 'curious laugh' (pp. 130, 129). Later still she is to sense that 'my chamber door was touched; as if fingers had swept the panels' (p. 182). All of these elements recur in 'The Turn of the Screw' but their return is consistently accompanied by a differentiating turn. The governess remembers that she 'slept little' on her first night at Bly and this initial inversion ushers in a sequence of others (*CT*, x, 24). Rather than distinctly hearing a woman's laugh, the governess detects, 'faint and far, the cry of a child'; rather than sensing that her door has been brushed by a hand, the governess finds herself 'just consciously starting as at the passage, before my door, of a light footstep' (p. 25). The governess's experiences parallel those of Jane Eyre, but only in impacted and distorted ways. Jane witnesses Rochester's arrival at Thornfield and renders assistance when his horse slips on a sheet of ice. In 'The Turn of the Screw', however, this famous meeting is warped almost to the point of travesty. The governess is retrospectively informed of (and is not present at) the death (not injury) of the valet (not master) after a fall on the ice (see *CT*, x, 52). *Jane Eyre* glissades into 'The Turn of the Screw' only to signal the later text's deviations. One almost feels that 'The Turn of the Screw' alludes to *Jane Eyre* in order *not to be* the precursor-text. Negating or inverting the analogies it establishes, 'The Turn of the Screw' contains deep differences from *Jane Eyre* at the heart of its likenesses. Rochester's arrival fills up 'the blanks of existence' for Jane (*Jane Eyre*, p. 181). But for the governess the blanks remain because the master simply never turns up to be resisted, wounded and redeemed. Rochester and Jane become engaged during a walk in the orchard at Thornfield. It is Midsummer Eve. A storm breaks, and the couple return to the house at midnight. Mrs Fairfax observes them embracing in the hall. Rochester advises Jane to 'take off your wet things' and, thinking of the 'amazed' housekeeper, Jane then runs upstairs, telling herself that 'explanation will do for another time' (p. 322). Lacking a master to become engaged to, the governess in 'The Turn of the Screw' must stage a reduced-cast version of this incident. After her first encounter with Quint in mid-June, the governess circles the grounds for some time before returning to the house. She is alone; darkness has fallen. She meets a 'surprised' Mrs Grose in the hall, does not mention what has happened, and pleading 'wet feet' goes up to her room (*CT*, x, 38, 39). The governess's reconstruction of the scene in *Jane Eyre* would suggest that she is in some sense seeking to become her literary predecessor. This attempt is frustrated partly by a lack of basic materials and partly because other elements and configurations in 'The Turn of the Screw' relentlessly warp the model-text. One could argue that the appearance of Quint has already destroyed the possibility that the experience of the governess will follow the same pattern as *Jane Eyre*. The governess is not, as in her fantasy, to meet the master at a turn of the path. She meets Quint instead, and must subsequently attempt to enforce a parallel with *Jane Eyre* through her allusion to the 'unmentionable relative kept in unsuspected confinement' (p. 38). Seen in this way, her return to Bly becomes a dramatic attempt to restore the desired plot, to put the narrative back on the rails. Other attempts to promote analogies with *Jane Eyre* are to follow. The children's charades (see pp. 68–9) appear to replace those acted out by the adults in *Jane Eyre*. When, towards the end of 'The Turn of the Screw', the governess exclaims that Miss Jessel is 'as big as a blazing fire!', she seems to make a supreme final attempt to establish herself as Jane by identifying her predecessor at Bly with the incendiary Bertha Mason (p. 115). This linkage, however, has already been extensively undermined and compromised. To read one text through the other is to encounter the glimpse of a suggestion that the governess is dispossessed of Jane's role, which falls instead to Miss Jessel. When, having returned from church, the governess encounters Miss Jessel for the third time, she notices that her predecessor's arms 'rested on the table' whilst her hands 'supported her head' (p. 97). To rest one's head in one's hands or to cover one's face with one's hands is almost as common an action in James as turning one's back: indeed, Hortense Bernier performs both actions in 'A Tragedy of Error', James's first tale (see *CT*, I, 28). Though more conventionally or at least less idiosyncratically significant, the covered face veils and reveals almost as many meanings as the turned back: shame, possibly; but also despair, deprecation, tact, or even simply thoughtfulness. Yet however common it is as a motif, Miss Jessel's posture uncannily echoes that of Jane Eyre, who, after the marriage to Rochester fails to take place, goes to her room: 'I leaned my arms on a table, and my head dropped on them' (*Jane Eyre*, p. 373). At this point the governess seems to detach herself from the Jane Eyre image, dismissing Miss Jessel as her 'vile predecessor' and deciding that she 'must stay' at Bly whilst Jane (and Miss Jessel) had opted to leave (*CT*, x, 97). Even as the governess attempts to distance herself from *Jane Eyre*, however, she seems to become locked into and associated with inappropriate elements of the relinquished model-text and is unable even to control the drift of her inverted references to references made within *Jane Eyre*. Alluding to I Samuel 16. 14–23, Rochester tells Jane that 'if Saul could have had you for his David, the evil spirit would have been exorcised without the aid of the harp' (*Jane Eyre*, p. 561). Both Oscar Cargill and E. A. Sheppard have noticed that the governess reverses the sense of the biblical text and the reference to it in *Jane Eyre* (see ' "The Turn of the Screw" and Alice James', p. 243, note 24; *Henry James and 'The Turn of the Screw'*, p. 59). 'David playing to Saul could never have shown a finer sense of the occasion', she remarks when Miles offers to play the piano (*CT*, x, 107). The implication of this reference is damaging, since the governess presents Miles as David whilst reserving for herself the place of Saul, possessed by an evil spirit. Read through *Jane Eyre*, the governess's allusion has the odd effect of creating an analogy between Miles and Jane. Curiously enough, this analogy has already been suggested at an earlier point in the tale. The scene in which Miles and the governess walk to church could be read as a disfigured version of the failed wedding in *Jane Eyre*. Yet during this incident the governess seems no longer to be playing the part of Jane. Having pinned Miles to her shawl in order 'to provide against some danger of rebellion' (p. 90), she takes on a peculiar resemblance to Rochester, who holds Jane's hand in 'a grasp of iron' as he hurries her to church (*Jane*

Eyre, p. 363). Once again these ghostly echoes of *Jane Eyre* stray from the narrative paths which the governess seems to want to follow, defeating her attempt to repeat established plots, roles and patterns. Indications that the children play an important part in these unruly deviations occur quite early in 'The Turn of the Screw'. The image of Miles left indoors to finish a book 'on the red cushion of a deep window-seat' (*CT*, x, 53) seems to fuse with the image of Flora concealed behind the window-blinds (see pp. 72, 75) to recall the opening scene of *Jane Eyre*, in which the young Jane sits in a window-seat behind a 'red moreen curtain', escaping from the oppressive environment of Gateshead into Bewick's book on birds (*Jane Eyre*, p. 4). Even as the governess tries, fails and abandons the attempt to become the adult Jane, both the children upstage her by acting out a plausible and relatively undistorted version of the young Jane's career. When the governess asks Flora 'why did you pull the curtain . . . ?' (*CT*, x, 73), it is Flora who looks like Jane as a child whilst the governess reminds one of the bullying John Reed, who asks Jane 'what were you doing behind the curtain?' (*Jane Eyre*, p. 7). One might possibly disinter suggestions that the governess is engaged in a rearguard action against inappropriate analogies derived from the Gateshead period in *Jane Eyre*. Her strategy seems to involve projecting Miles as another version of John Reed. Yet even here 'The Turn of the Screw' puts up defences against the governess, inserts a twist into her narrative drive. Miles and John Reed cannot be neatly superimposed because they may well be opposites or mirror images of each other. John Reed's schoolmaster is called Miles: a fact which already, in the context of 'The Turn of the Screw', insinuates a deviation (see *Jane Eyre*, p. 6). One wonders what the name of Miles's schoolmaster might have been, and perhaps there is a clue in the uncle's letter to the governess:

This, I recognise, is from the head-master, and the head-master's an awful bore. Read him, please; deal with him; but mind you don't report. (*CT*, x, 28)

For 'read him' one could read 'he is Reed', creating a faint and almost certainly extravagant suggestion that the relation between Miles and John Reed is reflective rather than simply repetitive. I do not want to push this particular possibility too far; nevertheless, the tightly packed rehandlings of early scenes in *Jane Eyre* which one finds in 'The Turn of the Screw' create a growing impression that, rather than progressing from Gateshead to Ferndean, there is a partially concealed narrative thread in 'The Turn of the Screw' which inexorably winds back from Thornfield to Gateshead, turning the prior text and the narrative desires of the governess back on themselves. At the beginning of the final scene in 'The Turn of the Screw', Miles, his forehead against the window, contemplates 'the dull things of November' just as Jane looked out, in the opening chapter of Charlotte Brontë's novel, at 'the drear November day' (*CT*, x, 129; *Jane Eyre*, p. 4). Shutting Flora up and later sending her away, the governess displays a kinship less to Jane than to the proud and tyrannical Mrs Reed, who punishes Jane's demonic protests against injustice by locking her into the red room and sending her away to school at Lowood.

The allusions to and deviations from *Jane Eyre* in 'The Turn of the Screw' leave the governess marooned in a narrative which refuses to satisfy her imaginative demands. One way out of this impasse would be to extend one's repertoire of possible plots. When the governess starts to investigate the 'roomful of old books' at Bly, one senses that she is attempting to open up new narrative options (*CT*, x, 70). The text she picks is Henry Fielding's *Amelia*, and Oscar Cargill as well as E. A. Sheppard have suggested that the governess is trying to forge a link between herself and Fielding's virtuous but sexually beset heroine.[55] The governess may also want to connect the fallen Mrs Bennet, who bears 'a strong Resemblance' to Amelia,[56] with Miss Jessel – a woman 'almost as young and almost as pretty' as the governess herself (*CT*, x, 30). Mrs Bennet's husband dies partly as a result of 'a dreadful Wound in his Head': a fact which anticipates the history of Miss Jessel and Peter Quint, who dies after receiving 'a visible wound to his head' (*Amelia*, p. 299; *CT*, x, 52). But the governess is no more successful in controlling the implications of *Amelia* than she has been with *Udolpho* or *Jane Eyre*. The figure of Mrs Bennet offers no conclusive corroboration for the governess's description of Miss Jessel as her 'vile predecessor' (p. 97). In fact Mrs Bennet provides Amelia with a timely warning of the conspiracy between Mrs Ellison and the anonymous lord by whom Mrs Bennet has herself been previously seduced. If the governess wants to keep a firm grasp on the role of Amelia, then one way to follow Fielding's script would be to think of Miss Jessel in the same way that Amelia thinks of Mrs Bennet: as 'an innocent and an unfortunate Woman' (*Amelia*, p. 304). By rejecting this interpretation, the governess relinquishes any parallels between herself and the forgiving Amelia. More intriguingly, however, the narrative of the governess also calls up vestigial resemblances between *herself* and Mrs Bennet. The fact that Mrs Bennet's son has died partially anticipates the relation between the governess and the doomed Miles, and certainly works against the parallels between Mrs Bennet and Miss Jessel. The governess is 'the youngest of several daughters of a poor country parson' from Hampshire (*CT*, x, 19). This family history recalls that of Mrs Bennet in *Amelia*, who describes herself as 'the younger of two Daughters of a Clergyman in *Essex*' (*Amelia*, p. 268). The governess moves from Hampshire to Bly, in Essex, at the age of twenty (see *CT*, x, 19–20). Mrs Bennet moves from Essex to Hampshire at the age of nineteen (see *Amelia*, p. 272). Should one read these echoes in terms of reflection and opposition or repetition and identification? The fact that the governess becomes 'deeply interested' in *Amelia* and sits up 'horribly late' to read it is prefigured within the covers of Fielding's novel not by the heroine herself, but once again by Mrs Bennet, whose 'Delight lies in Books' and who also happens on one occasion 'to sit up very late' (*CT*, x, 70; *Amelia*, pp. 260, 264). These faint resemblances do not necessarily suggest that the governess, any more than Miss Jessel, is an iniquitous monster. Indeed, one could argue that the analogy between the governess and Mrs Bennet invites the reader to extend the same generosity towards the former as Amelia extended to the latter. Nevertheless, the connection between the governess and Mrs Bennet is not entirely compatible with the sort of role which the governess wishes to reserve for herself. Fielding emphasizes that Mrs Bennet is 'desirous of inculcating a good Opinion of herself, from recounting those Transactions where her Conduct was unexceptionable, before she came to the more dangerous and suspicious Part of her Character' (p. 268).

Fielding's Mrs Bennet may be 'dangerous and suspicious' and yet she may also, at least for Amelia, be 'innocent and ... unfortunate' (pp. 268, 304). In her attempt to create an analogy between Mrs Bennet and Miss Jessel, the governess chooses to adopt only one of these interpretative possibilities. Yet the fact that the governess can herself be linked to Mrs Bennet creates a problem within the narrative, setting up a circulation of likenesses amongst the three women, an unforeseen and perhaps uncontrollable play which undermines the governess's attempt to establish an orderly system of exclusive differences. If Miss Jessel resembles Mrs Bennet, then one could argue that she may be innocent and unfortunate rather than (or perhaps as well as) dangerous and suspicious. Correspondingly, the governess herself might well be seen as dangerous and suspicious rather than (or perhaps as well as) innocent and unfortunate.

WOMEN AND THE GHOSTLY

Like Mrs Bennet, the governess is a woman who narrates her own past. This fact alone goes some way towards accounting for the polarized reactions to both characters, for the idea of women as tellers of stories, and in particular of ghost stories, has frequently aroused deeply divided responses. On the one hand, female narrators are seen as innocent and threatened figures. Aubrey regretted the fact that painting, literacy and the Civil War had created a climate in which 'fabulous stories ... of Sprights and walking of Ghosts' were no longer 'derived down from mother to daughter (quoted in Dick's introduction to Aubrey's *Brief Lives*, p. xxix; see p. 10 above). The disappearance of such narratives was closely linked in Aubrey's mind with the loss of certain ways of communicating history, which in 'the old ignorant times' had also been 'handed down from Mother to daughter' (quoted by Dick, p. xxix). The threat to the narrative link between mother and daughter is still more intense in Goldsmith's 'The Deserted Village'. Enclosure and rural depopulation leave the narrating mother as a sad and solitary 'historian of the pensive plain' whilst the listening daughter has lost her virtue in the city (Goldsmith, *Collected Works*, IV, 292, line 136; see p. 299, lines 326–31). By the time of Wordsworth, the female narrator had become a female vagrant. In spite of this material dispossession, however, the female narrator continues (at least in the eyes of the male creator) to communicate oracular knowledge and to make sibylline revelations. She seems closely connected with poetry's attempt to move from text to voice, with the sources and resources of the literary imagination, and with an uncanniness which feeds creativity.[57] By witnessing and reporting the appearance of a giant spectral hand at the top of a staircase, Bianca in *The Castle of Otranto* – despite the fact that she is the butt of numerous witticisms concerning the credulity of servants – takes on something of the role of Walpole himself, who began his novel after dreaming that he had seen 'a gigantic hand' at the top of 'a great staircase'

(letter to William Cole of 9 March 1765, quoted in Lewis's introduction to *The Castle of Otranto*, p. ix). One could also argue along
similar lines that another servant full of supernatural tales, Annette
in *The Mysteries of Udolpho*, is a diminutive fragment of Ann Radcliffe herself, a coded confession of the writer's implication in the
superstitions she eventually disperses.

Women who tell ghost stories may on the other hand be deeply
threatening figures, dangerous and suspicious narrators. Even
Aubrey reluctantly admitted that 'old wives fables are grosse things'
(quoted by Dick, p. lxv; see p. 28 above). Addison also argued that
'Stories of Spirits and Apparitions' were merely 'old Womens
Fables' (*The Spectator*, I, 53). These are relatively gentle, if patroniz-
ing ways of dismissing the female narrator of ghost stories. But
Hobbes mounted a full-scale assault on the idea of 'dead men's
ghosts . . . and other matter of old wives' tales' (*Leviathan*, p. 398; see
p. 10 above). In the implication that 'old wives' survive to speak of
'dead men', one may detect a sense of the threat to which Hobbes is
reacting. For Locke, the dangers of female narrative began in
childhood when the 'foolish Maid' inculcated '*Ideas* of *Goblines* and
Sprights' on the mind of a child, interrupting the development of
masculine reason (*Human Understanding*, II, 33, 10; see p. 13 above).
Hoffmann's 'The Sandman' could be read as an extended study of
the damaging effects of such narratives. In 'The "Uncanny"', Freud
notes that Nathaniel's mother first mentions the Sandman as a
'figure of speech' (*SE*, XVII, 228). The trope is subsequently amplified, endowed with 'gruesome attributes' and placed within a fearful
narrative by Nathaniel's nurse (p. 228). For Freud, therefore, the
mother's metaphor, and the nurse's elaboration of it, lie at the root
of Nathaniel's development and at the origin of his later symptoms.
Although he chooses to emphasize the role of the father in
Nathaniel's castration complex, Freud concedes that later manifestations of this complex are partly the result of 'the persisting influence of his nurse's story' (p. 228). One could therefore argue that the
Sandman, who blinds and also gives the tale its title, operates at one
level as a token of 'unenlightened' female narrative. Hoffmann is
not, of course, engaged in the same sort of attack on superstition as
Locke since he delights in the aesthetic possibilities of interrupting
reason, or at least in exaggerating the consequences of such inter-
ruptions to the point of madness. It is Freud the rationalist who,
rather unexpectedly, draws out Lockeian elements in Hoffmann's

tale, demonstrating the persistence of the perceived threat from the ghostly tales told by nurses, the enduring tendency to associate stories of the dark, told at night, superstitious and irrational tales, with narrators who themselves belong to the shadows cast by the defining light of any particular culture. For Aubrey, Addison, Hobbes and Locke, for Hoffmann and for Freud, ghost stories are tales told by women, shadows of the narratives related by men; women, moreover, who tend not to be defined within marital, procreative or bourgeois systems of order: old wives, foolish maids, ignorant nurses. Freud takes this process of expulsion a stage further, finally associating the uncanny and the figurative with 'painted women' (*SE*, XVII, 237; see p. 26 above).

One might expect that governesses could readily be added to the series of female narrators described above and that they too would be the subject of polarized responses. Eventually this was true; at first, though, the governess was very much a daughter of the Enlightenment. Children of monarchs and the upper echelons of the aristocracy had been taught by women since at least the fourteenth century but the role of the governess was only institutionalized in a recognizable form during the eighteenth century, when governesses began to be employed by upper-middle-class families and a school-room was added to the nursery within the bourgeois home.[58] First translated into English in 1719, Charles Perrault's fairy stories were 'Tales of Mother Goose'. By the middle of the eighteenth century, however, as Iona and Peter Opie have shown, Mother Goose's presiding role as the narrator of fairy-tales was being challenged by the professional educationalist.[59] In Sarah Fielding's *The Governess* (1749), fabulation gave way to instruction, the play of delight and dread to useful work and practical precept, the fireside and the bedside to a well-lit school-room efficiently patrolled by Mrs Teachum, 'the widow of a clergyman', who tells one of her pupils not to be 'carried away' by the 'high-sounding language' of fairy-tales, since 'supernatural assistances in a story, are introduced only to amuse and divert'.[60] It is true that 'Morals' had been appended to the tales of Mother Goose. But Mrs Affable, the governess in Madame Le Prince de Beaumont's *The Young Misses Magazine* (1761), intersperses her fairy-tales with interminable 'proper Reflections' in her attempt to 'enlighten' her pupils' understandings with 'Useful knowledge'.[61] The enlightened governess turns up again as Madame de Rosier in Maria Edgeworth's 'The Good

French Governess'. In order to promote 'a love for industry' in young Herbert Harcourt, she buys radish seeds from a '"rational toy-shop"'.[62] To some degree all such governesses were women turned against women, female speakers who occupied front-line positions in reason's attack on dangerous and suspicious female narratives. They policed the threshold between the rational and the irrational.

Madame de Rosier is rationalism's obedient servant, but the similarly-named Madame de la Rougierre of Sheridan Le Fanu's *Uncle Silas* (and the shift from 'rose' to 'rouge' warns that Rousseau's vision of natural goodness may well have been superseded by painted artifice) deliberately terrifies Maud Ruthyn with her ghoulish tales. A 'good' French governess gives way to an equally and oppositely 'bad' one, tutoring to torturing, and the figure of the governess becomes exposed to the same sort of antithetical treatment accorded to earlier female narrators. The divergent channels which determined the career of the nineteenth-century governess appear in numerous ways and in many other texts. She could be a mocked dog's-body like Miss Merry in *Daniel Deronda*, a housekeeper in all but name; or a figure of towering malevolence, a confidence trickster like Flora de Barral's governess in Conrad's *Chance*. The governess quite literally crossed borders. In *Villette*, Lucy Snowe takes a job abroad as governess in a private school. In Mrs Henry Wood's *East Lynne*, on the other hand, Isabel Vane acts as a governess on the Continent before returning (in disguise) to fulfil the same function for her own children in England. Socially as well as geographically mobile, the governess tended to be the subject of extreme and rapid changes of status. She could fall to the level of a vagrant only to become a wealthy married woman like Jane Eyre, or rise to be the wife of a baronet-to-be only to find herself abandoned in impoverished middle age, like Becky Sharp in *Vanity Fair*. Writing in the *Quarterly Review* of 1848–9, Elizabeth Eastlake observed that the governess could either be the daughter of an aristocratic family in decline or of aspiring bourgeois parents.[63] In 1865 Bessie Rayner Parkes described the profession of the governess as 'a platform on which middle and upper classes meet, – the one struggling up, the other drifting down'.[64]

The role of the governess epitomizes nineteenth-century anxieties concerning social and sexual borders. Simultaneously *both* one thing and the other and *neither* one thing nor the other, the governess is the liminal figure par excellence: always, to recall Victor Turner's phrase, 'betwixt and between' (see p. 20 above). In the Countess of Blessington's novel *The Governess* (1839), a somewhat hostile house-keeper describes the governess as 'neither fish or flesh, lady or servant'; in Elizabeth Sewell's *Principles of Education* (1865) she is 'not a relation, not a guest, not a mistress, not a servant – but something made up of all'.[65] The predicament of the governess was 'equivo-cal',[66] 'artificial' 'anomalous', 'ambiguous', 'unnatural', 'unquiet'[67] and 'undefined' (Sewell, *Principles of Education*, II, 240). Yet her position and possibilities could also be determined in highly pola-rized ways. The governess could by turns be apotheosized or demon-ized, welcomed into the dominant order or violently expelled from it. She was like the strange term in metaphor, an alien who made herself uncannily at home within literality. Even in her day-to-day life, the governess trod a perilous tightrope. An outsider within the family, often a foreigner within the familiar, she did not quite belong either above or below stairs, either with the adults or the children, either amongst men or with other women. 'A private governess', as Charlotte Brontë declared to her sister Emily in a letter of 8 June 1839, 'has no existence, is not considered as a living rational being'.[68] For Elizabeth Eastlake the governess was a 'tabooed woman'.[69] For Alfred W. Pollard she was 'a cypher or a butt'.[70]

The ambiguous and contradictory social position of the governess has been commented on in a number of recent studies.[71] Yet it is not simply that the governess is between categories. As Mary Poovey has recently argued, the governess was also asked to police the borders between categories, to provide a boundary which fixed the lower limit of the middle class and to erect a 'bulwark against immorality and class erosion'.[72] Much of the debate concerning the role of the governess in Victorian England concerned the dual problem of how to reserve education by governesses for middle-class children and how to prevent 'low born, ignorant, and vulgar governesses' from entering the profession.[73] This double-sided problem became increasingly acute from the mid-century onwards, when there were growing indications of an over-supply of governesses.[74] M. Jeanne Peterson has argued that the opening of the Governesses' Resi-dential Home and the foundation of Queen's College for the edu-cation of governesses were a twin-pronged attempt to professionalize governessing, therefore reserving it for 'true gentlewomen' and excluding 'upwardly mobile daughters of tradesmen and clerks' and to maintain 'the fiction that members of the gentle classes were not sinking into the class beneath'.[75] According to a notice placed in *The Times* of 22 April 1869, the objects of the Governesses' Benevolent Institution were to assist cases of distress and 'to raise the character of governesses as a class'.[76]

These exercises in social engineering can be seen as attempts to deploy the liminal figure of the governess in the interests of the ruling order and its categorial systems. Yet it is hardly surprising, in terms of Victor Turner's notions of liminality, to find the governess also being associated with disorder, misrule, inversion, and ultimately with the manifestations of social or literary crisis outlined by Girard in his account of sacrifice and Todorov in his analysis of the fantastic. The opening of the Governesses' Residential Home and the foundation of the Queen's College (in 1846 and 1847 respectively); the publication of *Vanity Fair* and *Jane Eyre* (both in 1847): the proximity of these events to those of the year of revolutions did not go unobserved. The author of *The Story of the Governesses' Benevolent Institution* makes it clear that the idea of advancing the education of women smacked of revolutionary unrest in Victorian conservative circles.[77] The governess was meant to be a bulwark but, as Mary Poovey points out, Victorian society was anxiously aware that she could also potentially be a 'conduit through which working-class habits would infiltrate the middle-class home' ('The Anathematized Race', p. 129).[78] Customs officers are best placed to act as smugglers and far from preserving categorial purity the governess could erase, contaminate or corrupt the discrete with her own indiscretions. Whilst nineteenth-century culture denied to the governess the status which, in Charlotte Brontë's view, made possible existence as a 'living rational being', Victorian writers endlessly elaborated on the governess's tendency to ill-health, discontent, nervousness, morbidity, hysteria and insanity.[79] Elizabeth Sewell bemoaned the fact that 'our lunatic asylums, our workhouses, and – alas for England that it should be so! – even our penitentiaries, are too often homes for decayed, distressed, destitute governesses' (*Principles of Education*, II, 245–6). The governess could fall from reason into madness, from employment into destitution and from legality into criminality. She could also, as Sewell seems delicately to hint, fall from propriety into sexual delinquency. Peterson points out that 'metaphors of prostitution are not uncommon in relation to governesses' and her observation certainly seems to be

unconsciously confirmed by the author of *The Story of the Governesses'
Benevolent Institution*, who claims that the governess belongs to 'the
oldest honourable profession in the world open to women' ('The
Victorian Governess', p. 210, note 39; *The Story of the Governesses'
Benevolent Institution*, p. 1).[80] Writing in Henry Mayhew's *London
Labour and the London Poor* (1861–2), Bracebridge Hemyng vigorously
denied that prostitutes had once been 'either a seduced governess or
a clergyman's daughter'.[81] But Hemyng testified less to statistical
facts than to the strength of collective beliefs.

The governess as lunatic or prostitute, a painted woman? This
was a vivid possibility in the Victorian popular imagination at least,
and Mary Poovey has drawn attention to the fact that Jane Eyre
potentially resembles both Rochester's ex-mistress Cline Varens and
the insane Bertha Mason, his previous wife (see 'The Anathematized
Race', p. 136). In this sense the nineteenth-century governess can be
linked not only to 'the figure who epitomized the domestic ideal' but
also to 'the figure who threatened to destroy it' (p. 127). The
professional supplement to the mother could potentially replace her
as mistress or second wife. On occasion (and one thinks not only of
Jane Eyre and Becky Sharp, but also of the tediously dignified
Gertrude Walcot, who marries Sir Herbert Lyster in *The Governess;
or, Politics in Private Life*, and of Clara Mordaunt, the 'pensive yet
angelic' heroine who marries Clarence Seymour at the end of the
Countess of Blessington's *The Governess*), the governess was able to be
accepted by or to insinuate herself into the governing order (*The
Governess*, 1, 15). According to Mary Heath, the Lady Super-
intendent of the Home and Foreign Governesses' Institute, the
'ladylike' governess protected children from the 'vulgar coarseness'
of female domestic servants who were apparently intent on 'lengthy
flirtations with the butler of coachman'.[82] But perhaps the governess
was already herself flirting with her colleagues, as in Blanche
Ingram's anecdote in chapter 17 of *Jane Eyre*. Or with the master.
Or – alas for England that it should be so – with her pupils. Even in
1849, Mary Maurice's *Governess Life: Its Trials, Duties, and Encourage-
ments* was drawing attention to 'frightful instances ... in which she,
to whom the care of the young had been entrusted, instead of
guarding their minds in innocence and purity, has become their
corrupter ... the first to lead and to initiate into sin'.[83]

Saint or incubus? Hovering in the space between divergent,
almost mythic archetypes, the governess is both picaresque anti-

heroine and melodramatic *ingénue*. She combines equal elements of Mother Goose and Medea, fairy godmother, cruel stepmother and wicked witch. She is both the obedient servant and the adventuress, the reactionary and the revolutionary, puritan and prostitute, victim and violator, seduced and seducer. Poovey concludes that the governess cannot mark 'the boundary between ... two groups of women' ('The Anathematized Race', p. 147). Belonging to both groups, the figure of the governess undermines 'the very possibility of an opposition' (p. 147).

Long before writing 'The Turn of the Screw', James had begun to connect the figure of the governess with a number of the ambivalences and threshold problems outlined above. In *Watch and Ward*, Hubert Lawrence counts governesses amongst the 'civilized influences' (*Novels, 1871–1880*, p. 25). Yet as early as 'De Grey', Margaret Aldis (a paid household assistant, though not actually a governess) displays a more problematic combination of wildness and tameness, vulnerability and fatality, innocence and dangerousness. These ambiguous mixtures were to recur in James's later female characters and to be focussed with still greater intensity in his governesses. One of the correspondents in the epistolary tale 'A Bundle of Letters' (1879) describes how Lady Battledown renames her children's governesses 'Johnson' in order to ensure that they do not have 'a nicer name than the family' (*CT*, IV, 453). One wonders whether Johnson will act as cordon sanitaire or conduit in this nominal limbo. She could of course act as both, using her virtual anonymity to move between roles and poles. To be such a fluid and adaptable figure would only be to perform the associations involved in the name of a nursemaid mentioned in 'A Bundle of Letters'. If her name is anything to go by, 'Travers' should move easily between the available oppositions. She might protect the upper-class family – and here the name of one of the Principino's nurses in *The Golden Bowl*, 'Noble', becomes significant – or she might threaten its progeny in some way, a possibility which may vestigially be present in the name of another nurse in *The Golden Bowl*: 'Bogle'. The play between these bifurcating possibilities is indicated in wonderfully impacted form by the name of another governess cited in 'A Bundle of Letters'. 'Turnover' is the name of somebody who might overturn established social structures, who might even bring Lady Battledown down in battle. Yet the name also carries rather different connotations. Rather than acting outside the law to overturn her employers, Miss Turnover might turn them over, exposing their transgressions to legal retribution. A punitive governess of this sort had already featured as the first-person narrator of James's early frame story, 'Master Eustace' (1871). Dangerously vindictive and suspiciously prurient, this governess wants to give her young charge 'a taste of bad luck' (*CT*, II, 351). Unearthing the secret of Eustace's illegitimacy, she gains vicarious enjoyment from speculating about the skeletons in bourgeois cupboards. 'Turnover' is also, however, the name of somebody who might herself, socially, sexually or legally, be overturned or turned over. James was to develop this possibility in 'Sir Dominick Ferrand' (1892), in which Mrs Ryves is the illegitimate daughter of a governess seduced by the aristocrat of the title. Nominally as well as vocationally, Miss Turnover also prefigures the upwardly-mobile Miss Overmore of *What Maisie Knew*. *Maisie* seems to open the impacted ambivalences of 'Turnover' into a more developed dialectic. Miss Overmore possesses something of Becky Sharp's talent for social climbing. Without her predecessor's wit, however, she also looks like a flashy descendant of Edgeworth's Madame de Rosier. '"Qualified"' to 'say lots of dates straight off' and to 'state the position of Malabar', Miss Overmore's teaching methods reduce rational radish-planting to the rote learning of trivia (*NYE*, XI, 27). Mrs Wix, in contrast, takes refuge on 'the firm ground of fiction' (p. 27). One might think that Mother Goose has finally turned governess, but Mrs Wix's looming, somewhat sinister shabbiness and desperate tenacity faintly recall the ghoulish Madame de la Rougierre.

The ambivalent implications of the name 'Turnover' are revived and extended in 'The Turn of the Screw'. In 'The Ambiguity of Henry James', Edmund Wilson took the line of Hobbes and Locke, seeing the tale as a study of an irrational, dubious and dangerous female narrator. In 'The Freudian Reading of "The Turn of the Screw"', on the other hand, Heilman's governess was an innocent and unfortunate figure. Heilman's second essay on the tale, '"The Turn of the Screw" as Poem', even joins forces with Aubrey and Goldsmith. Because the governess's narrative, in Heilman's view, re-enacts the fall of man, she is closely associated with mythic truth and the restoration or re-presentation of such truths. Like Goldsmith's sad historian, the governess speaks (notably in the final lines of the narrative) of dispossession. This play of alternative descriptions might seem relatively satisfactory were it not for hints that the governess herself has a negative attitude to woman as fabulist and mythmaker. To take over the education of the children from a 'Mrs Grose' is to be but a letter away from being the enlightened successor of 'Mother Goose'. One only needs to change another letter in 'Grose' to see the governess superseding the teller of what Aubrey called 'grosse' fables (see pp. 28, 147 above). The governess is no radish planter but her curriculum, vaguely though it is described, seems equally distant from Miss Overmore's perfunctory professionalism and Mrs Wix's unorthodox devotion to fabulation. Miles and Flora study orthography (see *CT*, x, 29), music (see pp. 69, 107), letter-writing (see p. 89), arithmetic, geography and history (see p. 106). Flora even seems to be familiar with the works of Mrs Marcet, author of numerous 'useful' educational textbooks for children (see p. 74). It is true that the children are allowed to read fairy-tales without being treated to morals in the manner of Mrs Affable. But Flora's Sea of Azov games (see p. 54), the charades involving 'Romans . . . Shakespeareans, astronomers and navigators' (p. 68) and the memorizing and recitation of '"pieces"' (p. 68) all seem to belong to a relatively balanced if somewhat free-wheeling educational programme. Locke would certainly have approved of the governess's reference to 'the criminality of those caretakers of the young who minister to superstitions and fears' (p. 79). Sidney Lind has shown that James's immediate source for this typical Enlightenment attitude may well have been Alice Meynell's *The Children* (1897), which recommends dismissing 'the nurse who menaces a child with the supernatural' (quoted in 'The Supernatural Tales of Henry James', p. 293). Early in 1897, shortly before discussing Charlotte Brontë in the first of his 'London Notes', James mentioned *The Children* and described Meynell as 'an observer of singular acuteness' (*LC*, I, 1391).

Yet the governess's implicit dismissal of old wives' tales and nurses' stories is qualified by the fact that she herself tells the children about a 'Goody Gosling', repeating the 'celebrated *mot*', if not of Mother Goose herself, then of her daughter (*CT*, x, 86). Furthermore, from the point of view at least of Sewell's *Principles of Education*, the governess's performance as a teacher has serious shortcomings. The problems that face Sewell's governess are not unlike those that face the governess in 'The Turn of the Screw' but one does not, I think, need much close analysis to realize that her conclusions and solutions are hardly those of Sewell. Throughout

her *Principles of Education*, Sewell argues against a Manichean opposition between good and evil, seeing the latter merely as 'distorted or
exaggerated good' and emphasizing the inextinguishable possibility
of regeneration (I, 140; see p. 141). She warns that, 'in striving to
destroy a fault', the teacher should never 'overlook the virtue of
which it is the indication' (pp. 141–2). For Sewell there is no
'natural love of falsehood in the young'; the 'love of truth' is part of
our 'original nature' (p. 235).[84] Untruthfulness in children results
from 'want of moral courage'[85] or vanity, since children 'are fond of
making themselves heroes and heroines' (pp. 245, 251). The teacher
should always lead by positive example, particularly in the case of
truthfulness: 'if sorrow is coming upon the family, – illness, poverty,
separation, do not let us attempt to dress up the trial in any false
garb' (p. 248). In cases of suspected impurity the teacher should be
aware that 'the very fact of examination' can 'create the evil which
is dreaded' (II, 77). 'We dread that which contaminates us', she
adds, but – it is a suggestive line in the context of 'The Turn of the
Screw' – 'the sense of contamination arises from something in our
own hearts' (p. 83).

The governess clearly departs in various ways from the comparatively progressive liberalism of Sewell's educational theories.
More importantly and more generally, however, she is finally
unable to fulfil her social and cultural role by policing the frontier
between the rational and the irrational, the light and the dark.
James was to claim in his Preface that the governess 'has "authority"' (*LC*, II, 1186). This comment looks forward to his 1906–7
essay 'The Speech of American Women', in which the female voice
is again in question, although now in a quite literally lingual sense.
The Early- and Mid-Victorian governess was, he wrote, 'the closed
vessel of authority, closed against sloppy leakage'.[86] Is the governess
of 'The Turn of the Screw' to be identified with this 'purblind
transmitter' of 'a precious ripe tradition' ('The Speech of American
Women', pp. 18–19)? Her handwriting if not her diction has,
according to the frame narrator, a 'fine clearness' (*CT*, x, 22). Yet
the governess seems a beleaguered vessel rather than a merely frail,
delicate or closed one. Far from successfully resisting 'sloppy
leakage', she is eventually to feel that the cup which for weeks she
has 'held high and full to the brim' has overflowed 'in a deluge'
(p. 113).

I suggested some pages ago that the nineteenth-century governess could be seen in terms of the picaresque tradition (see pp. 152–3 above). According to Barbara A. Babcock, the picaresque has its own particular relationship to the concept of liminality. Since the narrative of the governess possesses a number of characteristics which links it to the descriptions of the liminal phase put forward by Arnold van Gennep and Victor Turner, this suggests that 'The Turn of the Screw' may have a relation to the picaresque.[87] Babcock argues that the hero of romance must 'go beyond the margins of society' and undergo a 'liminal experience' in order to achieve status and power.[88] In the picaresque narrative, the trajectory of romance is 'perverted in the total extension and elaboration of liminality into a rhythm of "continuous disintegration"' (Babcock, 'Liberty's a Whore', p. 101). The picaro remains betwixt and between fixed points. He is, according to Babcock, often an 'unreliable' narrator with a 'limited and distorted perspective' (pp. 108, 107). The picaresque narrative is often couched in the form of 'a first-person autobiographical reminiscence' (p. 108). The picaro uses a language of dissimulation which renders 'primary categories' such as good and evil or life and death ambiguous or indistinguishable (p. 110). Clearly picaresque liminality relates not only to the role of the governess in nineteenth-century culture but also, and in intriguingly specific ways, to the structure and nature of the governess's narrative in 'The Turn of the Screw'.

Elliott Schrero has argued that the governess would have been seen by Victorian readers as a shield between the children and the corrupted, corrupting servants. This is certainly the cultural convention to which the governess herself appeals and to which another critic of 'The Turn of the Screw', Robert W. Hill, has also drawn attention.[89] Yet Schrero's admission that Victorian governesses could also be seen as corrupting influences weakens his disambiguating argument that the governess is merely showing a 'proper concern for the moral welfare of her pupils'.[90] Perhaps this is the moment to return to Mary Maurice's reference to those 'frightful instances' in which the governess had become the corrupter of children, 'the first to lead and to initiate into sin' (quoted by Hughes in *The Victorian Governess*, p. 126). It is not particularly difficult to speculate about the possible nature of these frightful instances. Both Jonathan Gathorne-Hardy and Kathryn Hughes have discussed the way in which Victorian society was periphrastically and euphemistically aware of the possibility of sexual relations between children

and their nannies or governesses.[91] In his Preface James described
how in 'The Turn of the Screw' he had avoided 'weak specifications'
and attempted to make the reader '*think* the evil' (*LC*, II, 1188). He
went on to claim that his having been 'assaulted ... with the charge
of a monstrous emphasis, the charge of all indecently expatiating'
was an indication of his success '(p. 1188). James's blanks have
certainly not led to a shortage of speculation about the sexual nature
of corruption at Bly. On 5 January 1899 an anonymous reviewer in
the *Independent* (in all probability the assailant referred to by James
in his Preface) produced the following extraordinarily suggestive
account of the experience of reading 'The Turn of the Screw':

> The feeling after perusal of the horrible story is that one has been assisting
> in an outrage upon the holiest and sweetest fountain of human innocence,
> and helping to debauch – at least by helplessly standing by – the pure and
> trusting nature of children. Human imagination can go no further into
> infamy, literary art could not be used with more refined subtlety of spiritual
> defilement.[92]

The reviewer appears to be blaming James for the spiritual defilement and himself for unwilling complicity in debauching the nature
of children. His terms are vaguely but indubitably sexual in their
connotation. In a letter to Oliver Lodge of 28 October 1894 which
has recently been discovered by Peter G. Beidler, F. W. H. Myers is
still more explicitly reading James's blanks in terms of sexual corruption. For Myers, however, the defilement and debauchery are
blamed on Peter Quint and Miss Jessel, who are said to have
initiated and encouraged homosexual desires on the part of the
children.[93] Myers's idea that Miss Jessel 'kills herself in pregnancy' is
developed by Robert W. Hill, who thinks that it is a 'reasonable
assumption' that Miss Jessel was 'pregnant and died from an abortion' and Ned Lukacher, who speculates that 'Miss Jessel became
pregnant with Quint's child and was sent home, where she presumably died, as the result of either a miscarriage or an abortion'.[94]
Yet still other critics find still other secrets. John Clair suggests that
Miles and Flora are the illegitimate children of the master and Miss
Jessel.[95] For Allen Tate, the governess is trying to seduce Miles.[96]
For Hill, in contrast, it is Miles who is trying to seduce the governess
and, furthermore, 'it is not improbable that Miles witnessed Quint
and Miss Jessel copulating' ('A Counterclockwise Turn', p. 57).
Lukacher would agree that the primal scene which haunts the
governess is that of the children witnessing 'the spectacle of *coitus*

flagrante' ('"Hanging Fire"', p. 117). Sexual spectacle, outrage, illegitimacy; homosexual seduction of children by adults; heterosexual seduction of children by adults, of adults by children, of superiors by inferiors and inferiors by superiors: if all these speculations have equal value, the sexual life of the residents at Bly, past and present, has clearly been richly and busily transgressive. I am not trying to argue that these ideas have no value, that they are simply to be dismissed as extra-textual fantasies. There is of course a distinction to be made between those critics who seriously think that they have discovered what is 'really' going on beneath the surface at Bly or what 'actually' happened before the governess arrives and those, like Schrero, Hill and Lukacher, who attempt more culturally and historically self-conscious reconstructions. As I have already argued, however, James's ghost stories and frame stories do indeed frequently mediate or blank out archetypal sexual plots (see pp. 95–7 above).

Seeing '*The Turn of the Screw*' as 'a frank appeal to prurient speculation', Mark Spilka has criticized Freudian readings of the tale for failing to recognize its exploration of infantile sexuality.[97] Looked at in this way, the Wilson/Heilman debate, just as it recapitulates the polarized representations of women and governesses in the nineteenth century, also seems to repeat something of the Victorian ambivalence towards children. Discussing William Acton's description of the 'normal functions of childhood' in *The Functions and Disorders of the Reproductive Organs* (1857), Steven Marcus writes in *The Other Victorians* that 'on the one hand, children are spoken of as pure and innocent and sexually quiescent; on the other, they are described as constantly threatened by horrid temptations, open to stimulation and corruption, and in danger of becoming little monsters of appetite'.[98] There is, as Marcus points out, 'nothing to mediate between these two extreme states, no middle ground or connection between them' (*The Other Victorians*, p. 15). In the context of '*The Turn of the Screw*' this is highly significant phraseology, for this is precisely the attitude of the governess and her earlier critics. Marcus goes on to point out that the Victorian governess was often used as a stock character in fears or fantasies concerning the temptation, stimulation or corruption of children (see p. 255). His observations about the pornographic possibilities of the governess as dominatrix are certainly borne out by *Harriet Marwood, Governess*, a (presumably Victorian) titillation novel which

I have only encountered in a modern, distinctly unscholarly edition, the name of whose heroine may well derive from the flagellating courtesan Helen Marwood, onetime companion of the author of *My Secret Life* (see *The Other Victorians*, p. 124).

Marcus suggests that the flagellating mother-surrogates of late Victorian pornography replace the father, displacing him from the pornographic fantasy and thus providing a 'last-ditch compromise with and defence against homosexuality' (p. 260). One might add that such fantasies of a compliant or responsive juvenile sexuality may also replace or defend against the recognition of the sexual abuse of children by adults. In a forthcoming article, Allan Lloyd Smith approaches 'The Turn of the Screw' very much along these lines. For him, Shoshana Felman's account of 'The Turn of the Screw', which so emphasizes the way in which the master preserves his authority by disappearing, would celebrate rather than evaluate the way in which patriarchal power perpetuates itself by subtle censorship instead of direct repression. In Smith's view, Felman's depiction of the text's elusive phallicism re-enacts a 'systematic not-knowing'.[99] The argument turns on the incident at the end of chapter 6 during which Flora tightens a piece of wood into a hole in another piece of wood. For Felman, this scene is to be read as a challenge to and critique of those like Wilson and the governess who seize the signifier, translate it into a literal signified and thus become trapped by mastery, its play of sliding signifiers and its refusal of straightforward meaning (see 'Turning the Screw of Interpretation', pp. 168–74, 204–5). In contrast, Smith argues that the scene is not so much an emblem of the devious strategies of patriarchal power play but an enactment of what culture refuses to recognize or articulate. The action performed by Flora articulates what has been done to her, presumably by Quint (see 'A Word Kept Back', p. 3). Smith then proceeds to read the blanks in 'The Turn of the Screw' in terms of their 'implications of child sexual abuse' (p. 11). Miles is expelled from school because he says things which indicate 'graphic personal knowledge of homosexual practises between a child and an adult' (p. 4). He too has been abused by Quint. Miss Jessel apparently colluded in this and has herself, like Miles and Flora, 'obviously been abused by Quint' (p. 10). Using Nicholas Abraham and Maria Torok's theories of the phantom (see pp. 5–9), Smith argues that the governess sees 'ghosts of the actions of the abuser' (p. 4). In the final scene of the tale,

Miles dies as a result of having his secret history exposed as 'disgusting or evil' by the governess (p. 15).

Smith does not imply that the characters in 'The Turn of the Screw' have a life outside the text; nor is his account a violent demystification of the tale's manifold mysteries. Yet the intriguing idea, drawn from Abraham and Torok, that one may be haunted by the secrets of others does not seem to me to provide an entirely satisfactory methodological solution to the problem of extra-textual inference. If one accepts that the sexual abuse of children is the crucial instance of what is not talked about within nineteeth-century culture, then Smith may well be right to argue that there is 'a strong current of suggestiveness' regarding the 'probable content' of the blanks (p. 19). Yet, given the fact that there are other taboos, there are other equally plausible and historically justifiable readings of the blanks. Why, for instance, does Smith not recognize the possibility of *heterosexual* abuse in Miles's case? Perhaps because if too many postulated transgressions remain in play, one runs the risk of over-determining the content of the blanks almost to the point of absurdity. Furthermore, given the reading of 'The Turn of the Screw' put forward by Myers, Smith's claim that the sexual abuse of children epitomizes what nineteenth-century culture refused to recognize may well be exaggerated. Of course, Myers did suggest sexual compliance on the part of Miles and Flora and the characterization of the abused child as wicked and corrupt represents a typical Victorian displacement. Smith himself explores nineteenth-century apprehensions about the sexual exploitation of children, although admittedly these concern child prostitution and not the abuse of children by carers within the home (see pp. 16–17). More importantly, it seems to me that the patterns involved in child abuse raise wider issues. Smith claims that the governess is 'drawn into a repetition of the servants' sadistic use of the children' (p. 18). This observation has a very specific relation to the issue of abuse. It would seem that those (like Marietta Higgs in the recent Cleveland child abuse case) who claim to have detected the signs of abuse in others often fall victim to a mirror logic which represents them in terms analogous to those applied to the abuser. This logic recalls that of the unpardonable sin: a problem which reaches back to Salem. It is significant that Maxwell Geismar compares the governess to 'one of those fanatical inquisitioners seeking out sin, as in the old witch trials' whilst in the next sentence finds something 'almost witchlike' in the governess herself.[100] This mirror logic, as well as these blind spots and instances of violence or displacement, are bound to remind one of the 'crisis of distinctions' described by Girard (*Violence and the Sacred*, p. 49; see p. 19 above). When social workers become abusers and inquisitioners become witches one would appear to have encountered something resembling the disruption of the sacrifical trajectory which for Girard is often associated with the figure of the double (see *Violence and the Sacred*, pp. 116, 143–4). Smith gives a new specificity to a long tradition of reading 'The Turn of the Screw' in terms of sexual transgression but his argument ultimately seems less like a key to the text than a replica of its lock. Though by no means irrelevant or unilluminating, the child abuse angle on 'The Turn of the Screw' provides no privileged analytical path. Indeed, the effacements of difference so closely associated with abuse are already amply set out in 'The Turn of the Screw' itself. Just as the text undermines the governess's revival of past narratives, so it also undercuts her attempts to make selections and distinctions amongst the spectrum of governess possibilities, to retain the role of the 'good' governess and to cast Miss Jessel as the 'bad' governess. Instead, the desired opposition of forces – an opposition which was present between Miss Overmore and Mrs Wix in *Maisie*, although already in rather complicated ways – gives way to circulating paradoxes, impacted and fused ambivalences. With the governess of 'The Turn of the Screw', as with the governess in nineteenth-century culture at large, 'the very possibility of an opposition' (to recall Mary Poovey's phrase) is put in doubt ('The Anathematized Race', p. 147).

TRANSGRESSIONS

In 'The Turn of the Screw' the descriptive power of an oppositional logic is radically challenged. Rather than attempting to immobilize the play of polarities or to invert the governess's distinctions between the innocent and the dangerous, one might instead consider the implications of making such oppositions in the first place. The fact that the governess sees Miss Jessel as 'bad' is itself richly suggestive, providing as much information about the spectator as about the spectre she perceives. Here is the governess's account of Miss Jessel's third appearance:

She rose ... with an indescribable grand melancholy of indifference and detachment, and, within a dozen feet of me, stood there as my vile predecessor. Dishonoured and tragic, she was all before me; but even as I fixed and, for memory, secured it, the awful image passed away. Dark as midnight in her black dress, her haggard beauty and her unutterable woe, she had looked at me long enough to appear to say that her right to sit at my table was as good as mine to sit at hers. (*CT*, x, 97)

A number of phrases in this passage – 'vile predecessor', 'dishonoured and tragic', 'awful image', 'dark as midnight', 'haggard beauty', 'unutterable woe' – border on the melodramatic. Similarly stereotyped phrases and images characterize other female ghosts in James. In 'A Passionate Pilgrim', the ghost of the seduced curate's daughter is 'young, dreadfully pretty, pale and ill, with the sadness of all the women who ever loved and suffered' (*CT*, II, 287). Unlike Searle, the governess feels terrified rather than ecstatic, threatened rather than privileged. She is capable of detecting Miss Jessel's beauty and her woe but the ghost of her predecessor (a woman who has perhaps also loved and suffered) seems only to destabilize her own identity, prompting a 'wild protest' which recalls the violent unveiling of the false ghost (another sexual transgressor) in 'The Ghostly Rental' (*CT*, x, 97). The narrator of that tale finds before him 'a beautiful woman' with a 'long black dress' and a 'pale, sorrow-worn face' (*CT*, IV, 83). By demystifying this ghost, the narrator raises a second spectre, 'the punishment of my indiscretion – of my violence' (p. 84). In contrast, the governess accepts neither her indiscretion nor its punishment: her violent protest is against the role of the 'intruder' that has been forced on her (*CT*, x, 97).

Some time after the publication of *The Scarlet Letter* in 1850, the young James was taken to an exhibition of pictures at the National Academy. In *Hawthorne*, he was to remember having seen a representation of Hester Prynne, 'a pale, handsome woman, in a quaint black dress and a white coif' (*LC*, I, 402). The pallor, the beauty, the combination of black and white: this iconic portrait of the transgressive woman would seem to influence or at least to prefigure the depiction of the ghost in 'A Passionate Pilgrim' as well as the false apparition in 'The Ghostly Rental' and Miss Jessel in 'The Turn of the Screw'. One is reminded also of Margaret Aldis in 'De Grey', who is first encountered as a 'young girl, pale, alone, and dressed in mourning' (*CT*, I, 394). Once again, however, James's responses are more complex than those of the governess. Miss Jessel is simply a 'pale and ravenous demon' (*CT*, x, 114). James had been 'vaguely frightened' ,by the picture of Hester Prynne but the book itself, which he had not yet read, exercised 'a mysterious charm' (*LC*, 1, 402). I have suggested that the governess would have been an unsympathetic reader of 'Gabrielle de Bergerac' (see pp. 110–11 above). One might now suspect that she would have responded as coolly to *The Scarlet Letter*, as well as to 'A Passionate Pilgrim' and 'The Ghostly Rental', with their ghostly scapegoats and penitents.

The allusion to Hawthorne in *The Tragic Muse* foreshadowed James's renewed investigation of his predecessor's legacy in 'Sir Edmund Orme', 'Owen Wingrave' and 'The Way it Came'. Is there a Hawthorne element in 'The Turn of the Screw'? James had certainly been thinking about his predecessor as recently as 1896, when he wrote an introduction to a volume of extracts from Hawthorne published in Charles Dudley Warner's *Library of the World's Best Literature*. Much of this introduction was taken up with a discussion of Hawthorne's investigation into 'the secret play of the Puritan faith' and its 'ingrained sense of sin, of evil, and of responsibility', its 'pressing moral anxiety' (*LC*, 1, 459). These are all suggestive phrases in the context of 'The Turn of the Screw', and of course a number of critics have described the governess in usually rather general terms as a puritan.[101] Others have seen Hawthornean elements in 'The Turn of the Screw'.[102] But 'The Turn of the Screw' owes far more specific debts to *The Scarlet Letter*. Although the narrative of the governess is extensively underwritten by *Jane Eyre*, Bly is a veritable house of fictions.

Ghostly notes of *The Scarlet Letter* begin to sound at a very early point in the tale. According to Douglas, the governess's manuscript is written 'in old, faded ink, and in the most beautiful hand' (*CT*, x, 17). When the package enclosing the manuscript arrives, it contains 'a thin old-fashioned gilt-edged album' with a 'faded red cover' (p. 22). The packet, the red and the gold, the faded ink and cover: these elements seem designed to raise memories of 'The Custom-House', Hawthorne's own frame to *The Scarlet Letter*. Surveyor Pue's 'mysterious package' contains Hester's letter: an 'affair of fine red cloth, much worn and faded', with 'traces about it of gold embroidery' (*CE*, 1, 31). Just as the 'I' of 'The Custom-House' is separated from Hester Prynne by Surveyor Pue, so the 'I' of the introductory chapter in 'The Turn of the Screw' is divided from the governess by

Douglas. Both frame chapters involve the unearthing of a narrative, the discovery of an enigma and (in both senses) a letter. Both concern the search for a title which describes this letter. In both texts the letter is to be repeatedly and uncannily evoked. Unlike Hawthorne's blazoned 'A', however, James's 'O' turns in upon itself, leaving only absence. The 'A' of *The Scarlet Letter* could be read as a prefix which connotes negation or exclusion: things asocial or anomic. In 'The Turn of the Screw', the 'O' replaces these negatives with blanks and turns, converts the 'ah' of involved sympathy, of cathartic pity and dread, into the 'oh' of detachment, of mystified surprise and suspended meaning. Hawthorne's 'A' suggest *a* meaning, *a* truth, a certain singularity. It is an indefinite article whose ambiguous nature needs to be defined, a riddle with a series of possible answers: adulteress, certainly, but also 'Angel' and 'able' in *The Scarlet Letter*, 'Admirable' in 'Endicott and the Red Cross', and, according to Marius Bewley at least, 'Artist' (*CE*, I, 158, 161; IX, 435; *The Complex Fate*, p. 62). But if 'A' is the sign of sin, then 'O' is the disappearance of signs of sin. James's 'O' may well be a non-existent article, an ellipse or cipher in which meaning has turned its back.[103] If 'A' embraces a range of possibilities which James might have identified as typically American – negativity, singularity, literality and a rigorous policing of transgression – then the cipher 'O' adds potentially innumerable, quintessentially European secrets and values to any given figure.

Discussing 'The Turn of the Screw' in his Preface, James described the 'process of *adumbration*' which enabled him to avoid presenting evil in terms of 'the offered example, the imputed vice, the cited act, the limited deplorable presentable instance' (*LC*, II, 1187). He had raised similar objections to the presentation of specific transgressions in *Hawthorne*, excusing the use of 'the familiar combination of the wife, the lover, and the husband' in *The Scarlet Letter* only because Hawthorne had dealt with the 'moral situation' of his characters 'in the long years that were to follow' (*LC*, I, 403). Shoshana Felman points out that the governess is a detective who tries to track down familiar combinations, 'the definitive, literal or proper meaning of words and of events' ('Turning the Screw of Interpretation', p. 153). One could argue that the governess is trying to find the 'A' behind the 'O', to impute specific vice, to elicit a scarlet letter instead of all the blanks and turns.

The governess's account of the events at Bly permits one to

establish a partial analogy between Peter Quint and Roger Chillingworth. Both are hovering, blighting, persecuting presences. Both
are watchers who seem at one level to stand for the plots and dark
arts of the writer (see pp. 39–40, 107–8 above). When Quint is
described as 'a sentinel before a prison' (*CT*, x, 133), the phrase
recalls a scene at the beginning of *The Scarlet Letter* during which
Chillingworth observes Hester's temporary release from prison and
subsequent public ordeal. Yet there is an important difference
between Chillingworth and Quint which simultaneously establishes
and breaks the analogy between them, marking a transition from
the 'A' to the 'O'. Chillingworth possesses a 'slight deformity': one of
his shoulders is 'higher than the other' (*CE*, 1, 60). Quint's back is
also misshapen, but only by absence: he has, according to the
governess, a 'villainous back that no hunch could have more disfigured' (*CT*, x, 72).

The relation between Quint and Chillingworth suggests the con-
comitant possibility of a connection between Miles and Dimmesdale. It is perhaps significant in this context that Dimmesdale's
successor in *Blithedale* (itself a suggestive name with regard to 'The
Turn of the Screw') is Miles Coverdale. The governess is quick to
note Miles's 'great glow of freshness' and his 'positive fragrance of
purity' (p. 32). Read alongside *The Scarlet Letter*, such a passage is
bound to raise questions about Miles's moral well-being, since
Dimmesdale conceals his sin beneath his 'simple and childlike'
exterior, with its 'freshness, and fragrance, and dewy purity' (*CE*, 1,
66). But the letter of the law in 'The Turn of the Screw' is quite
different from that in *The Scarlet Letter*. Whilst Dimmesdale apparently develops a scarlet letter which imprints itself on his breast,
Miles shows neither a 'trace' nor, in the revised version of the text, a
'wound' to signify his wickedness, suffering or punishment (*CT*, x,
41; *NYE*, xii, 182). During his vigil on the scaffold, Dimmesdale
looks upwards and sees in the night sky 'an immense letter, – the
letter A, – marked out in lines of dull red light' (*CE*, 1, 155). In order
that he should be thought 'for a change – *bad!*', Miles in 'The Turn
of the Screw' also goes out at night (*CT*, x, 80). He too looks
upwards. But no revelatory 'A' appears; there is only, according to
the governess, a moon which makes the night 'extraordinarily pene-
trable' (p. 76). Miles has apparently said things which were 'too
bad' to write about (p. 137). These words remain unspecified
although it seems clear that they 'came round' to Miles's masters (p.
137). Elided and elliptical, Miles's language must be distinguished

from that of Dimmesdale, who at one point is tempted to teach the children of Boston 'wicked words' (*CE*, I, 220). These words are not defined by the 'O', by the blank or the turn. They are scarlet words which make the author 'blush to tell', the products, perhaps, of a devil's bargain signed in blood (p. 220). 'Bly' could be read as a secretive contraction of 'Blankley' (see p. 116 above). But in a world of imperfectly suppressed violence and obscenity, 'Bly' (Bl...y) could also stand in for 'bloody'.

I have argued that the governess's attempt to become Jane Eyre is jeopardized by Flora, who recalls the young Jane at least as much as she recalls Adèle (see pp. 140, 143–4 above). The narrative of the governess also raises parallels between Flora and Hawthorne's Pearl. In *The Scarlet Letter*, Pearl uses 'the unlikeliest materials, a stick, a bunch of rags, a flower' in her games, adapting them to 'whatever drama occupied the stage of her inner world' (p. 95). She makes 'little boats out of birch-bark' and also constructs models of the 'A' out of burdock burrs and eelgrass (p. 177; see pp. 134, 178). Flora also plays with sticks and makes boats. Shortly before her first encounter with Miss Jessel, the governess glances towards Flora who, in her game, has 'turned her back to the water':

She had picked up a small flat piece of wood, which happened to have in it a little hole that had evidently suggested to her the idea of sticking in another fragment that might figure as a mast and make the thing a boat. This second morsel, as I watched her, she was very markedly and intently attempting to tighten in its place. (*CT*, x, 55–6)

Yet this is no dramatization of a scarlet letter; it is a very precise rendering of the turn of a screw. Just as Pearl rewrites the 'A' which affects her, so Flora replicates the 'O' which determines her text. Resemblances between Flora and Pearl do, however, continue to accumulate. Pearl sometimes looks like 'a much older child' (*CE*, I, 96). At least when she is in communication with the ghosts, Flora is, according to the governess, 'not a child' (*CT*, x, 111). Both Flora and Pearl have a demonic side to them, and Hester Prynne imagines that her daughter is possessed by 'an evil spirit' (*CE*, I, 97). Just as Pearl will sometimes 'harden her small features into a stern, unsympathizing look of discontent', so Flora displays a 'small mask of reprobation' which makes her seem 'hideously hard' (*CE*, I, 93; *CT*, x, 116). In a sense, however, these echoes only serve to emphasize the fact that both children faithfully follow their respective texts to their respective letters. This correlative insistence on the 'A' and the 'O' (the middle letters, incidentally, of Pearl and Flora's names)[104] is focussed with the greatest clarity in chapters 19 and 20 of 'The Turn of the Screw'. Accompanied by Mrs Grose, the governess makes a circuit of the lake to reach Flora. Shortly afterwards Miss Jessel appears for the last time. I have already suggested that this scene represents an attempt on the part of the governess to align Miss Jessel with Bertha Mason in *Jane Eyre* (see p. 141 above). Yet 'The Turn of the Screw' is a palimpsest, and beneath this second, partially effaced text there are traces of a third, spectral script. The spatial relationship between Miss Jessel and Flora reminds one of a scene in chapter 19 of *The Scarlet Letter* during which Hester (accompanied by Dimmesdale) calls out to Pearl, who has appeared on the opposite side of a brook. A crisis is to follow in both *The Scarlet Letter* and 'The Turn of the Screw', but whilst Pearl bursts into 'a fit of passion' because Hester has removed her badge, Flora's anger is directed at the governess for having committed herself to 'the monstrous utterance of names' (*CE*, I, 210; *CT*, x, 88). Both Pearl and Flora counter the attempts of their elders to disavow the letter that rules them, yet because the letters are different this identity of effort produces entirely divergent results. Pearl is enraged by the absence of the 'A' and the presence of a blank on Hester's breast. Flora, in contrast, is upset by the loss of the 'O' and the introduction of a specific presence. It is this 'A' of naming which has previously made the governess 'crimson' (p. 88).

Intriguingly, however, it would seem that Flora does not only use the scene by the lake to enforce blanks. She also turns the relationships which obtain in *The Scarlet Letter*, establishing an analogy not between Miss Jessel and Hester Prynne but between Hester Prynne and the governess. Struck by the 'bareheaded aspect' of the governess, Flora provides a workable link between her current preceptress and Hawthorne's heroine, who removes her cap at the same time as taking off the scarlet letter (p. 113). It is only having established this subversive analogy that Flora begins to dictate blanks by refusing to speak first, by noting the absence of Miles (Dimmesdale) and by protesting at the naming of Miss Jessel. The possibility that the governess is more closely related than Miss Jessel to Hester Prynne is raised as early as the introductory chapter of 'The Turn of the Screw', with its analogy between the governess's manuscript and Hester's scarlet 'A' (see p. 164 above). Several subsequent passages tend to develop and confirm the impression that the governess is, in spite of herself, taking on the role of her transgressive literary predecessor. Hester Prynne embroiders gloves; the governess mends them (see *CE*, I, 100; *CT*, x, 41). Hester Prynne is a self-ordained 'Sister of Mercy'; the governess wants to be a 'sister of charity' (*CE*, I, 161; *CT*, x, 102). Dimmesdale mounts the scaffold in order to stand where Hester Prynne has stood. When Miles stands on the lawn and looks upwards at the tower he seems to be taking the place not of Miss Jessel but of the governess, who occupied a similar position during her first encounter with Quint. Finally, of course, Miles dies in the arms of the governess just as Dimmesdale dies in the arms of Hester Prynne.

REVERSALS

There is, naturally, a danger of overplaying the allusive aspects of 'The Turn of the Screw'. I have tried to show, in the case both of *Jane Eyre* and *The Scarlet Letter*, that James had indeed been meditating on the work of his predecessors in the period between his notebook entry on 'The Turn of the Screw' in 1895 and the publication of the tale in 1898. I am not, however, particularly concerned with the question of whether James is consciously referring to certain texts. What I am trying to do is to assess how James (perhaps unconsciously) transformed those texts and, ultimately, how 'The Turn of the Screw' reads *if* one sees it through the lens of a particular work. The connections between *The Scarlet Letter* and 'The Turn of the Screw' would seem to implicate the governess in the transgressions she projects onto others, drawing her into an ever-closer community with that which she seeks to expel. If one chooses to read the governess as the governess reads Miss Jessel then she would in turn become a 'pale and ravenous demon'. But evil in 'The Turn of the Screw' is not an essence or a core; it is the effect of a particular reading – a reading which takes on the responsibility of detecting and punishing sins and in doing so commits them. The governess is not simply a passive victim of the blanks or of the text's strange law. She bounds around Bly (see pp. 42, 93, 137), seizing and grasping characters or concepts (see pp. 115, 133, 138), gripping, catching and dashing (see pp. 30, 67, 72), throwing herself on people and flinging herself about (see pp. 88, 104). She figuratively delivers blows to the stomach (see p. 56), pushes people to the wall (see p. 63) and holds them under fire (see p. 79). The governess seeks not only to enforce borders but also to overrun them, to 'push my way through it to the end' and to take 'the straightest road out' (p. 69). She tries to constitute herself as a screen but she also wants to give 'the last jerk to the curtain', to make a 'breach of the silence' which she likens to 'the smash of a pane of glass' (pp. 63, 113). Once the governess sees the curtain rise on 'the last act of my dreadful drama', surfaces and borders are increasingly threatened (p. 91). She senses that she has hurt herself 'beyond repair' and can now 'patch up nothing' (p. 95). She feels her sense of ruin 'pierced through' by 'a prodigious private triumph' (p. 115). The richly material image of the screen gives way to the recognition of 'material testimony to Flora's rupture' (p. 118).

The governess is a passionate interpreter who actively manipulates patterns in accordance with her own designs. Driven by her beliefs and her desires, she tries to fill in the blanks, which she reads not as mere voids but as screens which conceal a meaning. Shortly after Flora and Mrs Grose have driven away from Bly, the governess notices that 'the maids and the men looked blank' (p. 125). This blankness is taken as 'a confused reflection of the crisis' (p. 125). Blankness, in other words, is not nothing but something, not a window but a mirror, not an 'O' but an 'A'. Absence is so material a thing for the governess that her inductions can be raised to the level of proofs. 'Not seeing' the boat in its usual mooring-place is 'the strongest of proofs' that Flora has taken it to cross the lake (p. 111). Yet the apparent rigour of this logic seems distinctly strained when, having woken to find her light out, the governess reaches 'an instant certainty that Flora had extinguished it' or when she argues that, because Miles is looking up at the tower, 'there was clearly another person above me' (pp. 75, 76).[105] To describe Flora's removed belongings as 'material testimony' to her rupture is to engage in a sort of inferential conjuring in which absence becomes a form of presence (p. 118).

The governess's reading of blankness depends on the presupposition that what the veil covers is vile or evil, that Bly sets up blinds between a blithe surface and a blighted depth. Flora seems partially aware of this assumption when she tells the governess that her absence makes her 'naughty' (p. 72). Such a view also seems to determine Miles's midnight escapade, since it is his absence that should make the governess think him 'for a change – *bad!*' (p. 80). A similar underlying proposition about the nature of absence recurs when the governess fails to join the children in church and imagines them calling her a 'naughty, bad thing' (p. 96). Blankness, it seems, can only be interpreted in one way. The fact that the masters 'go into no particulars' about Miles's expulsion can have 'only one meaning': that the boy was 'an injury to the others' (p. 29). The absent past can only be the 'evil time', the 'dreadful days', the 'bad time' (pp. 52, 82). What is obscure must be obscene; what is hidden must necessarily be 'hideous' (p. 69). 'Depth' is 'depravity', 'silence' is 'flagrantly ominous' and the 'systematic silence' of the children convinces the governess that they 'perpetually meet' Quint and Jessel (pp. 82, 112, 81).

The difficulty with absence, however, is not that it may arouse suspicions but that it is not necessarily always suspicious. Although Mrs Grose's 'quick blankness' turns into a significant blush, her 'dumb emotion' seems to be a sign not of guilty knowledge but of dumbfounded incomprehension and her 'blank' face can later be seen simply to signify 'scared ignorance' (pp. 28, 29, 107). The text (but not the governess) offers a host of motives for remaining silent other than that of concealing guilt. The frame narrator points out that not speaking may indicate that one has had 'a scare' (p. 17). When the governess decides not to mention Quint's first appearance to Mrs Grose, the reason for her silence seems to be the house-keeper's 'plain heartiness' and 'comfortable face', which prompt, by contrast, an anxiety which she is reluctant to communicate and therefore multiply (p. 38). To be silent is also to obey the master's injunction not to 'trouble him' (p. 22). Mrs Grose's reluctance to 'tell tales' seems to be founded on the master's dislike of 'tale-bearing' (pp. 31, 51). Perhaps Miles and Flora are only taking a leaf out of their uncle's book when they ask Mrs Grose to 'say nothing', arguing that the governess will 'like it better' (p. 98). When Douglas fails to confirm the speculation that the governess's silence was a result of her scare, the frame narrator immediately provides another explanation of her reserve: that she was 'in love' (p. 17). Silence, therefore, may signify deep affection, and it may also be a way of furthering one's erotic desires: not troubling the master is, for the governess, part of 'the fine machinery I had set in motion to attract his attention to my slighted charms' (p. 84). Yet though the master's silence may reveal the flattering extent of his 'trust' in the governess, she herself later accepts that it is 'an odd way' to demonstrate his high opinion of her (pp. 89, 120). The master's uncommunica-tiveness might equally well result from the fact that, as the governess tells Miles, 'I don't think your uncle much cares' (p. 94). The text also links reticence with the desire to avoid vulgarity. The entire narrative, as Douglas points out, '*won't* tell ... in any literal vulgar way' (p. 18). The governess feels that to break down in 'the monstrous utterance of names' would be to violate the children's 'instinctive delicacy' (pp. 54, 88). Yet there is also a 'criminality' in ministering to 'superstitions and fears' by speaking to children of ghosts (p. 79). To emphasize only the silence which signifies guilty knowledge is to exclude the silences which are ignorance and run the risk, in reacting to the evil that one has detected, of breaking out into violent speech.

The silences and absences in 'The Turn of the Screw', then, do not have only one possible meaning; they are ambivalent no-places occupied by fear and trust, love and indifference, obscenity and delicacy, obedience and transgression. When absences become stressed with such contradictory meanings there are grounds for bewilderment but also opportunities for manipulation, and there are very few fissures in the text which exclude the governess's interpretative insinuations. On her first day at Bly the governess notes that Mrs Grose is glad to see her: 'so glad', in fact, that she is 'positively on her guard against showing it too much' (p. 24). The smallest crevice, the slightest hesitation or restraint, 'with reflection, with suspicion', becomes full of uneasy meanings (p. 24). The children are 'like the cherubs of the anecdote, who had – morally, at any rate – nothing to whack!' (p. 40). To have no punishable surface and no moral bottom is to be cherubically good, but the governess's analogy contains even now an undertow of suggestion that the children are morally bottomless. Flora initially has 'placid heavenly eyes that contained nothing to check us' but this empty gaze shifts by quarter-turns into a suspiciously 'fathomless charity' and possibly cunning 'depths of blue'; eventually one finds the governess referring to the children's 'false little lovely eyes' (pp. 26, 62, 96).

To a large extent the narrative of the governess records her attempts to master the logic of the turn. Although the inference that Miles has been an injury to others is temporarily abandoned because he is 'incredibly beautiful', it is not long before his manifest charms – with reflection, with suspicion – suggest the absent; and the absent, in turn, suggests the opposite (p. 32). Miles's beauty no longer testifies against the original hypothesis of his evil but actually confirms it. The governess argues that the children's beauty is 'more

than earthly' and that their apparent goodness is 'absolutely unnatural' (p. 82). Miles must have been expelled for 'wickedness ...
what else – when he's so clever and beautiful and perfect?' (p. 100).
The boy is 'exquisite – so it can be only *that*' (p. 100). To assume that
beauty and goodness are identical is perhaps no more but certainly
no less disquieting a procedure than to argue that they are incompatible. To turn from one strategy to the other, however, is to have
one's interpretative cake and eat it, to read the same sign in two
quite different ways.

The argument that absence is an inversion of presence becomes
the governess's key to translating events at Bly. If the manifest sign
reverses the latent significance, then meaning can be restored by
simply inverting the manifest sign. Thus ostensible blankness signifies concealed knowledge, overt beauty or goodness signify covert
ugliness or evil, and Miles's 'lies' make up the governess's 'truth' (p.
132). The fact that Miles has 'no history' at first persuades the
governess to reject her initial suspicions, since the absence of
manifest signs of evil seems in these early days sufficient evidence of
the boy's goodness (p. 41). 'I found nothing', she writes, 'and he was
therefore an angel' (p. 41). It is not long, however, before the
governess reflects that Miles's reticence about Quint has a sinister
significance. From now on it is precisely the fact that Miles has
'scarce even made a reference to anything in your previous life'
which becomes conclusive evidence of the justice of her suspicions
(p. 103). Absence is not the lack of guilt but the concealment of
guilt.

The governess is therefore, as William Goetz puts it, capable of
reading 'signs of omission or negation ... as their opposites, as
avowals' (*Henry James and the Darkest Abyss*, p. 128). She is also able
to reverse her interpretation of particular items of evidence. Yet one
could go further: in order to sustain identical conclusions, the
governess is quite willing to reverse her supporting evidence.[106]
During the first scene by the lake the governess employs her standard epistemological method. She waits for an 'innocent sign' from
Flora which will indicate that the child is interested in or alarmed
by Miss Jessel's presence (*CT*, x, 55). The fact that 'nothing came'
then provides sufficient grounds for the reflective turn (p. 55). To be
apparently unaware of Miss Jessel cannot signify innocence: it is the
very fact that Flora said 'not a word' which indicates that the
children 'know' (p. 56). The distressed Mrs Grose counters that

Flora's behaviour might be 'just a proof of her blest innocence' (p. 58). The housekeeper's straightforward belief that an apparent lack of awareness of evil must signify innocence brings the governess 'almost round' (p. 58). The consequences of being able to derive a proof of awareness in others from the absence of any signs of such awareness are of course already extremely far-reaching, since on this basis knowledge and ignorance, guilt and innocence, good and evil are indistinguishable if not practically identical. But the strategy of the governess becomes doubly dubious when she defends herself against Mrs Grose's challenge to her reading by reversing the evidence which supported it. At first it was Flora's silence which convinced the governess of the child's concealed and therefore guilty awareness. Faced with Mrs Grose's literalism, the governess soon alters her review of events by the lake by recalling Flora's attempts 'to divert my attention', attempts which include 'the singing, the gabbling, of nonsense' (p. 62). Although the governess may now be remembering the events which followed Flora's silence at the end of chapter 6, the change in her account is both noticeable and disturbing. A sinister silence which had failed to convince Mrs Grose is replaced by a diversionary noise which effectively seals the issue. The housekeeper, at least, can hardly maintain an identical argument when presented with a reversal of the evidence. The governess can, and with some ease, but her reversal of the signs provides no reassurance regarding the accuracy of the inferences. There is no way of demonstrating that Flora's gabbling of nonsense, like her earlier silence, is not a sign of her innocence – precisely the innocent sign which the governess had previously missed. Noisy or silent, Flora might be innocently unaware rather than guiltily knowing. Yet from now on, for the governess at least, 'the traceable increase' of the children's 'demonstrations' is just as suspicious as their silence, although towards the end of the tale, 'freshly upset' by the lack of a 'demonstration' on the part of Miles and Flora, she claims to like their dumbness 'worse' (pp. 67, 97–8). In the meantime, whilst the piano breaks into 'gruesome fancies', the governess lives in an obscuring 'cloud of music' (p. 69). But it is all an 'exhibition', 'a game ... a policy and a fraud' (pp. 83, 82). Silence is guilt. Yet noise is guilty too. If all manifestations of innocence are potentially fraudulent, then there is simply no room for manifest innocence.

The logic of the governess seems both fluid and too rigid, both subtle and too crude, both clear and yet too blurred. She pounces passionately on the conceptual relations of a given situation. When any change in these relations occurs (it usually takes the form of a reversal) she devotes herself to following through the play of correlations and inverted consequences. The mere speculation that 'the more I saw, the less they would' becomes a law in the psychic geometry at Bly, so that when the governess sees 'nothing, whether in or out of the house', she automatically draws the inference that 'Miles and Flora saw *more*' (pp. 53, 86, 89). Awareness and unawareness or noise and silence become elements in a system capable of generating virtually algebraic proofs. But it is of no consequence which particular term is manifested since the governess, by shifting and rehandling other binary oppositions, continues to draw the same conclusions. Noise becomes a turned version of silence, evil of good and vice versa. In this spectral logic presence and absence are virtually equivalent: to go to one end of the scale is to find oneself closer to the opposite end than to any more finely graduated intervening ground. Divine or infernal? Because the governess can use the terms almost synonymously (see p. 136 above) there may well be no distinct gap between the 'angel' Miles seems to be at Bly and the 'fiend' he apparently was at school (*CT*, x, 65). And if angels can be fiends, then fiends can be angels – or at least, 'though they were not angels', they pass, 'as the French say', in the same vocabulary (p. 88).

Reversals and transpositions have their limits, however, and the governess is often reluctant to read previous events in the light of new turns. Silence is suspicious but it does not follow that noise allays doubts. Not to mention one's school is dubious behaviour but to bring up the question of one's education is not by the same token innocent. Miles is suspiciously good but when he does something to make the governess think him '*bad*' there is only a brief trace of a retroactive reversal in the governess's recognition of Miles's 'reserves of goodness' (pp. 80, 81). The governess's refusal to read past events in terms of new inferences is particularly noteworthy in the case of Flora. When, after having got up at night for the first time, Flora claims that she has not seen anybody outside, the governess 'absolutely believed she lied' (p. 73). But when Flora rises a second time the governess becomes convinced that the child 'now saw – as she had not, I had satisfied myself, the previous time' (p. 75). Reversing her interpretation of the first scene allows the governess to repeat her original inference. She does not retrospectively exonerate Flora.

'Why did you pull the curtain over the place to make me think you were still there?', she asked initially, including the answer and the whole force of her strategy in the question (p. 73). The governess has already decided that the curtains surrounding Flora's bed have been drawn 'deceivingly' and do not, as she had thought at the beginning of the scene, cover 'the perfection of childish rest' (pp. 72, 70). If rest is perfection, then what is wakefulness? The conclusion seems to follow naturally from the given propositions, and when the propositions are repeated the same conclusion is drawn, even though the governess now feels that her first interpretation must have been mistaken. She does not for a moment question her original assumptions regarding the deceptive nature of screens. When the governess finds Flora behind the window-blind for a second time she becomes certain that the child is now 'face to face with the apparition we had met at the lake' (p. 75). Yet her accusation fails to stick even when it is reiterated: the figure on the lawn is that of Miles and not Miss Jessel. Once again the governess modifies her interpretation without withdrawing the accusation which has now been belied (Bly'd?) on two separate occasions. Although screens may well be deceptive it seems that one can also be misled by believing that they always deceive, or that they have been drawn with a deceptive intention, or that what is concealed behind the screen must necessarily be a portentous reversal of what exists in front of it.

Towards the end of the tale the governess writes that her 'equilibrium' depends upon an exercise of 'rigid will' in shutting her eyes 'as tight as possible to the truth that what I had to deal with was, revoltingly, against nature' (p. 127). Her predicament makes it necessary 'to supply, one's self, *all* the nature' (p. 127). At this late stage, however, it is almost impossible for the governess to recuperate the natural since she has already radically problematized conventional distinctions between the natural and the unnatural. It was in the midst of 'the mystery of nature' that Quint first emerged (p. 34). Miles's evasions, which one might have assumed lay at the heart of what is unnatural at Bly, were described as an outbreak of the 'natural man' (p. 66). Shortly afterwards all manifestations of goodness become 'absolutely unnatural' (p. 82). There are for the governess two ways to supply nature, and both irresistibly lead to the unnatural. No 'suppression of reference to what had occurred' can be natural, but nor can the governess 'make a reference' (as she has already done to Flora) without 'a new plunge into the hideous obscure' (p. 127). The governess decides on a middle course: neither speaking nor remaining silent, she makes Miles speak. Yet to risk 'the stretch of an angular arm' over Miles's character is to reveal a rigid, linear drive to rupture the screens every bit as intense as her 'breach of the silence' with Flora (pp. 127, 113). The governess's struggle to achieve 'equilibrium' fails at every point (p. 127). In the final scene, however, the perverse logic which she has previously turned on others is at last turned on herself. Having violated the borders, the governess seems finally to discover manifest wickedness in the children. Flora's 'childish beauty' vanishes as she turns 'common and almost ugly' (p. 116). The governess's prediction that the children 'say things that, if we heard them, would simply appal us' seems at last to be confirmed by Mrs Grose's discovery that Flora 'says things' and by Miles's confession to having 'said things' (pp. 110, 122, 135). If silence or misleadingly innocent noise have previously covered hidden evil, then there seems no reason why the revealed guilt of Flora's 'appalling language' or Miles's admission to having said things that were 'too bad' to write about should not signify the children's latent innocence (pp. 122, 137). Making her usual interpretative turn, the governess suddenly encounters the 'appalling alarm' that Miles is 'perhaps innocent' (p. 136). And if Miles is innocent, 'what then on earth was *I*?' (p. 136). So set are the governess's interpretative habits that she is prepared to contemplate the possibility of her own guilt rather than arresting the reflective turns of her reading. A victim of her own rationale, she seems as unable to demonstrate the salvation she wants to have wrought as she was of proving the damnation she previously fought. Her final 'positive certitude' of Miles's unconsciousness of Quint, which ought to be the crowning triumph of her attempts to screen the children, seems as groundless as her previous certainty of the boy's awareness (p. 134).

TURNS

What then on earth is the governess? To conclude that she is guilty and reverse her reading at every point would inevitably be to adopt her own dangerous logic, and maintaining that the blanks are never suspect is as doubtful a strategy as asserting that they always are. The governess turns the screw with such effect that the distinctions and oppositions on which she relies lose their integrity. If the divine and the infernal are not discriminable, then the question of whether the governess is 'good' or 'evil' no longer makes sense in the usual ways. One could very well give a further turn to the interpretative turns of the governess. But it may be more useful to examine how and with what effect the screw can be turned.

In the introductory chapter, Douglas comments on the way in which the child in Griffin's story 'gives the effect another turn of the screw' (*CT*, x, 15). The expression 'turn of the screw' seems to describe the results brought about by literary artifices, which in this case make use of the vulnerable figure of a child in order to solicit the reader's involvement and to intensify feelings of suspense, uncertainty and so on. Towards the end of the tale, the governess feels that her situation requires her to make 'another turn of the screw of ordinary human virtue' (p. 127). The repetition of the expression is accompanied by a turn in its sense, since the governess is not talking about the artifices of narrative but about her attempts 'to supply ... nature' (p. 127). The governess's (oddly mechanistic) metaphor details an active moral manifestation rather than a passive aesthetic response. In spite of these differences, however, both Douglas's and the governess's turns of the screw are essentially centripetal. The turn of the screw connotes various forms of restriction, intensification, enclosure, enforcement or constraint. This range of senses underlies a number of James's other uses of similar tropes. In 'A Most Extraordinary Case' (1868), the injured Mason feels that he is 'living by mere force of will, and ... if he loosened the screws for a single instant he should sink back upon his bed again and never leave it' (*CT*, I, 361). Maximus Austin, the predatory diarist of 'A Light Man' (1869), notes that Frederick Sloane, his patron and victim, has been through a straitened period in his youth: 'his turning the screw during those relatively impecunious years represents, I am pretty sure, the only act of resolution in his life' (*CT*, II, 76). In *The American*, Valentin observes that his family 'must have had to turn the screw pretty tight' in order to accept Newman as Claire's suitor (*Novels 1871–1880*, p. 674). These instances of the turning screw describe resolutions, acts of will and of self-control which involve the resistance to expenditures of desire. The financial implications associated with turning the screw suggest some form of connection to another centripetal dynamic in James: that of economic mastery. James found it entirely acceptable and even necessary to turn the screw in the interests of economic mastery and in order to secure the intensity suggested in Douglas's use of the phrase. In the notes on 'The K.B. Case' which James made in 1909 or 1910, he was happy to subject his ideas to 'the pressure and the screw' (*N*, p. 259). He admitted with some pride in the Prefaces that 'The Tree of Knowledge' had required an even greater number of 'full revolutions of the merciless screw' than 'The Middle Years' (*LC*, II, 1240). The economic master justifiably used techniques of compaction and restraint in his search for more intensely effective and affective forms of writing. He reduced life's leaden metals to the point where they became transformed into art and took on an immense increase in value. The results of this centripetal dynamic are the subject of indirect comment in the introductory chapter of 'The Turn of the Screw'. The fact that Douglas's story is 'horrible' gives it 'the utmost price' (*CT*, x, 16). Its 'dreadful – dreadfulness' makes it, to one of the listeners at least, 'delicious' (p. 16).

Yet if the screw is not turned in the literary and aesthetic interests of economic mastery then the conversion of pain into pleasure may not occur. If the screw is turned on living material, in order to enforce a particular moral standpoint or to restrain other beings, then it acquires distinctly negative associations for James. When George Flack rushes off to give 'a turn to one of his screws' in *The Reverberator* or, in one of the 'American Letters' of 1898, Theodore Roosevelt is said to be jingoistically attempting 'to tighten the screws of the national consciousness', James is describing narrow and exploitative if not downright sinister actions (*Novels 1886–1890*, p. 575; *LC*, I, 663). These more disturbing turns of the screw resemble those of the governess rather than those of Douglas or James, and pushed too far the screw is liable to turn into an instrument of torture rather than a compression tool. The telegraphist of 'In the Cage', for instance, describes Captain Everard's terrified pre-dicament in terms of 'twists and turns ... places where the screw drew blood' (*CT*, x, 224).

There is for James, however, another and quite different turn of the screw. In *The Golden Bowl*, Adam Verver looks back on his ascent of the 'hill of difficulty, the tall sharp spiral round which he had begun to wind his ascent at the age of twenty' (*NYE*, XXIII, 131). This is the familiar tightening spiral of a literally economic success. Having reached the pinnacle of business achievement, however, Adam gazes down on 'the kingdoms of the earth' and undergoes a further 'revolution of the screw', a sea change in which his sensibility recognizes 'the affinity of Genius, or at least of Taste' (pp. 131, 141).[107] Rather than resisting desire by centripetal turns, Adam falls in love with the realm of art. His revolution, which creates a new world of aspirations, extensions and expenditures, therefore seems to be related to the explosive principle rather than to economic mastery. The revolving wheel mentioned in *The Sacred Fount* appears to turn in a similarly centrifugal way, sending the narrator spiralling off into ineffable regions in pursuit of the artist's adventure (see p. 106 above). A further link between the turn of the screw and artistic ecstasy was made on 4 January 1910, when James recorded his encounter with the ghost or good angel of his work: 'my poor blest old Genius pats me so admirably and lovingly on the back that I turn, I screw round, and bend my lips to passionately … kiss its hand' (*N*, p. 268).

The screw can therefore turn in two quite different ways. Its centripetal revolution relates to economic mastery and to the descending, contracting nature of the Jamesian 'real', with its limitations and deferrals of gratification. Its centrifugal relation is related to the explosive principle and to the ascending, expanding spiral of the 'romantic', with its polymorphous fascinations and limitless aesthetic satisfactions. So which way does the screw turn in 'The Turn of the Screw'? For the governess it can only turn centripetally. Rotation is involution, a means to overcome the text's circumvallations and get through to the inner essence of things, the core, the origin. For James, on the other hand, the screw must necessarily be turned in both ways, since the screen of the text can only be woven from double movements, its lines only drawn by the interaction of two quite separate dynamics. As the economic master, James sets out (in the words of his Preface) 'to catch those not easily caught' (*LC*, II, 1185). Having argued that 'improvisation' is compromised 'from the moment its stream breaks bounds and gets into flood', James seeks to preserve a sense of 'the course and the channel', to improvise 'without the possibility of ravage, without the hint of a flood' (p. 1184). James haunts the subtle thresholds of the text whilst the governess seems unable to prescribe the borders she wants (see pp. 130–1 above). One could argue that there is a hint of James's controlling authorial presence in the bailiff who, as Mrs Grose points out, 'writes' (*CT*, x, 100). Peter Quint and Miss Jessel are more developed representatives of James's admonitory presence. They control the expansion of the governess's desire, restrict the extension of her plots, and in this sense fulfil the standard function allotted to the ghostly from 'Travelling Companions' to *The Portrait of a Lady*.

Yet there is also a centrifugal dynamic at play within 'The Turn of the Screw'. James wants, as his Preface points out, to allow the imagination (his own and the reader's but also that of the governess) 'absolute freedom of hand' (*LC*, II, 1183). Improvising with 'extreme freedom', he invites these imaginations 'to act on a perfectly clear field, with no "outside" control involved' (pp. 1184, 1183). If Quint represents the economic master, he also acts in the interests of the explosive principle. His 'freedom' works against the governess's attempts to tighten the screws (see p. 111 above). His first appearance sends the governess 'circling about' Bly (*CT*, x, 38). Quint quite literally imparts a centrifugal motion to the governess, displacing her from the geographical centre of her narrative, driving her to the edge. Miss Jessel's final appearance – the point at which the governess finally feels her brimming cup 'overflow in a deluge' – also belongs to this explosive dynamic, leaving the governess on the far side of the lake to contemplate its other bank, the 'blank, haunted edge' occupied by Miss Jessel at the relative centre of the plot (pp. 113, 117).

At this point it might be useful to shift perspectives in order to focus more clearly the problematic dynamic relationships at work in 'The Turn of the Screw'. I have already tried to show the fullness and complexity of James's response to the figure of the Victorian governess (see pp. 153–4 above). This is of course particularly true of 'The Turn of the Screw'. The network of allusions to *Jane Eyre*; the fact that at least fifty years has passed between the events at Bly and the reading of the governess's manuscript; Douglas's reference to the governess's two interviews in Harley Street: these three elements of 'The Turn of the Screw' establish a distinctly mid-ninetenth-century cultural provenance. In spite of the tale's geographically isolated setting and its chronological non-specificity, 'The Turn of the Screw' is deeply rooted in the period of *Vanity Fair*, *Jane Eyre*, the foundation of the Governesses' Benevolent Institution and the establishment of Queen's College (both, incidentally, in Harley Street). The sheer iconographic power and ubiquity of the governess figure in this period, not to mention the calibre of the contributors to the governess debate, suggests the extent to which discussions of the governess articulated a wide range of concerns about the form, content and extent of women's education, about the role of mothers, about women's leisure and women's work, women's rights, capabilities, aspirations and desires. The 'governess question', in short, was a synecdoche for the 'woman question'. The association of governesses with disorder, crisis, inversion and revolution was often extended to women in general. Much of the writing on the 'miseries of the governess' arose from an anxious perception that, if allowed to go unchecked, these miseries might 'swell that sickening clamour about the "rights of women," which would never have been raised had women been true to themselves'.[108] Attempts to control and contain the role of the governess clearly belonged to a larger effort to limit and determine women. At the same time, the tendency to see the role of the governess in highly polarized ways was part of a broader propensity to divide women into angels or monsters, to see them in stereotypical terms as embodiments of 'extremes of mysterious and intransigent otherness which culture confronts with worship or fear, love or loathing'.[109] As I have argued in the case of the Victorian governess, these cultural extremes and polarized paradigms have to a large extent determined subsequent criticism of 'The Turn of the Screw'. I am not trying to suggest that James is in any straightforward way outside or beyond such schematizations, free from ideology. Clearly the opposition between the worldly Countess of 'Benvolio' and Scholastica, who eventually becomes a 'pale-eyed little governess', plays quite self-consciously with these polarized stereotypings of women (*CT*, III, 400). In *The Portrait of a Lady* James is in part treating Isabel in the way that Osmond treats Pansy: as 'a sheet of blank paper' for his inscriptions (*Novels 1881–1886*, p. 477). He is, as Susan Gubar asserts, reinforcing 'myths of male primacy' by figuring Isabel as a created object, a work of art, specifically one framed as a portrait.[110] Is something similar happening in 'The Turn of the Screw'? As economic master, James does seem to be encaging the governess within the text, gazing down on her from 'the best point of view' (*CT*, x, 39; see p. 108 above). Simultaneously acting as the instigator of the explosive forces in the text, he also makes the governess into a scapegoat, drives her out of her own narrative.[111] There are distinctly violent implications in both dynamics and one might well argue that James is acting on behalf of a governing order bent on the repression or expulsion of governesses as a class, or indeed of women in general. At some level, then, Jamesian economic mastery could be compared to other nineteenth-century attempts to preserve and police borders and boundaries. For Sandra Gilbert and Susan Gubar, this would place James solidly alongside turn-of-the-century authors from Haggard to Joyce who, fearing 'the possibility of women's triumph' (a possibility which in James's case reaches back to 'De Grey'), produced 'especially ferocious fantasies about female defeat'.[112]

So is the governess in 'The Turn of the Screw' another blank page to be written on, framed and converted into a text by Henry James the master? Possibly; partially. But I think that there are two important reservations to be made here. For one thing – and it is a further instance of the shifting relationships between the vital distinctions in James's work – it would seem that the explosive principle can on occasions be used to guarantee economic mastery. This results, not in James enclosing his protagonists but in his displacing or expelling them and, in a sense, imprisoning himself. I shall return to this issue later on. Secondly, and perhaps more importantly, there is a strong sense in which it is the *governess* in 'The Turn of the Screw' and not James who is committed to reading women as either angels or monsters. It is she whose melodramatic stereotyping of Miss Jessel, the dark and dishonoured predecessor, invokes turn-of-the-century (male) fantasies of the *femme fatale*; she who wants to be the pale-eyed governess and rout the worldly Countess.[113] One might of course say that James is simply projecting his own prejudices onto the governess. Yet I still think that it is the governess and not 'James' who tries to enforce the hierarchical oppositions which Hélène Cixous sees as the characteristic conceptual mode of patriarchal thought.[114] It is the governess who produces linear, penetrative readings and writings; she who zealously takes on the counter-revolutionary border-guarding duties allotted to the governess within Victorian ideology. In this sense the blanks in 'The Turn of the Screw' do not enforce a restrictive view of women so much as they defend against the restrictive readings and inscriptions of one particular woman. It is not the 'feminine' that is defeated but something which very much resembles a 'masculine' logic.

One could argue that James paradoxically channels the governess by flooding the channel of her thoughts, that he contains her by exploding her narrative. Yet even if this is the case, the dynamic balance of James's fiction has undergone a sea change, an unprecedented revolution of the screw which is not best understood by nineteenth-century paradigms of polarity. James is no longer using the uncanny or the ghostly to turn the limiting screw on the imaginative aspirations of his characters as in 'Travelling Companions', *The American*, 'The Ghostly Rental' or *The Portrait of a Lady*; nor is he depicting the ghostly as an extension of experience for the protagonist as he did in 'Sir Edmund Orme' and 'Owen Wingrave'. Instead he seems, in other ways than the one he ostensibly meant in his Preface, to have cast his lot with 'pure romance', identified himself more closely than ever before with an explosive force which works against the powerfully centripetal instincts of the governess (*LC*, II, 1187). Of course one could object that James is simply setting up the governess for a fall. Nevertheless, if he is maintaining his own authority by undermining hers, he is not doing this by implementing the hierarchical oppositions described by Cixous. Quite the reverse. Whatever authority James achieves is bought by abandoning or exposing the traditional masculinist terms of that authority, perhaps even – I recognize that this is a somewhat impertinent suggestion – by producing a writing which, 'working (in) the in-between', deploys the very fluidities and resonances which Cixous associates with feminine writing.[115] The play of forces in 'The Turn of the Screw' does not come to an end in the governess's polarizations. James's text is a charged border which resists absolutes of difference or an exclusive commitment to a simple dynamic.

The transformed arrangement of the dynamic forces in James's fiction throws some light on the nature of the subterranean allusions to previous literary works in 'The Turn of the Screw'. It is tempting to argue that these allusions – particularly those to *The Scarlet Letter* – are part of what John Carlos Rowe sees as James's continuing attempt to free himself from the legacy of American romance (see *The Theoretical Dimensions*, pp. 30–57; see also pp. 50–1 above). I have tried to show that such endeavours played an important part in early tales like 'The Romance of Certain Old Clothes', 'De Grey: A Romance' and 'The Ghostly Rental' (see pp. 52, 66–7, 70–4 above). There is a sense in which James is trying to lay the ghost of Hawthorne as late as *The Tragic Muse*, and it was only because he believed that he had succeeded in dissociating himself from the formal strategies of romance that he felt able to readmit Hawthorne as a thematic influence in 'Sir Edmund Orme', 'Owen Wingrave' and 'The Way it Came'. Even so, James's relation to Hawthorne during the 1890s continued to be a source of anxiety; he knew that to beat the ghosts was often to join them. Rowe would argue that the '"Hawthorne style"' of 'The Turn of the Screw' and *The Sacred Fount* represents a continuing recourse to the works of the great American predecessor on the part of the belated James (*The Theoretical Dimensions*, p. 57). It is certainly true that the blanks, shifts, oppositions, inversions and deviations employed in 'The Turn of the Screw' remind one of Harold Bloom's 'revisionary ratios': the swerving away from or antithetical completion of precursor texts, the use of breaking devices or defensive self-emptyings and the uncanny return of dead predecessors within the work of the later writer (*Figures of Capable Imagination*, p. 10; see also p. 11). But the function of these devices within 'The Turn of the Screw' concerns the governess rather than Hawthorne. James does not raise the ghost of his predecessor in order to overcome it but in order to haunt his protagonist, to undermine her plots, to prompt and intensify her anxieties. James is, of course, still making Hawthorne's text speak in a particular way, and to this extent he is still concerned at some level with questions of influence. Sandra Gilbert and Susan Gubar have argued persuasively that the writers of Henry James's generation were the first to have 'female precursors' (*No Man's Land*, 1, 129). For many such writers these predecessors reinforced feelings of literary belatedness and the 'anxiety about the originatory power of the father' (p. 130). In support of this view one could point to *The Portrait of a Lady*, in which the influence of George Eliot looms large (see p. 51 above) or to James's somewhat baffled musings on George Sand, or indeed, as Alfred Habegger does, to the disquieting legacy of James's American female precursors.[116] Charlotte Brontë is obviously the crucial female predecessor in the context of 'The Turn of the Screw'. Yet I do not think that the role of *Jane Eyre* in the text can entirely be described in terms of an *anxiety* of influence. In 'The Turn of the Screw', James is no longer, if indeed he ever was, simply a usurper. Despite his comments on James's 'strong misreading' of Emerson, Harold Bloom seems to indicate as much when he argues that James 'seems not to have needed to restitute a wounded narcissism as an author'.[117] I would certainly agree with Carren Kaston that, particularly in his later works, and in spite of his numerous influences, James seems to have 'got beyond resistance' (*Imagination and Desire*, p. 166). If anything it is the governess in 'The Turn of the Screw' who is the belated Oedipal figure, seeking out an imaginative space which is denied her, a contractual mastery which is repeatedly exploded. This alone distinguishes her from those female writers discussed by Gilbert and Gubar who transform, resist, or break away from male anxieties of influence (see *The Madwoman in the Attic*, pp. 47–50; *No Man's Land*, 1, 165–79). One could argue that the denial of mastery to the governess represents a calculated paternal prohibition which allows James to allay his own anxiety of being influenced by female writers. Where the governess seeks to repeat the trajectory of *Jane Eyre*, James continually swerves away from the prior text, defeating the romance which the governess models on that of Charlotte Brontë. Once again, however, as in 'The Ghostly Rental' or *The American*, to defeat romance is often to reinscribe its power at other levels. Gilbert and Gubar claim that female writers like Charlotte Brontë often constructed 'the emblematic figure of an enraged but tormented madwoman in order simultaneously to repress and express' their 'feelings of anger' (*No Man's Land*, 1, 67; see also *The Madwoman in the Attic*, p. 78). Is the governess using Miss Jessel in this way, both identifying with and revising patriarchal conceptions of women? I do not think so. The ambivalence belongs to James and it is he, not the governess, who follows Charlotte Brontë here, his text which sees resemblances between the governess and Miss Jessel where the governess herself sees only exclusive differences. Indeed, by subtly allying Miss Jessel with Jane Eyre rather than Bertha Mason (see pp. 141–2 above) James hints at the mistaken and violent nature of the governess's stereotyping. In this sense his prohibitions preserve *Jane Eyre* and his authority defends some of Charlotte Brontë's insights. 'The Turn of the Screw' creates likenesses between those who seek to repress or expel and those who are excluded or imprisoned. In order to be an 'expiatory victim', the governess must make Miss Jessel into a violator (*CT*, x, 50). This act alone does much to place the governess in the camp of the violators. The governess's subsequent attempts to establish regimented differences generate a counter-turn of likeness so that, like the governess in Victorian society at large, the governess in 'The Turn of the Screw' functions, to recall Mary Poovey's terms, as a 'conduit' rather than a 'bulwark' ('The Anathematized Race', p. 129; see p. 151 above).

This is an appropriate moment to return, not to *Jane Eyre*, but to Charlotte Brontë's comment that the private governess is 'not considered as a living rational being' (see p. 150 above). I have already looked at the Victorian fear of irrationality in governesses. But the claim that they are not even considered as *living* beings seems particularly significant in the context of 'The Turn of the Screw'. Bearing in mind the synecdochic relation between the governess and women in general, one could understand this as part of the broad tendency in patriarchal thought to define the feminine in terms of absence and non-being. The 'plots' of male writers, as Susan Gubar puns, can often be places in which to bury female protagonists ('"The Blank Page"', p. 254). It may well be the lifeless domestic existence of the governess which leads Bea Howe repeatedly to refer to her in ghostly terms.[118] There was certainly an awareness in nineteenth-century society that, when acting as a conduit rather than a bulwark, the governess might be involved in spreading superstitions or ghostly tales rather than censoring or bowdlerizing them.[119] I think, however, that for a richer account of the rationale which underlies and makes possible Charlotte Brontë's observation one could go back to Victor Turner's Ndembu neophytes, 'neither living nor dead from one aspect, and both living and dead from another' ('Betwixt and Between', pp. 96–7; see p. 20 above). Not only were women in general and governesses in particular associated with misrule, monstrous inversion and numerous other departures from or threats to patriarchal order, they could also be associated with the uncanny and ghostly aspects of the liminal predicament. Indeed, the two associations may coincide. In *No Man's Land*, Gilbert and Gubar reproduce a poster by David Wilson depicting the vast and shadowy form of a woman hovering in the skies above the Houses of Parliament. The woman is holding a leaflet inscribed 'Votes for Women' and the title of the poster is 'The Haunted House' (see *No Man's Land*, I, 77).

James's ghosts had always been infectious figures; time and again they had converted ghost seers into ghosts. 'You see a man who has seen a ghost!', proclaims the jubilant Clement Searle in 'A Passionate Pilgrim' (*CT*, II, 287). Yet the narrator will always feel 'that I, too, have seen a ghost' and Searle has himself already exclaimed that 'I *am* a ghost!' (pp. 287, 272). Hovering around Captain Diamond's house, the narrator of 'The Ghostly Rental' feels 'very much like a restless ghost myself' (*CT*, IV, 68). In 'Sir Edmund Orme', Mrs Marden's 'white face' leads the narrator to think for a second that she is 'an apparition' (*CT*, VIII, 125). James's stage directions for *The Saloon* emphasize that Owen Wingrave should present 'a startling apparitional effect'.[120] In 'The Third Person', the ghost of Cuthbert Frush converts Susan and Amy Frush, his living witnesses, into 'wandering ghosts' (*CT*, xi, 153). By embroidering the 'strange and sinister' on the 'normal and easy' (*LC*, ii, 1264), James discovered that the strange often led back to ancient stories, hushed family secrets, originary traumas – things 'known of old and long familiar', to use Freud's expression (*SE*, xvii, 220). Unlike Freud, however, James knew that this relation was a circular one and that the normal was itself often strange. 'The Turn of the Screw' is his most developed dramatization of this rotation, and the tale makes it clear that there is no just measure, no impermeable border between the dead and the living, between the familiar and the unfamiliar. Such categories fuse in a characteristically uncanny way even in the name 'Quint', which suggests both the odd, the quaint, and also the 'queynte' – the place which Freud in 'The "Uncanny"' describes as 'the entrance to the former *Heim* [home] of all human beings' (p. 245).[121] Quint is certainly a strangely familiar presence, and the governess feels that it is 'as if I had been looking at him for years and had known him always' (*CT*, x, 42). She is 'inexplicably' but also 'intimately' connected with the master's dead servant (p. 39). 'Hideous' and simultaneously 'human', Quint is a 'detestable, dangerous presence' but also a 'living' one (p. 71).

If the dead resemble the living, then the living may also resemble the dead. The governess, Mrs Grose and Miles repeatedly display white faces which resemble the 'pale face' of Quint and the 'pale and dreadful' countenance of Miss Jessel (pp. 46, 57; see also pp. 43, 44, 133, 134). The living characters at Bly are connected to the dead in a ring of hatlessness which begins with Quint and extends to Flora, Mrs Grose and the governess (see pp. 46, 108–9, 113).[122] Miss Jessel too is 'always without' a hat, and although Miles does pick up his hat in the final scene he is never to put it on (p. 108; see p. 132). Hawthorne had examined the difference between humanity and monsters, concluding that those who commit the unpardonable sin of detecting the monstrous in others themselves take on a degree of monstrosity. James shifts his predecessor's inquiry to the problem of the difference between people and ghosts. In 'The Turn of the Screw' he concludes that there is something spectral about the spectator, something haunting about the haunted and something appalling about the appalled. Doubting 'if even *I* were in life', the governess cannot separate herself or others from the dead (p. 71).

On a number of occasions the governess quite literally stands in the place of the ghosts. By taking over Quint's position outside the dining-room window, she replicates the effect of a ghost, giving Mrs Grose 'something of the shock that I had received' (p. 43). The governess tells Mrs Grose that she saw Quint 'as I see you', that Miss Jessel 'might have been as close as you' and that Flora sees Miss Jessel 'even as I actually saw Mrs Grose herself' (pp. 46, 57, 62). She accuses Flora of being able to see Miss Jessel 'as well as you see me' (p. 114). Spectral experience initiates a play of reflections in which Mrs Grose stares into the eyes of the governess 'as if they might really have resembled' those of Miss Jessel and the governess gazes back into the eyes of the housekeeper as if, within them, 'Miss Jessel had again appeared' (pp. 58, 60). These mirrorings are the greatest threat to the governess's attempt to distinguish herself from the predecessor who was 'almost as young and almost as pretty' as herself (p. 30). Even if one leaves aside the alliance between the two governesses suggested by the ghostly echoes of *Amelia*, *Jane Eyre* and *The Scarlet Letter*, the resemblances between the governess and Miss Jessel are established at numerous other points.[123] The governess collapses on the stairs (see p. 96) in the same place and posture as Miss Jessel on her second appearance (see p. 74). She covers her face with her hands (see p. 88) exactly as Miss Jessel does on both her second and third appearances (see pp. 74, 97).

To see a ghost is to become a ghost. But 'The Turn of the Screw' gives a further twist to this insight. To see a ghost is also to become what one thinks ghosts are. Requiring a counterweight to found her own being and her own desire, the governess sees the apparitions in her image and then becomes the image of a ghost. She shares a 'common intensity' with Quint and in her 'fierce rigour of confidence' haunts Bly with something like the 'fury of intention' she attributes to Miss Jessel (pp. 71, 58). I have already examined some of the reasons for and implications of the Jamesian frame (see pp. 94–7 above). Yet perhaps the most significant effect of the device, certainly in 'Sir Edmund Orme', 'The Way it Came' and 'The Turn of the Screw', is that it establishes the fact that the narrator is dead. Both a violator and a victim of the turns in meaning, the governess speaks in her narrative as a voice from beyond the grave, from what Maurice Blanchot has called 'the imprecise space of narration – that unreal beyond where everything is apparition, slippery, evasive, present and absent'.[124]

CHAPTER 4

The haunted chamber

THE GHOST AT THE WINDOW

In the Victorian mind the figure of the governess repeatedly signalled uncertainty and potential catastrophe. Governesses dissemi-
nated the tenor of crisis and were often the vehicle of social, sexual or
linguistic disasters. One of the finer insights in 'The Turn of the
Screw' is the relation that James establishes between the governess
and the ghosts: both haunt the margins and are intimately associated with categorial anxieties. In spite of herself, the governess acts
as a medium of exchange, crossing borders and enabling borders to
be crossed. As a ghost seer and as the narrator of ghostly experiences,
she herself becomes an apparitional figure. At a more general level
one could argue that the writer of this ghostly narrator also endows
himself with a degree of spectrality, hovers near thresholds as a
mediatory, interstitial, half-glimpsed presence. Shoshana Felman
sees the writer of 'The Turn of the Screw' as a 'phantom master' or
'Master-Ghost' ('Turning the Screw of Interpretation', p. 206).
Neither providing nor claiming to possess the supreme key to
meaning either in the text or in his evasive comments about it
elsewhere, James establishes his mastery by disappearing from the
scene, leaving in his wake eddies of unfixable significance. For
Felman, James's ghostliness is that of the disappearing uncle in the
tale (see pp. 203–7). Yet ghosts are apparitions, not simply absences;
there is a rather more specific sense in which James could figuratively be linked to Peter Quint, the ghost who wears the master's
clothes (see pp. 107–8 above). Like Gilbert Osmond in *The Portrait of
a Lady*, Quint springs from the competitive rather than the collaborative phase of James's engagement with the centre of consciousness.
Unlike *The Portrait of a Lady*, however, the James of 'The Turn of the
Screw' seems to have altered the dynamic balance of the competitive

encounter. He haunts the text not only to restrain but also to counter restriction, not only to patrol the edge of the text but also to push outwards from the centre.

Like the governess in 'The Turn of the Screw', the telegraphist of 'In the Cage' (1898) is a borderline figure, a medium for the passage of messages. At one point she experiences 'a triumphant, vicious feeling of mastery and power' which recalls the governess's claim 'to have mastered it, to see it all' (*CT*, x, 154, 124). If James is to maintain his new investment in the centrifugal, one might expect that some form of explosively uncanny experience will challenge the telegraphist's sense of mastery, displacing her from the centre as in 'The Turn of the Screw'. In fact, however, the dynamics of 'In the Cage' are rather different from those of 'The Turn of the Screw'. Although she leads her life in 'framed and wired confinement', the telegraphist is granted a 'queer extension of... experience' (pp. 139, 152). Indeed, her literal confinement is to a large extent the condition of her extension. In the cage, fantastic fictions lurk in the numberless words which pass through her hands, two of them – 'Orme' and 'Haddon' – fragmentarily recalling other positively privileging ghostly encounters in James (p. 145). Setting out on the ' "subjective" adventure' (it is of the telegraphist that James used this expression in the Preface to volume xi of the *New York Edition*), she achieves through Captain Everard a vision of 'the unattainable plains of heaven' (*LC*, ii, 1170; *CT*, x, 180). In his Preface James described how 'In the Cage' had developed from his speculations about the 'range of experience' vicariously opened up to the staff at his local Post Office, the 'haunt of one's needs and one's duties' (*LC*, ii, 1168). This autobiographical anecdote leads Ralf Norrman to argue that 'Henry James ... was the model for the Olympian Hero, Captain Everard'.[1] Norrman's argument is too literal, but it would not be inaccurate to say that Everard models or stands in for a Jamesian presence. He certainly permits the telegraphist to glimpse if not to reach some celestial realm. In the Preface to *The American*, a similar kingdom is occupied by the writer, the sole subject of 'an intenser experience ... like that enjoyed on the flowery plains of heaven' (*LC*, ii, 1063). At one point of the tale in particular, the telegraphist seems almost to meet her maker:

She saw, straight before her, like a vista painted in a picture, the empty street and the lamps that burned pale in the dusk not yet established. It was into the convenience of this quiet twilight that a gentleman on the doorstep of the Chambers gazed with a vagueness that our young lady's little figure violently trembled, in the approach, with the measure of its power to dissipate. Everything indeed grew in a flash terrific and distinct; her old uncertainties fell away from her, and, since she was so familiar with fate, she felt as if the very nail that fixed it were driven in by the hard look with which, for a moment, Captain Everard awaited her. (*CT*, x, 185–6)

Everard's 'hard look' is shortly replaced by 'the pleasantest laugh' (p. 187), a laugh which recalls the fraternal smile of Ralph Touchett (see p. 82 above). In 'The Turn of the Screw', on the other hand, the governess finds that her fantasy of the master's approving smile is destroyed by the apparition of Quint, who fixes her with a 'hard' and unwavering gaze (*CT*, x, 37). The telegraphist's encounter with Everard produces feelings of certainty rather than bewilderment. The sense of the deathly felt in 'The Turn of the Screw' is replaced during the summer's twilight walk of the telegraphist by 'infinite possibilities', a rich 'perfection' (*CT*, x, 186). The populated perspective of the telegraphist is quite different to the 'vista without a human figure' which Newman gazes along in the last chapter of *The American* (*Novels 1871–1880* p. 867). In its hallucinatory quality, the scene looks back to the final chapter of *Watch and Ward*, in which Nora Lambert sees her guardian walking towards her 'down the bright vista of the street' and feels as if she has been given 'a dose of ether' (*Novels 1871–1880*, p. 159). But is Everard as benign an authority figure as Roger Lawrence? Does he offer the telegraphist 'another world, another consciousness, an experience that, as effective as the dentist's ether, muffles the ache of the actual' as novelists do for their readers according to one of James's 'London Notes' (July 1897) for *Harper's Weekly* (*LC*, 1, 1400)? The telegraphist's predicament is surely a more precarious one than that of the happily anaesthetized reader. To be literally outside the cage may well be to find the subjective extension under threat. The telegraphist's experience is a 'positive creation', but perhaps only of a 'dream' (p. 186). It is 'charming', to recall the governess's expression, but perhaps only a 'charming story' (*CT*, x, 35). Fixed by a nail if not a screw, the subject of violent emotion, the telegraphist's experience is already close to terror. Her meeting with Everard produces not only 'a fatal great rush' and 'a flood of tears' which overflow the confines of her day-dreams, making what she has 'imagined' become 'dreadful and overwhelming', but also, and increasingly, an uncanny movement of contraction (*CT*, x, 191).

Wonder gives way to dread and a sense of danger, the dream turns to nightmare, and the telegraphist's imaginative extension begins to fail. Standing on the threshold of his chambers, Captain Everard seems to prevent any closer approach to the writer's room, to guarantee James's unchallenged occupation of the 'plains of heaven'. Far from sponsoring the expansion of the telegraphist's experience, Everard becomes an uncanny delegate of the economic master, changes allegiance from the side of Ralph Touchett to that of Gilbert Osmond, who blocks Isabel's attempts to reach the 'high places of happiness' (*Novels 1881–1886*, p. 629). Having subjectively escaped from her cage, the telegraphist must now return: 'to be in the cage had suddenly become her safety, and she was literally afraid of the alternate self who might be waiting outside. *He* might be waiting; it was he who was her alternate self, and of him she was afraid' (pp. 213–14). Whilst the governess in 'The Turn of the Screw' is driven out towards or beyond the edge, the telegraphist willingly retreats into the sort of enclosure once occupied by Isabel Archer, guarded and haunted by a defying and defining figure who ensures – to recall the Preface to *The Princess Casamassima* – her 'proper fusion with the fable' and denies her 'the superior nature of the all-knowing immortals' (*LC*, ii, 1095, 1090).

The use of the uncanny in 'In the Cage' therefore seems to represent a qualified return to the strategies of texts like 'Travelling Companions', *The American* and *The Portrait of a Lady*. By the time of *The Sacred Fount*, however, James appears to have performed another revolution of the screw. The imaginative consciousness achieved by the narrator during his evening walk approaches magical omnipotence (see p. 106 above). Whether the narrator represents the restrictive dynamic of an Osmond or the explosive force invested in Quint it remains true that he, like them, is the interceding gazer and not, like the governess or the telegraphist, the subject of another interrupting vision. Mrs Server may be 'the haunting principle' of his thought but he is the haunting, hovering, circling presence (*The Sacred Fount*, p. 97). Fewer restrictions are placed on the narrator's ability to satisfy the requirements of his imagination than in any other of James's novels. Unlike Christopher Newman or Isabel Archer, he never comes up against the dead wall of finitude and failure. Instead, he is 'overtaken by a mild artistic glow' and feels 'as inhumanly amused as if one had found one could create something' (p. 81). This amusement strongly reminds one of Osmond's callous mockery but it also recalls the governess's fantasy of the smiling uncle and the dreamlike presence of Captain Everard with his pleasant laugh. Whether engaged in a competitive or collaborative relationship with the other characters at Newmarch, the narrator's 'wizardry' (p. 97), his belief in his 'intellectual mastery' and his ecstatic feeling that he is capable of 'determining, almost ... creating results' closely allies him with the figure of the writer (p. 151).[2]

In 'Is There a Life After Death?' (1910), James described how the 'man of imagination' carried 'the field of consciousness further and further, making it lose itself in the ineffable' (pp. 224, 223). The man of imagination possessed 'the artistic consciousness and privilege' which shone 'as from immersion in the fountain of being' (p. 228). Despite the dangers he faces and the sacrifices he makes (see pp. 228–31 below), the narrator of *The Sacred Fount* is immersed in (or at least sprinkled by) this fountain and stands as James's closest fictional approximation to the creative consciousness. In his Preface to *The Ambassadors*, published two years before 'Is There a Life after Death?', James had remembered thrilling at the immeasurable opportunity 'to "do" a man of imagination' (*LC*, II, 1307). Unlike the telegraphist or the governess, neither Strether nor the narrator of *The Sacred Fount* rely on a single figure such as the master or Captain Everard for their experiential extension: both live their imaginative lives through everybody they meet. Nevertheless, Strether's imagination is, according to James's Preface, strictly 'comparative'; it does not enjoy '*supreme* command' (p. 1307). The relation between *The Sacred Fount* and *The Ambassadors* is therefore somewhat analogous to the relation between 'The Turn of the Screw' and 'In the Cage'. In each case the later text in some respects retrenches on the advances made by the earlier, re-emphasizes the importance of form and enclosure. Unlike the man of supreme imagination, the field of whose consciousness expands until it loses itself in the ineffable, Strether is, as the Preface announces, 'encaged' within the text (p. 1316). He cannot have 'the romantic privilege of the "first person" ' since in 'the long piece' this is 'a form foredoomed to looseness' and 'terrible *fluidity*' (pp. 1315–16). Strether knows that experience has a Coleridgean looseness and that he has been floating through measureless 'caverns of Kubla Khan' (*NYE*, XXII, 293). Yet he is also partially aware of the restrictions imposed upon him by his creator; life is for him 'a tin mould' which contains the 'helpless jelly' of consciousness (*NYE*, XXI, 218). Enclosed by the real, Strether must additionally resign himself to the exigencies of artistic form, of literary moulds. These creative strictures reveal themselves most explicitly in the river scene towards the end of the novel, during which Strether experiences 'a sharp fantastic crisis that had popped up as if in a dream' (*NYE*, XXII, 257–8):

> What he saw was exactly the right thing – a boat advancing round the bend and containing a man who held the paddles and a lady, at the stern, with a pink parasol. It was suddenly as if these figures, or something like them, had been wanted in the picture, had been wanted more or less all day, and had now drifted into sight, with the slow current, on purpose to fill up the measure ... The air quite thickened, at their approach, with further intimations; the intimation that they were expert, familiar, frequent – that this would n't at all events be the first time. They knew how to do it, he vaguely felt – and it made them but the more idyllic, though at the very moment of the impression, as happened, their boat seemed to have begun to drift wide, the oarsman letting it go. It had by this time none the less come much nearer – near enough for Strether to dream the lady in the stern had for some reason taken account of his being there to watch them. (*NYE*, XXII, 256–7)

In her analysis of this scene Ruth Bernard Yeazell detects forces which recall those at work in the Freudian uncanny. Through 'the inevitable surfacing of suppressed facts', Strether joins other characters in James's later work who must 'confront what in some part of themselves they have long since known'.[3] The river scene is the moment, beyond all others in *The Ambassadors*, when Strether becomes intensely aware that his imagination is not in supreme command, that he is not the author of his own experience. During his outing he has felt a rising sense of creative control as he realizes the Lambinet painting seen long ago in a Boston art dealer's, enters 'a land of fancy' which as yet he has only been able to appreciate 'through the little oblong window of the picture-frame' (*NYE*, XXII, 245). Strether's experience is 'mild enough' but it is nevertheless a 'romance' (p. 245). For a few hours the objects of his perception become entirely tractable, meeting and satisfying the requirements of his imagination. He has 'the sense of success, of a finer harmony in things' (p. 248). Everything is turning out 'according to his plan' and each new scene unfolds with 'a kind of inevitability' (pp. 248, 253). The culmination of Strether's adventure comes towards evening when he reaches an inn, orders a meal and, waiting in 'a small and primitive pavilion ... at the garden's edge', gazes along the river (p. 255). He sees 'exactly the right thing', and at this point the last element in the picture, the one that has been wanting all day, seems finally to have fallen into place (p. 256). Up to this moment, Strether's experience would seem to be running along lines similar to those recorded by the narrator of *The Sacred Fount* or the James of the Haddon Hall episode. Yet the boat which ministers to Strether's 'full impression' also gives him 'a sharper arrest' (p. 255). It contains Chadwick Newsome and Madame de Vionnet who, in the thickening air of Strether's intimations, seem more palpably and more intimately connected than he has been prepared to admit. Strether's crisis involves the realization that, however right he may have been in spirit, whatever his discretion and his tact, he has been wrong in fact. Little Bilham had classified the relation between Chad and Madame de Vionnet as a 'virtuous attachment' (*NYE*, XXI, 180). It now seems that this formula, to which Strether has clung throughout the novel, is 'simply a *lie*' or at best, as he later puts it to Maria Gostrey, 'a technical lie' (*NYE*, XXII, 262, 299). Strether conjures up the lovers' boat just as the narrator of *The Sacred Fount* evokes May Server. Yet in the earlier novel the meeting in the wood is the crowning triumph of the narrator's consciousness, the confirmation of his theory. For Strether, in contrast, the boat draws nearer only (like the theory of the virtuous attachment) to 'drift wide' (p. 256). Having become the object of an awareness on the part of others, Strether resembles the telegraphist or the governess more closely than the narrator of *The Sacred Fount*: just as the telegraphist's personal 'vista' suddenly becomes inhabited by Everard's gaze, so Strether's picture sends out a returning glance, an uncanny challenge to his own perspective (*CT*, X, 186). Madame de Vionnet and Chad seem suggestively to echo the eloping lovers mentioned in the Haddon Hall passage of *Transatlantic Sketches* (see p. 108 above). Strether is not another James since his experience is 'quite horrible', yet he does not respond to crisis and transgression with the centripetal single-mindedness of the governess in 'The Turn of the Screw': Chad remains, in however qualified or ironic a fashion, the 'hero of the idyll' (*NYE*, XXII, 258, 257). Although Strether's appreciation of the twilight scene does not entirely fade, there is nevertheless a distinct sense in which he has reached the limit of his possibility. His imagination must come to terms with the real, the actual, the familiar, the frequent. One could argue that James is engaged in the literary framing of Strether. Having felt during his outing that he has 'not once overstepped the oblong gilt frame' and that everything is 'a syllable of the text', even Strether's nearest approach to creative control never threatens the margins of literary form (pp. 252, 254). The gilded cage of art is a more ample space than the framed and wired enclosure of the telegraphist. Nevertheless, the James of *The Ambassadors*, unlike the James of *The Sacred Fount*, does seem to have partially revived the strategies of control so evident in *The Portrait of a Lady* or 'In the Cage'. Collaboration gives way to competition, extension to restriction. Although he is more conscious than Isabel of the illusory nature of freedom and less floored than the telegraphist by the unattainability of the 'plains of heaven', Strether would on this reading ultimately become another victim of the economic master. His first two names, borrowed from Balzac's 'Louis Lambert', imply not only that he is in some sense an *alter ego* of the author but also that his imaginative activity may lead to madness and incarceration.[4]

Strether's crisis on the river is an experience which borders on the uncanny but it would be easy to argue that he has not, at least on the surface, had an encounter with the ghostly representative of the writer, whether hostile or benign, admonitory or encouraging. I shall try to show later that this is not strictly true and that there are indeed echoes of a haunting Jamesian presence in the river episode (see pp. 236–9 below). This presence has in any case been registered at an earlier stage of the novel. Shortly after arriving in Paris, Strether has been taken by Chad to a garden-party held by the sculptor Gloriani:

The place itself was a great impression – a small pavilion, clear-faced and sequestered, an effect of polished parquet, of fine white panel and spare sallow gilt, of decoration delicate and rare, in the heart of the Faubourg Saint-Germain and on the edge of a cluster of gardens attached to old noble houses. Far back from streets and unsuspected by crowds, reached by a long passage and a quiet court, it was as striking to the unprepared mind, he immediately saw, as a treasure dug up; giving him too, more than anything yet, the note of the range of the immeasurable town and sweeping away, as by a last brave brush, his usual landmarks and terms. It was in the garden, a spacious cherished remnant, out of which a dozen persons had already passed, that Chad's host presently met them; while the tall bird-haunted trees, all of a twitter with the spring and the weather, and the high party-walls, on the other side of which grave *hôtels* stood off for privacy, spoke of survival, transmission, association, a strong indifferent persistent order ... Strether had presently the sense of a great convent ... a nursery of young priests ... of names in the air, of ghosts at the windows, of signs and tokens, a whole range of expression, all about him, too thick for prompt discrimination. (*NYE*, xxi, 195–6)

As the setting for Strether's 'live all you can' speech (p. 217), Gloriani's garden is, as James puts it in his Preface, 'planted or "sunk," stiffly and saliently, in the centre of the current' (*LC*, ii, 1304). The structural centre also coincides with the imaginative origin of the novel. In a notebook entry of 31 October 1895 James had recorded Jonathan Sturges's anecdote about William Dean Howells's advice to 'live all you can' (*N*, p. 141).[5] James claimed in his Preface that he had 'nipped the thread of connexion' between Strether and Howells, yet here in Gloriani's Faubourg Saint-Germain garden, Strether stands in the footsteps of his living model, transmitting the words once spoken by Howells in Whistler's garden in the Rue de Bac (*LC*, ii, 1307). One could number Whistler, Howells and Sturges as attendant spirits at this scene, hovering 'names', 'signs' and 'tokens' (*NYE*, xxi, 196). Yet it is the 'ghosts at the windows' who are the most arresting presences in Gloriani's garden (p. 196). Leon Edel has argued convincingly that James is himself one of these ghosts.[6] James had been a visitor at Madame Mohl's house in the Rue de Bac whilst in Paris during 1875–6; almost twenty years later – two years before Sturges told him the story about Howells – he had been one of Whistler's guests.[7] Protected by high walls, long passages and quiet courts, Gloriani's pavilion stands close to the centre of the labyrinth which is both Paris and the novel itself.[8] The pavilion stands 'on the edge of a cluster of gardens' which are 'attached to old noble houses' (*NYE*, xxi, 195). It is at the windows of these houses, in the dead centre of the novel, that the ghosts gather. One could argue that the Preface to *The Portrait of a Lady* uses this scene from *The Ambassadors* to provide an image of the position occupied by 'the consciousness of the artist' in its 'boundless freedom' (*LC*, ii, 1075). This consciousness is described as a 'watcher' at a window, a 'posted presence', a figure 'perched aloft' within 'the house of fiction' (p. 1075). In *The Ambassadors*, more definitively than in any of James's previous works except perhaps for 'The Private Life' or 'The Real Right Thing', the writer is imaged as a spectral spectator. More explicitly than ever before, the house of fiction has become a haunted place. The house and its ghosts had already been explored and encountered in such tales as 'The Romance of Certain Old Clothes', 'The Ghostly Rental' and 'Owen Wingrave'. There were distinct indications of

James's investment in ghostly or semi-ghostly figures like Gilbert Osmond, Ralph Touchett, Peter Quint and Captain Everard. The proximity between the ghost at the window and the seminary for young priests further recalls the final scene of *The American* in which Newman comes to a halt outside the convent in the Rue d'Enfer whilst James emblematically turns his back on his protagonist. In both *The American* and *The Ambassadors*, the house of fiction emerges as a sacred place. It is significant that James compares Flaubert to a 'Benedictine' in an 1893 review of his letters and speaks of his 'monastic cell' at Croisset in the 1902 introduction to *Madame Bovary* (*LC*, II, 308, 318). In a 1902 introduction to *The Two Young Brides*, Balzac too becomes 'a Benedictine of the actual' and in 'The Lesson of Balzac' (1905) he is further described as 'a Benedictine monk leading his life within the four walls of his convent' (*LC*, II, 93, 128).

Yet the ghost at the window in *The Ambassadors* is a more finely balanced presence than any of the previous apparitions. Standing at the centre of the maze, James guards the 'treasure' which strikes the 'unprepared mind' of Strether, but he also generously offers it to his protagonist as something already 'dug up' (*NYE*, XXI, 195). He erects 'high party-walls' and establishes the formal moulds of which Strether is shortly to speak, but he also fills the vessel and enriches the jelly of his protagonist's consciousness (p. 195). He implicitly associates himself with a 'strong ... persistent order' but also transmits to Strether 'a whole range of expression' (pp. 195, 196). The ghost at the window is simultaneously and even-handedly acting in the interests of economic mastery and of the explosive principle. It occupies the tensional and fusional intersection of the governing dynamics of Jamesian fiction without finally committing itself to a deviation in one direction or the other. Indeed, the ghost is in a certain sense 'indifferent': witnessing Strether rather than immobilizing or displacing him (p. 195). The ghost does not turn its back like Quint and, although 'the great artist' Gloriani is soon to show a 'charming smile', displays neither the intimately collaborative, fraternal smile of Ralph Touchett or the master in 'The Turn of the Screw' nor the mocking face of Gilbert Osmond (pp. 196, 197).

AN UNCANNY EDUCATION

Despite its refusal to curse or bless, the ghost at the window does retain the detachment which makes irony possible. Gloriani's pavilion – 'small' but 'polished', 'delicate and rare' – stands for

elaborate and expansive possibilities (p. 195). In the closing stages of
the novel, however, Strether finds himself entering a second and
more personal pavilion by the edge of the river. This structure –
'small' but 'primitive' and 'somewhat battered' – is an appropriate
stage for his recognition of limits (_NYE_, xxii, 255). Nevertheless, the
second pavilion does not present Strether with the dead wall which
both Isabel Archer and Christopher Newman come up against.
Indeed, the uncanny experiences in both pavilions serve an educa-
tive rather than punitive function, educing rather than restraining
Strether, drawing him out and drawing him on. In Gloriani's
garden he feels his 'usual landmarks' swept away; the atmosphere is
'too thick for prompt discrimination' (_NYE_, xxi, 195, 196). This
hesitation about making distinctions is itself part of a learning
process, since for much of the earlier part of the novel Strether is
occupied almost exclusively in noticing and accounting for contrasts. The 'difference' of Europe is 'much greater than he had
dreamed it would be' (p. 81). The first of the three uses of the word
'uncanny' in _The Ambassadors_ is closely connected to the problem of
evaluating such differences. When the door of the box at the
Français opens, Strether sees 'a gentleman, a stranger' (p. 135). He
is bewildered to discover that this alien figure is actually Chad and
later tells Maria that he has only his 'modest human means', adding
(at least in the revised version of the text) that 'it is n't playing the
game to turn on the uncanny' (p. 167).[9] The uncanniness of
Strether's experience lies in his perception of complete difference,
the 'sharp rupture of an identity', 'a case of transformation unsur-
passed' (p. 137). Everything seems 'totally different' (p. 149).
Chad's metamorphosis cannot easily be accounted for within the set
terms of Woollett, for whom Chad is, as Maria puts it, 'a young man
a wicked woman has got hold of' (p. 54). Chad's 'striking' air of
'good confidence' (p. 135), his deprecatory greeting, his discreet
patience: all these things suggest that there may be something in
Maria's earlier enquiry as to whether Woollett is sure that the
wicked woman is 'very bad' for Chad (p. 54). 'Of course we are',
responds Strether, who continues for some time to uphold Woollett's
view of 'the fundamental impropriety of Chad's situation', the
general 'badness' of the whole predicament and the possibility that
Chad is 'what shall I say? – monstrous' (pp. 54, 116, 117, 134).
Strether's mission lies in 'separating' Chad from the wicked woman,
making him 'break with everything' (pp. 54, 147). He has arrived in

Europe to bring an improper liaison to an end, to reimpose the values of Woollett, its categorial boundaries and distinctions. In some ways this conceptual logic, with its static absolutism, its Manichean oppositions ('perdition on one side, salvation on the other' as James summarized it in the Project for *The Ambassadors* which he submitted to Harper and Brothers in 1900), its reliance on the imagination of what Chad calls 'horrors', distinctly recalls that of the governess in 'The Turn of the Screw' (*N*, p. 551; *NYE*, xxi, 156). At this stage Strether, like the governess, tries to screen Chad from evil influences. Unlike the governess, however, with her world of angels and demons, Strether recognizes that he has entered a continent where finer gradations apply. Like the London theatre, Europe is 'a world of types' and Strether realizes that it is '"types" he should have to tackle' (p. 53). In Woollett the types are limited to 'the male and the female', with their individual varieties (p. 53). Men and women in Europe have the same 'personal and ... sexual range' but they also show the impress of 'a series of strong stamps ... applied, as it were, from without' (p. 53). Strether needs rapidly to acquire a language, to 'find names' capable of defining these typed denizens of the European scene (p. 49). He is assisted in this task by the easy eclecticism of Maria Gostrey, who strikes him as 'the mistress of a hundred cases or categories, receptacles of the mind, subdivisions for convenience, in which, from a full experience, she pigeon-holed her fellow-mortals with a hand as free as that of a compositor scattering type' (p. 11). With its manifold categories and subdivisions, Maria's logic challenges the dualism of Woollett, offering Strether a more flexible and plural way of apprehending the shaded and many-sided nature of European experience. To some extent his adoption of the notion of type already represents, at least in the eyes of Waymarsh, a betrayal of Woollett's values. Waymarsh sees Maria as 'a Jesuit in petticoats, a representative of the recruiting interests of the Catholic Church' (p. 41). For him the Catholic Church is 'the enemy, the monster of bulging eyes and far-reaching quivering groping tentacles' (p. 41). It is also 'society ... the multiplication of shibboleths ... the discrimination of types and tones ... in short Europe' (p. 41). For Waymarsh the very act of discriminating amongst types (and Maria is capable of making 'discriminations about a pair of gloves') is quintessentially European (p. 41). To multiply one's categories is to enter the enemy's camp, to be gripped by the tentacles of the European monster. Yet when, some time

later, Strether classifies Chad's uncanny transformation as 'a
miracle almost monstrous', he significantly departs from Waymarsh's inclusive dismissal of Europe (p. 167). Indeed, the recognition that the monstrous may actually be miraculous will eventually
make Strether himself seem 'monstrous' to Woollett (*NYE*, xxii,
201). Strether is particularly struck by Chad's grey hair, which to
him suggests 'refinement' (*NYE*, xxi, 140). This evaluation reveals
the extent to which he has already been drawn on by Maria's
discriminatory pigeon-holes and made a choice between the 'two
quite distinct things' which she suggests might have happened to
Chad: 'one is that he may have got brutalised. The other is that he
may have got refined' (p. 69). To some extent Maria's pairing of
alternative possibilities resembles the oppositional logic of Woollett.
Yet her categories open the way to more subtle, more surprising and
more challenging conclusions.

Throughout the first half of *The Ambassadors*, Strether rapidly
acquires a comparatively flexible and plural categorial logic. He
finds names to label Chad's transformation, to circumscribe the
miraculous in terms of type. The idea that Chad has become 'a man
of the world' is one 'formula' that comes 'in some degree to his relief'
(p. 152). The possibility that Chad is a 'Pagan' is another 'name'
gratefully 'seized' (pp. 156–7). The formula of the 'virtuous attachment' temporarily gives Strether 'almost a new lease of life' (p. 180).
He has been 'in search of the "word"' to describe Chad's 'change'
and at least Little Bilham's phrase seems to fit the 'confirmed
appearances' (p. 182). To have the right word is to have achieved a
certain mastery over the object. Little Bilham compares the transformed Chad to 'the new edition of an old book ... revised and
amended' (p. 177). Strether is not the author of Chad's text; indeed,
in spite of his occupation he must still ask 'who's the editor?' (p.
178). But he has at least, through his education in pigeon-holes and
subdivisions, achieved the status of a compositor in tolerably full
possession of the letters which make up the European text. By the
time of his encounter with the ghost at the window, Strether is
scattering type with as free a hand, if not so full an experience, as
Maria Gostrey. Gloriani affects him as 'a dazzling prodigy of type'
(p. 196). The garden-party in the Faubourg Saint-Germain is full of
'types tremendously alien, alien to Woollett' (p. 199). According to
Little Bilham, the guests comprise 'all sorts and sizes': ambassadors,
cabinet ministers, bankers, generals and 'even Jews' (p. 199).

Keenly discriminating *between* rather than against, Strether is fascinated by this multiplicity. If he is still hunting for monsters, however, his search may not be rewarded: Gloriani will sometimes invite 'an actress, an artist, a great performer – but only when they're not monsters' (p. 199).

Plenty of types but no monsters. To multiply labels and categories is a matter of 'convenience' for Maria Gostrey but for Strether it is an urgent necessity (p. 11). The danger of relying so heavily on the logic of types to give one new leases of life lies in a tendency to reduce the world to uselessly atomized and static particularity. If everything is different from everything else – if Chad is different even from himself – then consciousness becomes the apprehension of unalleviated alterity. Referring to the fact that Strether finds himself 'up to his middle in the Difference – difference from what he expected, difference in Chad, difference in everything', James wrote in his Project for *The Ambassadors* that 'nothing is manageable, nothing final – nothing, above all, for poor Strether, natural ... he has almost a sense of the uncanny' (*N*, pp. 562, 561).

This sense of the uncanny belongs not only to Strether's education in differences but also to his increasing awareness of resemblances. The ghost at the window hints at a 'range of expression ... too thick for prompt discrimination (*NYE*, xxi, 196). The very multiplicity of 'signs and tokens' in Gloriani's garden seems to make things less rather than more distinct: the more categories there are, the smaller are the crucial differences (p. 196). Pushed beyond a certain point difference becomes so generalized that it promotes identity, and the logic of type becomes a matter of fusions as well as tensions, of mergings as well as differentiations. The second use of the word 'uncanny' in *The Ambassadors* is closely connected to Strether's developing perception of resemblances. His first glimpse of Sarah Pocock at the railway station gives Strether 'a brief but vivid accent to her resemblance to her mother' (*NYE*, xxii, 73). Strether subsequently reflects that 'the immense, the uncanny part' of Sarah's resemblance to Mrs Newsome had been produced 'without her having so much as mentioned that lady' (p. 114). Strether first encountered Chad as a stranger who bore 'no resemblance' to Mrs Newsome (*NYE*, xxi, 140). His second uncanny encounter is therefore a complete reversal of the first: resemblance succeeds difference and the uncanniness of the unfamiliar, the unlike, gives way to the uncanniness of the familiar and the like. One could of course argue that Sarah and her mother resemble each other because they belong to the same type – female Woollett – and also because Sarah, as Maud Ellmann points out, 'condemns difference'.[10] Yet Strether's encounter with Sarah seems to challenge rather than confirm the sufficiency of a purely discriminatory, differential notion of category. Having studied the manifold distinctions of Europe, Strether has in fact already become partially aware that strangeness lies in similarities between separate types and not only in differences. At first he reads Little Bilham's serenity in terms of difference and the theory of monsters, labelling it as 'the trail of the serpent, the corruption, as he might conveniently have said, of Europe' (*NYE*, xxi, 125). But Maria Gostrey encourages Strether to re-pigeon-hole this convenient but restrictive categorization by arguing that Bilham's serenity is an intense Americanism, 'a special little form of the oldest thing they knew' (p. 125). For Strether this almost Freudian insight into the familiarity of the strange produces 'a sharper turn of the screw than any yet' (p. 125). With this resoundingly significant rotation Strether leaves behind the Manichean oppositions applied by the governess in 'The Turn of the Screw'. It is Sarah Pocock who inherits the role of the governess, and it is significant that her pressurizing of Strether, which amounts to moral blackmail, is described in the Project for *The Ambassadors* as 'the turn of that screw' (*N*, p. 567). Sarah's centripetal screw is finally to prompt the centrifugal 'revolution' on the part of Strether which James referred to in his initial 1895 notebook entry on *The Ambassadors* (*N*, p. 142). Yet the turn of the screw already instigated by Maria represents an even earlier shift to an opening spiral. Moving from difference to resemblance, from the European serpent to the oldest thing he knows, Strether completes a hermeneutic circle.[11] In principle he has become aware of the importance of generality as well as particularity. Rather than acting as an emissary to separate the types, Strether has become an ambassador who moves between categories with comparative ease. He is, like the governess, a figure who dwells on thresholds but unlike her he attempts to be a medium rather than a screen. His is a tropic consciousness which embraces both the 'is' and the 'is not' of metaphor – that figure which Ellmann describes as 'a rhetorical ambassador' ('The Intimate Difference', p. 105).

Strether's first encounter with Madame de Vionnet is an object-lesson in the resemblances which override differences. When Little

Bilham tells him that Gloriani invites 'the right *femmes du monde*', Strether encounters a new 'category' which strikes him as 'romantic and mysterious' (*NYE*, XXI, 199–200). Yet when Madame de Vionnet actually appears, Strether notices that she '*differed* less' than he has expected from women like Mrs Newsome and Sarah Pocock (p. 212). Madame de Vionnet does not seem to belong to the 'unfamiliar phenomenon of the *femme du monde*' and certainly does not project the 'perpetual monstrous haunting image' which, according to James's Project, Mrs Newsome contemplates from the perspective of Woollett (*NYE*, XXI, 213; *N*, p. 548). Madame de Vionnet is not an easily definable other, an uncanny outsider. She is uncanny by virtue of her very familiarity and rather than being 'vividly alien' impresses Strether with her 'common humanity' (*NYE*, XXI, 214, 213). As one of 'the ladies of the type' she strangely comes out as 'the usual thing' (p. 213). In Gloriani's garden Strether's conveniently clear-cut if increasingly plural categories give way to the perception of surprising similarities. 'In the light of Paris', as Miss Barrace informs him, 'one sees what things resemble' (p. 207).

Up to this point, Strether has been a somewhat timid maker of connections. When he remembers telling Mrs Newsome that, with her ruche, she resembles Queen Elizabeth, his simile is about as far as the figurative has been pushed in Woollett, at least by a 'gentleman of his age' (p. 52). Having met Maria Gostrey, Strether extends simile into analogy by thinking of his new acquaintance as Mary Stuart (see p. 52). Yet this gratifying antithesis is in some respects only a milder version of Waymarsh's Catholic monster (see p. 201 above). Having been alerted to the difficulty of making rigid discriminations by the ghost at the window and having received some preliminary training in resemblance from Maria Gostrey and Miss Barrace, Strether is able to see Gloriani as 'the glossy male tiger, magnificently marked' (p. 219). This is a metaphor of a wild animal but it could be described as a 'tame' metaphor in the orderly way it organizes an exchange between nature and culture. Strether's image has the fearful symmetry which Woollett would have been proud of: at last, in spite of Little Bilham's disclaimer, he has found a monster in the jungle of Europe. At the same time, however, Strether is in the presence of more richly compounded figurative structures. Here is Miss Barrace:

She seemed, with little cries and protests and quick recognitions, movements like the darts of some fine high-feathered free-pecking bird, to stand
before life as before some full shop-window. You could fairly hear, as she
selected and pointed, the tap of her tortoise-shell against the glass. (p. 204)

Miss Barrace is not being compared to a bird in the same way that
Gloriani is compared to a tiger. She is being compared to a bird out
shopping, a creature that pecks with eyes made out of the shell of a
reptile. One could describe this as a 'wild' metaphor since the
fantastic creature which results from it collapses zoological taxono-
mies, subverts the hierarchies of genus and species, fuses distinct
categories.[12] When, shortly afterwards, Miss Barrace describes
herself as the 'Great Father', her rhetorical transvestism completely
sabotages Woollett's efforts to limit types to the male and the female
(p. 206).

Ultimately, however, the proliferation of uncanny resemblances
poses as many dangers for Strether as the multiplying differences
inherent in any sophisticated notion of type. A world of absolute
resemblance would be a world of pure flux, lacking the moulds and
borders which give it comprehensible form. Consciousness needs
resemblance *and* difference; indeed, in many ways it *is* the play of
these twin dynamics. Although Madame de Vionnet at first strikes
Strether as strange by virtue of her surprising familiarity, he eventually achieves a sense of another strangeness: that of her 'rare
unlikeness to the women he had known' (p. 246). Ultimately,
therefore, Madame de Vionnet comprises both familiar and unfamiliar elements; she is simultaneously similar and different. Having
taken Strether's 'categories by surprise', Madame de Vionnet is
increasingly apprehended in terms of confluences and bifurcations
(p. 271). Strether reflects that she creates 'an effect that might have
been felt by a poet as half mythological and half conventional'
(p. 270). She is 'various and multifold ... an obscure person, a
muffled person, one day; and a showy person, an uncovered person
the next' (p. 271). Obscure and showy, muffled and uncovered,
partly divine and partly human, partly fantastic and partly conventional: Madame de Vionnet is 'a mixture of lucidity and mystery'
(*NYE*, xxii, 115). Sometimes it seems to Strether 'as if her art were
all an innocence' but at other times he feels that it is 'as if her
innocence were all an art' (p. 116). By a 'turn of the hand', Madame
de Vionnet converts her 'encounter' with Strether into a 'relation':
something interstitial, oscillating, determinable on the basis neither

of absolute and exclusive difference nor resemblance (*NYE*, XXI, 249). She is an incarnation of the contrasts and comparisons which create relational meaning rather than the syntheses or antitheses which govern so many conceptual systems.

For many of James's previous characters, the erasure of difference brought crisis: one thinks of Margaret Aldis's 'feverish transitions from ... exaltation to despair' in 'De Grey', Brooke's 'mingled sense of exaltation and dread' in 'Travelling Companions' and the governess's 'confusion of curiosity and dread' in 'The Turn of the Screw' (*CT*, I, 420; II, 221; X, 38). Numerous other characters in James are defined in terms of opposed and potentially conflicting capacities. Christopher Newman has

an eye in which innocence and experience were singularly blended. It was full of contradictory suggestions, and ... you could find in it almost anything you looked for. Frigid and yet friendly, frank yet cautious, shrewd yet credulous, positive yet skeptical, confident yet shy, extremely intelligent and extremely good-humoured, there was something vaguely defiant in its concessions, and something profoundly reassuring in its reserve. (*Novels 1871–1880*, p. 517)

In *The Portrait of a Lady*, James lists similarly dissonant qualities when he describes Isabel's 'confidence at once innocent and dogmatic, her temper at once exacting and indulgent, her mixture of curiosity and fastidiousness, of vivacity and indifference ... her combination of the delicate, desultory, flame-like spirit and the eager and personal young girl' (*Novels 1881–1886*, p. 242). The eye of Newman and the character of Isabel are analysed in terms of subtly discordant pairings. On the one hand they possess an outward-looking tendency which involves qualities such as innocence, friendliness, frankness, credulity, positiveness, confidence, indulgence, curiosity, vivacity and good-humour. On the other hand they are defined in terms of an inward-looking movement involving qualities like frigidity, caution, shrewdness, scepticism, shyness, defiance, reserve, dogmatism, fastidiousness and indifference. In *The Ambassadors*, Lambert Strether is introduced in somewhat similar terms. He is said to possess 'the oddity of a double consciousness', to have 'detachment in his zeal and curiosity in his indifference' (*NYE*, XXI, 5). Yet there are at least two features of this description which differentiate Strether from Isabel or Newman. Whereas the dualities of the two earlier characters were expressed in perceptual or temperamental terms, Strether's doubleness is explicitly a matter of consciousness. More importantly, though, the terms of Strether's double consciousness are arranged in a more complex and subtle manner than was the case in *The American* or *The Portrait of a Lady*. Placed at the mid-point of a single spectrum, Newman and Isabel were presented through the divergent and confluent qualities that together comprised their personal predicament. Strether also combines the divergent tendency towards an outward-looking zeal and curiosity on the one hand and an inward-looking detachment and indifference on the other. In his case, however, the relations between the different facets of his consciousness are determined in what one could call a doubly double way.[13] Strether does not simply oscillate between the centrifugal and centripetal tendencies of his consciousness. There is detachment *in* his zeal, curiosity *in* his indifference, an inwardness within his outwardness and an outwardness within his inwardness. The different aspects of Strether's consciousness are never discrete and single; they exist in terms of their dynamic relations with other aspects. His double consciousness is responsible for his recognition of likenesses behind differences and differences behind likenesses, of the art in Madame de Vionnet's innocence and the innocence in her art. 'Proportions', as he himself philosophizes, 'were at all times ... the very conditions of perception, the terms of thought' (*NYE*, xxii, 49).

With his potential to handle relations in this syncopated way, Strether comes close to the James who delighted in 'a deep-breathing economy and an organic form' (*LC*, ii, 1108). James describes his fiction, like Strether's consciousness, in a doubly double way: developing from within and held from without, it is simultaneously restricted and inflatable, mechanically controlled and yet full of life. Its meanings are relational, comprising fissile and fusile interactions between economic mastery and the explosive principle. Whilst the predicament of a Newman or an Isabel is staged in terms of the comparatively limited two-term logic of synthesis and antithesis, Strether and James occupy a more sensitively attuned and finely stressed borderland. As he moves towards the crisis on the river, it nevertheless remains true that Strether does not always experience a Jamesian delight in the double dynamic. He is in a sense condemned to turn the screw both ways, wounded by what propels him, bewildered by seeing things in their unexpected and repeatedly uncanny relations, 'burdened' by his double consciousness (*NYE*, xxi, 5).

On 9 August 1900, James told William Dean Howells that, with *The Sacred Fount*, he had recently completed 'a fine flight . . . *into* the high fantastic' (*L*, IV, 159). He had decided to abandon work on *The Sense of the Past* because he was 'preoccupied with half a dozen things of the altogether human order now fermenting in my brain' (p. 159). One of these things was of course *The Ambassadors*. Yet if this novel belongs to the human order it also echoes some of the fantastic elements in *The Sacred Fount*.[14] The relationship between Chad and Madame de Vionnet seems to superimpose the two sacred fount relationships detected by the narrator of the earlier novel so that each half of the virtuous attachment shows signs of being both vampire and victim. Like Briss, Chad seems to have aged; like Gilbert Long, he has become more refined. Like Mrs Brissenden, Madame de Vionnet seems, if not younger than she was, then at least younger than her actual years. In the flurried encounter that follows the meeting on the river, however, Madame de Vionnet also resembles May Server in her nervous volubility, and as the novel draws to its close she seems increasingly to have become a sacrificial victim. Just as Strether ponders the case of absolute difference presented by Chad, so the narrator of *The Sacred Fount* follows up Mrs Brissenden's observation that there is a 'difference' in Gilbert Long and Obert's word that May Server is 'different' (*The Sacred Fount*, pp. 21, 28). On first seeing Mrs Brissenden and her husband, he thinks that both are 'unknown' to him (pp. 18, 28). How can one account for these uncanny differences and failures of identification? As early as the second chapter the narrator is 'on the track of a law, a law that would fit, that would strike me as governing the delicate phenomena' (p. 30). It is significant that this law also involves four terms arranged in two pairs, within each of which the relation between lover and loved or between repletion and depletion is understood as a dynamic exchange.[15] Just as Strether's consciousness doubles the dualities of Newman or Isabel, so the narrator's law doubles the single vampire-victim pairings of early tales like 'The Story of a Year', 'Poor Richard', 'A Most Extraordinary Case', 'De Grey: A Romance', 'Osborne's Revenge' or 'Longstaff's Marriage'. Unlike Strether, the narrator of *The Sacred Fount* does not first attempt to explain difference through the static notion of type. He immediately grasps things in terms of interactions, using the torch of his analogy to illuminate change by a series of almost syllogistic deductions or extrapolations in which observations regarding one of the partners in a vampire-victim pairing are correlatively applied to the corresponding partner in the other pairing.[16] The narrator therefore sees intriguing connections between Briss and May Server as well as between Mrs Brissenden and Gilbert Long. In spite of the fact that James saw the novel as an exercise in the 'high fantastic', his narrator explains the uncanniness around him in terms of 'intimacy . . . intensity of relation (*L*, IV, 159; *The Sacred Fount*, p. 26). Appearances at Newmarch may be fantastic but it is human intimacy which enables the fount to flow. This insight establishes an important contrast between the narrator of *The Sacred Fount* and Strether in *The Ambassadors*. Although the latter novel addresses the 'human order', Strether at first sees both differences and similarities as uncannily miraculous and magical (*L*, IV, 159). He feels 'extremely wonderful', 'quite fantastic', and even 'mad' (*NYE*, XXII, 40). On the 'question of Chad's improvement', he wonders whether he is 'fantastic and away from the truth' (pp. 80–1). 'Intimacy of course had to be postulated' reflects the narrator in *The Sacred Fount* (p. 34). By contrast, Strether's idea of the virtuous attachment avoids postulating such intimacies. It is only on the river that Strether recognizes 'the deep, deep truth of the intimacy revealed' (*NYE*, XXII, 266). At this point Strether realizes that he has 'dressed the possibility' of a relationship deeper than that of the virtuous attachment 'in vagueness, as a little girl might have dressed her doll' (p. 266). His initial response to the revelation of 'the facts' which his theory has discreetly ignored is a negative one (p. 261). He feels 'mixed up with the typical tale of Paris', with what is morally 'sinister' in 'the vast, strange life of the town' (pp. 270–1). Yet though Mrs Newsome has continued to imagine 'horrors' and Sarah to keep up 'the theory of the horrible', Strether refuses to fall back on Woollett's monster-haunted logic (pp. 241, 242). 'I moved among miracles', he ruefully tells Maria Gostrey: 'it was all phantasmagoric' (p. 301). But there is no 'revulsion in favour of the principles of Woollett' (p. 296). Throughout the central sections of the novel, Strether has seen Madame de Vionnet as the source of Chad's miraculous transformation, the very principle of magical conversion. Now he recognizes that, 'however admirable', Madame de Vionnet's reconstruction of Chad is work 'of the strict human order' (p. 284). Through imaginative failure Strether eventually achieves the insight into the human order and the human intimacy which James and the narrator of *The Sacred Fount* began with. In doing so,

Strether also reaches a deeper understanding of the uncanny, which is no longer entirely a matter of strange and surprising differences or similarities. The revelation that human intimacy lies at the root of miraculous appearances does not reduce matters to a homely literality which entirely excludes the magical. Strether learns that there is something miraculous, or at least mysterious, in intimacy, familiarity, or at the most general level in life. The 'poor dear old life' which Strether has momentarily seen at work behind Chad's uncanny alteration becomes more enigmatic than the change itself (*NYE*, xxi, 168). There is something irreducibly mysterious in 'the terrible life' behind Gloriani's 'charming smile' (p. 197). Although Madame de Vionnet is reduced from the status of a demi-goddess to that of 'a maidservant crying for her young man', Strether finds that he has lost his more naively miraculous illusions only to become aware of still greater enigmas (*NYE*, xxii, 286). Chad may belong to the human order but even though the agent of his transformation is a victim, she is exploited by 'mysterious forces' – and 'at the end of all things, they *were* mysterious' (p. 284). Such is the human mystery in the human order, the uncanniness in life, that Madame de Vionnet remains for Strether 'the finest and subtlest creature, the happiest apparition, it had been given him, in all his years, to meet' (p. 286).

THE OTHER SELF

The third and final use of the word 'uncanny' in *The Ambassadors* occurs shortly after Strether's reception of the Pococks. Discussing Jim Pocock's view of the situation with Madame de Vionnet, Strether observes that 'men of my age, at Woollett – and especially the least likely ones – have been noted as liable to strange outbreaks, belated uncanny clutches at the unusual, the ideal' (p. 119). This final instance of the uncanny is closely associated with the 'good time', the American's belated indulgence in the artistic delights and sensory pleasures of the European scene (p. 119). Jim's good time is to be had 'at the Varieties' (p. 88). Waymarsh makes his 'tribute to the ideal' by buying Sarah Pocock expensive meals and then attending the circus (p. 137). Strether is capable of meeting the demands of the Théâtre Français, but he too accepts Chad's '*panem et circenses*' (*NYE*, xxi, 193). A thick-crusted bread roll or a play, a coarse-textured napkin or a bookstall: these things are virtually sublime to Strether, who with increasing pleasure takes in Paris orally as well as intellectually, from the watery beer of his first evening in the city (see p. 77) to the comparatively exotic '*côtelette de veau à l'oseille*' prepared by the landlady of the Cheval Blanc during his day in the country (*NYE*, xxii, 252). At first sight these 'belated, uncanny clutches' do not seem to be particularly uncanny. Indeed, such pleasures are *heimlich* in sense (c) of the definition from Sanders's *Wörterbuch* which Freud quotes in 'The "Uncanny"': 'intimate, friendlily comfortable; the enjoyment of quiet content, etc., arousing a sense of agreeable restfulness and security' (*SE*, xvii, 222). Nevertheless, as Freud points out, the *heimlich* also possesses senses which could easily be called *unheimlich*. Something of a movement towards the uncannier associations of the *heimlich* occurs during the scene by the river in *The Ambassadors*. Strether's quiet contentment gives way to the recognition of one of the examples cited by Sanders: a '*heimlich* love-affair, love, sin' (p. 223). His belated clutch at the ideal eventually results in the discovery of something which initially seems sinister. Throughout the novel, however, the good time has had a dubious, illicit side. Strether is not in Paris 'to dip, to consume', to enjoy sensory pleasure (*NYE*, xxi, 94). Nor is he there for aesthetic delight; in fact he has an 'odious ascetic suspicion of any form of beauty' (pp. 193–4). On Jim's part the anticipated good time at the Théâtre des Variétés gives rise to a vague but aggressive 'play of innuendo' (*NYE*, xxii, 88). One suspects that this ambivalence towards the European circus has a similar source to the imperfectly suppressed fascination displayed by Freud during his uncanny encounter with the 'painted women' (*SE*, xvii, 237). Strether himself sees a 'bad woman in a yellow frock' when he visits the theatre in London (*NYE*, xxi, 53). Waiting in Chad's apartment towards the end of the book, Strether finds a 'lemon-coloured and tender' novel with an 'ivory knife athwart it like the dagger in a contadina's hair' (*NYE*, xxii, 209). He feels 'as sad as if he had come for some wrong, and yet as excited as if he had come for some freedom' (pp. 210–11). The *contadina* may not be a painted woman but she too prompts a dual response, a mingling of sadness and excitement. Just as Freud's anecdote could be read as an encounter with the dangerously seductive nature of the figurative, or at its most general level the literary (see pp. 26–7 above), so Strether's metaphor magically transforms a book into an inviting but dangerous woman. His other experiences of the uncanny serve to educe but this third form of uncanny experience seems to seduce.

Literature as a beckoning *contadina* equipped, like a latterday Medusa, with a castrating knife? The encounter with the painted woman certainly produces a 'sense of helplessness' on Freud's part (*SE*, XVII, 237). Strether also feels an 'uneasiness' in Paris: to enjoy his surroundings might be to 'give one's authority away' (*NYE*, XXI, 89).

In 'The "Uncanny"', Freud cites *A Tramp Abroad* for its account of Twain's disorientated wanderings around a darkened hotel room in Europe.[17] Freud sees the scene as a comic version of a typically uncanny experience. Leon Edel has plausibly connected the figure of Waymarsh in *The Ambassadors* with Twain.[18] Adopting a defensive 'rigour' and refusing to 'float', Waymarsh treats Europe as an 'ordeal' (*NYE*, XXI, 26). More open to sensory fluidities, Strether experiences a certain pleasure in 'floating ... into society' (p. 41). He goes through a phase of virtually intra-uterine rapture during which the seeds of his past, 'buried for long years in dark corners', seem to have 'sprouted again' (p. 86). But sharper anxieties accompany these soft ecstasies. Strether finds himself 'often at sea' (p. 116). He moves like 'a sinking swimmer' in a 'fathomless medium' (p. 172). He realizes that he is standing 'on ground not of the firmest' (p. 266). Strether has entered 'a maze of mystic closed allusions' in which people hold onto their threads and seize their clues (p. 279). Like Freud in the Italian town, he experiences an increasing sense of geographical unease, begins to suspect that he has strayed from what Freud calls 'the marked or familiar path' (*SE*, XVII, 237). During his early days in Paris, Strether feels 'lost' without the assistance of Maria Gostrey, who, in the Parisian 'maze', acts, according to James's Preface, as the most 'abandoned of *ficelles*' (*NYE*, XXI, 120; *LC*, II, 1317). Maria can educate Strether out of his Partridge-like response to the play in London, yet ultimately she is an unhelpful Ariadne whose confident 'there we are' testifies mostly to Strether's sense of placelessness and relates only to the fact that women are 'abysses' (*NYE*, XXI, 234). Strether finds himself, as both Preface and novel state, in a 'false position' (*LC*, II, 1309; *NYE*, XXII, 190). Gradually and vertiginously the metaphors move towards a looming spatial catastrophe, foreboding a traumatic rebirth or an Icarian descent out of 'the upper air' (*NYE*, XXI, 216). The sound of Madame de Vionnet's thanks makes Strether 'fairly feel as if he had been tripped up and had a fall' (p. 276). Soon afterwards, whilst lunching with her on the left bank, he begins to anticipate a 'smash' (*NYE*, XXII, 15).

In 'The "Uncanny"', Freud describes a number of reasons for the

formation in adult life of doubles, apparently detached and persecuting or monitoring presences. In some cases what is usually called
'"conscience"' may be experienced as a malevolent other, 'observing and criticizing the self ... exercising a censorship' (*SE*, xvii,
235). When the conscience seems to have become a distinct, external
being, the ego may fall prey to 'delusions of being watched' (p. 235).
There is something of this uncanny doubling in *The Ambassadors* and
one could argue that Mrs Newsome represents Strether's New
England conscience, that she is, as James put it in his original
notebook entry on the novel, 'the reflection of his old self' (*N*,
p. 142). According to James's Project for *The Ambassadors*, Strether
is to be 'haunted with an inward *malaise*' (*N*, p. 556). In the novel
this malaise materializes in the form of Mrs Newsome's importunate
'ghost' (*NYE*, xxii, 47). At one point Strether feels as if Mrs
Newsome is 'in the room, and ... conscious, sharply and sorely
conscious, of himself' (p. 144). The victim of her scrutiny, Strether is
'oppressed, haunted, tormented' by 'the impression everything
might be making on her' (p. 237). After the arrival of the Pococks,
Strether is exposed still further to Woollett's interrogatory gaze and
moral weight. He begins to suspect that Sarah, whose looming
approach has already made him 'afraid of himself' (p. 61) and who
seems herself to be feeling 'the fixed eyes' of her mother 'fairly screw
into the flat of her back', will 'alight from her headlong course more
or less directly upon him' (p. 162).

Freud also mentions a number of other reasons for the formation
of doubles in later life. In 'The "Uncanny"' he cites 'all the
unfulfilled but possible futures to which we still like to cling in
phantasy, all the strivings of the ego which adverse external circumstances have crushed, and all our suppressed acts of volition which
nourish in us the illusion of Free Will' (*SE*, xvii, 236). Although
Strether arrives in Chester with 'a consciousness of personal
freedom' and, having reached Paris, seems 'again to find himself
young', one could argue that the strivings of his ego have indeed
been crushed by external circumstances and that his has been a
lifetime of suppressed acts of volition (*NYE*, xxi, 4, 81). In the first
chapter of the novel he searches his pocket for 'something, possibly
forgotten' (p. 8). This object may be his watch or his past, still more
the past possibilities which he has not fulfilled. It may be his card or
his identity, and still more the other self that he has suppressed, the
youth he has lost, the freedom he never used. Within forty-eight

hours of arriving in Paris, Strether is comparing his 'meagreness' to an 'unmapped Hinterland' (p. 87). As a young man he had dreamed of raising a 'temple of taste' (p. 87). He has never carried this structure further than the door and having returned to Paris, his past – like the destroyed palace of the Tuileries – seems an 'irremediable void' (p. 79). Strether is haunted by 'old ghosts of experiments ... old drudgeries and delusions' and by 'the pale figure of his real youth' (pp. 85, 83–4). The sight of 'some fair young man just growing up' makes him 'wince with the thought of an opportunity lost' (p. 84). Strether is, as James put it in his Project, 'vaguely haunted by the feeling of what he has missed' (*N*, p. 543). Yet Strether is not only haunted by his own old self, by his failures of fulfilment; once in Paris he seems to inaugurate a quest, not for the self who lost, but for a lost self who might freely have experienced a youth of sensory and even sensual satisfactions. He begins a search, not for his 'real youth', but for a more generalized other: 'the stray spirit of youth' (*NYE*, xxi, 84, 94). Strether experiences something of the self he might have been through Little Bilham's 'youth' (p. 97). In one sense Bilham replaces Strether's 'stupidly sacrificed' son, ultimately becoming the inheritor of 'every penny of my own' (*NYE*, xxi, 84; xxii, 167). Through the medium of Bilham, Chad immediately gains a 'pronounced association with youth' (*NYE*, xxi, 98). Strether's second other, Chad is the 'rare youth he should have enjoyed being "like"' (p. 220).[19] Towards the end of the novel, whilst waiting for Chad in the Boulevard Malesherbes apartment, Strether's rendezvous with the seductive *contadina* of literature is followed by a further and still more ghostly meeting, an encounter with the invoked 'spirit of the place':

The freedom was what was most in the place and the hour; it was the freedom that most brought him round again to the youth of his own that he had long ago missed ... represented the substance of his loss, put it within reach, within touch, made it, to a degree it had never been, an affair of the senses. That was what it became for him at this singular time, the youth he had long ago missed – a queer concrete presence, full of mystery, yet full of reality, which he could handle, taste, smell, the deep breathing of which he could positively hear. (*NYE*, xxii, 211)

Rather than remembering the past that he has had, the youth that missed and lacked, Strether creates a phantom of the youth that he has missed and might have been, the fuller freedom he might have had. To encounter this other self as a 'concrete presence' involves a certain sacrifice (p. 211). Strether's 'affair of the senses' is an indirect and subjective one (p. 211). His freedom is the 'freedom of appreciation': a passive experience rather than an active actuality (p. 188). 'Making up late for what I did n't have early' involves giving certain things up; it presumes the belated predicament, with its 'uncanny clutches at the unusual, the ideal' (pp. 51, 119). It is only through a 'tribute' to 'youth' that Chad and Madame de Vionnet, through the circuit and subterfuge of Strether's thought, become 'my youth' (p. 51). Strether's subjective experience of the free self depends on objective limitations and renunciations, on not being in Paris 'for his own profit – not, that is, the direct', on having 'a life only for other people', on being the person who 'finally paid' whilst 'it was others who mainly partook' and finally on Strether's adherence to his 'only logic': 'not, out of the whole affair, to have got anything for myself' (*NYE*, xxi, 94, 269; *NYE*, xxii, 186, 326). All these sacrifices are the very condition of the experience of freedom, enabling Strether to live by means of imaginative detours through other lives. Chad has both youth and freedom in actuality but there is a hint that he cannot fully experience these things since, according to Strether, he has 'no imagination' (p. 225). Strether's imagination is, on the other hand – though not in the sense of Woollett – 'monstrous' (p. 241). Requiring lack to create its plenitude and limitation to create its freedom, it is precisely the 'irremediable void' in the garden of the Tuileries which sets Strether's 'historic sense ... freely at play' (*NYE*, xxi, 79).

In Gloriani's garden Strether claims that he is without even the memory of 'the illusion of freedom' (p. 218). The trajectory of *The Ambassadors* and the dynamics of Strether's consciousness enable him, through sacrifice, renunciation and loss, as well as through certain forms of confinement, to evoke the ghost of a memory of an illusion. Strether comes to realize that it is the voids and the lost opportunities which, in Freud's words, 'nourish ... the illusion of Free Will', which uncannily contribute to the construction of an unconfined *alter ego*, permit the invention of alternative selves, phantasms of freedom and fulfilment (*SE*, xvii, 236).

'THE JOLLY CORNER'

When Strether is not acting as the ambassador between Woollett and Paris, he is the ambassador between himself and his own past, between his actual self and his imagined self. It is significant that

Europe is the scene of his brushes with this *alter ego*; the place, too, where Strether encounters the ghost at the window, the authorial other within the house of fiction. For Strether, Europe is a haunted landscape, a continent of uncanny differences and similarities, a place of literary resonances, a richly figurative scene. Like Freud's Italian town, Strether's Europe is the site of uncanny 'voyages of discovery', the place of 'adventure' (*SE*, xvii, 237).

For weal and woe, Europe continued to be the most proper scene in the world for the appearance of ghosts in *The Wings of the Dove*. It is in Venice that Merton Densher is haunted by the 'conscious watchful presence' of Kate Croy, obsessed by a 'hallucination' of intimacy (*NYE*, xx, 235, 236). Having returned to London, he becomes increasingly aware of a detached other, the figure of 'a young man far off ... hushed, passive ... half understanding, yet dimly conscious of something immense' (p. 342). Densher's ineffaceable impression of Milly Theale has made him 'a haunted man – a man haunted with a memory' (p. 343). He lingers in 'the stillness of his rooms' to cherish the sound of 'a faint far wail' (p. 396). Ghostly experience continues to be the prerogative of residents of Europe in *The Golden Bowl*. The occupants of Fawns undergo a crisis which hovers in the corridors of the house 'after the fashion of the established ghost' (*NYE*, xxiv, 211). With distinct echoes of 'The Turn of the Screw', Maggie becomes aware of an impression which lurks 'in the manner of a spying servant, on the other side of the barred threshold' (p. 43). The ghostly presence of Peter Quint is still more strongly felt when looming evil is compared to 'some bad-faced stranger surprised in one of the thick-carpeted corridors of a house of quiet on a Sunday afternoon' (p. 237).[20] Fawns is certainly 'a haunted house' but ultimately it is haunted as much by Maggie as by 'sombre ghosts of the smothered past' (pp. 288, 74). Gaining something of 'the constructive, the creative hand' (p. 145) and seeing those around her as 'figures rehearsing some play of which she herself was the author' (p. 235), it is Maggie who becomes an authorial ghost at the window, gazing down from her 'perched position', from an 'outlook' which is compared to that of 'some castle-tower', on Charlotte Stant, the 'far-off harassed heroine ... with a part to play' (pp. 306–7).[21]

In his Preface to *The Ambassadors*, James spoke of 'the *trivial* association' of Paris, the platitude involved in using the city of lost illusions as the stage for a drama concerning transformation and conversion, the collapse of moral schemes (*LC*, ii, 1312). Paris, he

claimed, was 'a minor matter, a mere symbol for more things than
had been dreamt of in the philosophy of Woollett' (p. 1312). The
allusion, of course, is to the ghost scene in *Hamlet* (see I. v. 166). It is
significant that further references to *Hamlet* crop up in the text of *The
Ambassadors*. As an emissary from America, the land of the dead,
Strether tells Maria 'the very secret of the prison-house' (*NYE*, XXI,
66; see *Hamlet*, I. v. 14). Yet Strether the ghost is later a ghost seer
who reflects that he is seeing the *femme du monde* 'in her habit as she
lived' (*NYE*, XXI, 270; see *Hamlet*, III. iv. 135). Even if it was 'a minor
matter', the James of *The Ambassadors*, quite as much as the James of
'Travelling Companions' or 'A Passionate Pilgrim', was playing on
the connection, not only between Europe and the exotic, the unfamiliar, the romantic – Europe as the stage for the subjective adventure – but also between Europe and the uncanny, the ghostly.
Woollett, in contrast, is haunted not by ghosts but by the imagination of the monstrous. It is the place of an icy moral austerity, a
sensory limbo of stark literality where, throughout the 'great desert'
of his middle years, Strether has edited the *Woollett Review*, with its
moneyed yet indigestible and fruitless 'kernel of economics, politics,
ethics' (*NYE*, XXI, 87).

Even as James was working on the novels of the major phase,
however, his attitude to the relation between America and Europe
was undergoing a revolution. In 'The Ghostly Rental' he had amply
demonstrated his dissatisfaction with the fabricated veils of
American romance. From the high-shouldered wall in the final
chapter of *The American* to the haunted pane in 'The Turn of the
Screw' and the ghost at the window in *The Ambassadors*, James had
found his charged thresholds in Europe. By the time of *The Golden
Bowl*, however, the Prince can compare his American friends – in an
image which explicitly recalls Poe's *Narrative of Arthur Gordon Pym* –
to 'a great white curtain' (*NYE*, XXIII, 22). The American veil exists,
and it is no longer to be torn aside so easily.

On 21 December 1902 James wrote to Sarah Butler Wister that
'my native land, in my old age, has become, becomes more and
more, romantic to me altogether: *this* one, on the other hand has,
hugely and ingeniously ceased to be' (*L*, IV, 259).[22] This sense of a
reversal in values surfaces throughout *The American Scene* (1907).
Although James is still disturbed by the 'underlying unity' of his
native country, its lack of contrasts and differences, he repeatedly
presents America in language which some years previously could

only have referred to Europe.[23] No longer 'hard and dry and thin', America seems full of 'latent poetry', veritably 'Arcadian' (*The American Scene*, pp. 19, 28, 14). Europe has become 'familiar', lost its 'mystery' and ceased to be 'strange' (pp. 365–6). Its 'romantic essence' seems 'enfeebled, shrunken and spent' (p. 366). America, on the other hand, has begun to appeal to 'the faculty of wonder' (p. 366). In the Prefaces it was this 'faculty of wonder' which was responsible for the fascination of the ghostly (*LC*, II, 1256). Certainly, the notebook entries which record James's return to America in 1904–5 overflow with a pervasive sense of the past as 'a pale pathetic ghost', 'a sphere peopled with old ghosts' and with 'strange little intensities of history' which defy 'economy' (*N*, pp. 238–9). In *The American Scene*, James invokes the 'lurking ghosts' of Harvard's Union Hall and senses the presence of 'the old Cambridge ghosts' (pp. 60, 68). He encounters 'special ghosts on the staircase' at the Vernon house in Newport and 'old ghosts' in Philadelphia's Independence Hall (pp. 218, 293).

One could go on for ever tracking down and discussing ghostly references in later James. What I want to emphasize here is that, for the first time since 'The Ghostly Rental', James's ghosts have begun to appear in an American locale. It is true that in 'The Aspern Papers' James had tried to create a 'dim and charming ghost' for the 'lean prime Western period' (*LC*, II, 1181). Yet the presence of this spectre can only be felt in Venice. James's renewed deployment of a spectral vocabulary in relation to America is, however, perhaps not as important as the context in which it took place. Like Strether in reverse, the James of *The American Scene* was setting out on a quest for his own self, engaging in a 'belated romance' (p. 52). The past 'gaps' in his 'experience' and 'consciousness' produced in the mature writer 'an infinite penetration of retrospect, a penetration productive of ghostly echoes as sharp sometimes as aches or pangs' (p. 52). One of the most notably uncanny instances of these belated and subjective penetrations takes place when James revisits Ashburton Place in Boston to see the house in which he spent two years towards the end of the Civil War and gained his 'earliest fond confidence in a "literary career"' (p. 229). On the scene of his origin as a writer, James attempts 'to recover on the spot some echo of ghostly footsteps – the sound as of taps on the window-pane heard in the dim dawn' (p. 229). Like the idea for the story about the knock at the door, these taps suggest that James is trying to recover or recapture the ghosts which had haunted his beginnings. It was, after all, in his 'chamber of application' in Ashburton Place that, on the day of Hawthorne's death in 1864, he had experienced a 'pang' which reduced him to tears (*Autobiography*, p. 478; see p. 50 above). I have argued that 'The Ghostly Rental' simultaneously breaks with the American romance tradition and acknowledges or foretells the persistent influence of the past. To demystify and exorcise American romance is to conjure up another ghost within the house of fiction as the punishment for one's transgressive violence. This second apparition waits, as yet unseen, beyond a closed door. In the years that followed 'The Ghostly Rental', James no longer needed to mount such self-assertive raids on the house of fiction. His characters repeatedly approached the haunted chamber of the writer, opened the door to encounter a spectral presence but were unable to cross the threshold, to enter the sacred place or to usurp the position of its occupant. The narrator of 'The Death of the Lion' (1894) develops 'an almost superstitious objection' to allowing the prowling journalist Pinhorn to cross 'the threshold of my friend's little lonely, shabby, consecrated workshop' – a room which is shortly to be described as Neil Paraday's 'haunted study' (*CT*, IX, 91, 94). Literary interlopers are turned back or, as in 'The Private Life', encounter a turned back. On occasions, however, the haunted study contained a more aggressive and fearful presence. In 'The Real Right Thing' (1899), George Withermore works in the study of the recently-dead Ashton Doyne, a writer 'gilded ... with greatness' (*CT*, x, 472). Rather than being the 'young priest' at Doyne's 'altar', however, Withermore tries to convert his literary god into a 'discreet librarian' (p. 478), a mere 'mystic assistant' (p. 479). Doyne is the 'dead host' possessed by a debilitating parasite, the sacred figure made into a sacrificial victim (p. 478). 'We lay him bare', Withermore tells Mrs Doyne, 'we serve him up' (p. 483). Initially Withermore believes that he is 'drawing many curtains, forcing many doors, reading many riddles' (p. 478). Eventually, however, the young biographer is confronted by a figure 'on the threshold – guarding it' (p. 485). 'Immense', 'dim', 'dark' and 'dreadful', Doyne's ghost protests against invasion and unveiling, forbids access to the chamber of writing (p. 485). These representations of the writer's chamber add further resonance to the pagoda scene which introduces the second book of *The Golden Bowl*. Before she gains the creative upper hand and becomes something like the author of a play in rehearsal,

Maggie figures herself approaching a building which, rather like the many-windowed house of fiction, has 'apertures and outlooks' but 'no door' to grant access from her level (*NYE*, xxiv, 4). The tower-pagoda-mosque, which at one level represents her 'situation', also stands for the sacred place occupied by authoritative authors; Maggie becomes aware of the possibility 'of one's paying with one's life if found there as an interloper' (pp. 3, 4).

The inaccessibility of the writer and the scene of writing's origin is a constant motif in James's work, and of course it also plays a part in tales like 'The Aspern Papers', 'The Figure in the Carpet' and 'John Delavoy'. James consistently criticized biographical attempts to cross the threshold into the writer's chamber, arguing that meaning was passed on by the work and not the workplace, still less the birthplace. Fully aware that a wall is required to balance the sense of strangeness and familiarity so vital to the experience of the '*visitable* past', and that closed doors create the thresholds which prohibit purchase on the objective actual, encouraging the subjective detour and thereby providing the grounds for relational meaning, the James of *The American Scene*, unlike the transgressive narrator of 'The Ghostly Rental', does all he can to preserve the veils (*LC*, ii, 1177). He wants 'not to press ... through any half-open door of the real' (*The American Scene*, p. 59). In Salem he feels a 'sacred terror ... that stayed me from crossing the threshold of the Witch House' (p. 268). This sacred terror is shortly to communicate itself to Hawthorne's birthplace: looking up at the window of the house, James reflects that 'wild horses ... wouldn't have dragged me into it' (p. 270).

In 'The Jolly Corner' (1908), Spencer Brydon fantasizes that the encounter with his *alter ego* will involve 'opening a door ... into a room shuttered and void, and yet so coming ... on some quite erect confronting presence ... planted in the middle of the place and facing him through the dusk' (*CT*, xii, 198). Having compared himself to 'some monstrous stealthy cat', Brydon runs his other self to ground in the last of a series of rooms at the back of his house (p. 211). He pauses on 'the nearer threshold' and contemplates 'applying his hand to a latch, or even his shoulder and his knee ... to a panel' (pp. 216, 218). Invasive, prowling, predatory: Brydon reminds one of George Withermore and seems initially to anticipate[24] the 'awful agent, creature or presence' encountered by James during his 'dream-adventure' in the Galerie d'Apollon and recalled in *A Small Boy and Others* (*Autobiography*, pp. 197, 196). This night-mare could be read in many different ways,[25] but it is significant that, like Brydon's ghostly other, James finds himself in a closed annexe at the end of a gallery where he defends himself against an intruder by 'the push of my shoulder against hard pressure on lock and bar from the other side' (p. 197). At this point, however, the paths of 'The Jolly Corner' and of the Louvre dream begin to diverge. With an explosive energy that recalls the final scene in 'The Romance of Certain Old Clothes', James thrusts open the door of his room in 'pursuit ... of a just dimly-descried figure that retreated in terror before my rush and dash' (p. 196). Having successfully guarded the threshold and preserved the inviolability of his chamber, James bursts out to take full possession of the great hall of art. Having expelled the biographer, he now becomes capable of autobiography and of new fictions.[26] In 'The Jolly Corner', on the other hand, Brydon proves himself capable of performing the re-nunciation which Withermore refused to make until it was too late. He gazes at the 'blank face' defiantly presented by the closed door, realizes 'the value of Discretion', and – like Newman and others before him – decides to turn away (*CT*, XII, 218). Declining to follow in the footsteps of Viola, who in 'The Romance of Certain Old Clothes' entered the attic and unlocked the chest in order to seize her dead sister's finery, Brydon avoids being disfigured and defeated by the explosive contents of Pandora's box. He refuses to commit the transgressive unveiling performed by the narrator of 'The Ghostly Rental'.

James's 1914 notes for the continuation of *The Sense of the Past* speak of Brydon 'turning the tables' on a 'haunting apparition' as if Brydon's role in 'The Jolly Corner' was equivalent to James's in the Louvre dream, where an aggressive dash ensured that 'the tables turned' upon his visitant (*N*, p. 507; *Autobiography*, p. 197).[27] This identification between James and Brydon works against com-parisons between James and Brydon's other, but it is not a strictly accurate one. Brydon initially believes that he has 'turned the tables' on his apparitional opponent but the notes for *The Sense of the Past* forget that the tables are turned once more in the climactic scene of 'The Jolly Corner' (*CT*, XII, 211).[28] Brydon's renunciation cannot save him from a second ghostly encounter. He reaches the front door of his house, 'the last barrier to his escape', only to find 'the prodigy of a personal presence' (p. 224).

Peter Buitenhuis has argued that James in 'The Jolly Corner' is in some sense finally encountering the American ghost he had left behind in 'The Ghostly Rental' (see *The Grasping Imagination*, pp. 86–7). James's comments on 'The Jolly Corner' in the Prefaces certainly set up an echo of 'The Ghostly Rental'. Brydon's malaise seems 'incongruous and discordant' in the context of New York's 'prosaic prosperous conditions' (*LC*, II, 1264). This phrase stirs memories of a house seen by the narrator of 'The Ghostly Rental' during his walks; a house which seems to stand for the American real and which 'is in no sense haunted ... has no sinister secrets, and knows nothing but blooming prósperity' (*CT*, IV, 53). Prosaic prosperity and blooming prosperity: both these phrases in turn look back to Hawthorne's remarks in the Preface to *The Marble Faun* concerning 'the difficulty of writing a Romance' about a country which knew nothing but 'common-place prosperity' (*CE*, IV, 3). Hawthorne's romances had attempted to achieve a neutral and liberated standpoint. Frequently, however, Hawthorne had felt trapped within his haunted chamber, imprisoned by 'viewless bolts and bars' (*CE*, XV, 495; see p. 43 above). At the time of 'The Ghostly Rental', James's predicament had been somewhat different. Rather than being shut in he had felt shut out, excluded from the American real. The downtown New York of 1875 had, as the Prefaces recalled, been 'bolted and barred' to him (*LC*, II, 1198). By 1898 this exclusion, and the consequent unfamiliarity of the downtown world, had led to an extraordinary reassessment of the American businessman. In 'The Question of the Opportunities', James began to endow this figure with the metaphors of romance. The American businessman was an 'epic' hero 'seamed all over with the wounds of the market and the dangers of the field', a 'diver for shipwrecked treasure' (*LC*, I, 655):

The American 'business-man' remains, thanks to the length and strength of the wires that move him, *the* magnificent theme *en disponibilité*. The romance of fact, indeed, has touched him in a way that quite puts to shame the romance of fiction. (p. 656)

In *The American Scene* the paradoxically romantic status of the real is even more apparent, and it is not limited to more obviously picturesque, rural scenes. Examining 'the hungry, triumphant actual', 'the monstrous form of Democracy' and commenting on the presence of 'the unmitigated "business man"', James describes urban

America as 'a huge Rappaccini-garden, rank with each variety of the poison-plant of the money-passion' (*The American Scene*, pp. 53, 54, 64, 57). The prosaic prosperous conditions of New York *were* a Hawthornean romance. By an extraordinary rotary subterfuge, James experiences 'a really romantic thrill' when he enters New York's City Hall to see the portraits of its 'florid ghosts', its 'Mayors, Bosses, Presidents, Governors' (p. 98).

The New York of 'The Jolly Corner' is another Rappaccini's garden of capitalism, an 'overgrown' and 'fantastic' landscape, a 'vast wilderness of the wholesale' (*CT*, xii, 196). Brydon's *alter ego* would have had the opportunity to develop his own long-latent 'capacity for business' (p. 195), would have been the 'full-blown flower' grown in the jungle of 'the rank money-passion' (p. 204). In the upper rooms at the back of the house, Brydon reaches the heart of the labyrinth and stands on the other side of the door defensively shut by the artist. In the hallway at the front of his house, however, Brydon eventually has a direct encounter with a rather different presence: a 'monstrous' figure, a 'stranger' who advances 'as for aggression', and before whom Brydon falls back under 'the roused passion of a life larger than his own, a rage of personality before which his own collapsed' (p. 226). The looming and eventually uncovered face of Brydon's businessman *alter ego* represents more than an encounter with a monstrously amplified Jim Pocock.[29] It stands for the emphatic return of the artist as economic master. Unlike the ghost of Ashton Doyne, who looks out from an inner sanctum, Brydon's other self stands at an open door looking inwards from the outer threshold of the fiction and the house in order to trap the expanding or escaping subjectivity. Yet this authoritarian figure who turns the screw inwards does not represent the mere actual so much as the romance of the real. The ghost is compared to one of the 'fantastic images projected by the magic lantern of childhood' (p. 226). Although Brydon's businessman *alter ego* hoards meaning and increases value through restriction and compression, he is also a figure out of Edmund Spenser, a 'black-vizored sentinel guarding a treasure' (p. 224).[30] The once starkly literal America has become a fabulous scene of densely compounded transformations, and Brydon's experience follows a quite different trajectory to that of Christopher Newman in *The American* or Brooke in 'Travelling Companions'. Brydon does not face and then retreat from a dead wall of absolute limitation but is instead involved in a collision with his other self, with something more violently overwhelming than Strether's quiet contact with his *alter ego*. In 'The Jolly Corner' the hunter who became the hunted meets the trapped turned trapper in a four-term fusion which results in a belated rebirth. Coming to consciousness in Alice Staverton's lap, Brydon feels that he has been 'miraculously *carried* back – lifted and carefully borne as from . . . the uttermost end of an interminable grey passage' (p. 227). Delivered into the light from the 'dark other end of his tunnel', Brydon discovers that his encounter with the ghost of his other self has made possible a salvation and resurrection beyond death and dispossession (p. 227).

In *The Ambassadors*, it was to some extent James who acted as Strether's other self, who represented the possibility his protagonist lost by returning to America after his early visit rather than remaining in Europe like his progenitor. In 'The Jolly Corner', Brydon's *alter ego* represents a new stage in James's engagement with the centre of consciousness. Yet it is also true that, unlike Strether, Brydon follows in his master's footsteps by returning to America in later life, by re-entering the house of the past.[31] One could therefore argue that Brydon's other is at some level also James's other: not the self he was, the self whose gaps *The American Scene* retrospectively filled out, but the self he might have been, the writer he might have become had he remained in his native land. 'The Jolly Corner' certainly revives the figure which the James of the Prefaces confesses to having dodged: the American businessman who, in tales like 'A Passionate Pilgrim', 'The Madonna of the Future' and 'Madame de Mauves', had been 'made to wait as in the furthest and coldest of an infinite perspective of more or less quaint antechambers' (*LC*, II, 1204).

In 1893, William Dean Howells published an influential essay entitled 'The Man of Letters as a Man of Business', which described the way in which writers were reaching new forms of accommodation with the exigencies of the literary market-place in post-Civil War America. Howells argued that the American artist was in 'a transition state' between the 'classes' and the 'masses' and would increasingly be identified with the mass of wage-earners.[32] Following Taine, James had used the phrase 'man of business' at least as early as his 1875 essay on Balzac (see *LC*, II, 32). A few years after Howell's essay, James reverted to Taine's formula about Balzac being 'an artist doubled with a man of business' (p. 96). In doing so,

James too, although in different ways than Howells, was beginning to re-evaluate the writer's existence in transitional terms. Balzac was a 'poet' but also a 'critic' and 'economist' (p. 93), an 'artist' but also a 'historian' (p. 94). He had been caught up in a 'perpetual conflict' in which 'fusion is never complete' (pp. 94, 96). But he had also produced works in which it was impossible to tell whether he was being 'historic' or 'romantic' (p. 112), whether he smashed 'the window-pane of the real' or substantially preserved it (p. 113). James concluded that Balzac's dualities were fusions. It was impossible to separate Balzac the man of imagination from Balzac the man of business: 'we must give up looking for the difference' since Balzac succeeded in making such differences 'nought' (p. 113). Some of these insights into Balzac's 'monstrous duality' (*LC*, II, 96) had been reached by James as early as 1867 in a review of Anne E. Manning's *The Household of Sir Thomas More* and *Jacques Bonneval*. Balzac exemplified the historian who 'works in the dark ... as men work in coal-mines' (*LC*, I, 1154). Confined to this eminently 'realistic' workplace and the inevitable denseness of its surrounding matter, however, Balzac had also and simultaneously been capable of the fabulous: his incidents and characters were 'as fictitious as those of Spenser's "Fairy Queen"' (p. 1155).

When the Prefaces reported the failure to enter downtown's 'monstrous labyrinth' in order to write about the 'money-passion', James was in some sense confessing to a deficiency in the economic and historic aspects of the Balzacian self. Balzac had been an artist and a man of business. Was James all and only an artist or did he, like Brydon, have another latent self? Was there some strangely spectral realist waiting in the wings? This was perhaps one of the questions which James asked himself when in 1902 he reverted to Balzac as to the 'parental threshold' – just as six years later, in fiction, Brydon would return to the house of his fathers (*LC*, II, 91). In 'The Question of the Opportunities' James had cited Zola as an eminent recorder of the businessman figure (see *LC*, I, 656). A decade later he was more specifically pondering the possibility of an American Zola and by implication the American writer that he might have become (see *The American Scene*, pp. 82–3). Edmund Wilson has argued that at contact with the new America, the 'old Balzac in James revives'.[33] This resurrection must be staged indirectly, since James still finds himself 'hovering about' downtown New York in 'magnanimous wonder' and with the sense of 'an intellectual adventure forever renounced' (*The American Scene*, p. 80). It is only through the medium of 'The Jolly Corner' that he is able, as the man of imagination, to double himself with the man of business, to assert that he is both the self in the centre and the one on the edge, that he can move between the explosive and the implosive, the real and the romantic, performing his 'whole possible revolution' and creating the 'rich and mixed' current attributed to Balzac and Zola in the Preface to *The American* (*LC*, II, 1062). In this sense 'The Jolly Corner' could be seen as a New York fictional advertisement for the *New York Edition*. Brydon's course deviated from that of his other at the age of twenty-three when he left for Europe. In 'The Jolly Corner', the paths come full circuit, the selves rejoin each other in preparation for the projected twenty-three volumes of the *New York Edition* – a number which, as Edel points out, seems to have been derived from the twenty-three-volume definitive edition of Balzac's *Comédie Humaine*.[34] Accomplishing fusion and yet sustaining tension, James symbolically embraces the shade of Balzac and also of Hawthorne, the master left behind in 'The Ghostly Rental'.

Yet no dynamic balance is a final one in James; with each new text the circuits begin all over again. The fusion achieved in 'The Jolly Corner' is extended in *The Sense of the Past*, where Ralph Pendrel actually takes over the role of his other, exchanges his identity with that of his *alter ego*. According to James's 1914 notes for *The Sense of the Past*, Pendrel achieves a 'double consciousness' which involves the awareness 'of being the other and yet himself also, of being himself and yet the other other also' (*N*, pp. 504, 505). This would seem to be a more radical double consciousness than Strether's, and one might have thought that Pendrel's adventure represents the greatest triumph achieved by any of James's protagonists. Pendrel crosses the threshold which separates himself, the desiring subject, from his other, the model or desired object. He is able to fulfil his desire to 'remount the stream of time', to become the figure who turns his back, the figure whose portrait hangs in the house in Mansfield Square (*NYE*, XXVI, 48). Although Pendrel somewhat resembles the triumphant James of the Louvre dream, Tamara Follini has shown that he remains a comparative case of imagination.[35] It is, as Dennis Donoghue argues, precisely because Pendrel literally crosses the threshold that his imaginative sense of the past turns into a sense of disappointment and restriction.[36] Having changed places with his other, Pendrel becomes 'painfully

... disconnected', simultaneously 'shut in' and '*cut off*' (*N*, p. 507). It seems that consciousness of the other as another being is at least as important as consciousness of being the other. Pendrel discovers that he has created a new site of desire in the space that he has left behind; he becomes his own model and cannot get back to himself.

ACROSS THE BORDER

The narrator of *The Sacred Fount* finds himself on the track of 'a law that would fit, that would strike me as governing the delicate phenomena' (*The Sacred Fount*, p. 30). Eventually he discovers a 'fine symmetry', a point of command which he refers to as his 'kingdom of thought' (pp. 130, 176). Yet gaining this kingdom entails certain losses, not the least of which is that of the chance to share his insights with a fellow-interpreter like Ford Obert. The narrator allows Obert to continue in what from his point of view is the mistaken belief that May Server is the recipient in a sacred fount relationship (see pp. 56–9). He subsequently does little to dissuade Obert from thinking that May has returned to her old self and that her donor is not at Newmarch (see pp. 150–1, 155). Having somewhat carelessly provided his visually minded friend with 'a torch in the darkness', the narrator allows Obert to believe that he has emerged 'into the light of day' whilst actually making every effort to keep him in the dark (pp. 56, 156).

The costs of the narrator's kingdom of thought are even heavier in his discussions with Mrs Brissenden. Having shared with her his insight into Gilbert Long's transformation, the narrator falls prey to the fear that he has helped the violators to a fuller awareness of their situation, consequently tipping the balance still further in their favour (see pp. 130–1, 189–90, 202–3). In order to restore this balance or at least to prevent any acceleration in the dynamic of the fount, he invests much of his energy in preserving Mrs Brissenden's ignorance about the state of his thoughts whilst sustaining her belief that she has successfully misled him. He does not admit privately agreeing with her idea that May is Long's victim; indeed, he openly affects an opposition to this identification (see pp. 60–3). A later scene finds him 'paying' by enabling Mrs Brissenden to use the resources of his imagination in order to cover her own tracks and those of Long (p. 167). In the final chapter the narrator allows Mrs Brissenden to believe that she has persuaded him that Lady John is Long's donor (see pp. 207–10, 218).

One might feel that the narrator of *The Sacred Fount* gathers meaning in somewhat abstract ways and that, like the governess, his handling of conceptual relations and reciprocal inferences enables him simply to extract the meanings he wants. One could argue that he ranks alongside Long and Mrs Brissenden as a violator, and it is to some extent true that he drains meaning from others and hoards it in his consciousness. Yet the narrator also speculates, engages in imaginative expenditure. In this sense he could also be seen as one of the novel's victims.[37] The narrator must play the part of an 'exemplary Christian' by renouncing – or at least appearing to renounce – his 'perfect palace of thought' (pp. 192, 214). In the 'crystal cage' of civilization as it stands he is unable to defeat the logic of sacrifice, powerless to 'save' May Server or Guy Brissenden in the realm of the real (pp. 142, 189). He must actively dissimulate his sympathy for the victims by allowing Briss to think that '*I* stood for the hollow chatter of the vulgar world' (p. 158). Only through the detour of his theory can the narrator convert actual depletion into subjective repletion and guard 'to the last grain of gold, my precious sense of their loss' (p. 189). The narrator must at all costs 'save my priceless pearl of an inquiry' (p. 203). This is not simply a matter of intellectual greed: the narrator ultimately discovers that 'the condition of light' inevitably involves an internalized re-enactment of the sacrificial process, a 'sacrifice of feeling' (p. 203). He can save only by losing, by renouncing direct emotional involvement. This 'responsibility' is the 'price' of subjective light, 'of the secret success, the lonely liberty and the intellectual joy' (p. 203).

Everything has its price, even for a narrator whose geometry of relationships has much in common with James's doubly double dynamics. The Preface to *The Princess Casamassima* argues that the fictional centre of consciousness has to undergo that bewilderment without which 'there would never be a story to tell about us' (*LC*, II, 1090). A fictional subjectivity achieved heightened visibility owing to the blind spots in its consciousness, became representable through failing to satisfy its imaginative requirements. Christopher Newman and Isabel Archer are defined in terms of static oppositions which leave them dangerously exposed to splits and imbalances. Even Strether, who does develop an interactive, analogical or chiastic[38] conceptual ability and an ambassadorial sense of borders and relations, cannot achieve supreme imaginative command. Bewilderment in James's fiction takes many forms but, from 'The Romance of Certain Old Clothes' to 'The Jolly Corner', one of the most persistent of these is the ghostly. The ghost stands for the ability of texts to sustain their own peculiar laws; it defeats or transforms the laws formulated by James's protagonists in their attempts to establish coherent and harmonious patterns of meaning, to control or elude their fate. Coherent analogies are eventually completed within the text, but only by an uncanny inversion or revolution, a bewildering Jamesian turn which leaves the protagonists with a sense of loss and of the insufficiency of their own models of meaning.

Yet James's characters are not the only ones to suffer this sense of loss and insufficiency. In the Preface to *The Wings of the Dove*, James argued that fiction was a bridge which 'spans the stream ... in apparently complete independence of ... the principal grace of the original design (*LC*, II, 1295). The writer had necessarily to be a 'dupe' in order to be a 'master' (p. 1295). Since the artist in triumph was intrinsically unrepresentable, his mastery could only be demonstrated and achieved through the detour of narrative and in strictly figurative ways, through apparently sacrificing original designs and a literal presence in order to create a structure which seemed to exist independently of its designer. The narrator of *The Sacred Fount* reaches a somewhat similar insight. Having noted that his 'opposed couples balanced like bronze groups at the two ends of a chimney-piece', he becomes immediately aware that his 'fine symmetry' is a matter of 'artificial proportion' (*The Sacred Fount*, p. 130). 'Things in the real', he reflects, 'had a way of not balancing' (p. 130). This observation could of course be used to discredit the narrator's inductions.[39] But it also helps to explain why he allows himself to be driven 'into a corner' with his 'dangerous explosive', why he seems deliberately to open himself to charges of building 'houses of cards' or of being 'crazy' and why, in the final chapter, he appears to have surrounded himself with 'a mere heap of disfigured fragments' instead of his perfect palace of thought (pp. 196, 181, 192, 214). In order to be a master the narrator must become a dupe. If things in the real have a way of not balancing, then a certain imbalance and an apparent relinquishment of originary control are vital to sustain and save life, to create the air of reality.[40] In *The Sacred Fount* this imbalance and relinquishment emerge from within rather than being imposed from without. Rather than being driven to the edge by centrifugal forces acting against his centripetal desires, like the governess in 'The Turn of the Screw', the narrator of *The Sacred Fount* deliberately detonates his charged theoretical enterprise. In the final chapter of the novel he seems almost to stage his own disappearance, accepting from Mrs Brissenden 'the word that put me altogether nowhere' and planning his 'escape to other air' (p. 219). He cuts the umbilical cord connecting him with his work, abjures his potent art.[41] Only by doing so can Mrs Brissenden prosper in the world of his work, maintain the 'tone', the full force of presence, which in spite of his 'method', the narrator has 'fatally lacked' (p. 219). The narrator nevertheless leaves behind him the traces of his enterprise and even as he speaks regretfully of his disfigured fragments seems to be re-erecting a bridge through 'the rising magnificence' of his 'metaphor' (p. 215).

Frank Kermode has argued that the Romantic image seeks to effect 'a reconciliation of opposites', a 'mysterious resolution between outward and inward'.[42] In many cases, however, and particularly in the late-flowering Romanticism usually referred to as Symbolism, resolution occurs less through a triumphant synthesis, a moment of perceptual immediacy and unity, than through deferral and problematic interpretation. Unity gives way, not to mere dualities, but to shadowy analogies, correspondences, balances and relations. Something of what Kermode sees as 'the life-in-death, death-in-life of the Romantic Image' is invoked by the chiastically poised portrait described in *The Sacred Fount* (*Romantic Image*, p. 63). This picture could be entitled both 'the Mask of Death', in which case the face of the man holding the mask would represent life (unless, of course, it is Death's mask) and 'the Mask of Life', in which case the face would stand for death – or life (*The Sacred Fount*, p. 51). For Walter Isle the portrait represents 'both death and life, the reality of death-in-life of the face and the artifice of life-in-art of the mask'.[43] Like the narrator's theory and a number of James's most heavily-freighted formulations, the portrait is a doubly double structure. It suggests that works of art sustain an enigmatic relation between the living and the dead. In one sense the portrait acts like the narrator's theory, flagrantly excluding life in its organic, deep-breathing unpredictability and assymetry. To the extent that art is governed by the fixed patterns of a formalized economy it is artificial and deathly. Yet, just as the narrator believes that his theory can convert objective loss into subjective gain, so the portrait also suggests that the work of art, by temporarily arresting depletion, can sustain life, circuitously creating a subjective fullness. Nevertheless, production presumes consumption; fullness in one place implies emptiness in another. What the work of art saves through its dynamic poise must be lost or sacrificed elsewhere. Kermode describes how the romantic image is typically thought to exact 'a heavy price in suffering' (*Romantic Image*, p. 2). In order to create, the artist must be 'lonely, haunted, victimized' (p. 6). The theme of the artist-victim, as Kermode points out, deeply affects James's depiction of writers such as Neil Paraday in 'The Death of the Lion' and Ralph Limbert in 'The Next Time' (see *Romantic Image*, p. 22). Yet artistic sacrifice was not merely a matter for the frustrated writers in James's fiction. In his 1907 introduction to *The Tempest*, James described Shakespeare the triumphant artist as 'the monster and magician of a thousand masks' (*LC*, I, 1209). Shakespeare the man, on the other hand, had been 'locked up and imprisoned in the artist' (p. 1209). Although Shakespeare the writer had been a divinity on a pedestal who defied interpretative penetration with a 'vague flicker of derision', his Osmond-like attitude of superior imaginative authority was bought at the price of an entrapment as absolute as Isabel Archer's. For James there was an important sense in which the writer paid for his work with his life. Balzac had existed only in terms of his labyrinthine imagination and in the ramifying corridors of his work: he had 'no time for the real thing', he 'did *not* live – save in his imagination' (*LC*, II, 107).

Hawthorne had been deeply disturbed by the way in which writing took him out of the real world. Trapped in the haunted chamber, he felt as if he were 'already in the grave' (*CE*, xv, 494). For James, on the other hand, to work in the haunted chamber was to undergo, as a notebook entry of 23 January 1894 put it, an 'intimate battle with the particular idea' and through 'surrender' to become 'victorious' (*N*, p. 84). James celebrated his entombment in the depths of his study, which in a notebook entry of 22 October 1891 was described as his 'sacred and salutary refuge', his 'blessed and uninvaded workroom':

discouragements and lapses, depressions and darknesses come to one only as one stands *without* – I mean without the luminous paradise of art. As soon as I really re-enter it – cross the loved threshold – stand in the high chamber, and the gardens divine – the whole realm widens out again before me ... and I believe, I see, I *do*. (*N*, p. 61)

A further notebook entry written two days later finds James actively wanting to 'live *in* the world of creation – to get into it and stay in it – to frequent it and haunt it' (*N*, p. 62). In his fiction, James had often presented his protagonists with terminally blank walls. Yet from his study in Bolton Street, as he pointed out in a letter of 3 April 1878 to Mrs John Rollin Tilton, he had himself been faced by 'the great smutty blank wall of Lord Ashburton's house' (*L*, II, 163). In De Vere Gardens, according to the Preface to volume XIV of the *New York Edition*, James had looked out on the 'featureless' side of a house which continued in the 'high wall' of a court (*LC*, II, 1220). Far from shutting the writer out and prohibiting access to the place of mastery, however, these barriers had protectively enclosed him within the high chambers of the house of fiction, where his task was, as the Preface to *The Portrait of a Lady* puts it, to pierce 'holes in a dead wall' (*LC*, II, 1075).

The luminous paradise of art; a study looking out onto a conveniently neutral wall which 'hung there like the most voluminous of curtains', masking the 'stage of the great theatre of the town': these are relatively cheerful assessments of artistic activity (*LC*, II, 1220). Many of James's notebook entries read exactly like dispatches from beyond the threshold of the luminous paradise of art. In these terms it would be easy to see James the master as a ghostly presence who looks down from the gods, one of the 'all-knowing immortals' of the Preface to *The Princess Casamassima* who was never bewildered, at least in the world of his work (*LC*, II, 1090). Sacrificing his characters or forcing them to make sacrifices, James is, as he put it to Henry Adams on 21 March 1914, 'that queer monster the artist, an obstinate finality, an inexhaustible sensibility' (*L*, IV, 706). In comparison to the split, exhausted or conceptually naive consciousness in his fiction, James was in supreme command of the fissile and fusile borderlands where relational meaning was born. He was obstinate and yet possessed of sensibility, final and yet also inexhaustible, simultaneously committed to a deep-breathing economy and an organic form. But the monster paid a price for his magic. James was more willing than Hawthorne to shoulder the responsibility of creative violence and to accept that writing always left traces of blood on the threshold. This was the artist's duty, his prerogative, even his privilege; but it was also his problem. In the Preface to *The Ambassadors*, James argued that the hero could not simultaneously be the historian (see *LC*, II, 1315). Yet according to the Preface to *The Tragic Muse*, it was also impossible for the artist to claim 'the privilege of the hero' (*LC*, II, 1118). The source and not the subject of representation, the man of imagination enjoyed something other than complete presence. To live in the world of creation was inevitably to be dead to other worlds.

In revising his works for the *New York Edition* of 1907–9, James spent the best part of four years living back 'into a forgotten state', breathing upon 'the dead reasons of things' and reviving what lay 'buried ... in the texture of the work' (*LC*, II, 1045). On one occasion at least, he found himself reviving the sense of his own 'revivalist impulse' (p. 1099). Characters such as Christina Light, who had first appeared in *Roderick Hudson* but had returned in *The Princess Casamassima*, resembled 'haunting ghosts' who walked round James's 'house of art ... feeling for the old doors they knew, fumbling at stiff latches and pressing their pale faces, in the outer dark, to lighted windows' (p. 1098). Coming full circle, the James of the Prefaces returns to his own house of fiction and finds it an uncanny place. He writes of the 'haunting presences' which reduce his 'revisiting, re-appropriating impulse' to 'a mere blurred, sad, scarcely consolable vision' (p. 1174). James was haunted by the ghosts he had raised, but the haunting presence most in question was often that of the writer he had been. To track or report back on this presence was a problematic affair. As the 'docile reader' of his more recent work, James's 'imaginative steps' sink comfortably into the footprints left by his writing self (p. 1329). Walking through his house of fiction, he becomes a happier version of Brydon, meeting his authorial other 'halfway, passive, receptive, appreciative, often even grateful; unconscious, quite blissfully, of any bar to intercourse' (p. 1329). But when he returns to the work of his earlier self it is often to tread out the steps of a 'very different dance' (p. 1329). In this case the encounter does not result in mutual recognition but instead produces a 'quite other kind of consciousness' (p. 1329). Because the artist in triumph was virtually unrepresentable, James often found himself looking back at his own turned back: a ghost in pursuit of a ghost, unable to catch himself in the act of creation. The writer may have possessed a plenitude of presence, but that presence was frequently elsewhere. He may have been an observing eye, but he could not easily inspect his own perceptual faculty. He may have been the origin of the work, but the work's origin (and this is especially true of the artist tales and the ghostly tales) was often not to be recaptured (see *LC*, II, 1081, 1103, 1166, 1228, 1232, 1241, 1246, 1250, 1261, 1262–3). Like Ralph Pendrel, James remounts 'the stream of time', although only 'to come back empty-handed'

(p. 1250). He repeatedly presents himself as the dupe rather than the master. Like the writers represented in his fiction, he can only become visible to himself at moments when he is 'deluded, diverted, frustrated or vanquished' (*LC*, II, 1118). When he pictures the room in which a particular book was written, his old self has often just stopped writing. This other writer paces to and fro, stands at windows, listens to faint but distinct noises which come in from without: a 'clatter of horse-pails' from the Piazza Santa Maria Novella in the Preface to *Roderick Hudson*, the 'rich rumble' of the Rue de la Paix in the Preface to *The Tragic Muse* (*LC*, II, 1043, 1110). In part these atmospheric, circumambient sounds represent the recollection of a filtering process on the part of James, who could not write of places 'under too immediate an impression' (*LC*, II, 1059). The man of imagination required 'the minimum of valid suggestion' and not the maximum (*LC*, II, 1175). Yet it is significant that the Prefaces repeatedly associate these mediated sounds of a city's life with interrupted rather than with achieved creation. In the Preface to *The American* James sees himself being drawn from his desk to his windows on the Rue de Luxembourg, from writing to the 'light Parisian click of the small cab-horse on the clear asphalt' and from the 'faded page' of his own text to its recollected 'interlineation of sound' (*LC*, II, 1058). In the Preface to *The Portrait of a Lady*, he again pictures himself at a window where, during 'the fruitless fidget of composition', he listens to 'the ceaseless human chatter of Venice' (*LC*, II, 1070). In a subsequent Preface it is the 'strong Venetian voice' which seems 'to say more in ten warm words ... than any twenty pages of one's cold pale prose' (*LC*, II, 1152).

Clatter, rumble, chatter: these auditory intermittences are not only about the failure to write, or more precisely to coincide with the self that wrote. The Prefaces swarm with ghostly echoes of James's predecessors: even the most perfunctory list would include the names of Shakespeare and Gray and Fielding, Gyp and Dumas and Scott, Byron and Shelley, Coleridge and Browning, Flaubert and Maupassant and Zola, George Eliot and Turgenev, Trollope and Tolstoy and Ibsen, even the unnamed Hawthorne. The return of the predecessors – through allusion, association or invocation – is often signalled by means of sound. Piccadilly's 'big human rumble' conjures up the world of Thackeray, whilst other parts of London seem to speak with 'the thousand voices' of Dickens (*LC*, II, 1220). A mention of Balzac leads almost immediately to memories of a 'light click and clatter, that sound as of the thin, quick, quite feminine surface-breathing of Paris' (*LC*, II, 1060).

James's later fiction possesses an often extraordinarily charged sense of the acoustic. In 'The Jolly Corner', Spencer Brydon listens for a 'dim reverberating tinkle as of some far-off bell hung ... in the depths of the house, of the past' (*CT*, XII, 209). In *The Sense of the Past*, Ralph Pendrel is alert to an almost impossibly tenuous echo: he wants to hear 'the very tick of the old stopped clocks' (*NYE*, XXVI, 49). Susanne Kappeler has argued that there is a shift from visual to auditory terms in *The Sacred Fount*.[44] In the Prefaces, as in the final lines of *The Sacred Fount*, it often seems that tone triumphs over method, speech over writing. James sacrifices any attempt to account for the origin of his work and chooses instead to concentrate on circuitous descriptions of its effect. Yet ultimately, perhaps, these uncanny resonances are the finest emblem of the dynamics of the Jamesian text. The light click from the Parisian street is not far distant from the 'little click' which, in a notebook entry of 22 October 1891, takes place in James's imagination as, 'pen in hand', he begins to look his subject 'in the face' (*N*, p. 62). In these terms, the windows which James reverts to in the Prefaces are not so much posts for observational supremacy as reverberating tympana which receive and transmit an interplay of presence and absence, inside and outside.

The Prefaces describe how their author watches himself looking out from the house of fiction. In *The Ambassadors*, by contrast, the ghost at the window is seen from outside and below. Yet the distance between James and his protagonist is not so great, and at various points Strether is to find himself both inside and above, at windows or on balconies. During these moments, as Tony Tanner points out, Strether achieves his creator's favoured position on the border between involvement and detachment (see 'The Watcher from the Balcony', pp. 40–3).[45] Strether has a Jamesian sensitivity to faint auditory percussions, to individual and cultural resonances, to what *The American Scene* calls 'the small silver whistle of the past' (p. 215). His Paris seems to 'reverberate' with 'the taste of history' (*NYE*, XXI, 228). Strether's attempts to 'reconstitute' the past do occasionally involve reducing it 'to the convenient terms of Victor Hugo' (*NYE*, XXII, 7). But there is no lack of Jamesian sophistication in his alertness to 'sounds and suggestions, vibrations of the air', to the meanings in the simultaneously human and dramatic 'tone' of Paris, to the 'far-off hum' and the 'sharp near click on the asphalt' (p. 24). Whilst the governess in 'The Turn of the Screw' seeks to pierce dividing membranes, Strether sustains them. He does not approach thresholds, stand at windows or listen at half-open shutters in order to break through to a meaning but to entertain the interpenetration which is meaning, to experience an intermingling of public and private, of past and present, perhaps even of ethics and aesthetics.

The later James shows an increasingly explicit investment in such borderlands, a growing commitment to what Mary Ann Caws has called an 'aesthetic sense of border'.[46] In *The Golden Bowl* the situation between Maggie and her father is described as a 'thin wall', an 'exquisite tissue ... stretched on a frame' (*NYE*, xxiv, 267). Endangered but ultimately preserved, this fragile membrane seems also to represent something still more important – the entire nature and possibility of textual, perhaps even of cultural meaning. A similar emphasis on edges and thresholds recurs in 'The Jolly Corner', where Brydon's activities are likened to setting 'some great glass bowl ... set delicately humming by the play of a moist finger round its edge' (*CT*, xii, 209). It is only in the 'indescribably fine murmur' made by the rim that 'the old baffled forsworn possibilities' achieve 'such measure of ghostly life as they might still enjoy' (p. 209). This image represents a virtual dramatization of the revolution in which the real becomes the romantic and the romantic becomes the real.

Strether's auditory sense of the past is also a sense of the present and even, on occasions, a sense of presence. The ghost at the window above Gloriani's garden is in itself a sufficient visual token of this presence, but the uncanniness of the scene is significantly heightened by a reference to the 'bird-haunted trees' (*NYE*, xxi, 195). Quite as much as the high walls, the birds in Gloriani's garden speak of 'survival, transmission, association' (p. 195). They are vernal, noonday, twittering creatures: less sombre presences than the birds heard by the narrator of *The Sacred Fount* during his evening walk, less strident than the rooks which 'wheeled and clamored' in the sky above Haddon Hall, less portentous than the rooks which circle and caw above 'the clustered tree-tops' at Bly (*The Sacred Fount*, p. 128; *Transatlantic Sketches*, p. 26; *CT*, x, 23). However different their atmospheric charge, all these references to birdsong – like the 'solitary Birds' heard by Addison during his twilight wanderings – seem to conjure up a faint sense of some Orphic presence (Addison,

The Spectator, I, 453). Onomatopoeia gives way to prosopopoeia and the text, interlineated with sound, becomes the writing of a listening to some phonic after-effect or belated sonic resurrection. The birds which haunt the trees in Gloriani's garden are far from threatening. On occasions, however, the resonances detected by Strether can become more ominous visitations. Towards the end of the novel, he calls on Madame de Vionnet in the Rue de Bellechasse. Through the open windows he hears 'the vague voice of Paris' (*NYE*, xxii, 274). Yet this voice no longer prompts mere mellow appreciation. Strether's 'historic sense' associates these sounds with 'omens' and 'beginnings', with 'days and nights of revolution' (p. 274).

Sound also presages crisis, though Strether is not aware of it beforehand, during his day on the river. It is true that he is reviving his memories of the Lambinet painting and that his country outing is at first predominantly a visual affair. Gradually, however, the sounds begin to gather. Poplars and willows start to 'rustle' (pp. 247, 253). Strether's walk becomes a 'murmurous' experience (p. 248). These auditory intermittences intensify when he reaches the pavilion at the edge of the river, listens to the 'lap' of the water, the 'ripple' of the river and the 'rustle' of the reeds (p. 255). Yet this is precisely the point at which Strether, a strictly comparative case of the imagination, begins to be unable to sustain a Jamesian resonance. As Chad and Madame de Vionnet drift into view along the river, a sudden hush seems to fall upon the scene. One is reminded of the governess's first encounter with Quint, during which 'the rooks stopped cawing' and a deathly stillness ensued (*CT*, x, 36). Quint is the manifestation of this silence, an unrecognizable intruder whose appearance is compared to 'the spring of a beast' (p. 34). In contrast, Strether's crisis involves the detection of the familiar in the strange. He suddenly recognizes Chad and Madame de Vionnet, and feels that his perception breaks the 'stillness' like 'some unprovoked harsh note' (*NYE*, xxii, 258). Whilst James destroys the governess's appreciation of 'the last calls of the last birds' by abruptly imposing silence, he registers the ironic distance between himself and Strether by subjecting his protagonist to a sudden harsh noise (*CT*, x, 35). In both texts the central consciousness is displaced from the fulcrum where auditory absence and presence satisfactorily meet and mingle.

There is something of the author as violent and primitive deity in these passages. James signals his judgements in thunderous rumbles and ominous silences or, more subtly, indicates his unseen presence in rustling leaves. In the 1877 version of *The American*, Newman enters Notre Dame and merely hears 'far-away bells chiming off, at long intervals, to the rest of the world' (*Novels 1871–1880*, p. 868). In the revised version of the text, however, he hears something more resounding: 'the big bronze syllables of the Word' (*NYE*, II, 533). The Logos is uttered by the creator. It demands sacrifice and renunciation. The word completes Newman's text, provides a 'formal conclusion' which enables him to 'close the book and put it away' (*Novels 1871–1880*, p. 868).[47]

James had repeatedly projected himself as the model for the desiring subjectivities featured in his fiction. Yet one cannot finally determine the echoes and resonances either in the fiction or in the Prefaces as the signs of a godlike creative plenitude or self-coincidence. Jamesian presence is partial, intermittent, ghostly. James represented himself through his ghosts but these did not provide for a self-enclosed and independent existence. Just as ghosts need human beings to see them, so writers need their readers. Quint may enjoy the best point of view, but he can only come into existence through the governess. As a writer, James must take a similar detour through others in order to come into being. Only by representing himself as the other for others could he become a master, an occupant of the plains of heaven. To be such a master, however, was inevitably to posit oneself as absent, as a being mediated by ghosts and texts. In a certain sense, the artist did not belong in life. The source of representation was not within the field of the representable. James's autobiographical writings are a sustained investigation of the artist's partial emptiness and absence, of how the small boy lived through others to become the man of imagination – that figure who had 'haunted' James since before *The Ambassadors* and who finally turned up in a shape 'almost too familiar ... for recognition' (*Autobiography*, p. 455). So familiar as to be almost unrecognizable, and even unrepresentable. The Prefaces speak of the idea of writing a history of the growth of the imagination as a 'subtle' but also as a 'monstrous' thing (*LC*, II, 1076). The autobiography makes it clear that an extraordinary contortion was required to turn the historian into the hero, to convert the man of imagination who was the source of representation into the subject of representation. To make this figure 'objective', James had to 'turn nothing less than myself inside out' (*Autobiography*, p. 455). This

existential unfolding and re-folding obviates any need to represent
the man of imagination as an interior from the interior. The sources
and the 'life' of James's subject are always elsewhere; the inside
becomes a matter of outsides. Time and again in *A Small Boy and
Others* and *Notes of a Son and Brother* it is the others who possess
presence. James acquires what being he has through consciousness,
and this consciousness is almost always consciousness of the
consciousness of others, consciousness of others as the site of full
being. Shut out from the 'richer consciousness' he imputes to others,
he observes life as if through a 'confectioner's window; unattainable,
impossible' (p. 101). The James who acted as a model in his fiction
was himself the yearning and frequently bewildered subject of
mimetic desire. He was both haunted and haunting, the subject of
phantasmagoric experience and fruitful alterities, yet also a disembodied spectator, a spectral observer. Cut off from 'direct performance' and 'direct participation', he lived through indirection,
through substitutive and figurative modes of existence, through 'the
beautiful circuit and subterfuge' of his 'thought' and 'desire', as he
put it in the Preface to *The American* (*Autobiography*, pp. 111–12; *LC*,
ii, 1063). Far from turning his back on the others, as he often did in
his fiction, it was the others in his life – and notably his brother
William – who repeatedly turned their backs on him, who seemed
'already beforehand', 'already seated' at their tasks, 'always round
the corner and out of sight' (*Autobiography*, pp. 7–8).

I have argued that the Louvre dream recounted in *A Small Boy and
Others* should be read in terms of its commitment to the centrifugal,
boundary-breaking imagination, to an artistic victory achieved by
means of the explosive principle. But one must also read the dream
in terms of economic mastery, foreshortening, perhaps even suppression. For the scene in the Galerie d'Apollon converts that
unattainable figure of the other, 'always round the corner and out of
sight', into a vanquished opponent. James transforms his exclusion
into a triumphant expulsion. But has the historian really become the
hero? If he has, there is a sense in which he gains one role at the cost
of another, sacrifices complete and self-enclosed presence in the
interests of oscillation, rotation and intermittence. The figure
encountered in the dream is not only some invasive monster, some
emblem of active force, of William and the others. It also represents
the situation of the Prefaces, in which James finds himself confronted
by his own turned back. In these terms the 'just dimly-descried

figure', the 'awful ... presence' who flees down the long diminishing perspective of the dream is not simply an imaginary being, a symbol, but a figure for the man of imagination's monstrous imagination, a force and a presence always elsewhere, always disappearing (pp. 196, 197). It is only by displacing or sacrificing this presence that James turns himself inside out and preserves the possibility of representation by retaining a figure on the threshold who lives to see the after-effect of the artist's presence. In other cases, however, the encounter with the writing self is more like a death or a blind spot. As the Prefaces make clear, the public form of Clare Vawdrey is ' "cut dead" ' on reaching 'the threshold of the closed study' (*LC*, II, 1254). Rather than defeating his other, Vawdrey is extinguished by it, annihilated by the 'waiting spirit' of his literary *alter ego*, the 'real great man ... a presence known ... all and only to himself – unseen of other human eye' (p. 1254). Taken over by the writing self, Vawdrey enters on a sort of posthumous existence. In quick succession he experiences the 'rare extension of being' provided by ghostly experience, the 'great extension' of artistic experience and the 'great extension' offered by the prospect of immortality (*CT*, IX, 400; *LC*, II, 1061; 'Is There a Life After Death?', p. 221).

Throughout this book I have been trying to evaluate the role of the ghostly in James's fiction, and this has often involved assessing the extent to which James was haunted by the writings of his predecessors. Yet one could also say that James himself was a not inconsiderable ghost in the minds of his literary successors. Any comprehensive description of James's influence would of course be the subject of another book than the one I have written. Briefly and finally, however, I should like to indicate in inevitably sketchy terms the way in which James appears to have haunted the work of his countryman T.S. Eliot. What is intriguing is that Eliot is particularly influenced by James's registrations of ghostly and uncanny experience. This is certainly the area to which Eliot seems drawn in 'The Hawthorne Aspect' (1918), which discusses the ghostly elements in late James, notably *The Sense of the Past*. I have the impression that the uncanny street encounters in *Watch and Ward* and 'In the Cage' are being called to mind in the half-deserted streets of 'The Love Song of J. Alfred Prufrock' (1917); Nora Lambert's sunset sensation of having been given a dose of ether prefigures the more grimly portentous etherized patient in the opening lines of 'Prufrock'. One might also recall the reference to a not very 'jolly corner' in *The Family Reunion* (1939).[48] Most interestingly of all, compounded echoes of the Galerie d'Apollon dream, as well as of 'The Private Life', 'The Real Right Thing', 'The Jolly Corner' and *The Sense of the Past* seem to be stirring in the encounter described by Eliot in 'Little Gidding' (1942). Here, in 'the uncertain hour before the morning',

> I met one walking, loitering and hurried
> As if blown towards me like the metal leaves
> Before the urban dawn wind unresisting.
> And as I fixed upon the down-turned face
> That pointed scrutiny with which we challenge
> The first-met stranger in the waning dusk
> I caught the sudden look of some dead master
> Whom I had known, forgotten, half recalled
> Both one and many; in the brown baked features
> The eyes of a familiar compound ghost
> Both intimate and unidentifiable.
> So I assumed a double part, and cried
> And heard another voice cry: 'What! are *you* here?'
> Although we were not. I was still the same,
> Knowing myself yet being someone other –
>
> (*The Collected Poems and Plays*, p. 193)

James spent a lifetime struggling to achieve artistic immortality, a life after death through others and by means of textual ghosts. The phrase 'across the border' crops up in his last dictation, as if death was some further version of the act of crossing 'the loved threshold' into his study (*N*, pp. 584, 61). 'It's the *living* ones that die; the writing ones that survive', he had observed to his brother after the death of Minny Temple in 1870 (*L*, I, 228). He did indeed survive – as a ghost in the haunted chamber of literature.

Postscript

I hope that my work on James has its own specific value and that my readings of his writings can be seen as relatively free-standing affairs. Nevertheless, there remains the issue of placing what has been said in more direct relation to some of the theoretical perspectives which were introduced on a pragmatic, *ad hoc* basis. This is not so much a matter of tying up loose ends as of examining a number of theoretical knots that may not themselves have been thematized in earlier chapters. It could well be a matter of my own critical inadequacy, but I would be tempted to describe these knots as limit problems.

Throughout this book I have found myself repeatedly reverting to ideas about sacrifice, violence and the scapegoat. René Girard's thoughts about the role of the model in the mimetic structure of desire seemed to shed light on James's complex relations with his fictional centres of consciousness. In particular, the idea of the sacrificial crisis (elaborated, I would argue, in Tzvetan Todorov's description of the fantastic) recognized the importance of the ghostly as well as providing it with a coherent function in social and narrative practices. There was, however, a further analogue to Todorov on the fantastic and Girard on the tragic trajectory. Arnold van Gennep's concept of liminality, especially as developed in the work of Victor Turner, afforded a useful way, not only of thinking through James's own complex, often paradoxical thresholds and of looking at the multiplication of sacred borders in the Jamesian text, but also, in ways that seemed to contribute to a fuller understanding of 'The Turn of the Screw', of defining the problematic predicament of women in general and governesses in particular within Victorian society.

For Victor Turner, liminality belongs to 'communitas', which he defines as social anti-structure (see *The Ritual Process*, pp. 97, 111, 129; *Dramas, Fields, and Metaphors*, pp. 45–57). In rites of passage 'men are released from structure into communitas only to return to structure revitalized by their experience' (*The Ritual Process*, p. 129). Although the liminal phase concerns anti-structure it always paves the way for a return to structure through elevation and incorporation or through expulsion and the recognition of irreconcilable divisions. In all cases, therefore, the liminal crisis discloses a communitas which reinforces the old structure or creates a new one. Particularly when one sees it in terms of chronological or narrative sequence, liminality is in other words ultimately normative, at least if one accepts what Barbara A. Babcock calls 'the functionalist steam-valve explanation' of rituals of reversal.[1] On this view, rites of reversal may involve an element of protest against structure but ultimately preserve or reinforce it. The idea of liminality, at least as it is usually presented, therefore bears a strong resemblance not only to Girard on sacrifice but also to Aristotle on catharsis. Like sacrifice, tragedy prevents the relentless accumulation of chaos or violence within society. Sacrificial expulsion and cathartic purgation act in the interests of social, political and perhaps also of philosophical order. Far from representing or expressing mythic or aesthetic freedom, therefore, ritual and art would serve an essentially normative function by recouping difference and deviance for the unified body of order, accounting for the ghostly and the figurative as diversions or detours.

I have already attempted to raise a number of questions about these hierarchies. From a rather different point of view, however, the functionalist explanation of ritual as a release of subversive energies which might otherwise have created the potential for revolutionary change has been challenged by a number of anthropologists (see Babcock's introduction to *The Reversible World*, p. 23). Although Turner sees 'liminoid' leisure genres such as carnival, festival and drama as the authentic descendants of liminal rites, he is prepared to accept that they may open the possibility of change in a way that liminal (that is to say, pre-industrial) forms do not (see *Dramas, Fields, and Metaphors*, p. 16; 'Comments and Conclusions', pp. 281, 295). Art can therefore escape the exigencies of structure in a way that ritual cannot. Natalie Zemon Davis would go somewhat further. Although she concedes that ritual inversions may in part 'reinforce hierarchical structure', she argues that the figure of the unruly woman as well as instances of gender inversion during crises in early industrial society are 'not so much a release from the tensions of stable hierarchical control as an expression of the struggle over change'.[2] For Davis, ritual inversions may subvert rather than confirm tradition.

Caroline Bynum's discussion of the concept of liminality takes rather a different line. For her, the potential for change emphasized by Davis and stated with more reservation by Turner simply does not exist. Bynum argues that liminality (she is specifically referring to symbolic gender reversals in Christian religious initiations) is not a universal pattern of ritual but a product of the Western, Christian patriarchal tradition. Rather than liberating and empowering, the liminal phase is 'an escape for those who bear the burdens and reap the benefits of a high place in the social structure'.[3] At least implicitly, however, Turner himself understands that patriarchal order thinks of women as liminal beings in order to facilitate male initiations and enact social resolutions in the interests of male institutions. In a sense, therefore, Bynum is not so much contesting the idea of liminality itself as she is criticizing Turner's vision of the interrelationships between structure and anti-structure for not sufficiently emphasizing the thoroughgoing way in which the latter serves the former. Identifying the concept of liminality with a structure/chaos binarism (see 'Women's Stories', p. 118) which reminds one of Cixous on male hierarchical oppositions, Bynum reveals not only the complicity between theories of liminality and their objects but also the continuity and inclusiveness of those normative forces which she deplores. The practice and the theory of the liminal becomes part of patriarchy's game.

How does the debate about liminality affect one's evaluation of the Jamesian text? To the extent that it creates areas which seem to exist between schismatic oppositions and hierarchies, that it represents inversions and turns, ghosts or uncanny crises, that it produces or valorizes charged thresholds, then clearly it is doing something which one could describe in terms of liminality. But what status or *telos* do these liminal tropes, this borderline sense of consciousness and the literary text have? Does Sharon Cameron's vision of a Jamesian consciousness which inhabits an 'undemarcated space' and undoes or eradicates conventional oppositions ultimately shape itself within the logic or demarcation and opposition (*Thinking in Henry James*, p. 81)? Are James's ghosts to be seen as temporary deviations which appear in the interests of the governing *status quo*? Or as part of some potentially more subversive attempt to escape from or undermine order and structure?

In chapter 2 I attempted to distinguish James's characteristic conceptual manoeuvres from those of the writers and thinkers I had looked at in the first chapter. James was not interested in expelling the irrational or in creating absolute, hierarchized oppositions. Yet nor, on the other hand, did his circuitries validate writing as a simple escape from power. Mark Seltzer would be unlikely to agree with this view. Indeed, *Henry James and the Art of Power* reads like a massive elaboration of theories of sacrificial, tragic or liminal normalization in terms of Henry James. Seltzer makes James into a supreme representative of precisely the tradition from which I have tried to distinguish him. For Seltzer, the nineteenth-century novel in general and the Jamesian text in particular stage a 'normalizing detour into abnormality'.[4] The second book of *The Golden Bowl*, for instance, is to be read as a 'rectification of the monstrous and perverse' (*Henry James and the Art of Power*, p. 90). Seltzer would certainly disagree with Turner and Davis, who want to see liminoid genres in terms of their capacity to produce genuine change and to escape from the replication of power structures. Following Foucault, Seltzer believes that literature's very claim to be external to the political merely confirms and reinforces the power it purports to oppose (see pp. 173–5). In the case of James's writing, art and power 'are not opposed ... but radically entangled' (p. 13). Seltzer argues that those critics who claim that James 'resists the impositions of power in the name of a radical (literary) freedom' collaborate in the operation of power by sustaining the dissimulations and disavowals that make power tolerable (p. 15; see also p. 115). 'The notion that the literary always and in principle stands apart from and subverts structures of power may function ideologically in support of the very power it seems to resist' (p. 132). For Seltzer, therefore, Jamesian dynamics are essentially regulatory and normative; they ultimately produce equilibrium, order, stability and closure. James maintains his narrative authority through recession and dispersal; his 'rule of organic form provides a way of disavowing the violence of authorial manipulation and control even as regulation is secured at every point' (p. 86). Seltzer argues that James's often celebrated 'resistance to the law in the name of an absolute novelistic liberty ... in fact works as a "cover" for a discreet and comprehensive entanglement between strategies of representation and exercises of power and law' (p. 18). His book therefore sets out to trace the manifold forms of this entanglement.

I share Seltzer's reservations concerning those critics who merely

see 'a radical opposition or polarization' in Jamesian dynamics
(p. 156). I am also inclined to agree with his view that approaching
James in terms of 'ambiguity' may well be to screen the guilty
affiliation of art and power (see pp. 156, 184). One can certainly
accept the idea that the literary is not in essence something which
works against philosophical, social or political order. In terms of my
own area of interest there is a very strong tradition for which, rather
than representing crisis, chaos and transgression (or indeed, more
interestingly, precisely *because* they represent crisis, chaos and transgression) ghosts preserve and sustain structure. Furthermore, it is
indeed true that James often represents the experience of writing as,
on the author's part, an experience of freedom. What I would
contest in Seltzer's account is the idea that James conceals the
complicity between art and power by opposing them. In principle
one can of course accept the idea that power may be more effectively
maintained when its implication in the aesthetic is concealed or
denied. In challenging this oppositional discourse, Seltzer goes so far
as to assert that art and power are in many respects tautologous (see
p. 156). I am not sure that this superimposition is particularly
helpful, yet if there is some kind of circular interrelationship
between art and power, as Seltzer more cautiously asserts (see p.
184), then I would argue that James's work recognizes and dramatizes this rotary mutuality rather than concealing it. For Leo
Bersani, certainly, James's novels are not so much the appropriate
object for a Foucauldian critique as a prescient demonstration of
Foucault's ideas about power as knowledge and discourse.[5]
However, Seltzer provides a strong argument against those critics
who claim that James at least covertly acknowledges his complicity
in power by acts of ironic self-subversion. For Seltzer, these ironies
register an affiliation with power which James then seeks to evade by
escaping into 'romance' (see pp. 135–6, 138). Romance is, to use
James's own word, a 'subterfuge', a way of wielding power in covert
ways (*LC*, II, 1063). Seltzer is evidently quite right to argue that
romance, insofar as it concerns individual desire, has often been held
to resist institutionalized forms of power (see *Henry James and the Art
of Power*, p. 139). But it seems unfair to criticize James for disavowing power through the language of romance, since the Preface to *The
American* describes the romantic as a 'circuit' as well as a subterfuge
and, in surprising terms, explicitly relates the romantic to the issue
of power:

It is as difficult, I said above, to trace the dividing-line between the real and the romantic as to plant a milestone between north and south; but I am not sure an infallible sign of the latter is not this rank vegetation of the 'power' of bad people that good get into, or *vice versa*. (*LC*, II, 1067)

It is true that James adds as a rider the comment that 'it is so rarely, alas, into our power that any one gets!' (p. 1067). But I don't think that we need to read this as a serious authorial disavowal: James is talking about himself as a member of a community, not as a writer. Speaking of himself as a writer, James is perfectly explicit about his implication in the play of power. Moreover, since this power is rooted in the writer's freedom, since Jamesian dynamics are circular and interactive, I cannot see James as the oppositional thinker described by Seltzer. In the Preface to volume XVIII of the *New York Edition*, James does seem to imply that the relationship between the explosive principle and economic mastery is to be thought in time. In this sense, the economic master does finally foreclose on the liberated expansions he had once sponsored. Such a sequence of events sounds distinctly normative and yet, looked at in the context of James's other discriminations, this passage does not finally corroborate Seltzer's idea that James screens the practice of power by proposing areas where it does not function. The one term presupposes the related existence of the other. To think of freedom is to consider what limits it, to commit oneself to control is to consider that which resists control. For James, the genre often associated with freedom – the romance – necessarily involves the exercise of power. Considered internally and in isolation, the romance may well dissimulate its disconnections, using representations of liberated experience to conceal or disavow the operation of authorial power. Externally and in the context of James's poetics of the novel in its entirety, however, the romantic is always related to, returning to or departing from the real. James may not, like Seltzer, see art and power as equivalent. But nor does he disconnect art and power in the way that Seltzer claims. 'Not to be disconnected', as he puts it in the Preface to *The Golden Bowl*, the artist 'has but to feel that he is not; by his lightest touch the whole chain of relation and responsibility is reconstituted' (p. 1340). I take the line out of context, yet it seems to be representative. In contrast to the bleak and devious oppositionalism seen by Seltzer, I think that one could express James's recognition of relationships and complicities in the chiastic formulation used by Hillis Miller to describe James's evaluation of writing and conduct: 'where we seem more responsible we are bound by a necessity which makes us in fact irresponsible, while where we are most free, untied, we are able to be more responsible, or are in fact, whether we will or not, responsible, since it is open to us to take responsibility or not'.[6]

Seltzer is quite right to argue that, 'far from being opposed, love and power in *The Golden Bowl* are two ways of saying the same thing' (*Henry James and the Art of Power*, p. 66). One can accept that power is productive and may even appear in benevolently caring rather than merely repressive forms, that it operates through what screens it and not simply behind the screens (see p. 134). More importantly, Seltzer's argument elegantly transcends the somewhat sterile question of whether Maggie is a saint or a dictator. For him the two roles are equivalent and *The Golden Bowl* affirms the normative trajectory by finally rectifying the monstrous and perverse. Just as sacrificial expulsion preserves order it would seem that adultery constitutes or creates marriage (see p. 80). Yet James is not concealing this, although it may well be more comfortable for the critics to assert that *The Golden Bowl* is either about love or power, saints or dictators. James knows as well as Turner or Girard or Seltzer that transgression can maintain the force of contract, and it seems unfair to blame him for scrutinizing what may well amount to something like the grand narrative of human culture. This, then, could be defined as a limit problem. The very attempt to 'break out of' the sacrificial trajectory may well introduce the notion of a transgression which confirms and reinforces contract.

Seltzer sees 'The Turn of the Screw' as another story which concerns the complicity of power and love (see pp. 66, 157). Once again, one can see that the classic debate over the tale screens its continuities. Seltzer identifies the governess as a representative of the major Foucauldian power structures. As tutor, nurse, confessor and analyst, she occupies 'the power roles of the "medico-tutelary complex"' (p. 157). This is a view to give one pause, for if the governess represents the productive and 'caring' side of power one can only conclude that structures of authority are highly unstable and that they carry dissent within themselves. As I have argued, the nineteenth-century governess was often seen to present a direct threat to social hierarchies and cultural borders. Seltzer defends Foucault against the criticism that he has 'an overly monolithic conception of power' (p. 193). For him, Foucault 'insists on the local and unstable moves of often conflicting apparatuses of discipline, administration, and regulation' (p. 193). But one rarely sees the local instabilities and conflicting apparatuses in his account of James. Seltzer makes considerable play of Foucault's description of the panopticon and the complicity between institutionalized power structures and novelistic acts of surveillance. It is true that the gaze may indeed be a powerfully mastering thing in James. Yet it is not always so. To see without being seen (as in Isabel Archer's vision of Gilbert Osmond and Serena Merle) may be to begin to recognize the extent of one's subjection – a form of power in itself, of course, but one which defines itself in relation to another source of power which is not, on this occasion at least, a specular one. Elsewhere in James it is often the aversion of the gaze which constitutes the most typical final gesture of those in authority. It is possible that Seltzer's account of power in the Jamesian text may not be inclusive enough. It certainly emphasizes the links between power and surveillance or power and discourse at the expense of the equally important association between power and blindness or power and silence. The variable attributes of power and the different ways in which it can be exercized suggest that the concept of authority in James will potentially be subject to rapid shifts and inversions. A good example of this, particularly in relation to the disciplinary theme, is to be found in 'The Turn of the Screw'. The governess thinks of herself as a gaoler but is eventually to find herself inside a figurative prison (see *CT*, x, 90, 133). Power has become powerless. It hasn't disappeared but, no longer issuing solely from conventional or institutionalized sources, it does seem to have become more mobile. At this point I would suggest, first, that this inversion (not to mention others in the Jamesian text) is not straightforwardly normative in effect, and second, that by recognizing the way in which power produces its authors as well as its subjects, James is addressing precisely those complicities which Seltzer accuses him of concealing.

I am not even sure whether Seltzer's idea of the dissimulated collusion between art and power really helps to explain pre-Jamesian versions of a 'middle ground', a neutral territory which in Seltzer's view maintains the fiction of art's apolitical independence (p. 190). In a novel such as *The Blithedale Romance* the normalizing trajectory is explicitly being called into question. Hawthorne creates a network of criminal conflicts and mutualities which enfolds Fourier the political radical, Hollingsworth the prison reformer,

Coverdale the spectator/novelist and Zenobia the proto-feminist. Hawthorne's 'unpardonable sin' anticipates Seltzer's references to the 'shame' or 'crime' of power and the 'criminal continuity between art and power' (*Henry James and the Art of Power*, pp. 15, 147, 150, 148). And if Hawthorne can recognize these continuities, then so can James. So far from positing art as a domain outside and radically opposed to power, the James of the Prefaces explicitly describes how he subjects himself to techniques of restraint. It is his ideas which require 'full revolutions of the merciless screw' (*LC*, II, 1240). It is his own 'accretions' which make him feel like 'some warden of the insane engaged at a critical moment in making fast a victim's straitjacket' (p. 1238). Seltzer sees the house of fiction as a 'prison house' with James as the panoptic gaoler (see *Henry James and the Art of Power*, pp. 48, 124). But if James can be the victim as well as the torturer, the madman as well as the warder, then surely he can also take on the role of the prisoner as well as that of the gaoler. Aligned in this way, of course, he would bear an uncanny resemblance to the governess in 'The Turn of the Screw'.

I have already argued along rather different lines that the governess could be seen as the perpetuator of masculinist oppositions and that James's blanks defeat her linear, phallic readings. Seltzer does not explicitly gender his analysis of power. If we do look at power in terms of patriarchy, however, I think that we can see more clearly the local instabilities, conflicts and internal shifts which determine James's complex relation to authority. Sandra Gilbert and Susan Gubar are right to point out, in a specific allusion to Jamesian terminology, that Victorian women were indeed 'constricted and restricted by the ... Houses of Fiction male writers authored' (*The Madwoman in the Attic*, p. xi). 'The Turn of the Screw' does address the polarized patriarchal view of women as angels or monsters and indeed one could argue that it shows a very typical fear that the angels are really half monsters (see *The Madwoman in the Attic*, p. 29). Perhaps James was indeed, like Joyce and Eliot in Gilbert and Gubar's account, transcribing female language 'in order to transcend it' (*No Man's Land*, I, 236) or, through 'the occulting of common language', attempting to intuit 'the ghost of a patriarchal *Ur-sprache* which has been lost or forgotten' (pp. 258, 256). Possibly the omissions in 'The Turn of the Screw', following the pun which Gilbert and Gubar derive from *Ulysses*, are to be seen as emissions (see p. 231). Perhaps, misogynistically, James is forcing

the governess's narrative open, creating lack, castrating or determining her as castrated. Perhaps his 'O' relates to the impulse in
male *fin de siècle* art to link women with circular figures, with what
Bram Dijkstra calls the 'vulval round'[7] or with an 'O' which for
Gilbert and Gubar signifies 'the emptiness and the openness of an
obediently serviceable woman' (Gilbert and Gubar, *No Man's Land*,
I, 47). Yet the evaluation of the 'O' may well depend on one's
evaluation of patriarchy, and the questions one can raise about the
nature of patriarchy recall the debate about the nature of liminality.
Is patriarchy a monolithic structure without internal difference or is
it sometimes capable of registering genuine dissent or producing
authentic change? Bynum and Seltzer or Turner and Davis? Nina
Auerbach argues that the feminist response to patriarchy and the
mythic has undergone a significant shift. Once seen almost entirely
in terms of a patriarchal assault upon women, myth has been
re-evaluated and revalorized, not least in Auerbach's own work, but
also in that of writers like Gilbert and Gubar.[8] For Auerbach,
patriarchal myth-making escapes from itself and glorifies what it
seems to suppress (see *Woman and the Demon*, p. 9; see also Gilbert and
Gubar, *No Man's Land*, I, 28). One could read this 'dual perspective'
of explicit abasement and implicit exaltation as an example of what
Seltzer would call a 'double discourse' (Auerbach, *Woman and the
Demon*, p. 168; Seltzer, *Henry James and the Art of Power*, p. 132 and
passim). Yet in terms of a feminist analysis, this covertly exalting
narrative, whilst not entirely escaping the play of power, is by no
means to be seen as merely a detour in support of that power. The
shift in the feminist account of patriarchal myth may well enable
one to re-evaluate the 'O's in 'The Turn of the Screw', although I do
not think that one is bound to see James's registrations of the
instabilities of patriarchy or his implicit exaltation of the feminine as
a matter of mere inadvertence. Blankness can, as Susan Gubar
points out, 'expose how woman has been defined symbolically in the
patriarchy as a *tabula rasa*, a lack, a negation, an absence' (' "The
Blank Page" ', p. 256). But it can also, in James as much as in
Dinesen, be 'an act of defiance, a dangerous and risky refusal to
certify purity', a multivalent and subversive 'voice of silence' (pp.
256, 260). The 'O', as Gilbert and Gubar point out, can exemplify a
positive femininity, a 'cave of female desire' that defies decoding (*No
Man's Land*, I, 270; see also p. 269). I accept that James's depiction of
the monstrous woman (whether Miss Jessel or the governess) may be

seen as part of a male attempt to allay anxiety (see *No Man's Land*, I, 28). Yet if, as Gilbert and Gubar argue, the madwoman in Victorian literature can operate as 'in some sense the author's double', then James may be revising as well as identifying with patriarchally enforced definitions (*The Madwoman in the Attic*, p. 78).

One could put the case in specifically genital terms. If Quint is a representative of (male) authority then why does his name suggest a Middle English word for the vagina? Should we read this, as Gilbert and Gubar might well do, as an instance of the castration anxiety so prevalent amongst turn-of-the-century writers? Does Quint resemble the Kurtz of 'Heart of Darkness', whose name, as Gilbert and Gubar point out, suggests 'cut off or curtailed' (*No Man's Land*, II, 44)? The fact that Quint has 'no hat' may certainly be seen as a castration symbol (*CT*, x, 46). In *The Interpretation of Dreams* Freud argues on two occasions that hats can stand for male genital organs (see *SE*, v, 355–6, 360).[9] Ultimately, however, I do not think that Quint can be explained in terms of a castration anxiety understood either (via Freud) as a fear of woman as lack or (via more recent commentators such as Susan Lurie) as a fear of female reproductive power.[10] This does not necessarily mean defaulting to Shoshana Felman's celebratory vision of the elusiveness and ineluctability of paternal authority in which the James of 'The Turn of the Screw' defends against, defeats and punishes the Oedipal attempt to arrest meaning and to assert interpretative mastery with castration, blindness and death, voids, losses and ghosts (see 'Turning the Screw of Interpretation', pp. 178, 192–3, 198). James is not only the master censor, not simply repressive: he also disseminates blanks. If pushed, I would therefore want to identify James with the hole in Flora's piece of wood rather than the mast which, for Felman, insists on its status as signifier and problematizes all attempts to fix meaning. James's blanks are not mere lacks or absences. They set up a multiplicity of 'O's which almost convinces me that 'The Turn of the Screw', like Luce Irigaray's description of woman, has 'sex organs just about everywhere'.[11] James's partial break with phallicism and his investment in these rhetorical invaginations does not, it seems to me, constitute the version of bisexuality which Hélène Cixous criticizes and which defines women as neuter in order to ward off the fear of castration (see 'The Laugh of the Medusa', p. 253; 'Sorties', p. 84). It is, as I have argued, much more like her account of female bisexual writing, 'working (in) the in-between' through dynamic exchanges and not fixed sequences ('The Laugh of the Medusa', p. 254).[12] Now there is reason to suppose that this may not be saying all that much: as S.H. Clark has argued, 'the more general claims made for the female temperament as being more physical, fluid, unbounded, are eminently compatible with traditional forms of gender idealisation' and there is, perhaps, 'nothing more predictable than being perpetually enigmatic'.[13] Nevertheless, there is certainly an unusual mobility and chiastic poise in James's gendering of authorship. In her handling of conceptual relationships, perhaps even in her alignment with Rochester, the governess in 'The Turn of the Screw' is, to put it in inevitably simplistic and stereotypical terms, a manly woman. Yet the placing and naming of Quint as well as the deployment of the 'O' in the text indicate that the authorial role is that of a womanly man. The Jamesian author may well be an Osmond looking down on the represented subjectivity from the plains of a patriarchal literary heaven in which, as James expresses it in an early letter to Thomas Sergeant Perry, 'there are no women' (*L*, I, 49). And yet, by interposing a blank wall between himself and the protagonist, James may well also, at least in the case of *The American*, be quietly identifying himself with Claire de Cintré and the nuns who inhabit the Carmelite convent in the Rue d'Enfer, subtly converting himself into a conventual authorial counterpart to the monastic literary selves of Balzac and Flaubert.

I am not trying to argue that James entirely and absolutely escapes the Oedipal narrative or refuses to collaborate in a liminality which serves the interests of order. In *The End of the Line*, Neil Hertz produces an account of the sublime which has numerous points of resemblance to the sacrificial crisis, the fantastic and the liminal phase. For Hertz, the sublime involves an encounter with a chaotic multiplicity, with inversion, crisis, disintegration, blockage, the 'transgression of conventional limits' and the 'dissolution of hierarchical difference'.[14] In Oedipal terms this is a moment of intense castration anxiety. The sublime crisis is often represented as a disorderly woman, a threateningly assertive femininity, a version of Medusa (see *The End of the Line*, pp. 45, 162, 165). It is followed by a re-establishment of boundaries and an 'aggressive reassertion of the subject's stability' which is 'bought at some other's expense' (p. 223; see also p. 14). This other – the scapegoat – is often but not always a woman (see p. 233). For Hertz, the compensatory positive movement found in sublime experience is also to be understood as the quintessential autobiographic moment in the sense that, through renunciation or expulsion, it creates the distinctions and stabilities of a post-Oedipal world (see p. 230). In Jamesian terminology, the sublime would result in the 'small boy' becoming detached from his 'others'. It is therefore appropriate that the Louvre dream recalled in *A Small Boy and Others* involves a moment of aggressive expulsion following anxiety and crisis, a triumph which should, as I have already argued, be seen as the key which opens the door to James's late autobiographical writings (see p. 222 above). If one wanted to examine this sublime autobiographical moment in terms of Freudian topographies one could describe it as a wishful reversal of the process of regression as set out by Freud in *The Interpretation of Dreams* (see *SE*, v, 534–49). One could say that James wishfully masters the perception–consciousness system, conquers the monster of the unconscious by pushing it out of the perceptual system into the field of expression. James speaks of his 'recovery' of the dream, but his recollection is therapeutic as well as mnemonic (*Autobiography*, p. 196). In his dash through the Galerie d'Apollon he seems to have recaptured the corridor of mnemic traces, or in other words his childhood. Regression is not only the mechanism but also the theme of James's dream and, within the dream, a fearful retreat is converted into progression and assertion. Stimulus leads to innervation and perception to action. James dreams, in fact, that he has mastered the dream. The hallucination that he has woken up to face and eventually outface his assailant confirms the desire to triumph in reality. For James, in the Louvre dream itself, in 'The Jolly Corner' and in the notes on *The Sense of the Past*, the tables can be turned (see p. 222 above). This trope of tropes can also be read persuasively in Freudian terms. In *The Interpretation of Dreams* Freud accounts for his dream of 'turning the tables' as a fulfillment of his wishes for grandeur and power (*SE*, IV, 193; see also p. 192). He quite correctly suggests that dreams of inversion and reversal 'include a reference to the contemptuous implication of the idea of "turning one's back on something" ' (*SE*, IV, 327).

It would be hard to read the Galerie d'Apollon dream as some radical repudiation of the phallic, although one does not necessarily need to conclude that James is affirming an exclusively heterosexual version of masculine power. In *The Interpretation of Dreams* Freud notes that 'it is remarkable to observe ... how frequently reversal is employed precisely in dreams arising from repressed homosexual impulses' (*SE*, IV, 327). Nevertheless, James's assertions of power are usually couched in less distinctly phallic terms. To be a master is not always to be a man, nor is it inevitably to defeat women and determine them as castrated. It may well be to be a dupe, a victim, a prisoner. To turn one's back may not only signify an authoritative and conclusive contempt. It may also act as an unusual variant on the apotropaic display of genitals described by Freud in 'Medusa's Head'. Genital display may have an apotropaic effect in Freud's view because it exhibits precisely what the male spectator finds most horrifying and threatening: Medusa's head, translated as the female genitals, specifically those of the mother. Through catching sight of his mother's genitals, the boy comes to fear his own castration at the hands of his father. He realizes that he is in competition with the father for the attentions of the mother and, through fear of the punishment which she is seen as having undergone, that he must forego her as the object of desire.

Freud's analysis of the Oedipal subject has been criticized by Susan Lurie who, in 'Pornography and the Dread of Women', argues that the boy's fear is not that the mother is castrated or lacking but that she is not castrated and is yet powerful. For Lurie, the subsequent life of the Oedipal subject depends on encoding the feminine as mutilated and weak and on valuing or over-valuing the penis as a sign of or compensation for the traumatic separation from the mother. What I want to concentrate on here, however, are the curious ambivalences and instabilities in 'Medusa's Head'. Freud argues that the fear of the Medusa is symbolically equivalent to the fear of castration. The snakes which are conventionally used to represent Medusa's hair, however, as well as standing for female pubic hair, are also a 'mitigation' of the horror of the head itself because they 'replace the penis, the absence of which is the cause of the horror' (*SE*, XVIII, 273). This seems to contradict or at least qualify Freud's idea that 'a multiplication of penis symbols signifies castration' (p. 273). In this case, in the very midst of the moment of castration anxiety, a multiplication of penis symbols signifies a wishful erasure of castration. The second apparent contradiction in 'Medusa's Head' involves the idea that the sight of Medusa petrifies the spectator or renders him 'stiff with terror' (p. 273). Freud again reads this element of the myth in a paradoxical way. For him, the spectator's stiffness represents a compensatory erection, a further

transformation or warding off of the fear of castration. Thus phallicism appears to be reinvigorated at exactly the moment when it is
most seriously under threat.

In 'The "Uncanny" ' Freud makes it clear that the encounter
with the female genitals is an – perhaps *the* – archetypically uncanny
experience. These insights provide intriguing ways of thinking
through the complexities of Jamesian mastery in sexual terms. One
could see James as the horrified spectator of his protagonists' desires,
as a writer who interposes blank walls in order to turn away desire or
to turn away from it. In this case, the back-turning gesture of the
master would be virtually equivalent to the recognition of castration. Or perhaps one should rather see the blank walls of the house
of fiction, possibly lacking windows and certainly without external
projections, as a more comprehensive refusal of genitality, of an
Oedipal sexuality predicated on castration anxiety. In this sense the
secret beyond the Jamesian threshold is not, as Edmund Wilson and,
more recently, Allon White and Alfred Habegger would have it, the
sexual itself (see pp. 5–6, 96–7 above). Yet nor, since desire remains,
in front of the wall, stimulated and interrupted by the wall, could one
follow Mark Seltzer's perception of the 'omission of power and sexuality' in the Jamesian text (*Henry James and the Art of Power*, p. 168).

What then is behind the wall? A feminine, bisexual or homosexual
self? A self that has castrated itself or stalled the phallic trajectory?
Similar paradoxes hold sway in 'Medusa's Head'. Freud appears
almost to superimpose absence and presence, the penis and the
vagina, wishes and fears, fantasies and anxieties, castration and
empowerment, weakness and strength. It is as if he is arguing, in the
words of Derrida's *Glas*, that 'the "assumption" or denial of castration' comes down 'to the same'.[15] The man who has been circum-
cised and therefore symbolically castrated may also apotropaically
castrate his enemy, exhibiting 'castration as an erection that defies
the other' (Derrida, *Glas*, p. 46). For Derrida the paradox of the
apotropaic involves 'castrating oneself *already*, always already, in
order to be able to castrate and repress the threat of castration'
(p. 46). It means 'renouncing life and mastery in order to secure
them ... losing in advance what one wants to erect' (p. 46). In many
ways these comments provide an extraordinarily incisive description
of Jamesian dynamics. In 'The Jolly Corner', poorly sighted and
with an injured limb, Brydon's *alter ego* exhibits his symbolic castration as an erection that defies his other. And yet, within this

paradoxical landscape, James is capable of assuming still other authorial roles. He is not only the punitive father and the horrified or persecuted son. By turning his back and reflecting the desires of his subjects back upon themselves, the Jamesian author becomes a kind of Perseus who turns the tables on the apotropaic and petrifies the Medusa. Or, in the guise of Quint, he can also become the Medusa herself, allowing his governess a compensatory erection before finally turning away. Castrated but not lacking, he would then be the mother whose Oedipal subjects must renounce him/her as the object of desire.

One simply cannot pin the man down. He is all these things and more.

Notes

INTRODUCTION

1 James, *LC*, i, 742.
2 Sears, *The Negative Imagination*, p. 126.
3 See Anesko, *Friction with the Market*, p. 158.
4 James, *L*, iv, 512.
5 Retitled 'The Friends of the Friends' for inclusion in the *New York Edition*.
6 First publication dates of James's works are taken from Edel, Laurence and Rambeau, eds., *A Bibliography of Henry James*.
7 Lind, 'The Supernatural Tales of Henry James', p. 421; see also p. 425.
8 Wilson, 'The Ambiguity of Henry James', *Hound and Horn*, 7 (1933–4), 385–406 (p. 385). See Heilman, 'The Freudian Reading'. Wilson's essay was republished with minor alterations in *The Triple Thinkers* (London, 1938). It appeared for a third time, with major revisions and a postscript, in *The Triple Thinkers* (London, 1952). The 1952 text, with a further postcript dated 1959 which retracts the 1952 retractions, is included in Willen's *Casebook*. For an account of the evolution of Wilson's essay, see Slaughter, 'Edmund Wilson'. Wilson was not, however, by any means the first critic to advance a hallucination theory with regard to 'The Turn of the Screw'. See 'The Recent Work of Henry James' (anonymous review); Elton, *Modern Studies*, pp. 255–6; Pound, 'A Shake Down', p. 34; Pattee, *The Development of the American Short Story*, pp. 206–7; Goddard, 'A Pre-Freudian Reading' (published 1957, but written in the early 1920s); Kenton, 'Henry James to the Ruminant Reader'. Later exponents of Wilson's views include Lind, 'The Supernatural Tales of Henry James' (see pp. 255–93); Cargill, 'Henry James as Freudian Pioneer' and '"The Turn of the Screw" and Alice James'; Silver, 'A Note on the Freudian Reading'; Cranfill and Clark, *An Anatomy*. Edel puts forward a Freudian interpretation if not an explanation in 'The Point of View', *Stories of the Supernatural* (see pp. 427–34) and *The Treacherous Years* (see pp. 194–6). Heilman's arguments had also been anticipated by a number of critics. See Carroll, 'The Supernatural in the Writings of Henry James', p. 54; Fagin, 'Another Reading'; Waldock, 'Mr Edmund Wilson'; Liddell, 'The

"Hallucination" Theory'. Heilman's followers include Stoll, 'Symbolism in Coleridge'; Evans, 'James's Air of Evil'; Reed, 'Another Turn on James's "Turn of the Screw"'; Leavis, *What Maisie Knew*; Hoffmann, 'Innocence and Evil'; Miner, 'Henry James's Metaphysical Romances'; Jones, 'Point of View in "The Turn of the Screw"'; Mackenzie, '"The Turn of the Screw": Jamesian Gothic'; Vaid, *Technique* (see pp. 16, 90–2); Banta, *Henry James and the Occult* (see pp. 116–17).

9 See Bewley, *The Complex Fate*, pp. 99, 106; Firebaugh, 'Inadequacy in Eden', p. 57; Blanchot, '"The Turn of the Screw"', pp. 82–3; Geismar, *Henry James and his Cult*, p. 161; Enck, '"The Turn of the Screw"', p. 262; Bersani, 'The Jamesian Lie', pp. 65–6; McMaster, '"The Full Image of a Repetition"', pp. 127–8; Fryer, 'The Mother-Surrogates', p. 153; White, *The Uses of Obscurity*, p. 131; Bell, '"The Turn of the Screw" and the *Recherche de L'Absolu*', p. 65. But on Bewley and Geismar, see also chapter 3, note 13 below.

10 Brooke-Rose, *A Rhetoric of the Unreal*, p. 156; see also pp. 129–55, 157. Armstrong, 'History and Epistemology', pp. 697–8.

11 Briggs, *Night Visitors*, p. 22.

12 Heilman, 'The Freudian Reading', p. 434.

13 I am thinking in particular of Scarborough, *The Supernatural in Modern English Fiction*; Railo, *The Haunted Castle*; Praz, *The Romantic Agony*; Penzoldt, *The Supernatural in Fiction*; Fiedler, *Love and Death*; Miyoshi, *The Divided Self*; Keppler, *The Literature of the Second Self*; Todorov, *The Fantastic*; Miller, *Doubles*.

14 Black, *Models and Metaphors*, p. 227.

15 Poole, *Henry James*, p. 142; see also pp. 24–8.

16 Woolf, 'Henry James's Ghost Stories', pp. 288–9.

17 Hawthorne, *CE*, i, 36.

I THE THRESHOLD

1 Quoted in Dick's introduction to Aubrey's *Brief Lives*, p.xxix.

2 Hobbes, *Leviathan*, p. 398.

3 Tanner, *Adultery in the Novel*, p. 11.

4 Locke, *Human Understanding*, Book ii, Chapter 33, section 10.

5 De Man, 'The Epistemology of Metaphor', p. 21.

6 Quoted in Feidelson's *Symbolism and American Literature*, p. 78.

7 Plato, *Dialogues*, i, section 229.

8 'Like' derives from Teutonic *líko*, 'body', 'appearance', 'form' or 'shape'. But the cognate word 'lich' can mean 'a dead body; a corpse' (*OED* 1b) as well as 'the living body' (*OED* 1a). This first sense persists in German *Leiche*, 'dead body'.

9 See Derrida, *Dissemination*, pp. 72–3, 103–5, 137–9.

10 Aristotle, *Works*, xi, 1410. b. 30–5; 1411. b. 25–30.

11 Ricoeur, *The Rule of Metaphor*, p. 21; see also p. 152.

12 See Richards, *The Philosophy of Rhetoric*, pp. 94, 100; Black, *Models and Metaphors*, pp. 33, 37, 47, 236–9.

13 On Aristotle's use of the word '*kurion*', see Derrida, *Margins of Philosophy*, pp. 246–47; Ricoeur, *The Rule of Metaphor*, pp. 18, 285–6, 290–1, 326 note 21.

14 For Aristotle's list of incidents suitable for tragedy, see *Works*, XI, 1453. b. 19–21.

15 Girard, *Violence and the Sacred*, p. 37.

16 Van Gennep, *The Rites of Passage*, p. 11. I am indebted to Ian Bell for pointing out to me the relevance of the idea of 'liminality' in this context.

17 Turner, 'Betwixt and Between', pp. 96–7; see also p. 98. For further analysis of the complex relation between the living and the dead in the liminal phase, see also Turner's *Dramas, Fields, and Metaphors*, p. 259; 'Death and the Dead in the Pilgrimage Process', pp. 24–5.

18 On the inversion of relations between the sexes, see Turner, *The Ritual Process*, p. 111; *Dramas, Fields, and Metaphors*, p. 247. On status inversion, see *The Ritual Process*, pp. 97, 99, 102, 107, 167; *Dramas, Fields, and Metaphors*, pp. 53, 234. On the reversal of relations between the strong and the weak, see *The Ritual Process*, pp. 108, 168; *Dramas, Fields, and Metaphors*, p. 234. On youth/age reversals, see *Dramas, Fields, and Metaphors*, p. 273.

19 See Turner, *Dramas, Fields, and Metaphors*, p. 239.

20 See Turner, 'Betwixt and Between', p. 97; *The Ritual Process*, p. 109.

21 See also Turner, *Dramas, Fields, and Metaphors*, pp. 239, 256.

22 Turner, *Dramas, Fields, and Metaphors*, p. 37.

23 Girard acknowledges the resemblance between van Gennep's account of the liminal phase and his own ideas about the loss of difference during the sacrificial crisis but has little to say about Victor Turner other than to approve of the connections between ritual and drama made in his work (see *Violence and the Sacred*, pp. 281, 290–1).

24 Turner, 'Comments and Conclusions', p. 280; see also p. 282. Turner proposes to reserve the term 'liminal' for the description of ritual practices and suggests that the word 'liminoid' should be used for industrial or post-industrial 'symbolic inversions and expressions of disorder' (p. 287). On this terminology, see also *Dramas, Fields, and Metaphors*, p. 14.

25 See Turner, *The Ritual Process*, p. 201; *Dramas, Fields, and Metaphors*, pp. 16, 35.

26 On threshold contracts (culturally instituted borders between the subjective and the objective, the inside and the outside, reality and representation), see Cassirer, *Mythical Thought*, pp. 85–6, 98–9, 103–4.

27 Todorov, *The Fantastic*, p. 114.

28 Freud, *SE*, XVII, 219.

29 Hoffmann, 'The Sandman', pp. 120, 119.

30 Hertz, 'Freud and the Sandman', p. 311.
31 Longinus, 'On the Sublime', p. 85.
32 Carroll, 'Freud and the Myth of Origin', p. 516.
33 Cixous, 'Fiction and Its Phantoms', p. 527.
34 Spenser, *Works: The Faerie Queene*, II. 12. 42.
35 *The Spectator*, I, 53.
36 See Bloom, *Agon*, pp. 6–7, 12–15, on belatedness, the sublime and the uncanny.
37 Gray, *Works*, I, 78 (line 91); Goldsmith, *Collected Works*, IV, 303 (line 421).
38 Hartman, 'Words, Wish, Worth: Wordsworth', p. 193.
39 Wordsworth, *The Prelude*, line 308 (1805), line 309 (1850).
40 Burke, *A Philosophical Enquiry* (1757), p. 72.
41 Coleridge, *Collected Works*, VII, 2, p. 6.
42 Scott, *Novelists and Fiction*, p. 179.
43 Sutherland, *Defoe*, p. 144.
44 Swift, *Gulliver's Travels*, p. 269.
45 On ghosts as protectors of traditional values, see Briggs, *Night Visitors*, pp. 24, 29, 111.
46 See Schonhorn's introduction to *Accounts of the Apparition of Mrs Veal*, p. i.
47 See 'The "Uncanny"', in *SE*, XVII, 250; Frye, *Anatomy of Criticism*, pp. 50, 74–6, 135, 245; Ricoeur, *The Rule of Metaphor*, p. 226; Kermode, *The Genesis of Secrecy*, p. 113.
48 Fielding, *Tom Jones*, II, 853. See also 'A wonderful long Chapter concerning the Marvellous', which argues that ghosts in fiction are to be used with 'the utmost Caution' (I, 399).
49 See Wimsatt and Beardsley, *The Verbal Icon*, pp. 21–39.
50 Richardson, *Selected Letters*, p. 41 (quoted by Scott in *Novelists and Fiction*, p. 21).
51 Richardson, *Pamela*, II, v (quoted by Miyoshi in *The Divided Self*, p. 4).
52 Walpole, *Otranto*, p. 7.
53 Scott, 'Romance', p. 435 (quoted in Williams's introduction to Scott, *Novelists and Fiction*, p. 1).
54 Rosmarin, *The Power of Genre*, p. 14.
55 On the tendency for novels to be read as romances by later readers, see Frye, *Anatomy of Criticism*, pp. 49, 307; Beer, *The Romance*, p. 5.
56 Similar theoretical positions are maintained by Clara Reeve (see the Preface to *The Old English Baron*, p. 3), by Mary Shelley (see the Preface to *Frankenstein*, p. 13) and by Robert Louis Stevenson (see 'A Note on Realism', pp. 96–7).
57 Reeve, Preface to *The Old English Baron*, p. 4.
58 Scarborough, *The Supernatural in Modern English Fiction*, p. 6. See also Woolf, 'The Supernatural in Fiction', p. 294; Penzoldt, *The Supernatural in Fiction*, pp. 4–5. Fiedler uses similar ideas, although with greater attention to Gothic ambivalence, in *Love and Death* (see pp. 129–40).

59 Horace, 'The Art of Poetry', p. 300.
60 Lewis, introduction to Walpole's *Otranto*, p. xiii.
61 Scott, *Waverley*, I, 7.
62 Dekker, *The American Historical Romance*, pp. 50, 51.
63 Morris, 'Gothic Sublimity', pp. 302, 299. For discussion of the continuing fascination with the ghostly, the monstrous and other forms of categorial transgression in nineteenth-century fiction, see Todorov, *The Fantastic*, pp. 76–82, 113; Tanner, *Adultery in the Novel*, pp. 192–6.
64 Tanner, *The Reign of Wonder*, p. 24; see also pp. 355–9.
65 Melville, *Moby-Dick*, p. 1001.
66 Poe, 'The Premature Burial' (1844), p. 532.
67 Bell, *The Development of American Romance*, p. 29.
68 Fiedler, *Love and Death*, p. 144.
69 Chase, *The American Novel*, p. 19.
70 Colacurcio, *The Province of Piety*, p. 492.
71 For well-argued opposition to the view of Hawthorne as a thoroughgoing ironist and support for his worked ambivalences, see Dekker, *The American Historical Romance*, pp. 140–9, 166.

2 THE CHAMBER OF CONSCIOUSNESS

1 James, *Autobiography*, p. 478.
2 Bloom, *Figures of Capable Imagination*, p. 1; see Rowe, *The Theoretical Dimensions*, pp. 30–83. On James's hostility to Trollopeian realism, see Habegger, *Gender, Fantasy, and Realism*, p. 105, and, for a different view of the influences (which denies the primacy of such writers as Hawthorne, Eliot, Balzac, Flaubert and Turgenev whilst emphasizing James's 'realist' reaction against the American tradition of women's popular writing) see especially pp. ix, 54–6, 65, 108–9.
3 Eliot, *Daniel Deronda*, p. 461; see p. 502.
4 The 'man of imagination' is mentioned in the Prefaces (see *LC*, II, 1175, 1307); in a letter of 20 January 1909 to Shaw (see *L*, IV, 512); in 'Is There a Life After Death?' (see p. 224) and in *Notes of a Son and Brother* (see *Autobiography*, pp. 454–55). See Feidelson, 'James and the "Man of Imagination" '. See also pp. 3, 59, 75, 79, 82, 194, 227, 233, 235 and 239–41 above.
5 James had translated Mérimée's tale during the early 1860s. See 'Prosper Mérimée' (1898), in *LC*, II, 576–77; *Autobiography*, p. 292.
6 James, *CT*, I, 302.
7 Edel, *The Untried Years*, p. 254.
8 Discussing the dynamics of the James family, Carren Kaston argues that at one point Alice James also saw death as an assertion of independence (see *Imagination and Desire*, p. 20).
9 In a more recent analysis of 'The Romance of Certain Old Clothes', Kaplan counters Edel by arguing that James is to be allied with Lloyd's second wife, Viola (see *Henry James: The Imagination of Genius*, pp. 71,

91). If Perdita is therefore aligned with William, James is not fantasizing posthumous victories but entertaining the idea that his brother might exact revenge for any attempted usurpation. But for the fact that Perdita is the younger of the two sisters I would find Kaplan's account almost equally plausible. To the extent that James desires to defeat William and fears defeat by William he can, as Edel himself hints, be associated with both Perdita and Viola.

10 See Pound, 'Brief Note', pp. 7–8; Poirier, *The Comic Sense*, p. 187; Bersani, 'The Jamesian Lie', pp. 57–8.

11 Geismar, *Henry James and his Cult*, p. 7.

12 See Anderson, *The Imperial Self*, p. 166; Frye, *Anatomy of Criticism*, p. 267; Allott, 'Symbol and Image', p. 323; Bayley, 'Love and Knowledge', p. 259; Segal, *The Lucid Reflector*, p. 50; Buitenhuis, *The Grasping Imagination*, p. 261; Grover, *Henry James and the French Novel*, pp. 9, 177; Jameson, *The Political Unconscious*, pp. 154, 206, 219–24.

13 See Felman, 'Turning the Screw of Interpretation'; Kappeler, *Writing and Reading*; Brooke-Rose, *A Rhetoric of the Unreal*; Norrman, *The Insecure World*, pp. 75–6; Ellmann, 'The Intimate Difference'; Boone, 'Modernist Maneuverings', pp. 374, 379.

14 Blackmur, Introduction to *The Art of the Novel*, p. xxxviii. For Cameron, the Prefaces postulate the existence of a central, uniting, coherent and autonomous consciousness whilst the novels systematically subvert such a view of subjectivity (see *Thinking in Henry James*, pp. 41, 52, 59, 76, 77, 185 note 17).

15 Holland, *The Expense of Vision*, p. 155.

16 Carroll, *The Subject in Question*, p. 65.

17 Sherman, 'The Aesthetic Idealism of Henry James' (1917), pp. 92, 99.

18 See Matthiessen, *Henry James*, pp. 85, 94; Dupee, *Henry James*, p. 57; Poirier, *The Comic Sense*, pp. 166–7, 182, 224; Vaid, *Technique*, pp. 145–6; Sears, *The Negative Imagination*, p. 102; Appignanesi, *Femininity*, pp. 27, 56–7; Kappeler, *Writing and Reading*, pp. 22–4.

19 See Barzun, 'James the Melodramatist'; Nettels, *James and Conrad*, pp. 159–62, 171–80; Donadio, *Nietzsche, Henry James*, p. 3; Bradbury, *Henry James*, pp. 157–62.

20 See Fiedler, *Love and Death*, p. 131; Segal, *The Lucid Reflector*, p. 12 note 9; Banta, *Henry James and the Occult*, p. 81; Nettels, *James and Conrad*, p. 89.

21 See Trilling, *The Liberal Imagination*, pp. 62–63; Chase, *The American Novel*, pp. ix, 119, 125, 135; Paterson, 'The Language of "Adventure"', pp. 295, 299, 301; Nettels, *James and Conrad*, pp. 88–93; Stowe, *Balzac, James*, pp. 37–8, 53; Rowe, *The Theoretical Dimensions*, pp. 26, 160, 180–8.

22 See West, *Henry James*, pp. 24–25; Eliot, 'The Hawthorne Aspect'; Matthiessen, *American Renaissance*, pp. 292–305; *Henry James*, p. 71; Lind, 'The Supernatural Tales of Henry James', pp. 18, 31, 44, 61–6, 79, 114–16, 122, 206–10, 217, 418; Dupee, *Henry James*, p. 57; Bewley,

The Complex Fate, pp. 1–113; Fiedler, *Love and Death*, pp. 302–3; Long, *The Great Succession*; Rowe, *The Theoretical Dimensions*, pp. 30–57; Person, 'The Aboriginal Hawthorne'.

23 See Kelley, 'The Early Development of Henry James', p. 257; Frye, *Anatomy of Criticism*, pp. 42–3, 50, 117, 202; Holland, *The Expense of Vision*, pp. x, 68–73, 117, 143; Buitenhuis, *The Grasping Imagination*, pp. 38–40, 84, 102, 178; Nettels, *James and Conrad*, pp. 128–9.

24 Feidelson, 'James and the "Man of Imagination"', pp. 336, 343.

25 James had challenged the novel/romance opposition well before the Preface to *The American*. See his 1865 review of T. Adolphus Trollope's *Lindisfarn Chase* (*LC*, I, 1356) and 'The Art of Fiction' (*LC*, I, 54–5).

26 Feidelson makes a similar claim (see 'James and the "Man of Imagination"', pp. 335–6).

27 See Anderson, *The Imperial Self*, pp. 169, 174, 179, 190, 192.

28 See Stoll, 'Symbolism in Coleridge', pp. 229–33; Beebe, 'The Turned Back of Henry James', p. 521; Ward, *The Search for Form*, pp. 18–19; Banta, *Henry James and the Occult*, p. 73; Fogel, *Henry James and the Structure of the Romantic Imagination*, pp. 5, 25; Armstrong, *The Phenomenology of Henry James*, p. 46.

29 See Watson, 'Contributions to a Dictionary of Critical Terms', p. 207.

30 See Ward, *The Search for Form*, pp. 4–5, 12–13.

31 On Emerson, see *LC*, I, 257, 270; on Wordsworth, see *LC*, I, 773; on Sand, see *LC*, II, 700, 723, 725, 730; on Goethe, see *LC*, II, 947.

32 Kaston, *Imagination and Desire*, p. 178; see also p. 8.

33 Anesko, *Friction with the Market*, p. 87. See also pp. 134–8 and, for the analogies between James's state of suspension and divided characters such as Hyacinth Robinson in *The Princess Casamassima*, pp. 109, 115, 118.

34 McWhirter, *Desire and Love in Henry James*, p. 61; see also pp. 5, 62.

35 Cameron, *Thinking in Henry James*, p. 59; see also pp. 22–3, 63, 68, 81, 157–9.

36 Bell, *Henry James and the Past*, p. 40.

37 In spite of the contrast between James's and Locke's conceptions of the threshold, Raleigh makes some interesting connections between their ideas about experience (see 'Henry James: The Poetics of Empiricism'). For a rather different account of James's philosophical antecedents, see Griffin, 'The Selfish Eye'.

38 Tanner, 'The Watcher from the Balcony', p. 37. On the centrifugal and centripetal impulses in American fiction at large, see Tanner, *Scenes of Nature, Signs of Men*, pp. 28–39.

39 James, *Novels 1881–1886*, p. 379. The revised version of the novel has a more famous and precise line here: 'to meet the requirements of their imagination' (*NYE*, III, 261).

40 James, 'Is There a Life After Death?', p. 221.

41 See James's review of Bayard Taylor's *John Godfrey's Fortunes* (*LC*, I, 624–5); his Prefaces to *The Tragic Muse* and *The Ambassadors* (*LC*, II,

1118, 1315–16) and his 3 March 1911 letter to H. G. Wells (*The Letters of Henry James*, edited by Lubbock, II, 188–9). On James's misgivings concerning autobiography, see Holland, *The Expense of Vision*, pp. 136–7.

42 Goetz, *Henry James and the Darkest Abyss*, p. 25.

43 On James's ambivalence towards the imaginative aspirations of his characters, see Feidelson, 'James and the "Man of Imagination"', pp. 332–4.

44 For other readings of James in terms of Girard's theories of desire, see Seltzer, *Henry James and the Art of Power*, pp. 78–9; Cameron, *Thinking in Henry James*, p. 43; McWhirter, *Desire and Love in Henry James*, pp. 173, 200 note 1.

45 Shakespeare, *Hamlet*, I. i. 115. For other allusions by James to *Hamlet* and its ghosts, see p. 218 above.

46 James, *Transatlantic Sketches*, p. 304.

47 On 'Benvolio' as a debate between romance and realism, see Kelley, 'The Early Development of Henry James', p. 233. But see also Vaid, *Technique*, p. 148.

48 On the relation between realism and idealism in Eliot and Turgenev, see James's 1873 review of *Middlemarch* and his 1874 review of *Frühlingsfluthen. Ein König Lear des Dorfes* (*LC*, I, 965; *LC*, II, 974, 978). On Eliot's 'spontaneous' and 'artificial' aspects, see James's 1876 dialogue '*Daniel Deronda*: A Conversation' (*LC*, I, 985). On the relation between actual and imaginative experience in Balzac, and that between the spontaneous and the reflective, see James's 1875 essay 'Honoré de Balzac' (*LC*, II, 36, 44).

49 See Buitenhuis, *The Grasping Imagination*, pp. 86–7.

50 See Kelley, 'The Early Development', p. 246, note 4; Lind, 'The Supernatural Tales of Henry James', pp. 92, 97; Kerr, 'James's Last Early Supernatural Tales', p. 143.

51 On the image of the veil in Hawthorne, see Budick, 'The World as Specter', pp. 225–9; Miller, *Hawthorne and History, passim*.

52 See Frye, *Anatomy of Criticism*, pp. 37, 107, 186, 193. On romance and the omnipotence of thoughts, see also Beer, *The Romance*, pp. 3, 12.

53 James, *Novels 1871–1880*, p. 592.

54 Stowe, *Balzac, James*, p. 39.

55 On blank or dead walls in James, see pp. 81–2, 193, 200 and 233 above.

56 See Radcliffe, *The Italian*, pp. 118–19. A similar scene occurs in Balzac's 'The Duchesse de Langeais' (see pp. 161–3).

57 See Beebe, 'The Turned Back of Henry James'; Blackall, *Jamesian Ambiguity*, pp. 81–3; Cixous, 'Henry James: l'écriture comme placement', p. 37; White, *The Uses of Obscurity*, pp. 160–2; Poole, *Henry James*, pp. 31–3, 84. On turned backs in James, see also pp. 86, 107, 126, 128, 142, 166, 199, 220, 227, 234, 240 above and note 90 to this chapter.

58 James, *NYE*, II, 534. On this revision, see also Stowe, *Balzac, James*, pp. 53, 184 note 52. For a somewhat different account of the novel in

terms of doubling and imagery of the fantastic, see Rowe, 'The Politics of the Uncanny: Newman's Fate in *The American*'.

59 On James's transformation of the literally Gothic, romantic or melodramatic into metaphor, see Barzun, 'James the Melodramatist', pp. 518–21; Yeazell, *Language and Knowledge*, pp. 62–3; Nettels, *James and Conrad*, p. 93.

60 See Nettels, *James and Conrad*, p. 104.

61 For a different and intriguing account of this scene in terms of James's relations with the literary market-place, see Anesko, *Friction with the Market*, pp. 12–13, 67–8.

62 See Turner, 'The Haunted *Portrait of a Lady*', p. 230.

63 On the partial analogy between James and Ralph Touchett, see Habegger, *Henry James and the 'Woman Business'*, pp. 166–7, 173–6.

64 Binswanger, 'The Case of Lola Voss', p. 287. On 'extravagance', see Binswanger's essay of that name. Armstrong uses the distinction between the 'ethereal world' and the 'grave world' in his study of James (see *The Phenomenology of Henry James*, pp. 23, 74–89).

65 For a similar reading of James's investment in both Gilbert Osmond and Ralph Touchett, see Kaston, *Imagination and Desire*, pp. 43, 62.

66 In the revised text, this smile gives way to a 'responsive' but 'ironic' expression (*NYE*, IV, 59).

67 On frames and framing in James, see pp. 94–7 above.

68 On Vereker's smile, see Feidelson, 'Art as Problem', p. 49.

69 Habegger, *Henry James and the 'Woman Business'*, p. 178; see also p. 82. On the *Moods* review, see p. 73. On the guardian-ward theme in James's fiction, see pp. 26, 37, 80, 108, 133, 159. For a rather different account of the association between Osmond and Henry James Snr in terms of their mutual retreat from the market-place into a world of being as opposed to doing, see Anesko, *Friction with the Market*, pp. 30, 87.

70 On Daudet's smile, see Bell, *Henry James and the Past*, pp. 98, 135. On other smiles in James's fiction, see pp. 106–7, 192–4, 199 above. On Shakespeare's smile, see p. 232 above.

71 Tanner, 'The Fearful Self', p. 218.

72 It may be worth noting that this aside foreshadows the family history in 'Owen Wingrave' (see pp. 100–1 above).

73 On the periodical market, see Briggs, *Night Visitors*, p. 14. Briggs supplies a useful list of exponents of the ghost story in her bibliography. On the general supernatural ferment of the 1890s, see *Night Visitors*, pp. 76–97.

74 See Gauld, *The Founders of Psychical Research*, pp. 35, 51, 62.

75 On Victorian literature of duality, see Miyoshi, *The Divided Self*; Keppler, *The Literature of the Second Self*; Miller, *Doubles*, especially pp. 57, 135, 242–3.

76 On the trance lecturer Mrs Cora V.L. Hatch, see James's letter of 1 November 1863 to Thomas Sergeant Perry (*L*, I, 44–5). On table-

rapping, see his letter to Mrs Henry James Snr of May 1873 (*L*, I, 388). For James's variously intrigued and contemptuous comments on spirit communication, see his letter of 11 March 1906 to Paul Harvey (*L*, IV, 396–7), of 17 November 1906 to William James (*L*, IV, 425), of 12 January 1912 to Theodate Pope Riddle (*L*, IV, 599) and of 17 June 1915 to Lilla Cabot Perry (*L*, IV, 758–9).

77 Dorothy Scarborough was the first to suggest that 'The Turn of the Screw' was based on an incident reported to 'the Psychical Society' (*The Supernatural in Modern English Fiction*, p. 204). For more detailed development of the claim that James was familiar with psychical research and other aspects of contemporary psychology, see Lind, 'The Supernatural Tales of Henry James', pp. 108–11, 246–7, 302–3, 336; Roellinger, 'Psychical Research and "The Turn of the Screw"', especially p. 405; Cranfill and Clark, *An Anatomy*, pp. 36–41; Banta, *Henry James and the Occult*, pp. 7–27, 105, 135, 154–5, 175; Sheppard, *Henry James and 'The Turn of the Screw'*, pp. 9, 116–211, especially p. 133. For Lang's comments on the undramatic nature of the SPR ghosts, see *The Book of Dreams and Ghosts*, pp. viii, 108, 110. For James's similar observations, see *LC*, II, 1182, 1186. Gauld provides a general history of the SPR in *The Founders of Psychical Research*. For critical contemporary assessment of SPR data, see Parish, *Hallucinations and Illusions*.

78 On this incident, see James's letter of 7 October 1890 to Frederic W. H. Myers (*L*, III, 302) and of 7 November 1890 to William James (*L*, III, 305). On 20 October 1890 William was hoping that James's experience would start him on a new career of 'psychic apostolicism' (*L*, III, 306, ed. note 1). 'Psychical' jokes between the two brothers were still running in James's letter of 5 January 1895, written shortly before the opening of *Guy Domville* (see *L*, III, 507).

79 For similar remarks, see James's 21 December 1902 letter to Sarah Butler Wister (*L*, IV, 259), his 13 December 1903 letter to Grace Norton (*L*, IV, 301) and his 2 June 1912 letter to Rhoda Broughton (*The Letters of Henry James*, edited by Lubbock, II, 247).

80 James, *N*, p. 120.

81 See Edel, *The Middle Years*, pp. 75, 100; *The Life of Henry James*, II, 753; Buitenhuis, *The Grasping Imagination*, p. 158; Habegger, *Henry James and the 'Woman Business'*, p. 189.

82 *The Letters of Henry James*, edited by Lubbock, I, 287.

83 Lind notes some of these parallels (see 'The Supernatural Tales of Henry James', pp. 209–10, 217).

84 James's frame stories are: 'A Landscape-Painter' (1866), 'Gabrielle de Bergerac' (1869), 'Master Eustace' (1871), 'The Madonna of the Future' (1873), 'The Sweetheart of M. Briseux' (1873), 'Adina' (1874), 'The Path of Duty' (1884), 'The Solution' (1889–90), 'Sir Edmund Orme' (1891), 'The Visits' (as 'The Visit', 1892), 'The Way it Came' (1896), 'The Turn of the Screw' (1898), and 'Maud-Evelyn' (1900). The frame is not used in 'Owen Wingrave' or in later ghostly tales such

as 'The Real Right Thing', 'The Third Person', 'The Jolly Corner' and *The Sense of the Past*, which represent the supernatural through a third-person consciousness.

85 See, for example, Hawthorne's 'Legends of the Province House'; Irving, 'The Knight of Malta; The Grand Prior of Minorca'; Mérimée, 'Lokis'; Le Fanu, 'Green Tea'; Maupassant, 'The Hand'; Lee, 'The Legend of Madame Krasinska'; Hugh Walpole, 'Mrs Lunt'. For a discussion of framed ghost stories in Scott and Dickens, see Briggs, *Night Visitors*, pp. 35–8. Dekker also argues that Hawthorne's framing devices derive from Scott (see *The American Historical Romance*, p. 163). For a more general approach to literary frames, see Caws, *Reading Frames in Modern Fiction*.

86 Schug argues that narrative frames keep explosive forces 'within bounds' in *Frankenstein*, *Wuthering Heights* and 'Heart of Darkness' (see *The Romantic Genesis of the Modern Novel*, p. 61).

87 Briggs sees this as one of the major attractions of the genre for Victorian writers (see *Night Visitors*, p. 111).

88 On the connection between female desire and the metaphor of the flood in James, see Kaston, *Imagination and Desire*, p. 54; Boone, 'Modernist Maneuverings', p. 384.

89 White, *The Uses of Obscurity*, p. 154.

90 For interpretations of the back injury, see Rosenzweig, 'The Ghost of Henry James', pp. 438–41; Trilling, *The Liberal Imagination*, pp. 165–74; Edel, *The Untried Years*, pp. 176–85.

91 Habegger, *Gender, Fantasy, and Realism*, pp. 251, 252; see also p. 253.

92 Lukacher, '"Hanging Fire"', p. 128.

3 'THE TURN OF THE SCREW'

1 Edel and Tintner include Addison's *Essays* in their catalogue of the Lamb House library, but James's copy was not autographed until 1880 – five years after *Transatlantic Sketches* (see 'The Library of Henry James', p. 163).

2 James, *The Sacred Fount*, p. 97.

3 On the omnipotence of thoughts in James's characters, see Norrman, *The Insecure World*, pp. 130–2; Yeazell, *Language and Knowledge*, pp. 58–9; Goetz, *Henry James and the Darkest Abyss*, p. 125.

4 Lind draws attention to the parallels between Haddon Hall and Bly (see 'The Supernatural Tales of Henry James', pp. 332–4); see also Briggs, *Night Visitors*, p. 113. On garden scenes in James, see Troy, 'The Altar of Henry James', pp. 47–8; Heilman, '"The Turn of the Screw" as Poem', pp. 217–19; Gibson, 'Metaphor in the Plot of *The Ambassadors*', pp. 302–5; Kappeler, *Writing and Reading*, pp. 34–8, 60, 161–72.

5 See Felman, 'Turning the Screw of Interpretation', pp. 199, 205–6; Goetz, *Henry James and the Darkest Abyss*, p. 114.

6 O'Gorman raises but finally rejects the idea that the ghosts are not evil

(see 'Henry James's Reading of "The Turn of the Screw"', pp. 239–40).

7 For James's reminiscences of the French actor, see 'Coquelin'; *Autobiography*, pp. 228, 607.

8 Sheppard argues that Quint and Jessel could be seen as 'godless revolutionaries' and that Quint is a revival of Paul Muniment in *The Princess Casamassima* (*Henry James and 'The Turn of the Screw'*, p. 100).

9 On this point, see O'Gorman, 'Henry James's Reading of "The Turn of the Screw"', p. 238; Firebaugh, 'Inadequacy in Eden', p. 63.

10 This strategy is not unprecedented in accounts of the Jamesian uncanny. In 'The Ghost of Henry James', Rosenzweig reads 'The Jolly Corner' as a revised version of 'The Story of a Year'. Rosenzweig's 'The Ghost of Henry James: Revised' extends the theory of origins to 'A Tragedy of Error'.

11 See Briggs, *Night Visitors*, p. 151.

12 Felman, 'Turning the Screw of Interpretation', p. 98; see also pp. 97, 99–108 and Brooke-Rose, *A Rhetoric of the Unreal*, p. 132. Felman's work on 'The Turn of the Screw' owes much to the debate between Lacan and Derrida over Poe's 'The Purloined Letter' which had been conducted in earlier isssues of *Yale French Studies*. On this debate, and on the way in which Lacan and Derrida replicate the interpretative strategies they criticize, particularly with regard to filling in epistemological blanks, see Johnson, 'The Frame of Reference', especially pp. 116–17, 126.

13 See Bewley, *The Complex Fate*, pp. 84–7, 94–6, 110, 134, 148; Booth, *The Rhetoric of Fiction*, pp. 311–16, 339–46, 361; Geismar, *Henry James and his Cult*, pp. 159, 395; Samuels, *The Ambiguity of Henry James*, pp. 5–6, 22.

14 Krook, *The Ordeal of Consciousness*, pp. 319, 311.

15 Rimmon, *The Concept of Ambiguity*, p. 227.

16 For criticism of Rimmon's notion of ambiguity, see Falconer, 'Flaubert, James and the Problem of Undecidability', pp. 2–3, 6–8; Álvarez Amorós, 'Possible-World Semantics', pp. 60–4. White also questions the sufficiency of the notion of ambiguity in James criticism (see *The Uses of Obscurity*, pp. 17–18, 130–1).

17 See Firebaugh, 'Inadequacy in Eden', p. 60; Lydenberg, 'The Governess Turns the Screws', pp. 54, 58; Ward, *The Search for Form*, p. 43; Fryer, 'The Mother-Surrogates', p. 154; Norrman, *Techniques of Ambiguity*, p. 81; Brooke-Rose, *A Rhetoric of the Unreal*, p. 192; Millicent Bell, '"The Turn of the Screw" and the *Recherche de L'Absolu*', pp. 68–70.

18 See Brooke-Rose, 'Historical Genres/Theoretical Genres'; *A Rhetoric of the Unreal*, pp. 62–71; Siebers, 'Hesitation, History, and Reading', p. 558. Todorov's analysis of fantastic themes (see *The Fantastic*, pp. 107–39; see also p. 21 above) seems more productive, and is certainly distinct from, his ideas about genre. Todorov accords the idea of 'theoretic' as distinct from historical genre a 'diminished importance',

except as a 'heuristic strategy', in a subsequent essay ('The Origin of Genres', p. 170, note 2).

19 On the connection between the neutral territory and the fantastic, see Kerr, Crowley and Crow, introduction to *The Haunted Dusk*, p. 2.

20 See Dekker, *The American Historical Romance*, p. 136.

21 Chatman argues persuasively that Jamesian ambiguity is geometrically cumulative (see *The Later Style*, pp. 88–91).

22 Fagin, 'Another Reading', p. 200; Firebaugh, 'Inadequacy in Eden', p. 63; Lydenberg, 'The Governess Turns the Screws', p. 41. See also Ward, *The Imagination of Disaster*, pp. 69–72, but N.B. p. 88; Vaid, *Technique*, p. 121.

23 Cargill, '"The Turn of the Screw" and Alice James', p. 248. See Silver, 'A Note on the Freudian Reading', *passim*.

24 Todorov has also argued that 'the Jamesian narrative is always based on *the quest for an absolute and absent cause*' (*The Poetics of Prose*, p. 145).

25 For possible expansions of the syllable 'bly', see pp. 170, 176 above. The name 'Bly' may well have occurred to James during August or September 1897 when, shortly before beginning work on 'The Turn of the Screw', he spent some time at Dunwich in Suffolk, four miles from Blythburgh and six from Blyford. Also suggestive is the following sequence of names in James's notebooks for 1892: 'Gaye (name of house) – Taunt – Tant (Miss Tant, name of governess)' (*N*, p. 67).

26 In the revised version of the tale James further multiplied the intervening stages in the children's history by inserting a reference to some grandparents, who take care of Miles and Flora after the death of their parents and before their uncle (see *NYE*, XII, 153).

27 On the problem of origins and the relation between narrative and death in 'The Turn of the Screw', see Felman, 'Turning the Screw of Interpretation', pp. 122, 128.

28 See Fussell, 'The Ontology of "The Turn of the Screw"', p. 120.

29 On the temporal discrepancy in the introductory chapter of 'The Turn of the Screw', see O'Gorman, 'Henry James's Reading of "The Turn of the Screw"', pp. 133–5.

30 See Watt, 'The First Paragraph of *The Ambassadors*, pp. 257–8; Samuels, *The Ambiguity of Henry James*, p. 199.

31 Day 1 (pp. 23–6), Day 2 (pp. 26–8), Day 3 (pp. 28–32), Day 4 (pp. 32–3). Quint first appears on Day 5 (pp. 35–9). His second appearance occurs on Day 6 (pp. 41–52). Miss Jessel first appears on Day 7 (pp. 53–66). Quint appears for a third time on Day 8 (pp. 69–74). Day 9 (pp. 74–6), Day 10 (pp. 77–84). Miss Jessel's third appearance occurs on Day 11 (pp. 90–105) and her fourth appearance on Day 12 (pp. 106–18). The final encounter with Quint occurs on Day 13 (pp. 118–38). Days 1–4 are successive, as are Days 9–10 and 11–13. Gaps of time occur between Days 4 and 5, Days 5 and 6, Days 6 and 7, Days 7 and 8, Days 8 and 9, and Days 10 and 11. It is coincidental that

Costello detects a sequence of thirteen *non-chronological* units in the text (see 'The Structure of "The Turn of the Screw"').

32 See note 26 to this chapter.

33 See Felman, 'Turning the Screw of Interpretation', p. 144; Brooke-Rose, *A Rhetoric of the Unreal*, p. 397, note 5.

34 Brooke-Rose points out that Quint is never completely described in physical terms and, like the narrative, seems to be 'truncated' (*A Rhetoric of the Unreal*, p. 162).

35 On James's use of the dash to create ambiguity, see Norrman, *Techniques of Ambiguity*, pp. 29–32, 63–7 and, regarding 'The Turn of the Screw', pp. 153, 174.

36 Mansell, 'The Ghost of Language', p. 52.

37 For further discussion of the word 'turn' in 'The Turn of the Screw', see Caws, *Reading Frames in Modern Fiction*, pp. 146–7.

38 For the information in the above paragraph I am indebted to the Benders' *Concordance*, which uses the *New York Edition* text of 'The Turn of the Screw'.

39 Brooke-Rose discusses the governess's self-estranged formulations and her 'tendency to exteriorise inner feelings' (*A Rhetoric of the Unreal*, p. 192; see also pp. 193–4, 214–15 and 404–5, note 15).

40 Poole discusses the significance of various 'dividing membranes' in 'The Turn of the Screw' (*Henry James*, p. 29).

41 Felman, Brooke-Rose and Goetz discuss the problematic relation between in and out in 'The Turn of the Screw' (see 'Turning the Screw of Interpretation', p. 123; *A Rhetoric of the Unreal*, p. 166; *Henry James and the Darkest Abyss*, pp. 133–7). Felman's idea that the frame chapter of 'The Turn of the Screw' problematizes the difference between the inside and the outside is developed by Caws, who makes use of Derrida's work on frames, rims and borders (see Caws, *Reading Frames in Modern Fiction*, p. 13). On the paradoxical nature of the frame, see also Johnson, 'The Frame of Reference', pp. 128–9.

42 See O'Gorman, 'Henry James's Reading of "The Turn of the Screw"', pp. 135–7. For a detailed study of the iconography of inversion in Renaissance broadsheets, see Kunzle, 'World Upside Down', pp. 41–51.

43 Norrman also comments on the drift towards oxymoron in 'The Turn of the Screw' (see *The Insecure World*, pp. 153–5).

44 Sheppard, *Henry James and 'The Turn of the Screw'*, p. 114.

45 For information about the secondary material on the relation between 'The Turn of the Screw' and *Udolpho*, *Jane Eyre*, *Amelia* and *The Scarlet Letter*, see notes 48, 54, 55, 101 and 102 to this chapter. Numerous other sources, references and allusions have been detected. In '"The Turn of the Screw" as Poem', Heilman cites Milton, Keats and the Bible. Lind examines the influence of Maupassant's 'The Little Roque Girl' and Kipling's 'Baa, Baa, Black Sheep' (see 'The Supernatural Tales of Henry James', pp. 334, 342–5). Allott posits other literary references in

'Mrs Gaskell's "The Old Nurse's Story": A Link between *Wuthering Heights* and "The Turn of the Screw"'. In 'Henry James as Freudian Pioneer' and '"The Turn of the Screw" and Alice James', Cargill argues for the direct impact of Freud and Breuer's *Studies on Hysteria*. Egan analyses the influence of Ibsen's *Ghosts* (see *Henry James: The Ibsen Years*, pp. 89–113). Sheppard disinters echoes of *A Midsummer-Night's Dream* (see *Henry James and 'The Turn of the Screw'*, p. 27), *David Copperfield* (see pp. 93–4), Le Fanu's *Uncle Silas* and *The Cock and Anchor* (see note 51 to this chapter), and Ibsen's *The Lady from the Sea, Little Eyolf* and *Peer Gynt* (see pp. 36–41, 98). Most recently and surprisingly, Leon Edel has pointed out links between 'The Turn of the Screw' and Tom Taylor's *Temptation* (see *Henry James: A Life*, pp. 465–6).

46 Goddard, 'A Pre-Freudian Reading', p. 9.
47 Perrault, *Histories*, pp. 33, 73.
48 Cargill, '"The Turn of the Screw" and Alice James', p. 244, note 25.
49 Brontë, *Jane Eyre*, p. 536.
50 See Reeve, *The Old English Baron*, p. 42; Austen, *Northanger Abbey*, p. 88. On this appropriation of Gothic effects, see Briggs, *Night Visitors*, p. 158.
51 See Le Fanu, *Uncle Silas*, p. 52. On this and other resemblances between *Uncle Silas, The Cock and Anchor* and 'The Turn of the Screw', see Sheppard, *Henry James and 'The Turn of the Screw'*, pp. 27–8, 34, 269.
52 Robbins, 'Shooting Off James's Blanks', p. 197. For further discussion of the governess's Gothic sensibilities, see Hill, 'A Counterclockwise Turn', p. 56; Lukacher, '"Hanging Fire"', p. 127.
53 Radcliffe, *Udolpho*, p. 278.
54 See De la Mare, 'The Lesson of the Masters' (1915), p. 9; Liddell, 'The "Hallucination" Theory', p. 144; Cargill, '"The Turn of the Screw" and Alice James', pp. 243–4 (note 25), p. 249 (note 53); Edel's introduction to *CT*, X (p. 8) and *The Treacherous Years*, p. 195; Sheppard, *Henry James and 'The Turn of the Screw'*, pp. 42–60, 223 note 105; Tintner, 'Henry James's Use of *Jane Eyre* in "The Turn of the Screw"'; Briggs, *Night Visitors*, p. 152.
55 See Cargill, '"The Turn of the Screw" and Alice James', p. 248; Sheppard, *Henry James and 'The Turn of the Screw'*, p. 30.
56 Fielding, *Amelia*, p. 237.
57 On the debt of writers such as Dickens and Stevenson to the fantastic tales of nurses, see Gathorne-Hardy, *The Rise and Fall of the British Nanny*, pp. 129–30, 282–5. On the continuing potency of the figure of the old maid in post-Enlightenment culture, see Auerbach, *Woman and the Demon*, pp. 75, 111, 140.
58 See Howe, *A Galaxy of Governesses*, pp. 16, 83; anon., *The Story of the Governesses' Benevolent Institution*, pp. 1–4; Hughes, *The Victorian Governess*, p. 11.
59 See Iona and Peter Opie's introduction to *The Classic Fairy Tales*, pp. 24–5.
60 Fielding, *The Governess*, pp. 9, 52–3.

61 Le Prince de Beaumont, *The Young Misses Magazine*, title-page to volume I. Though opposing the Utilitarian inculcation of 'mere facts', the anonymous 'Notes of Lectures on Method in Learning and Teaching', published in *The Governess: A Repertory of Female Education* (1855), argues similarly that governesses should use fairy tales 'for the purposes of instruction' and in order to convey 'some deep spiritual truth' (pp. 373–4).

62 Edgeworth, *The Good French Governess*, pp. 117, 107.

63 See Eastlake, review of *Vanity Fair*, *Jane Eyre* and the Governesses' Benevolent Institution Report for 1847, p. 180.

64 Parkes, 'The Profession of the Teacher' (1865), p. 88.

65 The Countess of Blessington, *The Governess*, I, 136; Sewell, *Principles of Education*, II, 240.

66 *The Guide to Service: The Governess* (1844), p.6.

67 Jameson, 'On the Relative Social Position of Mothers and Governesses' (1846), pp. 252, 257–8, 272.

68 Quoted in Gaskell, *The Life of Charlotte Brontë*, pp. 187–8.

69 Eastlake, Review of *Vanity Fair*, *Jane Eyre* and the Governesses' Benevolent Institution Report for 1847, p. 177.

70 Pollard, 'The Governess and her Grievances' (1889), p. 511.

71 See Peterson, 'The Victorian Governess: Status Incongruence in Family and Society', pp. 5, 10–11; Michie, *The Flesh Made Word*, p. 47; Hughes, *The Victorian Governess*, pp. 85–6.

72 Poovey, 'The Anathematized Race', p. 129; see also pp. 127–8.

73 *The Governess; or, Politics in Private Life* (1836), p. 310. See also 'Hints on the Modern Governess System' (1844), pp. 582–3; Eastlake, review of *Vanity Fair*, *Jane Eyre* and the Governesses' Benevolent Institution Report for 1847, pp. 177, 180; *Hints to Governesses, By One of Themselves* (1856), p. 9; Martineau, 'The Governess: Her Health' (1860), p. 270.

74 See 'Hints on the Modern Governess System', pp. 573, 578–9; Martineau, 'The Governess: Her Health', p. 270; Edward Forbes, letters in *The Times*, 25 October 1864 (p. 7) and 4 January 1868 (p. 6); Francis Pigou, letter in *The Times*, 26 October 1864 (p. 10); anonymous letter in *The Times*, 14 September 1867 (p. 6).

75 Peterson, 'The Victorian Governess', pp. 18, 17. For further information on Queen's College and the residential home, see Neff, 'The Governess', pp. 176–82; anon., *The Story of the Governesses' Benevolent Institution*.

76 *The Times*, 22 April 1869, p. 9.

77 See *The Story of the Governesses' Benevolent Institution*, p. 17.

78 On these anxieties, see also Hughes, *The Victorian Governess*, pp. 19, 56–8.

79 See *The Guide to Service*, p. 345; 'Hints on the Modern Governess System', pp. 571, 573, 575; Jameson, 'On the Relative Social Position of Mothers and Governesses', pp. 253, 273, 290, 294; Eastlake, review of *Vanity Fair*, *Jane Eyre* and the Governesses' Benevolent Institution

Report for 1847, p. 177; Martineau, 'Female Industry' (1859), pp. 294, 307 and 'The Governess: Her Health', pp. 268–71; Parkes, 'The Profession of the Teacher', p. 91; Maxse, 'On Governesses' (1901), p. 400. On Charlotte Brontë's period of ill-health as a governess, see Gaskell, *The Life of Charlotte Brontë*, p. 189. Freud's analysis of the English governess Miss Lucy R. is also pertinent here (see *Studies on Hysteria*, SE, II, 106–24). For more recent commentary, see West, *Chapter of Governesses*, pp. 98–9; Howe, *A Galaxy of Governesses*, p. 116; Hardwick, *Seduction and Betrayal*, pp. 12, 22.

80 For euphemistic expressions of the 'temptations' and 'dangers' to which English governesses in Paris were exposed, see Edward Forbes, letter in *The Times*, 25 October 1864 (p. 7); Francis Pigou, letter in *The Times*, 26 October 1864 (p. 10). See also West, *Chapter of Governesses*, pp. 98–9; Hughes, *The Victorian Governess*, pp. 118–23.

81 Hemyng, in Mayhew's *London Labour*, IV, 217.

82 Heath, letter in *The Times*, 15 September 1868, p. 9.

83 Quoted in Hughes, *The Victorian Governess*, p. 126.

84 See also *The Guide to Service*, p. 125.

85 A point also made in *Hints to Governesses* (see p. 21).

86 James, 'The Speech of American Women', part III, p. 19. On this remark, see Habegger, *Henry James and the 'Woman Business'*, pp. 235–6; Poole, *Henry James*, p. 109.

87 For a rather different reading of the relationship between 'The Turn of the Screw' and picaresque fiction, see Heilman, 'The Lure of the Demonic', pp. 356–7.

88 Babcock, 'Liberty's a Whore', p. 101.

89 See Hill, 'A Counterclockwise Turn', pp. 57–8.

90 Schrero, 'Exposure in "The Turn of the Screw"', p. 269.

91 See Gathorne-Hardy, *The Rise and Fall of the British Nanny*, pp. 163–5; Hughes, *The Victorian Governess*, pp. 120, 123.

92 'The Most Hopelessly Evil Story', p. 175.

93 See Beidler, 'The Governess and the Ghosts', p. 96. For criticism which defines the nature of the blanks in 'The Turn of the Screw' in specifically homosexual terms, see also Forster, *Aspects of the Novel* (Appendix A), p. 171; Cargill, '"The Turn of the Screw" and Alice James', pp. 246–7; Schrero, 'Exposure in "The Turn of the Screw"', p. 271; Smith, 'A Word Kept Back', pp. 4, 11–12, 15.

94 Beidler, 'The Governess and the Ghosts', p. 96; Hill, 'A Counterclockwise Turn', p. 71, note 13; Lukacher, '"Hanging Fire"', p. 120.

95 Clair, *The Ironic Dimension*, p. 39.

96 Tate, 'James: "The Turn of the Screw"', p. 168.

97 Spilka, 'Turning the Freudian Screw', p. 246. For a similar argument, see Hill, 'A Counterclockwise Turn', especially p. 55.

98 Marcus, *The Other Victorians*, p. 15.

99 Smith, 'A Word Kept Back', p. 16.

100 Geismar, *Henry James and his Cult*, p. 164.

101 See Lydenberg, 'The Governess Turns the Screws', pp. 47, 58; Geismar, *Henry James and his Cult*, p. 14; Cranfill and Clark, *An Anatomy*, p. 82; O'Gorman, 'Henry James's Reading of "The Turn of the Screw"', pp. 237–9.

102 See Fagin, 'Another Reading', pp. 198–201; Rowe, *Theoretical Dimensions*, p. 57.

103 The idea that James is capable of alphabetic punning may seem unlikely, but on his use of 'P' and 'V', see Lock, '"The Figure in the Carpet"', pp. 168–9.

104 I am grateful to Adrian Poole for pointing this out to me.

105 Goddard also questions these inductions in 'A Pre-Freudian Reading' (see pp. 19–20). See also Fryer, 'The Mother-Surrogates', pp. 157–8; Norrman, *Techniques of Ambiguity*, p. 42.

106 Norrman also argues that the governess uses opposite propositions to reach identical conclusions and identical propositions to reach opposite conclusions (see *Techniques of Ambiguity*, pp. 157, 164–5).

107 For an alternative reading of these two rotations, see Anderson, *The American Henry James*, pp. 318–23, 349.

108 'Hints on the Modern Governess System', p. 573. On the woman question, the early stages of the suffrage struggle and the debate about female education in the mid-nineteenth century, see Gilbert and Gubar, *No Man's Land*, I, 9–21.

109 Gilbert and Gubar, *The Madwoman in the Attic*, p. 19; see also p. 15.

110 Gubar, '"The Blank Page"', p. 244; see also p. 245. For the pun on framing, see p. 254 and Gilbert and Gubar, *The Madwoman in the Attic*, p. 13. On women seen by men in terms of blankness, absence and negativity, see, for example, Gilbert and Gubar, *No Man's Land*, I, 22.

111 On the governess as scapegoat, see Goetz, *Henry James and the Darkest Abyss*, p. 124.

112 Gilbert and Gubar, *No Man's Land*, I, 4. The argument extends to include *The Bostonians* on pp. 26–7 and tales such as 'The Death of the Lion', 'The Next Time' and 'Greville Fane' on p. 135.

113 On the iconography of the *femme fatale*, see Praz, *The Romantic Agony*, pp. 189–286; Auerbach, *Woman and the Demon*; Dijkstra, *Idols of Perversity*; Gilbert and Gubar, *No Man's Land*, II, xiv, 4–9; Bronfen, *Over Her Dead Body*.

114 See Cixous, 'Sorties', pp. 63–4.

115 Cixous, 'The Laugh of the Medusa', p. 254.

116 See Habegger, *Gender, Fantasy, and Realism*, especially pp. vii–x, 3–65, 111; *Henry James and the 'Woman Business'*, especially pp. 26, 63–125.

117 Bloom, introduction to *Henry James*, pp. 3, 12.

118 See Howe, *A Galaxy of Governesses*, pp. 12, 78, 92, 113, 129.

119 For an example of the governess taking over from the nurse or old maid as a teller of ghost stories, see Neff, 'The Governess', p. 151.

120 James, *The Saloon*, p. 671.

121 As well as referring to the female genitals, Middle English 'queynte'

means 'strange', 'curious', 'artful' and 'sly'. On the significance of the related French words *'quinte'* and *'quinteux'* ('vagary', 'crotchet', 'whimsical', or 'fantastic'), see Lind, 'The Supernatural Tales of Henry James', p. 337. For other suggestions about the sources for or connotations of Quint's name, see Roellinger, 'Psychical Research and "The Turn of the Screw"', p. 411; Sheppard, *Henry James and 'The Turn of the Screw'*, pp. 27, 93, 98; O'Gorman, 'Henry James's Reading of "The Turn of the Screw"', pp. 240–1. One might add that the rotary motifs in James's tale indicate a possible reference to 'quintain', a dummy figure or target used in medieval tournaments which, when hit incorrectly, revolved to strike the tilting knight. On Miss Jessel's name, see Sheppard, *Henry James and 'The Turn of the Screw'*, p. 28; O'Gorman, 'Henry James's Reading of "The Turn of the Screw"', p. 241.

122 On the absence of hats in 'The Turn of the Screw', see Norrman, *Techniques of Ambiguity*, pp. 89–92; *The Insecure World*, pp. 170–1.

123 On the resemblances between the governess and the ghosts, see Edel's introduction to *CT*, X (p. 9); McMaster, '"The Full Image of a Repetition"', pp. 125–6; Banta, *Henry James and the Occult*, pp. 124–5; Mackenzie, *Communities of Honor and Love*, p. 79; Norrman, *Techniques of Ambiguity*, pp. 89, 160; *The Insecure World*, pp. 169–70; Brooke-Rose, *A Rhetoric of the Unreal*, pp. 168–9; Robbins, 'Shooting Off James's Blanks', pp. 196–7; Millicent Bell, '"The Turn of the Screw" and the *Recherche de L'Absolu'*, p. 72; Goetz, *Henry James and the Darkest Abyss*, p. 137; Poole, *Henry James*, pp. 142, 156.

124 Blanchot, '"The Turn of the Screw"', p. 82.

4 THE HAUNTED CHAMBER

1 Norrman, *Techniques of Ambiguity*, p. 122.

2 Most of the basically positive responses to the narrator of *The Sacred Fount* involve the argument that his role is analogous to that of the Jamesian artist. See Follett, 'Henry James's Portrait of Henry James'; Blackmur, *'The Sacred Fount'*; Allott, 'Henry James and the Fantasticated Conceit', especially pp. 79–81; Perlongo, *'The Sacred Fount'*; Finkelstein, 'The "Mystery" of Henry James's *The Sacred Fount'*; Tanner, 'Henry James's Subjective Adventurer'; Wiesenfarth, *Henry James and the Dramatic Analogy*, pp. 101–3; Gargano, 'James's *The Sacred Fount'*; Moon, 'Is *The Sacred Fount* a Symbolist Novel?'. Negative assessments of the narrator tend to emphasize the resemblances between him and characters like the governess in 'The Turn of the Screw'. See Wilson, 'The Ambiguity of Henry James', especially pp. 394–5; Anderson, *The American Henry James*, pp. 120–1; Cargill, *The Novels of Henry James*, pp. 289–95; Ward, *The Imagination of Disaster*, pp. 72–3; Blackall, *Jamesian Ambiguity*, pp. 33, 51–3, 80–1; Sears, *The Negative Imagination*, p. 178; Samuels, *The Ambiguity of Henry James*, pp. 27–8; Schneider, *The*

Crystal Cage, p. 66; Sklepowich, 'Gossip and Gothicism'; Norrman, *The Insecure World*, p. 132; Goetz, *Henry James and the Darkest Abyss*, pp. 125–6, 145–9.

3 Yeazell, *Language and Knowledge*, pp. 32, 33. For Ellmann the river scene represents a still more specifically Freudian 'return of the repressed' ('The Intimate Difference', p. 109). Goetz draws attention to the 'uncanny quality' of the passage (*Henry James and the Darkest Abyss*, p. 202).

4 On 'Louis Lambert' and *The Ambassadors*, see Anderson, *The American Henry James*, pp. 213–14; Tanner, 'The Watcher from the Balcony', pp. 39–40.

5 On this incident, see also Edel, *The Treacherous Years*, pp. 140–1.

6 See Edel, *The Master*, p. 73.

7 See Edel, *The Conquest of London*, p. 231; *The Middle Years*, p. 275.

8 On the labyrinth image in *The Ambassadors*, see Paterson, 'The Language of "Adventure"', pp. 299–300. For a discussion of the labyrinth figure in *The Golden Bowl* and analysis of the broader implications of the image, see Miller, 'Ariadne's Thread', especially p. 68. On the Theseus and Ariadne motif in *The Sense of the Past*, see Frye, *Anatomy of Criticism*, p. 190.

9 In the first edition the place of the word 'uncanny' is occupied by the word 'abnormal' (*The Ambassadors*, p. 124). But the use of the stronger and more distinctly ghostly term in the later text is worth noticing, particularly because it significantly contrasts with the second occurrence of the word 'uncanny' (see p. 203 above).

10 Ellmann, 'The Intimate Difference', p. 101.

11 On circles and circling in *The Ambassadors*, see Poole, *Henry James*, pp. 28, 47–8.

12 On 'savage' metaphor (i.e. catachresis), see Derrida, *Of Grammatology*, p. 276.

13 Sears discerns a movement from a 'twofold' to a 'fourfold' consciousness in *The Ambassadors* (*The Negative Imagination*, p. 107).

14 On the relationship between *The Ambassadors* and *The Sacred Fount*, see Cargill, *The Novels of Henry James*, pp. 295, 305; Finkelstein, 'The "Mystery" of Henry James's *The Sacred Fount*', pp. 772–4.

15 Goetz discusses the 'two times two' arithmetic of *The Sacred Fount* (*Henry James and the Darkest Abyss*, pp. 126–27).

16 On the narrator's use of logical, algebraic, geometrical and legal terminology, see Follett, 'Henry James's Portrait of Henry James', p. 2; Perlongo, '*The Sacred Fount*', p. 646; Segal, *The Lucid Reflector*, pp. 156–8; Norrman, *Techniques of Ambiguity*, p. 40.

17 See Freud, *SE*, XVII, 237; Twain, *A Tramp Abroad*, pp. 69–74.

18 See Edel, *The Master*, pp. 36–7, 72.

19 Sears argues that Gloriani, Chad, Waymarsh and Little Bilham are all *alter egos* for Strether (see *The Negative Imagination*, p. 142). On the motif

of the double in *The Ambassadors*, see Goetz, *Henry James and the Darkest Abyss*, pp. 193–4. See also note 29 to this chapter.

20 Krook implies that Maggie is a less avid version of the governess in 'The Turn of the Screw' (see *The Ordeal of Consciousness*, p. 263).

21 On Maggie as a restrictive author-figure, see Bersani, 'The Jamesian Lie', pp. 72–3; Boone, 'Modernist Maneuverings', pp. 374, 381–4. For an account of *The Golden Bowl* which emphasizes Maggie's resemblances to Isabel Archer as well as Gilbert Osmond, see Kaston, *Imagination and Desire*, p. 169.

22 See also James's 24 May 1903 letter to William James (*L*, IV, 272) and his 5 January 1903 letter to Mme Paul Bourget (*The Letters of Henry James*, edited by Lubbock, I, 419).

23 James, *The American Scene*, p. 117.

24 Edel conjecturally dates James's dream to 1910 (see *The Master*, pp. 448–9). The evidence for this comes from entries in James's pocket diary for 21 July 1910, 12 September 1910 and 15–21 September 1910 (see *N*, pp. 318, 321).

25 For interpretations of the Galerie d'Apollon dream, see Trilling, *The Liberal Imagination*, pp. 81–3; Anderson, *The American Henry James*, pp. 164–9; Bayley, 'Love and Knowledge', p. 236; Geismar, *Henry James and his Cult*, pp. 360–1, 390–2; Edel, *The Untried Years*, pp. 69–80 and *The Master*, pp. 448–9; Donadio, *Nietzsche, Henry James*, pp. 254–8; Rowe, *The Theoretical Dimensions*, p. 215. See also note 26 to this chapter on the views of Eakin and Follini.

26 Eakin argues that the Gallerie d'Apollon is 'the perfect emblem of James's autobiographical text' and that the dream is a preparation for 'a triumphant return to the house of fiction' ('Henry James and the Autobiographical Act', pp. 81, 125). For a similar view, see also Follini, '"Hero and Historian"', p. 165.

27 On the figure of the turned tables, see Esch, 'A Jamesian About-Face', p. 591.

28 On James's moment of amnesia, see Lind, 'The Supernatural Tales of Henry James', pp. 392–4; Allott, 'Symbol and Image', p. 331; Edel, *The Untried Years*, p. 76. Ward argues too simplistically that Brydon actually does achieve a victory over his other self (see *The Imagination of Disaster*, pp. 162–3).

29 Brooks compares Brydon and his other to Strether and Jim Pocock (see *The Pilgrimage of Henry James*, p. 47).

30 Rovit draws attention to the name 'Spencer' Brydon and describes 'The Jolly Corner' as a 'social' and 'international' 'Prothalamion' ('The Ghosts in James's "The Jolly Corner"', p. 72, note 11). Mackenzie has also seen resemblances between *The Ambassadors* and the 'Epithala-mion' (see *Communities of Honor and Love*, p. 192, note 7). On romance imagery in 'The Jolly Corner', see Miller, *Doubles*, p. 232. On the resurgence of romance patterns in late James, see Frye, *Anatomy of Criticism*, pp. 117, 202.

31 Lind states baldly, and I think with only partial accuracy, that 'James *is* Spencer Brydon' ('The Supernatural Tales of Henry James', p. 400).

32 Howells, 'The Man of Letters as a Man of Business', p. 35. See also p. 34.

33 Wilson, 'The Ambiguity of Henry James', in *The Triple Thinkers* (1938), p. 160. The line is not used in the original version of the essay, although Wilson does discuss James's ambition to be the American Balzac (see p. 402).

34 See Edel, *The Master*, pp. 329–32. Qualifying Edel's claim, Anesko has shown that the contemplated number of volumes in the collected edition was initially sixteen and that it was ultimately James's publisher who restricted him to twenty-three, or, in the event, twenty-four (see *Friction with the Market*, pp. 143–58).

35 See Follini, '"Hero and Historian"', p. 162.

36 See Donoghue, 'Attitudes Toward History', p. 119.

37 Cargill suggests that the narrator becomes depleted (see *The Novels of Henry James*, p. 295). For an extended version of this interpretation, see Kappeler, *Writing and Reading*, pp. 121–40.

38 For an extensive exploration of the implications of chiastic thinking in James, see Norrman, *The Insecure World*, pp. 137–84. On the links between chiasmus and romance, see Dekker, *The American Historical Romance*, p. 151.

39 See, for instance, Andreach, 'Henry James's *The Sacred Fount*', pp. 199–202; Isle, 'The Romantic and the Real', p. 257.

40 On the narrator's sacrifice, see Andreach, 'Henry James's *The Sacred Fount*', pp. 212–16; Holland, *The Expense of Vision*, p. 119.

41 Frye describes the narrator as 'an ironic parody of a Prospero figure' (*Anatomy of Criticism*, p. 180).

42 Kermode, *Romantic Image*, pp. 43, 59.

43 Isle, 'The Romantic and the Real', p. 260.

44 See Kappeler, *Writing and Reading*, pp. 132, 145.

45 On balcony scenes in *The Ambassadors*, see also Gibson, 'Metaphor in the Plot of *The Ambassadors*', pp. 297–300.

46 Caws, *Reading Frames in Modern Fiction*, p. 148.

47 For a rather different reading of this scene, see Kaston, *Imagination and Desire*, p. 25.

48 Eliot, *The Collected Poems and Plays*, p. 288.

POSTSCRIPT

1 Babcock, introduction to *The Reversible World*, p. 22.

2 Davis, 'Women on Top', pp. 171, 170.

3 Bynum, 'Women's Stories', p. 109.

4 Seltzer, *Henry James and the Art of Power*, p. 140.

5 See Bersani, 'The Subject of Power', p. 10.

6 Miller, 'Re-Reading Re-Vision', p. 107.

7 Dijkstra, *Idols of Perversity*, p. 129; see also pp. 130–4.
8 See Auerbach, *Woman and the Demon*, p. 12.
9 On another occasion, however, Freud argues that hats can symbolize female genitals (see *The Interpretation of Dreams*, *SE*, v, 362).
10 See Lurie, 'Pornography and the Dread of Women', pp. 160–72.
11 Irigaray, 'This Sex Which Is Not One', p. 103.
12 For an account of the explosive principle in terms of feminine writing and economic mastery in terms of male authorship as well as for discussion of the implicit bisexuality in James's construction of a dialogue between them, see McWhirter, *Desire and Love in Henry James*, pp. 61–2.
13 Clark, *Sordid Images*, pp. 19 (Introduction), 155 (Chapter 6).
14 Hertz, *The End of the Line*, pp. 1, 185; see also pp. 14, 40, 44, 57–60, 162, 230.
15 Derrida, *Glas*, p. 46.

Bibliography

WORKS BY JAMES REFERRED TO IN THE TEXT

The Ambassadors (London, 1903)
The American Scene (London, 1907)
Autobiography, ed. by Frederick W. Dupee (London, 1956)
  The Middle Years (1917), pp. 547–99
  Notes of a Son and Brother (1914), pp. 239–544
  A Small Boy and Others (1913), pp. 3–236
The Complete Notebooks of Henry James, ed. by Leon Edel and Lyall H.
  Powers (New York, 1987)
The Complete Tales of Henry James, ed. by Leon Edel, 12 vols. (London,
  1962–4)
  'Adina' (1874), III, 211–57
  'The Altar of the Dead' (1895), IX, 231–71
  'The Aspern Papers' (1888), VI, 275–382
  'The Author of "Beltraffio" ' (1884), V, 303–55
  'The Beast in the Jungle' (1903), XI, 351–402
  'Benvolio' (1875), III, 351–401
  'The Birthplace' (1903), XI, 403–65
  'A Bundle of Letters' (1879), IV, 427–65
  'The Coxon Fund' (1894), IX, 119–84
  'Daisy Miller: A Study' (1878), IV, 141–207
  'The Death of the Lion' (1894), IX, 77–118
  'De Grey: A Romance' (1868), I, 387–428
  'The Diary of a Man of Fifty' (1879), IV, 389–425
  'The Figure in the Carpet' (1896), IX, 273–315
  'The Friends of the Friends'. See 'The Way it Came'
  'Gabrielle de Bergerac' (1869), II, 97–170
  'The Ghostly Rental' (1876), IV, 49–86
  'The Great Good Place' (1900), XI, 13–42
  'Greville Fane' (1892), VIII, 433–52
  'In the Cage' (1898), X, 139–242
  'John Delavoy' (1898), IX, 403–42
  'The Jolly Corner' (1908), XII, 193–232

'A Landscape-Painter' (1866), I, 99–138
'The Last of the Valerii' (1874), III, 89–122
'The Lesson of the Master' (1888), VII, 213–84
'The Liar' (1888), VI, 383–441
'A Light Man' (1869), II, 61–96
'Longstaff's Marriage' (1878), IV, 209–42
'Madame de Mauves' (1874), III, 123–209
'The Madonna of the Future' (1873), III, 11–52
'Master Eustace' (1871), II, 341–73
'Maud-Evelyn' (1900), XI, 43–75
'The Middle Years' (1893), IX, 53–76
'A Most Extraordinary Case' (1868), I, 321–67
'My Friend Bingham' (1867), I, 165–90
'A New England Winter' (1884), VI, 87–152
'The Next Time' (1895), IX, 185–229
'Nona Vincent' (1892), VIII, 153–87
'Osborne's Revenge' (1868), II, 13–60
'Owen Wingrave' (1892), IX, 13–51
'A Passionate Pilgrim' (1871), II, 227–306
'The Point of View' (1882), IV, 467–519
'Poor Richard' (1867), I, 191–258
'The Private Life' (1892), VIII, 189–227
'Professor Fargo' (1874), III, 259–98
'The Pupil' (1891), VII, 409–60
'The Real Right Thing' (1899), X, 471–86
'The Romance of Certain Old Clothes' (1868), I, 297–319
'Sir Dominick Ferrand' (as 'Jersey Villas', 1892), VIII, 343–405
'Sir Edmund Orme' (1891), VIII, 119–51
'The Solution' (1889–90), VII, 351–407
'The Story of a Year' (1865), I, 49–98
'The Sweetheart of M. Briseux' (1873), III, 53–87
'The Third Person' (1900), XI, 133–69
'A Tragedy of Error' (1864), I, 23–47
'Travelling Companions' (1870), II, 171–225
'The Turn of the Screw' (1898), X, 15–138
'The Visits' (as 'The Visit', 1892), VIII, 323–41
'The Way it Came' (1896), IX, 371–401
'The Wheel of Time' (1892–93), VIII, 453–502
'Coquelin' (1887), in *The Scenic Art: Notes on Acting and the Drama*, ed. by
    Allan Wade (London, 1949), pp. 198–218
Embarrassments (London, 1896)
'Is There a Life After Death?', in *In After Days: Thoughts on the Future Life*,
    ed. by W.D. Howells (New York, 1910), pp. 199–233
Letters, ed. by Leon Edel, 4 vols. (vols. I–III, London, 1974–81; vol. IV,
    Cambridge, Mass., 1984)

The Letters of Henry James, ed. by Percy Lubbock, 2 vols. (London, 1920)
Literary Criticism; Essays on Literature, American Writers, English Writers, ed.
     by Leon Edel and Mark Wilson, Library of America (New York,
     1984)
Alcott, Louisa M., *Moods* (1865 review), pp. 189–95
'American Letters', 26 March 1898 ('The Question of the Opportuni-
     ties'), pp. 651–7; 23 April 1898, pp. 663–7
'The Art of Fiction' (1884), pp. 44–65
Braddon, Mary Elizabeth, *Aurora Floyd* (1865 review), pp. 741–6
Brooke, Stopford, *Theology in the English Poets* (1875 review), pp. 770–5
Cabot, James Elliott, *A Memoir of Ralph Waldo Emerson* (1887 review),
     pp. 250–71
'*Daniel Deronda*: A Conversation' (1876), pp. 974–2
Eliot, George, *Middlemarch* (1873 review), pp. 958–66
Emerson, Ralph Waldo. See Cabot, James Elliott
Hawthorne (1879), pp. 319–457
Hawthorne, Julian, *Idolatry: A Romance* (1874 review), pp. 295–300
Hawthorne, Nathaniel (1896 introduction), pp. 458–68
Hawthorne, Nathaniel, *Passages from the French and Italian Note-Books*
     (1872 review), pp. 307–14
Howells, William Dean. See 'William Dean Howells'
'London Notes', 15 January 1897, pp. 1387–92; July 1897, pp. 1399–1406
Manning, Anne E., *The Household of Sir Thomas More* and *Jacques Bonneval*
     (1867 review), pp. 1152–7
'The Question of the Opportunities'. See 'American Letters'
'Robert Louis Stevenson' (1888), pp. 1231–55
Shakespeare, William, *The Tempest* (1907 introduction), pp. 1205–20
Spofford, Harriet, *Azarian: An Episode* (1865 review), pp. 603–13
Stevenson, Robert Louis. See 'Robert Louis Stevenson'
Taylor, Bayard, *John Godfrey's Fortunes* (?1865 review; first published
     1957), pp. 621–5
Trollope, Anthony, *Miss Mackenzie: A Novel* (1865 review), pp. 1312–17
Trollope, T. Adolphus, *Lindisfarn Chase: A Novel* (1865 review), pp.
     1355–6
'William Dean Howells' (1886), pp. 497–506
*Literary Criticism; French Writers, other European Writers, the Prefaces to the New
     York Edition*, ed. by Leon Edel and Mark Wilson, Library of America
     (New York, 1984)
'Alphonse Daudet' (1883), pp. 223–49
Balzac, Honoré de, *The Two Young Brides* (1902 introduction), pp. 90–115
Balzac, Honoré de. See 'Honoré de Balzac' and 'The Lesson of Balzac'
Daudet, Alphonse. See 'Alphonse Daudet'
Flaubert, Gustave, *Correspondance* (1893 review), pp. 295–314
Flaubert, Gustave, *Madame Bovary* (1902 introduction), pp. 314–6
'George Sand' (1877), pp. 708–34

Goethe, Johann Wolfgang von, *Wilhelm Meister's Apprenticeship and Travels* (1865 review), pp. 944–49

'Honoré de Balzac' (1875), pp. 31–68

'The Lesson of Balzac' (1905 lecture), pp. 115–39

Mérimée, Prosper, *Derniéres Nouvelles* (1874 review), pp. 562–5

Mérimée, Prosper. See 'Prosper Mérimée'

Preface to *The Altar of the Dead, The Beast in the Jungle, The Birthplace, The Private Life, Owen Wingrave, The Friends of the Friends, Sir Edmund Orme, The Real Right Thing, The Jolly Corner, Julia Bride* (*NYE*, XVII), pp. 1246–68

Preface to *The Ambassadors* (*NYE*, XXI), pp. 1304–21

Preface to *The American* (*NYE*, II), pp. 1053–69

Preface to *The Aspern Papers, The Turn of the Screw, The Liar, The Two Faces* (*NYE*, XII), pp. 1173–91

Preface to *The Author of Beltraffio, The Middle Years, Greville Fane, Broken Wings, The Tree of Knowledge, The Abasement of the Northmores, The Great Good Place, Four Meetings, Paste, Europe, Miss Gunton of Poughkeepsie, Fordham Castle* (*NYE*, XVI), pp. 1238–45

Preface to *The Awkward Age* (*NYE*, IX), pp. 1120–37

Preface to *Daisy Miller, Pandora, The Patagonia, The Marriages, The Real Thing, Brooksmith, The Beldonald Holbein, The Story In It, Flickerbridge, Mrs Medwin* (*NYE*, XVIII), pp. 1269–86

Preface to *The Golden Bowl* (*NYE*, XXIII), pp. 1322–41

Preface to *Lady Barbarina, The Siege of London, An International Episode, The Pension Beaurepas, A Bundle of Letters, The Point of View* (*NYE*, XIV), pp. 1208–24

Preface to *The Lesson of the Master, The Death of the Lion, The Next Time, The Figure in the Carpet, The Coxon Fund* (*NYE*, XV), pp. 1225–37

Preface to *The Portrait of a Lady* (*NYE*, III), pp. 1070–85

Preface to *The Princess Casamassima* (*NYE*, V), pp. 1086–102

Preface to *The Reverberator, Madame de Mauves, A Passionate Pilgrim, The Madonna of the Future, Louisa Pallant* (*NYE*, XIII), pp. 1192–207

Preface to *Roderick Hudson* (*NYE*, I), pp. 1039–52

Preface to *The Spoils of Poynton, A London Life, The Chaperon* (*NYE*, X), pp. 1138–55

Preface to *The Tragic Muse* (*NYE*, VII), pp. 1103–19

Preface to *What Maisie Knew, The Pupil, In the Cage* (*NYE*, XI), pp. 1156–72

Preface to *The Wings of the Dove* (*NYE*, XIX), pp. 1287–303

'Prosper Mérimée' (1898), pp. 575–81

Sand, George, *Mademoiselle Merquem: A Novel* (1868 review), pp. 696–701

Sand, George. See 'George Sand'

Turgenev, Ivan, *Frühlingsfluthen. Ein König Lear des Dorfes* (1874 review), pp. 968–99

Notebooks. See *The Complete Notebooks*

Novels 1871–1880, ed. by William T. Stafford, Library of America (New
    York, 1983)
    The American (1876–77), pp. 515–872
    The Europeans (1878), pp. 575–1038
    Roderick Hudson (1875), pp. 167–511
    Watch and Ward (1871), pp. 3–161
Novels 1881–1886, ed. by William T. Stafford, Library of America (New
    York, 1985)
    The Bostonians (1885–6), pp. 803–1219
    The Portrait of a Lady (1880–1), pp. 193–800
    Washington Square (1880), pp. 3–189
Novels 1886–1890, ed. by Daniel Mark Fogel, Library of America (New
    York, 1989)
    The Princess Casamassima (1885–86), pp. 3–553
    The Reverberator (1888), pp. 557–699
    The Tragic Muse (1889–90), pp. 703–1255
The Novels and Tales of Henry James, New York Edition, 26 vols. (vols.
    I–XXIV, London, 1907–9; vols. XXV–XXVI, London, 1917)
    The Ambassadors, XXI–XXII
    The American, II
    'The Friends of the Friends', XVII, 323–64
    The Golden Bowl, XXIII–XXIV
    The Portrait of a Lady, III–IV
    The Sense of the Past, XXVI
    'Sir Edmund Orme', XVII, 367–408
    The Spoils of Poynton, X, 3–266
    'The Turn of the Screw', XII, 147–309
    What Maisie Knew, XI, 3–363
    The Wings of the Dove, XIX–XX
The Sacred Fount, ed. by Leon Edel (New York, 1959)
The Saloon, in *The Complete Plays of Henry James*, ed. by Leon Edel (London,
    1949), pp. 639–74
'The Speech of American Women', *Harper's Bazaar*, 40 (1906), 979–82
    (part I), 1103–6 (part II); 41 (1907), 17–21 (part III), 113–17 (part IV)
Stories of the Supernatural, ed. by Leon Edel (London, 1971)
Stories Revived, 3 vols. (London, 1885)
Terminations (London, 1895)
Transatlantic Sketches (Boston, 1875)

OTHER WORKS REFERRED TO IN THE TEXT

Addison, Joseph, see *The Spectator*
Allott, Miriam, 'Henry James and the Fantasticated Conceit: *The Sacred
    Fount*', *Northern Miscellany of Literary Criticism*, 1 (1953), 76–86
    'Mrs Gaskell's "The Old Nurse's Story": A Link between *Wuthering Heights*
    and "The Turn of the Screw"', *Notes and Queries*, 206 (1961), 101–2

'Symbol and Image in the Later Work of Henry James', *Essays in Criticism*, 3 (1953), 321–36

Álvarez Amorós, José Antonio, 'Possible-World Semantics, Frame Text, Insert Text, and Unreliable Narration: The Case of "The Turn of the Screw"', *Style*, 25 (1951), 42–70

Anderson, Quentin, *The American Henry James* (London, 1958)

The Imperial Self: An Essay in American Literary and Cultural History (New York, 1971)

Andreach, Robert J., 'Henry James's *The Sacred Fount*: The Existential Predicament', *Nineteenth-Century Fiction*, 17 (1962–3), 197–216

Anesko, Michael, *Friction with the Market: Henry James and the Profession of Authorship* (New York, 1986)

Appignanesi, Lisa, *Femininity and the Creative Imagination: A Study of Henry James, Robert Musil and Marcel Proust* (London, 1973)

Arabian Nights. See *Tales from the Thousand and One Nights*

Aristotle, *The Works of Aristotle*, ed. by W.D. Ross, trans. by W. D. Ross and others, 12 vols. (Oxford, 1926–52)

De Poetica, trans. by Ingram Bywater, XI, 1447.a.–1462.b.

Rhetorica, trans. by W. Rhys Roberts, XI, 1354.a.–1420.b.

Armstrong, Paul B., 'History and Epistemology: The Example of "The Turn of the Screw"', *New Literary History*, 19 (1987–8), 693–712

The Phenomenology of Henry James (Chapel Hill, 1983)

Aubrey, John, *Aubrey's Brief Lives*, ed. by Oliver Lawson Dick (London, 1949)

Auerbach, Nina, *Woman and the Demon: The Life of a Victorian Myth* (Cambridge, Mass., 1982)

Austen, Jane, *Northanger Abbey* (1818), in *The Novels of Jane Austen*, ed. by R. W. Chapman, third edition, 5 vols. (London, 1933), V, 1–252

Babcock, Barbara A., 'Liberty's a Whore: Inversion, Marginalia, and Picaresque Narrative', in *The Reversible World: Symbolic Inversion in Art and Society*, ed. by Barbara A. Babcock (Ithaca, 1978), pp. 95–116

'Introduction', in *The Reversible World: Symbolic Inversion in Art and Society*, ed. by Barbara A. Babcock (Ithaca, 1978), pp. 13–36

Babcock, Barbara A., ed., *The Reversible World: Symbolic Inversion in Art and Society* (Ithaca, 1978)

Balzac, Honoré de, 'The Duchesse de Langeais' (1833–4), in *History of the Thirteen*, ed. and trans. by Herbert J. Hunt, Penguin Classics (Harmondsworth, 1974), pp. 157–305

Seraphita, ed. by George Saintsbury, trans. by Clara Bell (London, 1897)

'Louis Lambert' (1832), pp. 158–280

'Seraphita' (1842), pp. 1–157

The Wild Ass's Skin (1831), ed. and trans. by Herbert J. Hunt, Penguin Classics (London, 1977)

Banta, Martha, *Henry James and the Occult: The Great Extension* (Bloomington, 1972)

Barzun, Jacques, 'James the Melodramatist', *Kenyon Review*, 5 (1943), 508–21

Bayley, John, 'Love and Knowledge: *The Golden Bowl*', in *The Characters of Love: A Study in the Literature of Personality* (London, 1960), pp. 205–62

Beardsley, Monroe C. See Wimsatt, W. K.

Beebe, Maurice, 'The Turned Back of Henry James', *South Atlantic Quarterly*, 53 (1954), 521–39

Beer, Gillian, *The Romance*, Critical Idiom, 10 (London, 1970)

Bell, Ian F. A., *Henry James and the Past: Readings into Time* (Basingstoke, 1991)

Bell, Ian F. A., ed., *Henry James: Fiction as History*, Critical Studies (London, 1984)

Bell, Michael Davitt, *The Development of American Romance: The Sacrifice of Relation* (Chicago, 1980)

Bell, Millicent, '"The Turn of the Screw" and the *Recherche de L'Absolu*', in *Henry James, Fiction as History*, ed. by Ian F. A. Bell, Critical Studies (London, 1984), pp. 65–81

Bender, Claire E. and Todd K., *A Concordance to Henry James's 'The Turn of the Screw'* (New York, 1988)

Beowulf, trans. by M. Alexander (Harmondsworth, 1973)

Bersani, Leo, 'The Jamesian Lie', *Partisan Review*, 36 (1969), 53–79
'The Subject of Power', *Diacritics*, 7 (Fall 1977), 2–21

Bewley, Marius, *The Complex Fate: Hawthorne, Henry James and some other American Writers* (London, 1952)

Binswanger, Ludwig, *Being-in-the-World: Selected Papers*, ed. and trans. by Jacob Needleman (New York, 1963)
'The Case of Lola Voss', trans. by Ernest Angel, pp. 266–341
'Extravagance (*Verstiegenheit*)', pp. 342–9

Black, Max, *Models and Metaphors: Studies in Language and Philosophy* (Ithaca, 1952)

Blackall, Jean Frantz, *Jamesian Ambiguity and 'The Sacred Fount'* (Ithaca, 1965)

Blackmur, Richard P., '*The Sacred Fount*', *Kenyon Review*, Old Series, 4 (1942), 328–52

Blackmur, Richard P., ed., introduction to *The Art of the Novel: Critical Prefaces by Henry James* (London, 1935), pp. vii–xxxix

Blanchot, Maurice, '"The Turn of the Screw"' (1959), in *The Sirens' Song: Selected Essays*, ed. by Gabriel Josipovici, trans. by Sacha Rabinovitch (Brighton, 1982), pp. 79–86

Blessington, the Countess of, *The Governess*, 2 vols. (London, 1839)

Bloom, Harold, *Agon: Towards a Theory of Revisionism* (Oxford, 1982)
Figures of Capable Imagination (New York, 1976)
'Introduction', in *Henry James*, ed. by Harold Bloom, Modern Critical Views (New York, 1987), pp. 1–14

Bloom, Harold, ed., *Henry James*, Modern Critical Views (New York, 1987)

Bloom, Harold, and others, eds., *Deconstruction and Criticism* (London, 1979)

'Blue Beard'. See Perrault, Charles

Boone, Joseph A., 'Modernist Maneuverings in the Marriage Plot: Breaking Ideologies of Gender and Genre in James's *The Golden Bowl*', *PMLA*, 101 (1986), 374–88

Booth, Wayne C., *The Rhetoric of Fiction* (Chicago, 1961)

Bradbury, Nicola, *Henry James: The Later Novels* (Oxford, 1979)

Briggs, Julia, *Night Visitors: The Rise and Fall of the English Ghost Story* (London, 1977)

Bronfen, Elisabeth, *Over Her Dead Body: Death, Femininity and the Aesthetic* (Manchester, 1992)

Brontë, Charlotte, *Jane Eyre* (1847), ed. by Jane Jack and Margaret Smith, Clarendon Edition (Oxford, 1969)

Villette (1853), ed. by Geoffrey Tillotson, Riverside Editions (Boston, 1971)

Brontë, Emily, *Wuthering Heights* (1847), ed. by Heather Glen, Routledge English Texts (London, 1988)

Brooke-Rose, Christine, 'Historical Genres/Theoretical Genres: A Discussion of Todorov on the Fantastic', *New Literary History*, 8 (1976–7), 145–58

A Rhetoric of the Unreal: Studies in Narrative and Structure, especially of the Fantastic (Cambridge, 1981)

Brooks, Van Wyck, *The Pilgrimage of Henry James* (London, 1928)

Brown, Charles Brockden, *Wieland; or, The Transformation*, ed. by Fred Lewis Pattee (New York, 1926)

Budick, E. Miller, 'The World as Specter: Hawthorne's Historical Art', *PMLA*, 101 (1986), 218–32

Buitenhuis, Peter, *The Grasping Imagination: The American Writings of Henry James* (Toronto, 1970)

Burke, Edmund, *A Philosophical Enquiry into the Origin of our Ideas of the Sublime and Beautiful*, ed. by J. T. Boulton (London, 1958)

Bynum, Caroline Walker, 'Women's Stories, Women's Symbols: A Critique of Victor Turner's Theory of Liminality', in *Anthropology and the Study of Religion*, ed. by Robert L. Moore and Frank E. Reynolds (Chicago, 1984), pp. 105–25

Byron, George Gordon, Lord, 'Oscar of Alva', in *Lord Byron: The Complete Poetical Works*, ed. by Jerome J. McGann, 3 vols. (Oxford, 1980–1), I, 54–66

Cameron, Sharon, *Thinking in Henry James* (Chicago, 1989)

Cargill, Oscar, 'Henry James as Freudian Pioneer', *Chicago Review*, 10, no. 2 (summer 1956), 13–29

The Novels of Henry James (New York, 1961)

'"The Turn of the Screw" and Alice James', *PMLA*, 78, no. 3 (June 1963), 238–49

Carroll, Benjamin Hawkins, 'The Supernatural in the Writings of Henry James' (unpublished M.A. dissertation, Louisiana State University, 1939)

Carroll, David, 'Freud and the Myth of Origin', *New Literary History*, 6 (1975), 513–28
  The Subject in Question: The Languages of Theory and the Strategies of Fiction (Chicago, 1982)
Cassirer, Ernst, *Mythical Thought*, in *The Philosophy of Symbolic Forms*, trans. by Ralph Manheim, 3 vols. (New Haven, 1953–7), III
Caws, Mary Ann, *Reading Frames in Modern Fiction* (Princeton, 1985)
Chase, Richard, *The American Novel and its Tradition* (London, 1958)
Chatman, Seymour, *The Later Style of Henry James*, Language and Style Series, 2 (Oxford, 1972)
'Cinderella'. See Perrault, Charles
Cixous, Hélène, 'Fiction and Its Phantoms: A Reading of Freud's *Das Unheimliche (The "uncanny")*', trans. by Robert Dennomé, *New Literary History*, 7 (1976), 525–48
  'Henry James: L'écriture comme placement; ou, De l'ambiguïté de l'intérêt', *Poétique*, 1 (1970), 35–50
  'The Laugh of the Medusa', in *New French Feminisms*, ed. by Elaine Marks and Isabelle de Courtivron (New York, 1981), pp. 39–54
  'Sorties: Out and Out: Attacks/Ways Out/Forays', in *The Newly Born Woman*, by Hélène Cixous and Catherine Clément, trans. by Betsy Wing (Minneapolis, 1975), pp. 63–132
Clair, John A., *The Ironic Dimension in the Fiction of Henry James* (Pittsburgh, 1965)
Clark, Robert Lanier. See Cranfill, Thomas Mabry
Clark, S. H., *Sordid Images: The Poetry of Masculine Desire* (forthcoming)
Colacurcio, Michael J., *The Province of Piety: Moral History in Hawthorne's Early Tales* (Cambridge, Mass., 1984)
Coleridge, Samuel Taylor, *The Collected Works of Samuel Taylor Coleridge*, ed. by Kathleen Coburn, Bollingen Series, 75, 14 vols. (London, 1971–90)
  Biographia Literaria (1817), ed. by James Engell and W. Jackson Bate, vol. VII, parts 1 and 2
  Lecture of 22 or 29 December 1812, in *Lectures 1808–1819 on Literature*, ed. by R.A. Foakes, vol. V, part 1, pp. 494–5
  'The Statesman's Manual' (1816), in *Lay Sermons*, ed. by R. J. White, VI, 3–114
  Lyrical Ballads. See Wordsworth, William
Conrad, Joseph, *The Uniform Edition of the Works of Joseph Conrad*, 22 vols. (London, 1923–8)
  Chance: A Tale in Two Parts (1912), XI
  'Heart of Darkness' (1899), V, 45–162
Costello, Donald P., 'The Structure of "The Turn of the Screw"', *Modern Language Notes*, 75 (1960), 312–21
Cranfill, Thomas Mabry, and Robert Lanier Clark, *An Anatomy of 'The Turn of the Screw'* (Austin, 1965)
Dalby, Richard, ed., *The Virago Book of Victorian Ghost Stories* (London, 1988)

Davis, Natalie Zemon, 'Women on Top: Symbolic Sexual Inversion and Political Disorder in Early Modern Europe', in *The Reversible World: Symbolic Inversion in Art and Society*, ed. by Barbara A. Babcock (Ithaca, 1978), pp. 147–90

Defoe, Daniel, *Moll Flanders*, ed. by G. A. Aitken, Everyman's Library (London, 1930)

Roxana: The Fortunate Mistress, ed. by Jane Jack, Oxford English Novels (London, 1964)

'A True Relation of the Apparition of one Mrs Veal', in *Accounts of the Apparition of Mrs Veal*, ed. by Manuel Schonhorn, Augustan Reprint Society, 115 (Los Angeles, 1965)

Dekker, George, *The American Historical Romance*, Cambridge Studies in American Literature and Culture (Cambridge, 1987)

De la Mare, Walter, 'The Lesson of the Masters' (1915), in *Private View* (London, 1953), pp. 7–11

De Man, Paul, 'The Epistemology of Metaphor', *Critical Inquiry*, 5 (1978), 13–30

Derrida, Jacques, *Dissemination*, trans. by Barbara Johnson (London, 1981)

Glas, trans. by John P. Leavey and Richard Rand (Lincoln, Neb., 1986)

Margins of Philosophy, trans. by Alan Bass (Brighton, 1982)

Of Grammatology, trans. by Gayatri Chakravorty Spivak (Baltimore, 1976)

Dick, Oliver Lawson, ed. See Aubrey, John

Dickens, Charles, *David Copperfield* (1849–50), ed. by George H. Ford, Riverside Editions (Boston, 1958)

Dijkstra, Bram, *Idols of Perversity: Fantasies of Feminine Evil in Fin-de-Siècle Culture* (New York, 1986)

Donadio, Stephen, *Nietzsche, Henry James, and the Artistic Will* (New York, 1978)

Donoghue, Dennis, 'Attitudes Toward History: A Preface to *The Sense of the Past*', *Salmagundi*, 68–9 (1985–6), 107–24

Dupee, F. W., *Henry James*, American Men of Letters (London, 1951)

Dupee, F. W., ed., *The Question of Henry James: A Collection of Critical Essays* (London, 1947)

Eakin, Paul John, 'Henry James and the Autobiographical Act', in *Fictions in Autobiography: Studies in the Art of Self-Invention* (Princeton, 1985), pp. 56–125

Eastlake, Elizabeth, review of *Vanity Fair, Jane Eyre* and the Governesses' Benevolent Institution Report for 1847, *Quarterly Review*, 84 (1848–9), 153–85

Edel, Leon, *Henry James: A Life* (London, 1985)

Henry James: The Untried Years, 1843–1870 (London, 1953)

Henry James: The Conquest of London, 1870–1883 (London, 1962)

Henry James: The Middle Years, 1884–1894 (London, 1963)

Henry James: The Treacherous Years, 1895–1901 (London, 1969)

Henry James: The Master, 1901–16 (London, 1972)

The Life of Henry James, 2 vols. (Harmondsworth, 1977)

'The Point of View', in *The Psychological Novel: 1900–1950* (London, 1955), pp. 38–46

Edel, Leon, ed., *Henry James: Stories of the Supernatural* (London, 1971)

Edel, Leon and Adeline R. Tintner, eds., 'The Library of Henry James, from Inventory, Catalogues, and Library Lists', *Henry James Review*, 4 (1982–3), 158–90

Edel, Leon, Dan H. Laurence and James Rambeau, eds., *A Bibliography of Henry James*, Soho Bibliographies, 8, third edition (Oxford, 1982)

Edgeworth, Maria, 'The Good French Governess'(1801), in *Tales and Novels*, 18 vols. (London, 1832–3), III, 93–214

Egan, Michael, *Henry James: The Ibsen Years* (London, 1972)

Eliot, George, *Daniel Deronda* (1876), ed. by Barbara Hardy, Penguin Classics (London, 1986)

'The Lifted Veil', *Blackwood's Edinburgh Magazine*, 86 (1859), 24–48

Eliot, T. S., *The Complete Poems and Plays of T. S. Eliot* (London, 1969)
  The Family Reunion, pp. 283–350
  'Little Gidding', pp. 191–8
  'The Love Song of J. Alfred Prufrock', pp. 13–17

'The Hawthorne Aspect', *Little Review*, 5, no. 4 (August 1918), 47–53

Ellmann, Maud, '"The Intimate Difference": Power and Representation in *The Ambassadors*', in *Henry James: Fiction as History*, ed. by Ian F. A. Bell, Critical Studies (London, 1984), pp. 98–113

Elton, Oliver, 'The Novels of Mr Henry James', in *Modern Studies* (London, 1907), pp. 245–84

Enck, John J., '"The Turn of the Screw" and The Turn of the Century', in *Henry James: 'The Turn of the Screw'*, ed. by Robert Kimbrough, Norton Critical Edition (New York, 1966), pp. 259–69

Esch, Deborah, 'A Jamesian About-Face: Notes on "The Jolly Corner"', *ELH*, 50 (1983), 587–605

Euripides, *The Medea of Euripides*, trans. by D.W. Lucas (London, 1949)

Evans, Oliver, 'James's Air of Evil: "The Turn of the Screw"', *Partisan Review*, 16 (1949), 175–87

Fagin, N. Bryllion, 'Another Reading of "The Turn of the Screw"', *Modern Language Notes*, 56 (1941), 196–202

Falconer, Graham, 'Flaubert, James and the Problem of Undecidability', *Comparative Literature*, 39 (1987), 1–18

Feidelson, Charles, 'Art as Problem in "The Figure in the Carpet" and "The Madonna of the Future"', in *Twentieth Century Interpretations of 'The Turn of the Screw' and other Tales: A Collection of Critical Essays*, ed. by Jane P. Tompkins (Englewood Cliffs, 1970), pp. 47–55

'James and the "Man of Imagination"', in *Literary Theory and Structure: Essays in Honor of William K. Wimsatt*, ed. by Frank Brady, John Palmer and Martin Price (New Haven, 1973), pp. 331–52

Symbolism and American Literature (Chicago, 1953)

Felman, Shoshana, 'Turning the Screw of Interpretation', *Yale French Studies*, 55–6 (1977), 94–207

Fiedler, Leslie, *Love and Death in the American Novel*, second edition (London, 1967)

Fielding, Henry, *Amelia* (1751), ed. by Martin C. Battestin, Wesleyan Edition (Oxford, 1983)

   The History of Tom Jones, A Foundling, ed. by Fredson Bowers and Martin C. Battestin, Wesleyan Edition, 2 vols. (Oxford, 1974)

Fielding, Sarah, *The Governess; or, The Little Female Academy* (London, 1765)

Finkelstein, Sidney, 'The "Mystery" of Henry James's *The Sacred Fount*', *Massachusetts Review*, 3 (1961–2), 753–6

Firebaugh, Joseph J., 'Inadequacy in Eden: Knowledge and "The Turn of the Screw"', *Modern Fiction Studies*, 3 (1957), 57–63

Fogel, Daniel Mark, *Henry James and the Structure of the Romantic Imagination* (Baton Rouge, 1981)

Follett, Wilson, 'Henry James's Portrait of Henry James', *New York Times Book Review*, 23 August 1936, pp. 2, 16

Follini, Tamara Louise, '"Hero and Historian": The Autobiographical Writings of Henry James' (unpublished Ph.D. dissertation, University of Cambridge, 1985)

Forbes, Edward, letter in *The Times*, 25 October 1864, p. 7

   letter in *The Times*, 4 January 1868, p. 6

Forster, E. M., *Aspects of the Novel* (1927), ed. by Oliver Stallybrass (London, 1962)

Freud, Sigmund, *The Standard Edition of the Complete Psychological Works of Sigmund Freud*, ed. and trans. by James Strachey and others, 24 vols. (London, 1953–74)

   'Beyond the Pleasure Principle' (1920), XVIII, 7–64

   'Creative Writers and Day-Dreaming' (1908), IX, 143–53

   'From the History of an Infantile Neurosis' (1918), XVII, 7–122

   The Interpretation of Dreams (1899, post-dated 1900), IV–V

   'Medusa's Head' (written 1922), XVIII, 273–74

   'Notes Upon a Case of Obsessional Neurosis' (1909), X, 155–249

   Studies on Hysteria (1895), II

   Totem and Taboo (1913), XIII, 1–161

   'The "Uncanny"' (1919), XVII, 219–52

Frye, Northrop, *Anatomy of Criticism: Four Essays* (Princeton, 1957)

Fryer, Judith, 'The Mother-Surrogates', in *The Faces of Eve: Women in the Nineteenth Century American Novel* (Oxford, 1976), pp. 153–73

Fussell, Edwin, 'The Ontology of "The Turn of the Screw"', *Journal of Modern Literature*, 8 (1980–1), 118–28

Gargano, James W., 'James's *The Sacred Fount*: The Phantasmagorical made Evidential', *Henry James Review*, 2 (1980–1), 49–60

Gaskell, Elizabeth, *The Life of Charlotte Brontë* (1857), ed. by Alan Shelston, Penguin English Library (Harmondsworth, 1975)

   'The Old Nurse's Story' (1852), in *The Virago Book of Victorian Ghost Stories*, ed. by Richard Dalby (London, 1988), pp. 4–21

Gathorne-Hardy, Jonathan, *The Rise and Fall of the British Nanny* (London, 1972)

Gauld, Alan, *The Founders of Psychical Research* (London, 1968)

Gawain. See *Sir Gawain and the Green Knight*

Geismar, Maxwell, *Henry James and his Cult* (London, 1964)

Gibson, William M., 'Metaphor in the Plot of *The Ambassadors*', *New England Quarterly*, 24 (1951), 291–305

Gilbert, Sandra M., and Susan Gubar, *The Madwoman in the Attic: The Woman Writer and the Nineteenth-Century Literary Imagination* (New Haven, 1979)

    No Man's Land: The Place of the Woman Writer in the Twentieth Century, 2 vols. (New Haven, 1988–9)

    The War of the Words, I

    Sexchanges, II

Girard, René, *Violence and the Sacred*, trans. by Patrick Gregory (Baltimore, 1977)

Goddard, Harold C., 'A Pre-Freudian Reading of "The Turn of the Screw"', *Nineteenth-Century Fiction*, 12 (1957–8), 1–36

Goetz, William R., *Henry James and the Darkest Abyss of Romance* (Baton Rouge, 1986)

Goldsmith, Oliver, 'The Deserted Village', in *Collected Works of Oliver Goldsmith*, ed. by Arthur Friedman, 5 vols. (Oxford, 1966), IV, 287–304

The Governess; or, Politics in Private Life (London, 1836)

Gray, Thomas, 'Elegy written in a Country Churchyard', in *The Works of Thomas Gray*, ed. by Edmund Gosse, 4 vols. (London, 1884), I, 73–80

Griffin, Susan M., 'The Selfish Eye: Strether's Principles of Psychology', *American Literature*, 56 (1984) 396–409

Grover, Philip, *Henry James and the French Novel: A Study in Inspiration* (London, 1973)

Gubar, Susan, '"The Blank Page" and the Issues of Female Creativity', *Critical Inquiry*, 8 (1981–2), 243–63

The Guide to Service: The Governess (London, 1844)

Gurney, Edmund, F. W. H. Myers and Frank Podmore, *Phantasms of the Living* (1886), ed. and abridged by Mrs Henry Sidgwick (London, 1918)

Habegger, Alfred, *Gender, Fantasy, and Realism in American Literature* (New York, 1982)

    Henry James and the 'Woman Business', Cambridge Studies in American Literature and Culture (Cambridge, 1989)

Hampden, John, ed., *Ghost Stories*, Everyman's Library (London, 1939)

'Hansel and Gretel', in *The Classic Fairy Tales*, ed. by Iona and Peter Opie (London, 1974), pp. 238–44

Harari, Josué V., ed., *Textual Strategies: Perspectives in Post-Structuralist Criticism* (London, 1980)

Hardwick, Elizabeth, *Seduction and Betrayal: Women and Literature* (London, 1974)

Harriet Marwood, Governess (London, 1969)

Hartman, Geoffrey H., 'Words, Wish, Worth: Wordsworth' in *Deconstruction and Criticism*, ed. by Harold Bloom and others (London, 1979), pp. 177–216

Hawthorne, Nathaniel, *The Centenary Edition of the Works of Nathaniel Hawthorne*, ed. by William Charvat and others, 20 vols. (Columbus, 1962–88)

The American Notebooks, ed. by Claude M. Simpson, VIII

'The Ancestral Footstep' (written 1858), XII, 3–89

'The Artist of the Beautiful' (1844), X, 447–75

The Blithedale Romance (1852), III, 1–247

'The Devil in Manuscript' (1835), XI, 170–8

'The Dolliver Romance' (written 1863), XIII, 449–97

'Dr. Heidegger's Experiment' (1837), IX, 227–38

'Edward Randolph's Portrait' (1838), IX, 256–70

'Endicott and the Red Cross' (1838), IX, 433–41

'Ethan Brand: A Chapter from an Abortive Romance' (1850), XI, 83–102

Fanshawe (1828), III, 333–460

'Grimshawe' (written 1861), XII, 343–471

'The Haunted Mind' (1835), IX, 304–9

'The Hollow of the Three Hills' (1830), IX, 199–204

The House of the Seven Gables (1851), II

'Howe's Masquerade' (1838), IX, 239–55

'Lady Eleanore's Mantle' (1838), IX, 271–89

'Legends of the Province House'. See 'Howe's Masquerade', 'Edward Randolph's Portrait', 'Lady Eleanore's Mantle' and 'Old Esther Dudley'

Letters (1813–43), ed. by Thomas Woodson, L. Neal Smith and Norman Holmes Pearson, XV

The Marble Faun (1860), IV

'The Minister's Black Veil' (1836), IX, 37–53

'My Kinsman, Major Molineux' (1832), XI, 208–31

'Old Esther Dudley' (1839), IX, 290–303

'An Old Woman's Tale' (1830), XI, 240–50

'The Prophetic Pictures' (1837), IX, 166–82

'Rappaccini's Daughter: From the Writings of Aubépine' (1844), X, 91–128

The Scarlet Letter (1850), I

'Septimius Felton' (written 1861–62), XIII, 3–194

'Sights from a Steeple' (1831), IX, 191–8

'Wakefield' (1835), IX, 130–40

'The Wedding-Knell' (1836), IX, 27–36

'The Wives of the Dead' (1832), XI, 192–9

'Young Goodman Brown' (1835), x, 74–90

Heath, Mary, letter in *The Times*, 15 September 1868, p. 9

Heilman, Robert B., 'The Freudian Reading of "The Turn of the Screw"', *Modern Language Notes*, 62 (1947), 433–45

'The Lure of the Demonic: James and Dürrenmatt', *Comparative Literature*, 13 (1961), 346–57

'"The Turn of the Screw" as Poem', in *Forms of Modern Fiction: Essays Collected in Honor of Joseph Warren Beach*, ed. by William Van O'Connor (Minneapolis, 1948), pp. 211–28

Hemyng, Bracebridge, 'Prostitution in London', in *London Labour and the London Poor*, by Henry Mayhew, 4 vols. (London, 1861–2), IV, 210–72

Hertz, Neil, *The End of the Line: Essays on Psychoanalysis and the Sublime* (New York, 1985)

'Freud and the Sandman', in *Textual Strategies: Perspectives in Post-Structuralist Criticism*, ed. by Josué V. Harari (London, 1980), pp. 296–321

Hill, Robert W., 'A Counterclockwise Turn in James's "The Turn of the Screw"', *Twentieth Century Literature*, 27 (1981), 53–71

'Hints on the Modern Governess System', *Fraser's Magazine for Town and Country*, 30 (1844), 571–83

Hints to Governesses, By One of Themselves (London, 1856)

Hobbes, Thomas, *Leviathan; or, The Matter, Forme and Power of a Commonwealth Ecclesiasticall and Civil*, ed. by Michael Oakeshott, Blackwell's Political Texts (Oxford, 1946)

Hoffmann, Charles G., 'Innocence and Evil in James's "The Turn of the Screw"', in *A Casebook on Henry James's 'The Turn of the Screw'*, ed. by Gerald Willen (New York, 1959), pp. 212–22

Hoffmann, E. T. A., *The Devil's Elixirs* (1816), ed. and trans. by Ronald Taylor (London, 1963)

'The Sandman' (1816), in *Tales from Hoffmann*, ed. by J. M. Cohen, trans. by Thomas Carlyle and others (London, 1951), pp. 109–45

Holland, Laurence Bedwell, *The Expense of Vision: Essays in the Craft of Henry James* (Princeton, 1964)

Homer, *The Odyssey of Homer*, trans. by Richmond Lattimore (New York, 1967)

Horace, 'The Art of Poetry', in *The Works of Horace*, trans. by C. Smart (London, 1850), pp. 299–325

Howe, Bea, *A Galaxy of Governesses* (London, 1954)

Howells, William Dean, 'The Man of Letters as a Man of Business', in *Literature and Life: Studies* (Port Washington, 1968)

Hughes, Kathryn, *The Victorian Governess* (London, 1993)

Ibsen, Henrik, *The Oxford Ibsen*, ed. by James Walter McFarlane, trans. by James Walter McFarlane and others, 8 vols. (London 1960–77)

Ghosts (1881), V, 344–422

The Lady from the Sea (1888), VII, 29–124

Little Eyolf (1894), VIII, 39–106

Peer Gynt (1867), III, 251–421

Irigaray, Luce, 'This Sex Which Is Not One' (1977), in *New French Feminisms*, ed. by Elaine Marks and Isabelle de Courtivron (Amherst, 1980), pp. 99–106

Irving, Washington, 'The Adventures of the German Student', in *Washington Irving: Bracebridge Hall, Tales of a Traveller, The Alhambra*, ed. by James W. Tuttleton, Library of America (New York, 1991), pp. 418–24

'The Knight of Malta; The Grand Prior of Malta: A Veritable Ghost Story', in *Wolfert's Roost, and Other Papers, Now First Collected* (New York, 1855), pp. 130–50

Isle, Walter, 'The Romantic and the Real: Henry James's *The Sacred Fount*' (1965), in *Henry James: Modern Judgements*, ed. by Tony Tanner (London, 1968), pp. 245–65

Jameson, Fredric, *The Political Unconscious: Narrative as a Socially Symbolic Act* (London, 1981)

Jameson, Mrs, 'On the Relative Social Position of Mothers and Governesses', in *Memoirs and Essays Illustrative of Art, Literature, and Social Morals* (London, 1846), pp. 251–98

Johnson, Barbara, 'The Frame of Reference: Poe, Lacan, Derrida', in *The Critical Difference: Essays in the Contemporary Rhetoric of Reading* (Baltimore, 1980), pp. 110–46

Jones, Alexander E., 'Point of View in "The Turn of the Screw"', *PMLA*, 74, no. 1 (March, 1959), 112–22

Kaplan, Fred, *Henry James: The Imagination of Genius, A Biography* (London, 1992)

Kappeler, Susanne, *Writing and Reading in Henry James* (London, 1980)

Kaston, Carren, *Imagination and Desire in the Novels of Henry James* (New Brunswick, 1984)

Kelley, Cornelia Pulsifer, 'The Early Development of Henry James', *University of Illinois Studies in Language and Literature*, 15 (1930), 1–309

Kenton, Edna, 'Henry James to the Ruminant Reader: "The Turn of the Screw"', in *A Casebook on Henry James's 'The Turn of the Screw'*, ed. by Gerald Willen (New York, 1959), pp. 102–14

Keppler, C. F., *The Literature of the Second Self* (Tucson, 1972)

Kermode, Frank, *The Genesis of Secrecy: On the Interpretation of Narrative* (Cambridge, Mass., 1979)

Romantic Image (London, 1957)

Kerr, Howard, 'James's Last Early Supernatural Tales: Hawthorne Demagnetized, Poe Depoetized', in *The Haunted Dusk: American Supernatural Fiction, 1820–1920*, ed. by Howard Kerr, John W. Crowley and Charles L. Crow (Athens, 1983), pp. 135–48

Mediums, and Spirit-Rappers, and Roaring Radicals: Spiritualism in American Literature, 1850–1900 (Urbana, 1972)

Kerr, Howard, John W. Crowley and Charles L. Crow, eds., *The Haunted Dusk: American Supernatural Fiction, 1820–1920* (Athens, 1983)

Kimbrough, Robert, ed., 'The Turn of the Screw', Norton Critical Edition (New York, 1966)

Kipling, Rudyard, 'Baa, Baa, Black Sheep', in *Wee Willie Winkie and other Stories* (London, 1895), pp. 260–98

Krook, Dorothea, *The Ordeal of Consciousness in Henry James* (Cambridge, 1962)

Kunzle, David, 'World Upside Down: The Iconography of a European Broadsheet Type', in *The Reversible World: Symbolic Inversion in Art and Society*, ed. by Barbara A. Babcock (Ithaca, 1978), pp. 39–94

Lang, Andrew, *The Book of Dreams and Ghosts* (London, 1897)

Langland, William, *Piers Plowman*, ed. by Elizabeth Salter and Derek Pearsall, York Medieval Texts (London, 1967)

Laurence, Dan H. See Edel, Leon, Dan H. Laurence and James Rambeau, eds.

Leavis, F. R., '*What Maisie Knew*: A Disagreement by F. R. Leavis', in *The Complex Fate: Hawthorne, Henry James and some other American Writers*, by Marius Bewley (London, 1952), pp. 114–31

Lederer, Laura, ed., *Take Back the Night* (New York, 1980)

Lee, Vernon, 'A Wicked Voice', in *Hauntings: Fantastic Stories* (London, 1890), pp. 195–237

'The Legend of Madame Krasinska', in *Vanitas: Polite Stories* (London, 1892), pp. 225–76

Le Fanu, Joseph Sheridan, *The Cock and Anchor* (1845), ed. by Herbert van Thal, First Novel Library (London, 1967)

'Green Tea', in *In a Glass Darkly*, 3 vols. (London, 1872), I, 3–95

Uncle Silas: A Tale of Bartram-Haugh (1864), ed. by Elizabeth Bowen (London, 1947)

Le Prince de Beaumont, Jeanne Marie, *The Young Misses Magazine, Containing Dialogues between a Governess and several Young Ladies of Quality her Scholars*, second edition, 2 vols. (London, 1767)

Lewis, W. S., ed. See Walpole, Horace

Liddell, Robert, 'The "Hallucination" Theory of "The Turn of the Screw"', in *A Treatise on the Novel* (London, 1947), pp. 138–45

Lind, Sidney Edmund, 'The Supernatural Tales of Henry James: Conflict and Fantasy' (unpublished Ph.D. dissertation, New York University, 1948)

Lock, Peter W., '"The Figure in the Carpet": The Text as Riddle and Force', *Nineteenth-Century Fiction*, 36 (1981–2), 157–75

Locke, John, *An Essay Concerning Human Understanding*, ed. by Peter H. Nidditch (Oxford, 1975)

Long, Robert Emmet, *The Great Succession: Henry James and the Legacy of Hawthorne*, Critical Essays in Modern Literature (Pittsburgh, 1979)

Longinus, *On the Sublime*, ed. and trans. by W. Rhys Roberts (Cambridge, 1899)

Lukacher, Ned, '"Hanging Fire": The Primal Scene of "The Turn of the

Screw"', in *Primal Scenes: Literature, Philosophy, Psychoanalysis* (Ithaca, 1986), pp. 115–32

Lurie, Susan, 'Pornography and the Dread of Women: the Male Sexual Dilemma', in *Take Back the Night*, ed. by Laura Lederer (New York, 1980), pp. 159–73

Lydenberg, John, 'The Governess Turns the Screws', *Nineteenth-Century Fiction*, 12 (1957–8), 37–58

Mackenzie, Manfred, *Communities of Honor and Love in Henry James* (Cambridge, Mass., 1976)

'"The Turn of the Screw": Jamesian Gothic', *Essays in Criticism*, 12 (1962), 34–8

Mansell, Darrel, 'The Ghost of Language in "The Turn of the Screw"', *Modern Language Quarterly*, 46 (1985), 48–63

Marcus, Steven, *The Other Victorians: A Study of Sexuality and Pornography in Mid-Nineteenth Century England*, Studies in Sex and Society, 1 (London, 1966)

Marks, Elaine and Isabelle de Courtivron, eds., *New French Feminisms* (New York, 1981)

Martineau, Harriet, 'Female Industry', *Edinburgh Review, or Critical Journal*, 109 (1859), 293–336

'The Governess: Her Health', *Once a Week*, 3 (1 September 1860), 267–72

Matthiessen, F.O., *American Renaissance: Art and Expression in the Age of Emerson and Whitman* (New York, 1941)

Henry James: The Major Phase (London, 1946)

Maupassant, Guy de, *A Day in the County and Other Stories*, ed. and trans. by David Coward, World's Classics (Oxford, 1990)

'Le Horla' (1887), pp. 275–302

'The Little Roque Girl' (1885), pp. 203–38

'The Hand' (c. 1875), in *Selected Short Stories*, ed. and trans. by Roger Colet, Penguin Classics (Harmondsworth, 1971), pp. 251–8

Maxse, Mary, 'On Governesses', *National Review*, 37 (1901), 397–402

Mayhew, Henry. See Hemyng, Bracebridge

McMaster, Juliet, '"The Full Image of a Repetition" in "The Turn of the Screw"' (1969), in *Henry James*, ed. by Harold Bloom, Modern Critical Views (New York, 1987), pp. 125–30

McWhirter, David, *Desire and Love in Henry James: A Study of the Late Novels* (Cambridge, 1989)

Melchiori, Giorgio, 'Cups of Gold for the Sacred Fount: Aspects of James's Symbolism', *Critical Quarterly*, 7 (1965), 301–16

Melville, Herman, *Moby-Dick; or, The Whale*, in *Herman Melville: Redburn, White-Jacket, Moby-Dick*, ed. by G. Thomas Tanselle, Library of America (New York, 1983), pp. 771–1408

Mérimée, Prosper, *The Venus of Ille, and other Stories*, ed. by A. W. Raitt, trans. by Jean Kimber, Oxford Library of French Classics (London, 1966)

'The Venus of Ille' (1837), pp. 1–32

'Lokis' (1869), pp. 126–69

Michie, Helena, *The Flesh Made Word: Female Figures and Women's Bodies* (Oxford, 1987)

Miller, J. Hillis, 'Ariadne's Thread: Repetition and the Narrative Line', *Critical Inquiry*, 3 (1976–7), 57–77

   Hawthorne and History: Defacing It (Oxford, 1991)

   'Re-Reading Re-Vision: James and Benjamin', in *The Ethics of Reading: Kant, de Man, Eliot, Trollope, James, and Benjamin* (New York, 1987), pp. 101–27

Miller, Karl, *Doubles: Studies in Literary History* (Oxford, 1985)

Miner, Earl Roy, 'Henry James's Metaphysical Romances', *Nineteenth-Century Fiction*, 9 (1954–5), 1–21

Miyoshi, Masao, *The Divided Self: A Perspective on the Literature of the Victorians* (London, 1969)

Moon, Heath, 'Is *The Sacred Fount* a Symbolist Novel?', *Comparative Literature*, 39 (1987), 306–26

Morris, David B., 'Gothic Sublimity', *New Literary History*, 16 (1985), 299–319

'The Most Hopelessly Evil Story' (anonymous review in the *Independent*, 5 January 1899), in *Henry James: 'The Turn of the Screw'*, ed. by Robert Kimbrough, Norton Critical Edition (New York, 1966), p. 175

Myers, F. W. H., see Gurney, Edmund

Neff, Wanda F., 'The Governess', in *Victorian Working Women: An Historical and Literary Study of Women in British Industries and Professions 1832–1850* (1929), second edition (London, 1966), pp. 151–85

Nettels, Elsa, *James and Conrad* (Athens, 1977)

Norrman, Ralf, *The Insecure World of Henry James's Fiction: Intensity and Ambiguity* (London, 1982)

   Techniques of Ambiguity in the Fiction of Henry James, with Special Reference to 'In the Cage' and 'The Turn of the Screw', Acta Academiae Aboensis, 54, no. 2 (Åbo, 1977)

'Notes of Lectures on Method in Learning and Teaching, Delivered at Queen's College, Harley-Street, London', *The Governess: A Repertory of Female Education*, 2 (1855), 183–8 (Lecture II), 373–6 (Lecture VI), 421–5 (Lecture VII)

O'Gorman, Donal, 'Henry James's Reading of "The Turn of the Screw"', *Henry James Review*, 1 (1979–80), 125–38, 228–56

Opie, Iona and Peter, eds., *The Classic Fairy Tales* (London, 1974)

Ovid, *Metamorphoses*, ed. by E.J. Kenney, trans. by A.D. Melville (Oxford, 1986)

Parish, Edmund, *Hallucinations and Illusions: A Study of the Fallacies of Perception* (London, 1897)

Parkes, Bessie Rayner, 'The Profession of the Teacher: The Annual Reports of the Governesses' Benevolent Institution, from 1843 to 1864', in *Essays on Women's Work* (London, 1865), pp. 87–109

Paterson, John, 'The Language of "Adventure" in Henry James', *American Literature*, 32 (1960–1), 291–301

Pattee, Fred Lewis, *The Development of the American Short Story* (New York, 1923), pp. 206–7

Penzoldt, Peter, *The Supernatural in Fiction* (London, 1952)

Perlongo, Robert A., '*The Sacred Fount*: Labyrinth or Parable?', *Kenyon Review*, 22 (1960), 635–47

Perrault, Charles, *Histories; or, Tales of Past Times told by Mother Goose* (1697), ed. by J. Saxon Childers, trans. (1719) by G. M. (London, 1925)
    'Blue Beard', pp. 30–40
    'Cinderilla; or, The Little Glass Slipper', pp. 72–86

Person, Leland, 'The Aboriginal Hawthorne: Mastering the Master from Beyond the Grave', *Henry James Review*, 12 (1991), 162–66

Peterson, M. Jeanne, 'The Victorian Governess: Status Incongruence in Family and Society', in *Suffer and Be Still: Women in the Victorian Age*, ed. by Martha Vicinus (Bloomington, 1972), pp. 3–19

Pigou, Francis, letter in *The Times*, 26 October 1864, p. 10

Plato, *Phaedrus*, in *The Dialogues of Plato*, trans. by B. Jowett, 4 vols. (Oxford, 1871), I, 561–615

Podmore, Frank, see Gurney, Edmund

Poe, Edgar Allan, *The Complete Poems and Stories of Edgar Allan Poe*, ed. by Arthur Hobson Quinn and Edward H. O'Neill, 2 vols. (New York, 1964)
    'The Fall of the House of Usher' (1839), I, 262–77
    'The Premature Burial' (1844), I, 532–42
    'The Purloined Letter' (1845), II, 593–607
  The Narrative of Arthur Gordon Pym of Nantucket (1838), ed. by Harold Beaver, Penguin English Library (Harmondsworth, 1975)

Poirier, Richard, *The Comic Sense of Henry James: A Study of the Early Novels* (London, 1960)

Pollard, Alfred W., 'The Governess and her Grievances', *Murray's Magazine*, 5 (1889), 505–15

Poole, Adrian, *Henry James*, Harvester New Readings (Hemel Hempstead, 1991)

Poovey, Mary, 'The Anathematized Race: The Governess and *Jane Eyre*', in *Uneven Developments: The Ideological Work of Gender in Mid-Victorian England* (London, 1989), pp. 126–63

Pound, Ezra, 'Brief Note', *Little Review*, 5, no. 4 (August 1918), 6–9
  'A Shake Down', *Little Review*, 5, no. 4 (August 1918), 9–39

Praz, Mario, *The Romantic Agony*, trans. by Angus Davidson (London, 1933)

Radcliffe, Ann, *The Italian; or, The Confessional of the Black Penitents: A Romance* (1797), ed. by Frederick Garber, Oxford English Novels (London, 1968)
  The Mysteries of Udolpho: A Romance, Interspersed with some Pieces of Poetry

(1794), ed. by Bonamy Dobrée, Oxford English Novels (London, 1966)

Railo, Eino, *The Haunted Castle: A Study of the Elements of English Romanticism* (London, 1927)

Raleigh, John Henry, 'Henry James: The Poetics of Empiricism' (1951), in *Henry James: Modern Judgements*, ed. by Tony Tanner (London, 1968), pp. 52–70

'The Recent Work of Henry James', *The Critic*, 33 (1898), 523–4

Rambeau, James. See Edel, Leon, Dan H. Laurence and James Rambeau, eds.

Reed, Glenn A., 'Another Turn on James's "The Turn of the Screw"', *American Literature*, 20 (1948–9), 413–23

Reeve, Clara, *The Old English Baron: A Gothic Story* (1778, but first published anonymously in 1777 as *The Champion of Virtue*), ed. by James Trainer, Oxford English Novels (London, 1967)

Renton, Alice, *Tyrant or Victim? A History of the British Governess* (London, 1991)

Reynolds, Frank E. and Earle H. Waugh, eds., *Religious Encounters with Death: Insights from the History and Anthropology of Religion* (University Park, Pa., 1977)

Richards, I. A., *The Philosophy of Rhetoric* (Oxford, 1936)

Richardson, Samuel, *Pamela*, ed. by M. Kinkead-Weekes, Everyman's Library, 2 vols. (London, 1962)

Selected Letters of Samuel Richardson, ed. by John Carroll (Oxford, 1964)

Ricoeur, Paul, *The Rule of Metaphor: Multi-Disciplinary Studies of the Creation of Meaning in Language*, trans. by Robert Czerny, Kathleen McLaughlin and John Costello (London, 1978)

Rimmon, Shlomith, *The Concept of Ambiguity: The Example of James* (Chicago, 1977)

Robbins, Bruce, 'Shooting Off James's Blanks: Theory, Politics, and "The Turn of the Screw"', *Henry James Review*, 5 (1983–4), 192–9

Roellinger, Francis X., 'Psychical Research and "The Turn of the Screw"', *American Literature*, 20 (1948–9), 401–12

Rosenzweig, Saul, 'The Ghost of Henry James', *Partisan Review*, 11 (1944), 436–55

'The Ghost of Henry James: Revised, with a Postscript, 1962', in *Modern Criticism: Theory and Practice*, ed. by Walter Sutton and Richard Foster (New York, 1963), pp. 401–16

Rosmarin, Adena, *The Power of Genre* (Minneapolis, 1985)

Rovit, Earl, 'The Ghosts in James's "The Jolly Corner"', *Tennessee Studies in Literature*, 10 (1965), 65–72

Rowe, John Carlos, 'The Politics of the Uncanny: Newman's Fate in *The American*', *Henry James Review*, 8 (1987), 79–90

The Theoretical Dimensions of Henry James (Madison, 1984)

Samuels, Charles Thomas, *The Ambiguity of Henry James* (Urbana, 1971)

Scarborough, Dorothy, *The Supernatural in Modern English Fiction* (New York, 1917)

Schiller, Friedrich von, *The Ghost-Seer; or, Apparitionist* (1789) [trans. by D. Boileau] (London, 1795)

Schneider, Daniel J., *The Crystal Cage: Adventures of the Imagination in the Fiction of Henry James* (Lawrence, 1978)

Schonhorn, Manuel, ed. See Defoe, Daniel, 'A True Relation of the Apparition of Mrs Veal'

Schrero, Elliot M., 'Exposure in "The Turn of the Screw"', *Modern Philology*, 78 (1980–1), 261–74

Schug, Charles, *The Romantic Genesis of the Modern Novel*, Critical Essays in Modern Literature (Pittsburgh, 1979)

Scott, Walter, *The Antiquary*, 3 vols. (Edinburgh, 1816)
 Novelists and Fiction, see *Sir Walter Scott on Novelists and Fiction*
 'Romance', in the Supplement to the fourth, fifth and sixth editions of the *Encyclopaedia Britannica*, 6 vols. (Edinburgh, 1824), VI, 435–56
 Sir Walter Scott on Novelists and Fiction, ed. by Ioan Williams (London, 1968)
 Waverley; or, 'Tis Sixty Years Since, 3 vols. (Edinburgh, 1814)

Search, Pamela, ed., *The Supernatural in the English Short Story* (London, 1959)

Sears, Sallie, *The Negative Imagination: Form and Perspective in the Novels of Henry James* (Ithaca, 1968)

Segal, Ora, *The Lucid Reflector: The Observer in Henry James's Fiction* (New Haven, 1969)

Seltzer, Mark, *Henry James and the Art of Power* (Ithaca, 1984)

Sewell, Elizabeth Missing, *Principles of Education, drawn from Nature and Revelation, and Applied to Female Education in the Upper Classes*, 2 vols. (London, 1865)

Shakespeare, William, *The Riverside Shakespeare*, ed. by G. Blakemore Evans (Boston, 1974)
 A Midsummer Night's Dream, pp. 222–46
 The Tempest, pp. 1611–36
 The Tragedy of Hamlet, Prince of Denmark, pp. 1141–86

Shelley, Mary Wollstonecraft, *Frankenstein; or, The Modern Prometheus* (1818), ed. by M. K. Joseph, Oxford English Novels (London, 1969)

Sheppard, E.A., *Henry James and 'The Turn of the Screw'* (Auckland, 1974)

Sherman, Stuart P., 'The Aesthetic Idealism of Henry James' (1917), in *The Question of Henry James: A Collection of Critical Essays*, ed. by F.W. Dupee (London, 1947), pp. 86–106

Siebers, Tobin, 'Hesitation, History, and Reading: Henry James's "The Turn of the Screw"', *Texas Studies in Literature and Language*, 25 (1983), 558–73

Silver, John, 'A Note on the Freudian Reading of "The Turn of the Screw"', *American Literature*, 29 (1957–8), 207–11

Sir Gawain and the Green Knight, ed. by R. A. Waldron, York Medieval Texts (London, 1970)

Sklepowich, E. A., 'Gossip and Gothicism in *The Sacred Fount*', *Henry James Review*, 2 (1980–81), 112–15

Slaughter, Martina, 'Edmund Wilson and "The Turn of the Screw"', in *Henry James: 'The Turn of the Screw'*, ed. by Robert Kimbrough, Norton Critical Edition (New York, 1966), pp. 211–14

Smith, Allan Lloyd, 'A Word Kept Back in "The Turn of the Screw"', forthcoming in *Diacritics*

The Spectator, ed. by Donald F. Bond, 5 vols. (Oxford, 1965)

Spenser, Edmund, *The Works of Edmund Spenser*, ed. by Edwin Greenlaw and others, 11 vols. (Baltimore, 1932–57)
    'Epithalamion', VIII (*The Minor Poems*, II), 241–52
    The Faerie Queene, I–VI
    'Prothalamion', VIII (*The Minor Poems*, II), 257–62
    'The Ruines of Time', VIII (*The Minor Poems*, II), 37–56
    'Two Cantos of Mutabilitie', VI, 151–81

Spilka, Mark, 'Turning the Freudian Screw: How Not to Do It', in *Henry James: 'The Turn of the Screw'*, ed. by Robert Kimbrough, Norton Critical Edition (New York, 1966), pp. 245–53

Stevenson, Robert Louis, 'A Note on Realism' (1883), in *Essays in the Art of Writing* (London, 1905), pp. 93–107
    Strange Case of Dr Jekyll and Mr Hyde, in *The Works of Robert Louis Stevenson*, Vailima Edition, 26 vols. (London, 1922–3), VII, 347–454

Stoker, Bram, *Dracula*, ed. by A. N. Wilson, World's Classics (Oxford, 1983)

Stoll, Elmer Edgar, 'Symbolism in Coleridge', *PMLA*, 63, no. 1 (March 1948), 214–33

The Story of the Governesses' Benevolent Institution (Southwick, 1962)

Stowe, William W., *Balzac, James, and the Realistic Novel* (Princeton, 1983)

Sutherland, James, *Defoe* (London, 1937)

Swift, Jonathan, *Gulliver's Travels*, ed. by Harold Williams (London, 1926)

Tales from the Thousand and One Nights, ed. and trans. by N.J. Dawood (Harmondsworth, 1973)

Tanner, Tony, *Adultery in the Novel: Contract and Transgression* (Baltimore, 1979)
    'The Fearful Self: Henry James's *The Portrait of a Lady*', *Critical Quarterly*, 7 (1965), 205–19
    'Henry James's Subjective Adventurer: *The Sacred Fount*', *Essays and Studies*, New Series, 16 (1963), 37–55
    The Reign of Wonder: Naivety and Reality in American Literature (Cambridge, 1965)
    Scenes of Nature, Signs of Men (Cambridge, 1987)
    'The Watcher from the Balcony: Henry James's *The Ambassadors*', *Critical Quarterly*, 8 (1966), 35–52

Tanner, Tony, ed., *Henry James: Modern Judgements* (London, 1968)

Tate, Allen, Katherine Anne Porter and Mark Van Doren, 'James: "The Turn of the Screw"', in *A Casebook on Henry James's 'The Turn of the Screw'*, ed. by Gerald Willen (New York, 1959), pp. 160–70

Thackeray, William Makepeace, *Vanity Fair: A Novel without a Hero*, ed. by Geoffrey and Kathleen Tillotson (London, 1963)

The Times, anonymous letter, 14 September 1867, p. 6

anonymous notice, 22 April 1869, p. 9

Tintner, Adeline R., 'Henry James's Use of *Jane Eyre* in "The Turn of the Screw"', *Brontë Society Transactions*, 17, no. 1 (1976), 42–5

Tintner, Adeline R. See Edel, Leon and Adeline R. Tintner, eds.

Todorov, Tzvetan, *The Fantastic: A Structural Approach to a Literary Genre*, trans. by Richard Howard (Ithaca, 1975)

'The Origin of Genres', trans. by Richard M. Berrong, *New Literary History*, 8 (1976–7), 159–70

The Poetics of Prose, trans. by Richard Howard (Oxford, 1977)

Tompkins, Jane P., ed., *Twentieth Century Interpretations of 'The Turn of the Screw' and other Tales: A Collection of Critical Essays* (Englewood Cliffs, 1970)

Turner, Alden R., 'The Haunted *Portrait of a Lady*', *Studies in the Novel*, 12 (1980), 228–38

Turner, Victor, 'Betwixt and Between: The Liminal Period in *Rites de Passage*', in *The Forest of Symbols: Aspects of Ndembu Ritual* (Ithaca, 1967), pp. 93–111

'Comments and Conclusions', in *The Reversible World: Symbolic Inversion in Art and Society*, ed. by Barbara A. Babcock (Ithaca, 1978), pp. 276–96

'Death and the Dead in the Pilgrimage Process', in *Religious Encounters with Death: Insights from the History and Anthropology of Religion*, ed. by Frank E. Reynolds and Earle H. Waugh (University Park, Pa., 1977), pp. 24–39

Dramas, Fields, and Metaphors: Symbolic Action in Human Society (Ithaca, 1974)

The Ritual Process: Structure and Anti-Structure (London, 1969)

Trilling, Lionel, *The Liberal Imagination: Essays on Literature and Society* (London, 1951)

Troy, William, 'The Altar of Henry James' (1943), in *Henry James: Modern Judgements*, ed. by Tony Tanner (London, 1968), pp. 46–51

Twain, Mark, *A Tramp Abroad* (1880), ed. by Norman Lewis (London, 1982)

Vaid, Krishna Baldev, *Technique in the Tales of Henry James* (Cambridge, Mass., 1964)

Van Gennep, Arnold, *The Rites of Passage* (1908), trans. by Monika B. Vizedon and Gabrielle L. Caffee (London, 1960)

Vicinus, Martha, ed., *Suffer and Be Still: Women in the Victorian Age* (Bloomington, 1972)

Waldock, A. J. A., 'Mr Edmund Wilson and "The Turn of the Screw"', *Modern Language Notes*, 62 (1947), 331–34

Walpole, Horace, *The Castle of Otranto: A Gothic Story*, ed. by W. S. Lewis, Oxford English Novels (London, 1964)

Walpole, Hugh, 'Mrs Lunt' (1933), in *Ghost Stories*, ed. by John Hampden, Everyman's Library (London, 1939), pp. 302–18

Ward, J.A., *The Imagination of Disaster: Evil in the Fiction of Henry James* (Lincoln, Neb., 1961)

   The Search for Form: Studies in the Structure of James's Fiction (Chapel Hill, 1967)

Watson, George G., 'Contributions to a Dictionary of Critical Terms: *Imagination* and *Fancy*', *Essays in Criticism*, 3 (1953), 201–14

Watt, Ian, 'The First Paragraph of *The Ambassadors*: An Explication', *Essays in Criticism*, 10 (1960), 250–74

West, Katharine, *Chapter of Governesses: A Study of the Governess in English Fiction, 1800–1949* (London, 1949)

West, Rebecca, *Henry James*, Writers of the Day (London, 1916)

White, Allon, *The Uses of Obscurity: The Fiction of Early Modernism* (London, 1981)

Wiesenfarth, Joseph, *Henry James and the Dramatic Analogy: A Study of the Major Novels of the Middle Period* (New York, 1963)

Wilde, Oscar, *The Picture of Dorian Gray*, ed. by Donald L. Lawler, Norton Critical Edition (New York, 1988)

Willen, Gerald, ed., *A Casebook on Henry James's 'The Turn of the Screw'* (New York, 1959)

Williams, Ioan, ed. See Scott, Walter

Wilson, Edmund, 'The Ambiguity of Henry James', *Hound and Horn*, 7 (1933–4), 385–406

   'The Ambiguity of Henry James', in *The Triple Thinkers: Ten Essays on Literature* (London, 1938), pp. 122–64

   'The Ambiguity of Henry James', in *The Triple Thinkers: Twelve Essays on Literary Subjects* (London, 1952), pp. 89–128

   'The Ambiguity of Henry James', in *A Casebook on Henry James's 'The Turn of the Screw'*, ed. by Gerald Willen (New York, 1959), pp. 115–53

Wimsatt, W. K., and Monroe C. Beardsley, *The Verbal Icon: Studies in the Meaning of Poetry* (Louisville, 1954)

Wood, Mrs Henry, *East Lynne* (1861), ed. by Sally Mitchell (New Brunswick, 1984)

   'Reality or Delusion?', in *The Virago Book of Victorian Ghost Stories*, ed. by Richard Dalby (London, 1988), pp. 89–103

Woolf, Virginia, *Collected Essays*, ed. by Leonard Woolf, 4 vols. (London, 1966–7)

   'Henry James's Ghost Stories' (1921), I, 286–92

   'The Supernatural in Fiction' (1918), I, 293–6

Wordsworth, William, *The Poetical Works of William Wordsworth*, ed. by E. de Selincourt, 4 vols. (Oxford, 1940–7)

   'The Female Vagrant' (i.e. 'Guilt and Sorrow; or, Incidents upon Salisbury Plain'), I, 94–127

'Hart-leap Well', II, 249–54

'Lines composed a few miles above Tintern Abbey', II, 259–63

'Resolution and Independence', II, 235–40

The Prelude: 1799, 1805, 1850, ed. by Jonathan Wordsworth, M. H. Abrams and Stephen Gill, Norton Critical Edition (New York, 1979)

Wordsworth, William and Samuel Taylor Coleridge, *Lyrical Ballads*, ed. by R. L. Brett and A. R. Jones (London, 1963)

Yeazell, Ruth Bernard, *Language and Knowledge in the Late Novels of Henry James* (Chicago, 1976)

Index